The Politics of Work
and
Occupations

D1226120

ANNEXE DE LA BIBLIOTHÈQUE
uOttawa
LIBRARY ANNEX

J Marshall
mgen
(Don)

The Politics of Work
and
Occupations

edited by
Geoff Esland
and
Graeme Salaman

Université d'Ottawa
BIBLIOTHEQUES
ANNEXE DE LA BIBLIOTHÈQUE
uOttawa
LIBRARIES
LIBRARY ANNEX
University of Ottawa

UNIVERSITY OF TORONTO PRESS
Toronto & Buffalo

Copyright © 1980 The Open University Press

First published in the United States and Canada by
University of Toronto Press 1980

ISBN 0-8020-5429-9

All rights reserved. No part of this work may be
reproduced in any form, by mimeograph or by any
other means, without permission in writing from
the publisher.

Typeset by
R James Hall Typsetting and Book Production Services
and printed by
Anchor Press Ltd, Tiptree, Colchester,
Great Britain

British Library Cataloguing in Publication Data
The politics of work and occupations.
1. Industrial sociology
I. Esland, Geoffrey II. Salaman, Graeme·
301.5'5   HD6955

HD
6955
P65
1980 b

Contents

Acknowledgements

This book grew out of an Open University course entitled *People and Work* DE351. The authors of the chapters in the book would like to thank all those members of the course team whose support and criticism were invaluable in the preparation of the original course: Roger Dale, Ben Cosin; Ken Patton; Gwyn Pritchard; Bharti Kansara; David Boswell. We are grateful to Richard Brown and Alan Fox for their comments on the various drafts of the original units during the preparation of the course and we would also like to thank Moira Hilder for her help in preparing the manuscript.

Grateful acknowledgement is made to the following for permission to reproduce material in this book:

Front cover: *Les Constructeurs* by Fernand Leger, © by S.P.A.D.E.M., Paris, 1979.

Pages 83, 85, 91: Tables reproduced by permission of the OECD, Paris.

Pages 94, 95, 125, 126: Reproduced by permission of the Controller of Her Majesty's Stationery Office.

Page 114: Figure 1 reproduced by permission of Pergamon Press Limited.

Page 129: Table 2 reproduced by permission of David Field.

Page 131: Table 3 reproduced by permission of the *Sociological Review.*

Page 201: Table 1 copyright © 1963 by the Free Press of Glencoe, a Division of the Macmillan Company. Reprinted by permission of Macmillan Publishing Co. Inc.

Page 90: Table 2 © G.S. Bacon (1972) reproduced by permission of the Oxford University Press, Oxford.

Appendix: Reprinted by permission of *The Guardian* newspaper.

Editors' Introduction

This collection is derived from a third-year Open University course entitled *People and Work* (DE351) which first appeared in 1976. The chapters in this book are updated and modified versions of some of the written 'units' of that course. The origination of the present publication in an Open University course has a number of implications. Firstly, the chapters included here — all original pieces — were designed to form an integrated whole. Each author, therefore, has seen and commented on the other chapters. The overall structure and themes of the original course — and hence of the book — emerged from numerous conversations among the members of the Course Team.

Secondly, the book was primarily designed as teaching material. We hope that it will also be of interest to our fellow academics. But its prime function is to convey to students some of what we consider to be the major themes and issues of a sociology of work. This particular area of sociology has recently been invigorated by numerous debates around Harry Braverman's book *Labor and Monopoly Capital*, which has served to re-awaken and redirect interest in the relationship between work structures and societal patterns of interest and domination. This work has many valuable features, not least that it emphasizes the close links between issues of work design and control, and argues for the political — i.e. class — nature of work arrangements and technologies. One of the major strengths of Braverman's work, and the research and discussion it has encouraged, is that it has brought back into the arena of sociological debate the nature and origins of work arrangements themselves, in all their complexity. All too often, previously, with some notable exceptions, the origins of work arrangements and technologies were ascribed to the inexorable working out of some non-social logic or rationality of technological development, or of industrialism. Braverman has repoliticized this debate, and it is to this question — of the political nature of work arrangements, and their impact on employees – that the chapters in this book are all, in their various ways, addressed. Our concern with the 'politics of work' takes a number of forms and directions, but throughout this collection the authors consider such issues as the processes of occupational development, and occupational placement, the meaning of work, the political significance of the professions, of 'dirty work', processes of control and resistance within organizations, the nature of humanized management policies, and so on, which all in their various ways deal with the relationship between work and the structures of class and domination.

One of the main aims of the first two chapters is to introduce various theoretical debates concerning the sociology of work as a whole, and to locate the various areas of analysis within an overall framework of the relationship of work to forms of social and political organizations and ideologies. Perhaps most significant is the concern with the notion of capitalism as an over-arching form of industrial organization. Chapters 3 and 4 continue this discussion in a more concrete way so that, in Chapter 3, a variety of dimensions analysing the distinction between socialist and capitalist forms of industrial development are outlined and discussed. The consideration of occupational placement in Chapter 4 is examined within the context of a largely privately owned economy which relies on the market mechanism as an effective and 'just' method of allocating human work 'resources'. Chapter 3 takes up the debate as to whether there is a 'logic of industrialism', leading to a convergence of industrial societies, with regard to their occupational structures. The discussion is focused on the theoretical implications behind Kerr *et al*'s thesis and compares this with the perspective of Bell (1974), Dalton (1974) and Galbraith (1974). In particular, the chapter examines the evidence given to support the statements that there has been a reduction in the agricultural workforce, an expansion in white-collar and service occupations, an increase in mobility rates and an increasing emphasis on education and training prior to entering the workforce.

This debate sets the scene for an empirical comparison of the range, nature and conditions of work in the USA, Russia and, in more depth, Britain. This is important, not just for the overall picture of the occupational structure it provides, but for indicating some of the consequences that that structure may have for members of particular social groups. Thus, the implications for two such groups – immigrants and women – are considered, as both immigrants and women are found to be substantially over-represented in certain occupations, and thus under-represented in others, and have been consistently afforded unequal opportunities in seeking entry to high status occupations.

The discussion in Chapter 3 implicitly suggests that the system of occupational opportunities and rewards is closely connected with wider aspects of the social stratification system. Apart from stratification by race and gender, the class-based nature of industrial societies has an important influence on the attitudes and orientations to work held by members of different social groups and on the differential opportunities open to them in entering employment. Chapter 4 turns to a specific consideration of this aspect of work – how individuals come to choose particular kinds of work and how entry into the occupational structure is stratified along class dimensions. Developmental psychology has proposed that an individual comes to choose, and subsequently enters the type of work that is seen to be most consonant with his self-concept and ambitions, and that will therefore most adequately fulfil his perception of himself. Following a discussion of this approach, this chapter presents the sociological perspective and evidence that argues that this situation is rarely the case for most individuals. It suggests that the family, via its ascriptive functions and socialization patterns, class cultures and the educational system, with its differential access to achievement and certification, maintains and perpetuates an occupational structure, entry into which is not determined by ambitions and the 'free' choice of self-fulfilling work, but by one's position within the class system.

Chapters 5 and 6 share an interest in the meanings that are attached to and develop within different sorts of work experiences, and each considers the ways in which different sorts of work become labelled and defined, with implications for those concerned. In Chapter 5, Alan Fox presents a comprehensive review of the relevant literature on the meanings people find in their work, and the values and interests which inform the design of work. This chapter advances an original analysis of the relationship between the meaning and nature of work and class interests. Chapter 6 considers the Hughesian concepts of 'deviant' and 'dirty' work, a type of work which involves its practitioners in major problems of self-justification and defence. As much of the literature in this tradition demonstrated, people who are involved in what others regard as deviant or dirty work redefine and interpret their everyday work activities and identities in ways which afford them some protection from the stigma which tends to be their lot. Janet Woollacott extends the discussion beyond the normal limits to include a detailed consideration of the most massive and obscene example of dirty work – the systematic extermination of Jews, and others, by Hitler's SS. It might seem strange to regard such an activity as work; yet for the SS it was exactly that. And Janet Woollacott's consideration of such 'work' and those involved in it constitutes an important and interesting application of the concepts and theories of Hughes's occupational sociology to a hitherto largely unconsidered variety of dirty work.

A central theme of the book is the *politics of work.* And while all the chapters can be seen as relevant to this overriding focus of interest, it is in the remaining chapters – 7,8,9,10, and 11, that the theme is most overtly and clearly discussed. These chapters are about the politics of work and occupations and are, therefore, centrally concerned with work and power, and work and conflict.

When we talk of the politics of work and occupations we mean two things: the relationship between a work activity or group and the distribution of interests and power in the society within which these occur; and the organizational or ideological conflicts and relationships of power and domination internal to these occupations. These are, of course, related. Conflicts at work mirror larger social conflicts; forms of work organization reflect societal patterns of interest and domination. Chapters 7 and 8 deal specifically with the professions. Geoff Esland's analysis of the basis of their power and prestige, and his arguments about the role such occupations play in supporting and buttressing capitalism, are a clear example of this argument. There are some sociologists who have studied professions from a point of view which reflects the preoccupations of the would-be aspirants to professional status. Such a perspective leads to an interest in the conflicts between professional and bureaucratic forms of authority, the methods by which occupations achieve professional status, what is involved in processes of professional socialization and training, and so on. But Geoff Esland is not primarily interested in these issues: his focus is firmly placed on the *political* functions of occupations which have gained professional recognition.

He argues that in producing knowledge professionals are acting politically, especially when their knowledge concerns the 'real' nature of people. A necessary part of the development of modern, monopoly capitalism, with its large organizations, emphasis on welfare services and increasing reliance on technical and expert management activities, has been the creation – or the massive enlargement – of the new professional class: a class which is increasingly employed in and by the large organizations – whether in industry or government. These experts, these professionals, are given positions of power, privilege and prestige – their reward for work as agents of capitalism. A great deal of the chapter is concerned with describing how professionals' work can be seen in these terms. In Chapter 7, for instance, it is argued that '. . . through its reliance on highly legitimated knowledge, protected by the rituals of expertness and licence to practice, professionalism becomes both an adjunct to bureaucratic administration and a form of political domination'. In the following chapter Geoff Esland attempts to demonstrate this process by reference to an examination of the nature and function of a particular category of professions — those that diagnose illness and provide therapy.

He argues that the use of psychology, and the sort of knowledge contained in this discipline, serve political ends. By defining problems in terms of the individual, and treating them on this basis, the patient/ client is misled as to the real causes of the problem, and indeed the real nature of the problem. Even the existence of the problem *qua* problem may be cast in doubt. There are, then, two elements in the argument: firstly, that capitalist society systematically produces certain sorts of conditions, circumstances, strains, events, etc., which are then defined as 'problems'. Secondly, once regarded as problems, these conditions, or whatever, are diagnosed and treated in terms of individual adjust- ment, psychology and pathology. The social basis of their existence, definition and treatment is assiduously disguised and denied by the agencies which are licensed to deal with these conditions.

In so doing the professionals concerned are operating as 'agents' of capitalism in two, interrelated ways, it is claimed: firstly, they are handling and processing a genuine social problem, one which is a product of the capitalist system to a great extent; secondly, they are doing so in ways which throw the burden, the responsibility for the problem, back on the victim. In so doing, they mystify both the prob- lem and the society which produced it.

As with Chapter 7, the analysis of the nature and function of 'personal service' professions involves reference both to the kind and consequences of the professional theory, and to the ways in which such knowledge and practice is organized and controlled. The professions under analysis rely upon, and are legitimated by, a form of knowledge which, it is claimed, is inherently and unavoidably political, in that its basic unit of analysis is the individual. But these professions are increas- ingly under the control and organization of the state — a state which is not the neutral institution it is sometimes presented as.

In Chapter 9, Theo Nichols continues the book's interest in work and politics by considering a new and apparently liberal management ideology. Like the author of Chapters 7 and 8, Nichols emphasizes the ideological aspects of knowledge — in this case management knowledge of workers and their motivation, needs, etc.

Nichols' basic argument is clear: 'words can be a poor guide to deeds'. He argues that the recent interest in 'industrial democracy', participation, etc., is a product of certain constraints and circumstances experienced by senior management. The basic problem is the one spelt out by Alan Fox: capitalism involves forms of work organization and arrangement which are alienating. They are boring, repetitious, depriving and frustrating, and the fact that these principles of work organization are retained and justified is an obvious indication of the real priorities of capitalism which emphasizes rapid economic growth as its prize goal. But although the capitalist organization of work (and its implicit priorities) destroys commitment, it also requires co-operation and involvement. And it is this contradiction that supplies the motivation for such managerial exercises as 'worker participation', 'job enrichment', and so on.

However, Nichols also notes that the organization of work under capitalism does not allow genuine worker control and participation. If it did, then it would obviously introduce the possibility – indeed the certainty – that the workers would choose goals and priorities other than those that were most profitable. If the workers were in control, then values such as efficiency, productivity and profit would be replaced, or redefined. The acceptability of the criterion of efficiency might be brought into question with the result that people might enquire 'efficiency for what or for whom?' In short, Nichols sees recent developments in management thinking – developments which have often been based on social science theories – as attempts to resolve *managerial* problems, and as mere ideology.

Chapter 10 is a clear statement of the nature of work under capitalism. It specifically focuses on the concept of control, for it is precisely workers' lack of control over their own work, products and the organization of work that characterizes capitalism. As Hyman remarks, 'Work within capitalism is at one and the same time an economic and political activity; it involves not only the production of goods and services but also the exercise of power.' Hyman goes on to note that power at work reflects access to material and ideological resources, and it is necessary for production to take place because in capitalism work involves the organization of labour for specific, sectional interests; interests which are at odds with those whose labour is bought and organized. Not surprisingly, therefore, struggle over control characterizes working relations, struggles which Hyman argues are often, but not always, mediated by trade unions.

It should be noted that Hyman questions the view that industrial relations conflicts are exclusively concerned with financial improvements for their members. This point is important because it suggests that the argument that unions have accepted capitalist values and abdicated any responsibility for genuine workers' control is erroneous. By focusing on the struggle for control at work, a struggle which occurs within and reveals the context of capitalism, Richard Hyman illuminates not only the real nature of capitalism, but more importantly the constant process of worker resistance to the values and organizational forms inherent in this economic-political system.

In the final chapter, Terry Johnson is primarily concerned with delineating and contrasting the Weberian and Marxian approaches to the sociology of work, and with using the latter in the analysis of professions. To a considerable extent this can be seen as a conclusion to the book in the sense that it brings together some issues that have occurred earlier, while at the same time proposing a particular conception of the politics of work, and in so doing, it elaborates an important development in class theory.

CHAPTER 1

Graeme Salaman

The sociology of work:
some themes and issues

Introduction

This chapter has one major aim : to describe the major features of an important perspective on the sociology of work in capitalism by considering the relevant contributions of the theorists who first outlined such an approach, and by discussing the influence of these contributions on recent developments in the sociology of work. The chapter will discuss the origins and current manifestations of an approach to the sociological understanding of work experiences and arrangements which will be described as concerned with the *politics of work*, in the sense that the approach in question, which draws mainly on the work of Marx, seeks to understand and locate the origins of inequalities of work in capitalism — inequalities in the distribution of work's rewards, frustrations, delights, dangers and deprivations — and the significance of these for the development of conceptions of the nature of society, and attitudes towards the experiences of deprivation and subordination.

A concern for the politics of work in capitalism insists on the relationship between work structures and events, and the structure of interests and power and values in the society at large. It analyses the role of ideology in mystifying and buttressing work hierarchies and inequalities. It seeks to discover the interests that lie behind the claimed rationality and neutrality of much work-based deprivation. Most important of all, it retains and applies a sense of outrage. Unlike some approaches to the nature and experience of work in modern industrial societies, it insists on taking seriously the possibility that the daily routine of men and women wasting their lives and their intellects to gain their livelihoods is a major social injustice, and one which, since it reflects other societal distinctions and inequalities, ought to be changed.

The sociology of work and industry is an important and central element in general sociology, for three reasons : its various empirical objects of interest — work, employing organizations, occupations, professions, etc. — constitute institutions and processes of major significance in modern industrial societies. No understanding of such societies is possible without knowledge of work and industry. Secondly, the theories with which such processes and institutions are approached are central to the discipline as a whole. And, thirdly, a great deal of sociological theory — its key concepts and problems — was developed in response to efforts to understand the implications of the change from pre-industrial to capitalist society.

Like all sociological enquiry, industrial sociology is inherently theoretical. Predictably, all the major theoretical traditions and positions can be found within the sociology of work. There has, however, been a tendency for particular specialisms to rely much more heavily on some theoretical positions than others, so that empirical specialization has, in some cases, coincided with theoretical monopolization (see Esland and Salaman 1975).

If the sociology of work is irretrievably theoretical it is also unavoidably political, in the sense that it is, ultimately, concerned to support or to criticize existing society and social institutions. The mission of sociology, wrote Mills, is to understand the connections between history and biography, between social structure and personal histories, between public issues and private troubles. Such understandings have definite political implications. The political nature of all sociology, and particularly of the sociology of work, derives from the fact that *any* theory of society immediately confronts '. . . the main dilemmas and questions posed by sociology about contemporary society, its conflicts, shared values and aims and the direction of its developments' (Parker *et al* 1977 p 11).

To argue for the importance of a concern for the politics of work under capitalism is not to assert that the various theorists whose work informs such an approach can be seen to constitute a unified movement. Indeed the differences between the major contributors to such a perspective are very substantial. Nevertheless, there are sufficient common interests, common foci of enquiry, among Marx, Weber and, to a lesser degree, Durkheim, to warrant viewing them as initiators of the perspective outlined in this chapter (see also Esland and Salaman 1975).

The writings of Marx and Weber on the sociology of work are important because they established the basic elements and parameters of a sociological study of the politics of work under capitalism which has been very influential, and which continues to inform and inspire sociologists working in this area. The writings of Marx and Weber on work, alienation, the labour process, bureaucracy, rationality and the division of labour are too well known to require lengthy exposition here. They are usefully summarized in Giddens (1973), Eldridge (1973), Eldridge and Crombie (1974), Mouzelis (1967), and Salaman (1978). In what follows, these theoretical contributions will be considered under two headings : the design of work, i.e. control and the division of labour; and the nature and implications of work experiences, both of which subsume a great deal of recent work in the sociology of work.

1 Work and Society

For Marx, and many later writers, it is the way in which the means of production are owned, and the nature of the relationship between employers and employees in production (the formally free labourer selling his labour to the owner who employs it in the pursuit of expropriated profit) that determine social and political structure and process. Others, however, have chosen to regard the 'state of the productive forces' — the design of work and technology — as the determinants of social and political structure. These writers categorize societies in terms of the type of work that predominates. Kerr *et al* (1973) in their study of the 'logic' of industrialization start their discussion with data on changes in the occupational structure and work patterns of nineteenth-century England. And although they admit other implications of industrialization (urbanization, a larger governmental role, ideological consensus, etc.) they place most emphasis on changes in occupational structure and the structure of the labour force.

> Industrialization in fact develops and depends upon a concentrated, disciplined industrial work force — a work force with new skills and a wide variety of skills, with high skill levels and constantly changing skill requirements. (Kerr *et al* 1973 p 44)

Furthermore,

> The dynamic science and technology of the industrial society creates frequent changes in the skills, responsibilities, and occupations of the work force. Some are made redundant and new ones are created. The work force is confronted with repeated object lessons of the general futility of fighting these changes, and comes to be reconciled, by and large, to repeated changes in ways of earning a living. (Kerr *et al* 1973 p 44)

All this activity is dominated by specialization, automation and technol-

ogy under the control of large-scale organizations — 'The technology
and specialization of the industrial society are necessarily and distinctively associated with large-scale organizations' (Kerr *et al* 1973 p 49).
Kerr and his colleagues define 'industrial society' in terms of changes
in the work activities of the mass of the population as technology and
inanimate energy are applied to productive activity. They argue that
industrial societies have, as a result of a common inherent 'logic' and
a dependence on the same basic determinants, important similarities,
which override ideological and cultural differences between types of
society. Although they admit that 'different societies have taken and
still take separate paths on the way to industrialization' (Kerr *et al*
1973 p 280), they also claim that these differences follow variations
in the nature of the elites that fashion the industrialization process, not
the ideology or culture of the society. In a postscript they write: '. . .
the forces of industrialization have appeared in many countries to be
stronger, and cultural factors somewhat less of a force, than we thought
in 1960' (Kerr *et al* 1973 p 280). One important area where the 'weakness' of ideology is asserted is that of industrial relations, where

> . . . the central problem of industrial relations around the world is
> not capital versus labour, but rather the structuring of the labour
> force — how it gets recruited, developed, and maintained . . . the
> similarities of actions belie the ideological conflicts. (Kerr *et al* 1973
> pp 280—1)

They thus emphasize the importance of technology in shaping certain
key features of industrial society, the others being determined by the
dominant industrializing elite. They grant that in market-oriented
(capitalist) economies the '. . . class situation of individuals and groups,
understood in terms of their economic power and resources will have
(an) effect on . . . life chances' (Kerr *et al* 1973 p 298). Nevertheless
in the long term 'economic forces', which are affected by the most
'effective' available technology, have a greater impact than 'political'
forces. Economic is used here to refer not to the means of economic
regulation operative in an economy, or to how the means of production
are owned or controlled, but to what these authors regard as inevitable
and unavoidable economic constraints and requisites of the process of
industrialization, such as the need for capital investment, etc.

There are a number of difficulties in this argument. It is true that
the use of inanimate energy in factory production has implications for
the nature of work activities and processes. But this argument under-
estimates the crucial significance of *the social and economic setting*
within which technology and productive process are applied. Technol-

ogy is after all a *means*, a system of techniques, and it is as important to consider the goals and interests lying behind the choice of technology and its application, as it is the technology itself. As Braverman puts it:

> . . . it is not the productive strength of machinery that weakens the human race, but the manner in which it is employed in capitalist social relations. It has become fashionable . . . to attribute to machinery the powers over humanity which arise from social relations. Society in this view is nothing but an extrapolation of science and technology, and the machine itself is the enemy. The machine, the mere product of human labour and ingenuity, designed and constructed by humans and alterable by them at will, is viewed as an independent participant in human social arrangements . . . This is the reification of a social relation; it is, . . . nothing but a fetishism . . . machinery embraces a host of possibilities, many of which are systematically thwarted, rather than developed, by capital. (Braverman 1974 pp 229–30)

Technology is not an autonomous force, but a method, or system of methods which is designed and employed in certain economic and political contexts:

> . . . the productive enterprise cannot be considered in isolation from the economy or the polity, since it is essentially an organization operating in an economic and political environment. (Haddon 1973 p 15)

The most important feature of Kerr *et al*'s argument is the authors' view that social, economic and other arrangements follow, in the long term, certain patterns determined by industrialization. In other words, as Haddon points out, choice and decision-making on the grounds of ideology and interest are ruled out. Presumably resistance to these inexorable developments is misguided; certainly unsuccessful. The thesis, as Haddon remarks, portrays a strangely depoliticized world. Basic conflicts between social values and ideas, fundamental differences of political philosophy, all become submerged by the logic of industrialization. This convergence thesis, however, requires modification when considered empirically. Even within capitalism, research has shown that significant variations between capitalist societies can occur. Dore's study of British and Japanese factories for example (Dore 1973) reveals important differences in employment practices, control systems, worker-management relations, etc. Such differences do not simply reflect different national cultures : they also reflect the fact that '. . . later industrializers can learn from the mistakes of others and get ahead by adopting new modes of organization' (Parker *et al* 1977 p 173). In other words, different societies may reveal different strategies in the face of the broadly similar problems of capitalist economic organization. Gallie's study of British and French oil refineries supports this view : the capitalist context, and similar technology, did not achieve a similarity in organizational, motivational, relational or other terms. Striking and far-reaching differences were found to exist (Gallie 1978).

An argument closely related to Kerr's argument asserts that recent changes in capitalist societies and economies mark the supersession of capitalism. Relevant developments include the expansion of state regulation of, and interference in, economic activity; the development of state ownership; the increase in public ownership; the development of welfare provision, etc. These developments are undeniable; though it is a mistake to regard all of them as recent developments : government regulation of economic activity has always been an integral element of capitalism, despite the rhetoric of those who desire a 'return' to unfettered laissez-faire capitalism. Certainly some of the worst social consequences of the early phases of industrialization have been ameliorated by trade unionism, collective organization, welfare provision and legislation. Certainly nineteenth-century capitalism has developed into capitalism that is massively managed and monitored by government and large-scale, possibly multi-national, corporations. And certainly the relative success of post-war capitalist economies (until recently) has resulted in a degree of affluence for many that is remarkable in comparison with nineteenth-century conditions.

But what difference do these developments make to the basic thesis that these economies remain, essentially, capitalist? Capitalism, as a form of economic and social arrangement, is not so historically specific to nineteenth-century arrangements that these changes represent anything other than a stage in the *development* of capitalism. Under capitalism the vast majority of the workers sell their labour power to employers who use it to extract profit. From these basics follow the major feature of capitalist societies : the division into classes. These facts have not changed. The private capitalist might, in some cases, have been replaced by the nationalized industry board, with its managers; but the priority of production remains the same : profit. Conditions and rewards might have improved, but the basic distinction between managers and managed, with all its implications for life-chances and relationships, remains. Recent developments, far from changing the basic nature of capitalism, can be seen as supporting and fulfilling it, enabling capitalist priorities and contradictions to survive in the face of increasing difficulties : '. . . any movement towards state "intervention" in economic life and . . . the acceptance of the legitimacy of collective bargaining in industry and the enfranchisement of the working class, represent some sort of partial supersession of capitalist society. The opposite is the case; capitalist society only becomes fully developed when these processes occur' (Giddens 1973 p 22). Later, the same author adds, 'Social democracy . . . is the normal form taken by the systematic political inclusion of the working class within capitalist society' (Giddens 1973 p 285).

But one difficulty remains. If it is accepted that the societies of the West remain capitalist, and that this has implications for work within such societies, it remains to be demonstrated that the work experiences of the worker in the USSR are substantially different from his counterpart in a capitalist society. From the point of view of the ordinary worker does it really make any appreciable difference whether he is a member of, and works within, the Soviet Union, or the USA? After all, as Dalton remarks :

> The government of the Soviet Union owns all the industrial factories and mineral resources as well as state farms, which are organized like factories and employ wage-workers . . . One could not tell from looking at Russia's capital facilities, its steel mills or banks in Leningrad, that they are differently organized from capitalist steel mills and banks in Manchester. They differ in the intangible rules of their organization and the way input and output transactions are decided, that is, how labour and natural resources are acquired by producing firms, how the volume and variety of production are decided and how products are allocated. (Dalton 1974 p 127)

It is far from clear that work in a Russian car factory is substantially different from working for Ford. The technology is the same. The size of the organization and its conditions will be broadly similar. There may be some differences in levels of reward of manual work in the two countries, if not absolutely, at least relative to other work and occupational groups, but the hierarchical nature of the organization and the specialization, subdivision and nature of actual work tasks will be very similar. And while events and decisions in the Ford plant will be governed by the company's drive for profit, in the Russian case such decisions follow the organization's attempts to fulfil the levels of output, input and efficiency that had been set by the centralized planning departments. In neither case, it would seem, does the ordinary worker play much, if any, of a part in determining the nature of his work, or its objectives, nor does he work for himself in any meaningful sense, despite the fact that in the USSR he ostensibly owns the means of production.

Ironically, this argument is strengthened by the fact that Lenin, one of the architects of the Soviet system, was an enthusiastic supporter of Frederick Taylor's theory of Scientific Management, a view of the nature, arrangement and subdivision of work tasks which not only has played a highly important role in inspiring the arrangement of factory and office work, but which also, by its emphasis upon breaking down jobs into their smallest possible ingredients, and totally separating the *execution* of tasks from their *design* and *conceptualization* represents the capitalist view of work: that it is a commodity which must be regarded only in terms of its profitability to the employer or owner.

This theory of work organization was highly considered by Lenin, and has become institutionalized in Soviet factory organization and work design.

Does this mean then that, as Kerr and his colleagues have argued, the sheer fact of industrialization *per se* must be regarded as the salient consideration, and that varieties of political, social and economic organization do not have the significance attributed to them earlier in this section? Presumably some would accept such an interpretation, but there are other possibilities which have greater appeal and utility.

First, the fact that in the Soviet Union capitalist forms of work organization and practice still survive does not mean that a form of industrialized socialist society which rejects such practices is not a possibility. As Braverman says, 'What is said of capitalism may also be said of "socialism", which does not yet exist anywhere in the classic Marxist sense' (Braverman 1974 p 22). It is difficult to consider, design and instigate a form of industrial work organization other than that which has been developed within the capitalist societies and which finds its purest expression in the USA. Simply because a society's economy is organized on a socialist basis does not mean that the form of work design and organization automatically sheds those features which Taylor described and recommended:

> Socialism, as a mode of production, does not grow automatically in the way that capitalism grew in response to blind and organic market forces; it must be brought into being, on the basis of an adequate technology, by the conscious and purposive activity of collective humanity. (Braverman 1974 p 23)

In short, the fact that work arrangements in some socialist societies, notably the USSR, appear to differ little from those in existence in capitalist societies does not mean that (a) such forms of work design and factory organization are an inevitable result of industrialization or

technology, or that (b) socialist societies *must* employ the work arrangements and practices that have been developed under capitalism, or that
(c) some socialist societies will not develop, indeed have not developed
already, forms of work arrangement and factory organization which
demonstrate a concern not simply for the achievement of efficiency
and profit, but also for the right of the worker to play some part in
the design, planning and execution of his everyday work. For some
writers it is the retention of capitalist forms of work organization, and
capitalist work relations and priorities, which, with other factors,
demonstrates the non-socialist nature of some ostensibly socialist
societies, as, for example, the USSR.

But is it really true that working in a Leningrad steel mill is no
different from working in one in Sheffield? The answer is complicated
because to conceptualize and describe 'what it is like' is by no means
unproblematic. Undoubtedly as discussed above there *are* similarities.
The nature and content of the jobs and the technologies are similar. So
are conditions, levels of dirt, noise, etc. But even in the USSR, which, as
pointed out above, does not by any means represent the 'purest' example of a socialist society, there are features of work which significantly
alter, in the view of the writer, the nature of work experiences. As
Giddens remarks, 'State socialism . . . does not represent the transcen-
dence of capitalism, but an alternative mode of promoting industrialization or achieving high rates of economic growth' (Giddens 1973 p 252).

Giddens goes on to argue that the direct control of the economy by
the political administration, and the abolition of private property has
not created a free society or eliminated differences, but it does mean an
extremely significant reduction in class differences (or class structura-
tion as he terms it). These differences concern such things as income
differentials, mobility opportunities, job security, fringe benefits, etc.
Giddens remarks for example, that :

> In most of the contemporary state socialist societies, it now appears
> to be the case that the economic rewards, not merely of skilled
> workers but, expressed in terms of median earnings, of manual
> workers *as a whole*, are higher than those of clerical and lower-level
> administrative employees. (Giddens 1973 p 230)

To summarize this section. It has been argued that an important
approach to the sociology of work is that which is concerned with
what has been termed the politics of work — the relationship between
work inequalities and deprivations, and social structures, and patterns
of societal interests and power. This approach focuses on the relationship between capitalism and work structures and experiences. Before

presenting the major elements of such an approach attention was paid
to the arguments that industrialization, not capitalism, was responsible
for major features of industrial societies, and that capitalism *per se* had
been superseded. Finally, some consideration of the implications for
this argument of the existence in the USSR of capitalist work forms
was included. It is maintained that none of these arguments seriously
weakens the propositions that the societies of the West remain capitalist,
and that this has important consequences for work organization and
experience. The next two sections will consider these implications.

2 The design of work, control and organization under capitalism

For Marx, the nature of capitalism has direct implications for the nature
of work. Under capitalism the labour power of the formally free workers is purchased by the employer and employed to make profit, which
belongs to the owner, and which is used to finance further employment,
further profit. Labour power is, according to Marx, a 'mental and
physical capability', and as such its use by the owners requires constant
direction and management. The 'potential' must be realized in line with
the owner's requirements. The use of directed and controlled labour
power to achieve profit creates an inherent and undeniable conflict of
interest between capitalist and employee.

These two basic features of work in capitalism : the purchase of
labour power (which necessitates management) and the conflict
resulting from the creation and expropriation of profit (which creates
conflict and necessitates control) have an important implication for the
design of work : it causes efficiency and control to become irredeemably interrelated. The search for greater efficiency – and the work
design and technology which assist this – are inherently sectional and
political, since they increase the efficiency with which the workers are
exploited. As Marx puts it :

> The directing motive, the end and aim of capitalist production, is
> to extract the greatest possible amount of surplus-value, and con-
> sequentially to exploit labour-power to the fullest possible extent.
> As the number of cooperating labourers increases, so too does their
> resistance to the domination of capital, and with it the necessity
> for capital to overcome this resistance by counter-pressure. The
> control exercised by the capitalist is not only a special function, due
> to the nature of the social labour-process, and peculiar to that
> process, but it is, at the same time, a function of the exploitation

of a social labour-process, and is consequently rooted in the unavoid-able antagonism between the exploiter and the living and labouring raw material he exploits. (Marx 1954 p 313)

Marx's analysis has particular relevance to a discussion of the division of labour. 'Intelligence in production expands in one direction because it vanishes in many others. What is lost by the detail labourers, is concentrated in the capital that employs them' (Marx 1954 p 341). The organization of work reveals a growing division between 'hand' and 'brain' work, the former reduced to repetitive, 'detail' work, the latter expanding into a monopolization of the work of design, and control. Under capitalism, management takes on functions specific to the needs and problems of controlling and directing the labour power of poten-tially recalcitrant employees to achieve profit.

Braverman suggests that the capitalist mode of production and work organization finds its truest expression in the principles of Taylorism. He asserts that Taylorism demonstrates three basic principles : first, work knowledge and theory are systematized into rules and procedures and thus expropriated from the worker, and formalized, or as Braver-man calls this '. . . the dissociation of the labour process from the skills of the workers' (Braverman 1974 p 113). Secondly, the design and conception of work are separated from the execution of work tasks. This allows for greater management control, as well as reducing the skill and authority of the workers. The third principle is '. . . the use of this monopoly over knowledge to control each step of the labour process and its mode of execution' (Braverman 1974 p 119).

According to Braverman these are the principles on which capitalist work is built. It will be seen that his argument closely follows that of Marx. However, it is likely that Braverman exaggerates the coincidence of Taylorism with capitalism. Certainly Taylorism represents one strategy whereby employees can be controlled and their labour directed and exploited. But other strategies are also possible, for example, the granting of work discretion to generate commitment and 'trustworthi-ness'. It is also possible that Braverman exaggerates the extent to which Taylorism represented a destruction of previous craft arrangements. As Littler has pointed out, in many cases these had already been reduced by the introduction of indirect forms of control such as subcontract (Littler 1978).

Nevertheless Braverman's work remains important as an attempt (a) to understand the basic principles underlying the design of work in capitalism, (b) to relate these to the nature of the society within which they occur, and (c) to look behind the ideological assurances of the neutrality and inevitability of current work forms, and to uncover the interests and powers that inform these practices.

Other writers have also contributed to these developments. Davis and Taylor (1972), on the basis of empirical research into work design criteria, report that design of technology — and work systems — reflect assumptions and values about the nature — and worth — of employees. Similar conclusions have been reached by Fox (1974, 1976) and Rose (1975). Recently numerous writers have asserted the political nature of technology, and the work and organizational forms which accompany it : see, for example, Gorz (1976), Dickson (1974).

From a somewhat different position Fox has sought to isolate the basic principles underlying the design of work in large organizations. He distinguishes high and low discretion work, differentiated by the extent to which it allows the worker to employ his own judgement and discretion. This concept allows a useful bringing together of the two strands of the Marxist critique of work in capitalism : the repetitive and standardized nature of 'hand' work, and the origins of this sort of work in the uncertain commitment of employees to work which is not in their own interests, or for their purposes. Furthermore, Fox usefully describes the connection between work design criteria and control.

A critique of work in capitalism must soon have to face the conventional argument that work forms are determined not by ownership or profitability, but by the exigencies of modern technology, used in the interest of the whole society, as consumers (see the chapter by Alan Fox in this volume). Conventional treatments of technology within organizational sociology have tended to regard it simply as a response to the organization's goals. Considerable attention has been given to the relationship between technology and work design and organizational structure. Very little attention, however, has been allocated to the origins of this technology. Recently, however, a more critical perspective has developed. Drawing again on the work of Marx (who pointed to the functions of technology in controlling employees, and deskilling them), the new perspective considers how far technology is required by production alone, and how far it is useful for disciplining and controlling the work force. Under capitalism, of course, these two functions are interrelated, as noted above. Major contributors to this debate are Dickson (1974) Gorz (1976) and Marglin (1974). In fact both notions of technology, and of efficiency remain remarkably primitive in their sociological applications.

A more critical analysis of the politics of work argues for the ideological nature of much that has passed for organizational analysis, seeing much conventional organization theory, for example, as buttressing and mystifying existing inequalities and deprivations (see Fox, in this volume). More recent organization theory has addressed the question of the nature and origins of organizational technology and its implications for organizational design. Child, in an important piece (Child 1972), has pointed to the role of choice in organizational structure. He argues that organizational structures (with all their inequalities and hierarchy) reflect the assumptions and interests of the dominant coalition. More recently it has been suggested that organizational structure (the design of work and control) represents efforts by the senior members to control and direct the labours of their recalcitrant employees; efforts which are constantly subject to resistance and attack (see Salaman 1979, and Hyman and Fox in this volume).

To summarize this section. Marx pointed to the inherently political nature of work design in capitalism. Work is designed in order to maximize profitability, to direct and regulate, and to control the activities of employees whose interests are at odds with those of their employers. Recently these notions have found new application in the work of sociologists of work, who have tried to move beyond the rather bland assurances of conventional sociology that work design reflects undeniable imperatives of modern industrial society, and have focused their attention on the principles underlying modern work : the role of technology, and the place of class interests and values. Some of these writers are included in this volume. Others have been mentioned above.

3 Work and class

Capitalist societies and economies have already been defined in terms of two interrelated features: private ownership of the means of production and the pursuit of profit. These defining features produce classes.

Class refers to the relationship between groups and the means of production, i.e. owners versus non-owners. As Giddens puts it,

> Property relations constitute the axis of this dichotomous system: a minority of 'non-producers', who control the means of production, are able to use this position of control to extract from the majority of 'producers' the surplus product which is the source of their livelihood. (Giddens 1973 p 28)

It is an important feature of capitalism that it results in the supremacy of the market and the search for profit. Under capitalism labour becomes a commodity which is bought and sold on the market, bought by those who own capital.

The significance of this model of classes is not simply that they emerge as central and direct features of the defining element of capitalism, but also that they play a part in the destruction of that form of society. Classes are not just aggregates of people with a similar relationship to the means of production — they are also, occasionally but very importantly, *groups*, comprising people who have become aware of their similar position within the economic system, and their relationship to the interests of members of the opposed class. Under these conditions of class consciousness class becomes a political factor of great importance.

Marxist analysis seeks to explain the essential nature of capitalist society, and its future, not to produce a description of any particular historical case. From this point of view it is hardly relevant that the analysis is not entirely satisfactory as a description of twentieth-century capitalist societies (or for that matter of nineteenth-century capitalist societies either) since it does not set out to be one. It does not alert us, for example, to the considerable expansion of the middle class in these societies; an expansion which is not part of the dichotomous Marxist model. Members of this class (professionals and managers) are clearly differentiated from members of the working class (although they may all be propertyless) by their life-style and life chances in general, their political views, and their identification with the interests and values of the capital owners. Members of the middle class differ from members of the working class in terms of their life chances. This is a Weberian concept referring to the sorts of experiences and circumstances that follow a class location. Aspects of life chances are such things as income, job security, etc. Classes differ in the life chances of their members, and this is an important factor in the development of class-conscious attitudes. Differences in life chances — in experiences of social and financial rewards and deprivations — reveal the exploitative nature of capitalism and the human costs of a form of social and economic organization that evaluates and rewards men in terms of profit, and the market.

Capitalist society is a class society not only in the sense that it gives rise to differences in levels of reward and life chances but also in the more significant sense that these differences are systematically related to, and an inevitable part of, a form of economic arrangement which involves the pursuit of profit, and the use of profit as the central criterion of evaluation through the employment of the privately-owned means of production. Furthermore, class differences of interest permeate many other aspects of social life, notably of course, politics. And these differences are, finally, sometimes responsible for the development of class consciousness among the working class.

The fact that capitalist societies are class societies has a number of important implications for work in capitalist society. First, capitalism involves the buying and selling of labour. Those who buy constitute one class: those who sell constitute the other. Those who sell their expertise, knowledge and commitment in exchange for a privileged position in the system constitute a middle group. These class memberships are systematically related to differences in life chances and variations in rewards and deprivation. They are also related to attitudes and values concerning the nature, structure and fairness of the employing enterprise and the society at large. Furthermore, of course, these class positions are closely tied to differences in work *experiences.* Since capitalism involves the buying and selling of labour power for purposes other than those of the sellers of labour it becomes necessary to organize and control work tasks and organizations in such a way as to ensure maximum output and efficiency, rather than to ensure the comfort, safety, delight, creativity, cleanliness, etc., of the workers concerned. The following sections will explore these issues in the light of certain selected relevant empirical studies.

4 The experience of work in a class society

According to Marx, work in a capitalist (class) society is characterized by 'alienation'. Marx used this concept to describe, among other things, the impact and meaning of capitalism on the nature of men — on their ability to realize themselves. More precisely it means a detachment, a separation, that develops, under capitalism, between man and his work, his product, his colleagues and his true self. Its features are described as follows:

> First, that the work is *external* to the worker, that it is not a part of his nature, that consequently he does not fulfil himself in his work but denies himself, has a feeling of misery, not of well-being, does not develop freely a physical and mental energy, but is physically exhausted and mentally debased. The worker therefore feels himself at home only during his leisure, whereas at work he feels homeless. His work is not voluntary but imposed, *forced labour.* It is not the satisfaction of a need, but only a means for satisfying other needs. Its alien character is clearly shown by the fact that as soon as there is no physical or other compulsion it is avoided like the plague. Finally, the alienated character of work for the worker appears in the fact that it is not his work but work for someone else, that in

work he does not belong to himself but to another person. (Marx 1932 pp 177–8)

Under capitalism the worker is alienated from his product since this object is not in any way the result of the worker's creativity, skill, or planning: '. . . it never is *his* product at all; he is merely the instrument of its production. In a word, it is *alien* to him' (Schacht 1971 p 85). Alienation is the result of the worker selling his labour power to accumulate capital for the owners of the employing enterprise.

The worker under capitalism is alienated from his product not only in the sense that he is uninvolved in its production, and uninterested in its nature and quality, but also in the sense that the product represents and helps to recreate the system itself. By producing a commodity which is owned by the employer and sold for a profit which then further supports the capitalist system, as well as helping to accumulate more capital for investment, the worker is producing a 'hostile force'. The alienation of workers under capitalism does not result simply from their involvement in an industrial system of production, but from a *capitalist* system of production.

The same is true for another aspect of the worker's alienation — alienation from his own labour. This describes the situation when men sell their labour power to an employer, and put themselves under his control, in exchange for a wage. By selling their labour as a commodity the workers lose their capacity to fulfil themselves in their work. Thus the division of labour, far from freeing men from a direct dependence on nature actually imposes new restrictions and deprivations. In particular work becomes more and more machine-like, and increasingly subject to 'rationalization' in the search for profit.

Marx's concept of alienation has played an important part in the sociology of work. The main features of his sense of alienation and his use of the concept, which have been an inspiration to later sociological writings, include a moral, humanitarian critique of life and work in a capitalist society and of the values and priorities which determine events and decisions within such a society; and a concern to uncover the personal meaning and significance of life within this type of system, and in particular the impact of work activities, events and decisions on those concerned.

A great deal of the sociology of work, whether overtly radical or not, contains a strong sense of outrage at the sorts of work activities and conditions to which many people are subjected. Consider for example Gouldner's remarks on the 'unemployed self':

For many in modern industrial society, for the member of parliament no less than the coalminer, the world of work . . . is one of human insufficiency or of downright failure in the midst of technological triumph, or personal confusion in the midst of detailed organizational blueprints. (Gouldner 1969 p 346)

He argues that people's reports on their work reveal a common sentiment 'that work as many know it, is nothing less than the wasting of life' (Gouldner 1969 p 346). This perception of work follows, Gouldner argues, not simply from the complex and highly differential division of labour that characterizes advanced economies, but from the predominance within such societies of the value of usefulness. Things, and people, are evaluated in terms of their use.

Gouldner notes that one of the devastating consequences of this emphasis on utility and efficiency (measured of course in terms of output or profit) is that individuals learn to 'market' themselves — '. . . the individual learns what the system requires; he learns which parts of himself are unwanted and unworthy; he comes to organize his self and personality in conformity with the operating standards of utility' (Gouldner 1969 p 349). The same point has been made by Eric Fromm. Fromm argues that the modern era is characterized by a highly prevalent marketing orientation. Everything, even personalities, are assessed in terms of their market value, as commodities in the market. Not surprisingly the result of this is that people begin to see themselves in terms of the value others place on them. 'Since modern man experiences himself both as a seller and as the commodity to be sold on the market, his self-esteem depends on conditions beyond his control. If he is "successful", he is valuable; if not he is worthless' (Fromm 1947 p 62). It has also been argued that education plays a broadly similar role.

These writers use the concept of alienation (or are inspired by it) to describe some of the sentiments and attitudes that people develop in a capitalist and market-oriented society. The same sort of inspiration is evident in Huw Beynon's book *Working for Ford*, in particular the section where he describes the ambivalence towards their product displayed by the Ford workers.

Living in a society ruled by the tyranny of the market place men frequently find themselves attracted yet at the same time repelled by features of that society. Nothing better demonstrates this state amongst Ford workers than their relationship with the motor car. (Beynon 1975 p 110)

Sennett and Cobb's recent study, *The Hidden Injuries of Class* (1973), is directly concerned with the relation between class and the attitudes and self-image of working class people. These authors argue

that the nature of working class work and life are severely damaging
to those concerned. They write:

> The terrible thing about class in our society is that it sets up a
> contest for dignity. If you are a working class person . . . you have
> had to spend year after year being treated by people of a higher
> class as though there probably is little unusual or special about you
> to catch their attention . . . (Sennett and Cobb 1973 pp 147–8)

Other writers however have interpreted the Marxist sense of alienation in a rather more specific way, i.e. they have attempted to give
operational definitions to the concept. Writers such as Blauner, Argyris,
Dubin and others have attempted to relate the various attitudes and
feelings described above ('. . . that work is external to the worker . . .
His work is imposed, forced labour', etc.) to specific structural features
of particular work situations.

This aspect of the sociology of work inspired by a concern for the
alienation of the worker under capitalism researches the nature of
workers' work attitudes and feelings, and attempts to relate them to
aspects of the social organization of the productive enterprise – its size,
supervisory style, communications systems, etc. – or to the work itself,
the technology, and so on. The most obvious example of this approach
is Blauner's *Alienation and Freedom*.

There have been a large number of studies which document the
alienating effects of work in a capitalist society. That is the theme of
Huw Beynon's book:

> Working in a car plant involves coming to terms with the assembly
> line . . . Walking along the floor of the plant as a stranger you are
> deafened by the whine of the compressed air spanners, you step
> gingerly between and upon the knots of connecting air pipes which
> writhe like snakes in your path, and you stare at the moving cars
> on either side. This is the world of the operator. In and out of the
> cars, up and over the line, check the line speed and the model mix.
> Your mind restlessly alert . . . But still a blank – you keep trying to
> blot out what's happening. (Beynon 1975 p 109)

This section is not, however, about the meaning of work, or the
nature of the satisfaction that people derive (or are unable to derive)
from work. It is about the various ways in which Marx's concept of
alienation in capitalist societies has given rise to, or can be seen to have
influenced or inspired, certain important discussions within the sociology of work (which is not to claim that all the sociologists concerned
have done justice to the sense of the original). These areas of study,
which have been sketchily treated here but which are represented else-

where in this book, are on the one hand attempts to delineate the values and priorities prevalent in a market-oriented society and their impact on members of that society, and on the other, studies which try to describe workers' attitudes towards their work, their employing organization, their colleagues, etc., and to relate these to their position within the productive process in general (and their work situation, work technology and employing organization), and the various experiences and deprivations this involves (see the next section).

To summarize: one important way in which work in capitalist societies is influenced by its social and economic context is through the alienating consequences of work and life in such societies. These consequences are evident in two related ways: through the nature and impact of the priority attached to the profit motive, and the market, and through the sorts of work experiences, events and conditions to which many members of society are exposed, and the attitudes and ideas that are related to them. The evidence suggests that for a great many people the remarks of Marx quoted earlier are still highly appropriate.

The next section will explore in more detail the nature of work experiences with special reference to the extent to which work experiences and rewards still differ on a class basis. It will be remembered that part of the claimed utility of the class concept rests on the existence of differences in life chances associated with market capacity (notably, of course, possession or lack of possession of capital).

5 Working class work experiences and rewards

Classes are based upon ownership or non-ownership of the means of production. This distinction is directly related to differences in life chances and work experiences. By 'working class' is meant those people who sell their labour to those who own capital. However, it is necessary to exclude from the working class those people whose ownership of expert and professional skills and knowledge enables them to obtain a privileged share of the prerogatives and rewards of capital, and thus attain a privileged life style. However, this exclusion of the middle class from direct consideration in this section should not be understood as also implying exclusion of all those who are sometimes or occasionally described as 'middle class'. The label 'middle class' is used here to refer to professionals and to middle and senior levels of management — those members of organizations and firms who are, it is true, employed, but who are employed as the agents of the owners to represent them and to design, monitor and control the work of the work force. Of course, many of the members of this middle class are closely identified with capital not only through their values, commitments and privileges but through their schooling, family and social networks. The term 'middle class' is not used here to include such non-manual workers as shop assistants, secretaries, clerks, punch-card operators and all the many other 'white-collar' jobs that have developed as a result of the automation and enlargement of the bureaucratic office. Certainly some white-collar workers enjoy work conditions and benefits that distinguish them from manual workers as Goldthorpe and his colleagues and Wedderburn and Craig have documented. But a close look at the actual work of such groups, such as conducted by C. W. Mills in his famous *White Collar* (Mills 1956), shows that like manual workers they are daily involved in the *execution* of repetitive and demeaning work activities which are designed by, and in the interests of, those who own and control the office, shop or enterprise. In some cases their work conditions might be better; but their essential position as people who sell their labour within a system which entails organizing, designing and assessing such labour power for the sake of profit remains. Furthermore some writers have argued that viewed broadly not all white-collar workers enjoy similar distinctive work advantages (see Braverman 1974 Chapter 15). Braverman argues of some white-collar workers that:

> The problem of the so-called employee or white-collar worker which so bothered early generations of Marxists, and which was hailed by the anti-Marxists as a proof of the falsity of the 'proletarianization' thesis, has thus been unambiguously clarified by the polarization of office employment and the growth at one pole of an immense mass of *wage-workers*. The apparent trend to a large nonproletarian 'middle class' has resolved itself into the creation of a large proletariat in a new form. In its conditions of employment, this working population has lost all former superiorities over workers in industry, and in its scales of pay has sunk almost to the bottom. (Braverman 1974 pp 355–6)

It is, of course, true that some differences in work rewards and conditions between 'white-collar' and manual workers survive. But as Lockwood's analysis of clerks emphasizes, the white-collar worker of today is more clearly and self consciously proletarianized than his nineteenth-century counterpart. Neither is the term 'middle class' used here to include workers in service occupations – transport, retail trade, hotels, etc. This occupational sector has grown enormously over the last seventy years, mostly through using female labour. There are no useful grounds for regarding office cleaners, janitors, waitresses, petrol **pump** attendants, hospital attendants, etc. as middle class in the way in which that term is used in this book.

Within capitalism, work for most people is employment. Many of the 'costs' and deprivations suffered by those who sell their labour (rather than their expertise or knowledge and commitment) to those who own and control capital, and the enterprise based on capital, derive from their being controlled by rules, regulations, bonus schemes, assembly lines, supervisors, security men, and so on. This control is always supported — more or less successfully — by ideologies legitimating the control, justifying it, explaining it. Relationships of control within organizations — even when most depersonalized and routinized — are depriving, since they involve some men controlling the activities of others in the pursuit of their own interests and advantages. Not surprisingly, therefore, the various mechanisms of control are a frequent source of resentment.

Fox has noted that members of organizations have orientations not only towards the '. . . work and its accompanying social relations, how it is to be done, its rights and obligations, and its rewards and prospects' (Fox 1971 p 8) which he calls substantive orientations, but also '. . . the individual may . . . have orientations towards the nature of the decision-making procedures themselves' (Fox 1971 p 9). Orientations of the latter kind, which concern the right of some men to control others, and the degree of involvement and participation in that decision-making desired by the controlled, Fox terms 'procedural'. The distinction is an interesting and important one — for example it has been suggested that trade unions are much more concerned with substantive issues than procedural ones in their claims and negotiations. Mann writes:

> As trade unions are organized toward the attainment of economic bargaining gains, they tend in practice to lose sight of control issues, whether these concern the immediate work situation or wider-ranging questions of industrial structure. (Mann 1973 p 21)

Indeed Mann argues that job control is viewed, '. . . as something which can be exchanged periodically for economic rewards' (Mann 1973 p 22).

However, from the point of view of management the controls that are an intrinsic part of the purchase and employment of labour in a market-orientated system are crucial. From management's point of view their 'right' to control is essential: it is an integral part of the structure and process of organizations.

> The reason why hierarchy is so crucial for the organization's leaders is that it facilitates the making of decisions over which they can hope to exercise some control. Acceptance of the norms covering

these relationships is therefore the key to the acceptance of all other norms . . . the problem of 'authority' is therefore understandably a central issue. (Fox 1971 p 34)

As Fox goes on to stress, this central problem — both for organizational members and leaders and social scientists — revolves around the question of legitimacy — the situation in which the controlled grants his controller the right to control him. Not surprisingly, therefore, a great deal of management effort goes into demonstrating and justifying this 'right'. It should be added that — as the workers discover for themselves sooner or later — when ideology fails, when management's right to manage is questioned too frequently, and orders consequently challenged, power in the form of coercive sanctions is employed. This situation has recently been described with reference to a particular case of redundancy by Martin and Fryer (1973) in *Redundancy and Paternalist Capitalism.*

Beynon's study is actually about the battle for control, the questioning — and development of ideologies — of 'rights' to control, on both sides; this battle taking place within a context of a market economy, and the pursuit of efficiency, productivity and profit. He writes, 'This conflict over "rights" is a fundamental one and permeates union-management relationships' (Beynon 1975 p 144). It takes many forms, and appears in many different aspects of daily work.

The most important feature of working class work is the work itself, which follows directly from the priorities and principles of capitalist management. Beynon's book is a useful description of working class work.

> If you stand on the cat walk at the end of the plant you can look down over the whole assembly floor. Few people do, for to stand there and look at the endless, perpetual, tedium of it all is to be threatened by the overwhelming insanity of it. The sheer audacious madness of a system based upon men like those wishing their lives away. (Beynon 1975 p 109)

But it isn't just the nature of working class work and the forms of control and supervision that surround it that are important. Other factors too play a significant part in moulding experiences and attitudes. Beynon, for example, in *Working for Ford* lays great stress on the significance of security in a work context. But he also makes the point that no amount of planning, or even, finally, of consideration for the workers, can help to eliminate fluctuations in demand, changes in levels of investment, etc. And these circumstances reflect the workings, the priorities, and the rationality of capitalism. When these bear upon a particular factory or farm or other enterprise the implications are usually felt most severely by the lower-level employees.

Another example of the relationship between a system of economic organization based on the pursuit of profit through mobilization of the privately-owned means of production, and work events, is Nichols' article 'The sociology of accidents and the social production of industrial injury' (1975). In this piece Nichols argues that industrial accidents cannot be understood simply or satisfactorily in terms of what he calls the forensic approach. They have to be seen in the context of some men being controlled by others for certain goals (productivity, efficiency, finally profit). The pressure to keep up production underlies the accidents discussed by Nichols. Capitalist industrial production necessarily involves such competitive pressure, a pressure which despite safety precaution measures, inevitably causes dangers for the 'units of labour' — the workers.

Working class work is also characterized by many other negative features which do not apply to middle class work. Wedderburn and Craig (1974) supply material evidence of class-based differences in work conditions and rewards.

The next section investigates the relationship between these features of working class work and the development of class consciousness. But how are they received by the workers themselves? The evidence points overwhelmingly towards workers being dissatisfied, frustrated and deprived in their work — if not directly damaged. The evidence for this view comes not just from satisfaction surveys, which are notoriously inaccurate, but from studies like Beynon's, where the workers speak directly, and from the high levels of absenteeism, sabotage, strikes, turnover, etc., that have been reported — for example by the *Work in America* report (1973).

Some writers have argued that these class-based differences in work conditions, rewards and attitudes are breaking down as a result of the gradual transformation of capitalist societies into middle class societies. This thesis forms the background to Goldthorpe *et al*'s study of *The Affluent Worker* which investigates the class situation and associated attitudes and behaviour of a sample of affluent workers. This study is concerned to examine the theory of the

> . . . *decline* and *decomposition* of the working class. As the development of industrial societies continued, it was suggested, the working class, understood as a social stratum with its own distinctive ways of life, values and goals, would become increasingly eroded by the main currents of change. The very idea of a working class had been formed in, and in fact belonged to, the infancy of industrial society; in the

era to come it would steadily lose its empirical referent. Social
inequalities would no doubt persist; but these would be modified
and structured in such a way that the society of the future would be
an overwhelmingly 'middle-class' society, within which the divisions
of the past would no longer be recognizable. (Goldthorpe *et al* 1969
p 6)

They note a number of causes that have been suggested for this 'decline
and decomposition' of class differences:

Three main types of change which have stimulated new thinking
have been alluded to: economic, technological and managerial, and
ecological. (Goldthorpe *et al* 1969 p 7)

For our purposes the most interesting of these are those which assert
the 'homogenization' of earnings and living standards. This argument
notes the

. . . marked increase in income that had been achieved, from around
the end of the 1940s, among many sections of the working class:
that is to say, the new middle-income group was to be seen as largely
the result of the relatively rapid economic advance of substantial
numbers of manual workers and their families. (Goldthorpe *et al*
1969 p 7)

This process of *embourgeoisement*, which is associated, it is claimed,
with changes in consumption patterns, family life and culture is
reinforced by changes in technology and industrial management. These
changes are, on the one hand, responsible for the increases in productivity which underlie the new affluence, and on the other, for bringing
about changes in the occupational structure and the demand for responsible, technically competent and knowledgeable workers. A further consequence of technological and organizational change is the reduction of
staff/shop-floor distinctions. The new technology produces greater
work-force integration and commitment: systems of control and
reward necessarily become more flexible and liberal. This, in highly
abbreviated form, is the argument that Goldthorpe *et al* set out to test.

The results are well known. The authors assert the importance of
distinctions between three aspects of class (and therefore of *embourgeoisement*); the economic, the normative and the relational. The economic variable refers to levels of income and consumption. They go on
to stress the need to distinguish between people's roles as producers
and as consumers. While it may or may not be true that working and
middle class people are *spending* their money in the same way, their
productive roles may differ drastically and importantly.

Despite the possibly levelling effects of some forms of advanced technology and of modern employment policies, the work situation of white-collar employees is still generally superior to that of manual wage earners in terms of working conditions and amenities, continuity of employment, fringe benefits, long term income prospects and promotion chances. Class position is not merely a matter of consumer power: the function and status of a group within the social division of labour must still be regarded as being of basic importance. (Goldthorpe *et al* 1969 p 24)

Goldthorpe and his colleagues go on to demonstrate how the productive role of working class people — however affluent — differs from that of middle class people. It is safe to assume that such differences are even greater for less affluent workers in more traditional industries and work communities.

The work of the workers studied by Goldthorpe was fragmented, 'rationalized' and monotonous, and was disliked by a high proportion of workers. They remained in it, however, because of the high level of pay. As the authors point out, this means that

. . . for many of the affluent workers we studied, affluence had been achieved only at a price: that of accepting work which affords little in the way of intrinsic rewards and which is likely to be experienced essentially as *labour* — as the expenditure of effort motivated simply by the extrinsic reward of payment. (Goldthorpe *et al* 1969 p 58)

However, these authors also point out that the actual nature of the work was not the only cost of their relative affluence. For this was paid for by long, and highly inconvenient and dislocating hours of work.

The work of working class and middle class people differs in other ways too: working conditions, promotion prospects, security, etc. Also very important are differences in work orientation and outlook: the affluent workers revealed a very instrumental orientation towards their work — 'The workplace was where they came to earn their living, to sell their labour for the best return they could get' (Goldthorpe *et al* 1969 p 67). For the middle class respondents work was more likely to be seen as a potential source of intrinsic satisfaction and social relationships. The work orientations of the affluent workers, furthermore, were of great importance in determining their attitudes towards their employing organization and the

. . . likelihood of their becoming at all highly integrated into their firms in the manner typical of many middle class employees . . . their relationship with their employer is a purely market or contractual one . . . The attachment of the majority of our affluent workers

to their firms was . . . very largely a matter of the cash nexus, and
their involvement in their employing organizations, of a markedly
calculative kind. (Goldthorpe *et al* 1969 pp 80—1)

Men's work expectations and orientations are most important in understanding their reactions to work events and rewards — or deprivations.
   The important feature of deprivations associated with working class
jobs and employment situations — relative to middle class jobs — is that
they result from the differential market power of these groups who sell
their labour within the society which is controlled by and in the interests of the owners of capital, and not by those who own only their
labour. Inevitably within such an economic system the worker is valued
in terms of his usefulness (his contribution to efficiency, productivity
and ultimately, profit).
   Finally it should be noted that our focus, in this section, has been
on class-based differences in work experiences, conditions, rewards,
activities, prospects, attitudes, etc. — differences which are not simply
random aspects of subordinate positions in a complex division of labour,
but are systematically related to the capitalist nature of the economy
and society. This contextual feature involves men selling their labour
to others who organize and use them in the pursuit of productivity and
profit. This means a constant potential clash of interest between the
sellers and buyers of labour, a clash which is revealed in the differential
allocation of work-based rewards and deprivations, which is directly
related to the market power of those concerned. At the same time
within the organization and the society, efforts are made to legitimate
the differential distribution of rewards, and the inevitable relationships
of super-and subordination: to preserve managements' right to manage.
   It is one of the features of class societies that deprivations (or
rewards) in one area of social life are highly associated with deprivations (or rewards) in other areas. So we would expect to find that those
who are deprived at work, in the sorts of ways described above, are also
deprived in terms of health, housing, education, etc. And such indeed is
the case. Furthermore these differences, these inequalities, are historically very stable, and are transmitted, in various ways, generationally.
   We have described how work experiences, in the widest sense, differ
in class terms. Many of these differences are dramatic, affecting many
aspects of life and personal happiness and health. We have also noted
that class is not merely a method of describing the allocation of
society's rewards and tribulations, but a way of understanding the
nature of a society, and explaining its history. That is why, in the
previous section, an attempt was made to relate work experience to
position, and market power, within a market-dominated economic

system. But a further task remains if we are to relate class to history; and that is to explore the link between class events and experiences and men's consciousness – or awareness – of these differences, and their origins.

6 Work and class consciousness

How do workers define and 'experience' the various deprivations to which they are subjected at work? Clearly an interest in this question has many practical and political implications. Practical, in the sense that, as noted above, the legitimacy of the structure and hierarchy of an enterprise is highly important from the point of view of the owners and controllers of the enterprise.

This brings out the political aspects of this topic. They were developed most fully by Marx with his suggestion that various features of capitalism, as it was experienced by the working class (notably endemic economic crises resulting in increasing deprivation), would result in the development of revolutionary, working class consciousness and political organization and the overthrow of the capitalist system. Class consciousness involves a number of elements which require exposition – Mann characterizes them in terms of class identity:

> . . . the definition of oneself as working class, as playing a distinctive role in common with other workers in the productive process. Secondly comes class opposition – the perception that the capitalist and his agents constitute an enduring opponent to oneself . . . Thirdly is class totality – the acceptance of the two previous elements as the defining characteristics of (a) one's total social situation and (b) the whole society in which one lives. Finally comes the conception of an alternative society, a goal toward which one moves through the struggle with the opponent. (Mann 1973 p 13)

How do these various elements relate to work activities and conditions? How are the sorts of deprivations and circumstances described in the last section actually experienced? As far as class consciousness is concerned it is clear that to a very considerable extent the working class is incorporated into the capitalist system. This is not to deny the occurrence of hostile outbursts, of smouldering resentment, of a reasonably widespread sense of a conflict of interest between those who sell labour and those who buy it. But it is to assert that, at least in Britain,

> The great English working class, this titanic social force which seemed to be unchained by the rapid development of English capitalism in the first half of the nineteenth century, did not finally emerge

to dominate and remake English society. Instead, after the 1840s it quickly turned into an apparently docile class. It embraced one species of moderate reformism after another, became a consciously subordinate part of bourgeois society, and has remained wedded to the narrowest and greyest of bourgeois ideologies in this principal of movements. (Nairn 1972 p 188)

Most explanations for the relative lack of militancy and class consciousness among the British working class refer to a number of features of twentieth-century British society. These include (i) the increase in standards of living, and the spread of citizenship rights; (ii) participation by a reformist political labour movement in parliamentary institutions; (iii) the increasing role of the state in modifying and avoiding some of the economic difficulties of capitalism, and the more damaging consequences of this system — unemployment, for example — and in supplying welfare, health and educational provisions; (iv) the institutionalization of class conflict through trade unions on the one hand and employers' federations on the other, with the state as the arbiter; (v) the significance of various 'sources of stability' as Parkin calls them, such as some degree of social mobility, the relative nature of people's expectations; (vi) various legitimating, or distracting, value systems, such as, traditionally, the established church.

Many writers explain the relative lack of revolutionary class consciousness among the working class of this country by reference to the culture, or ideology that is prevalent. Mann for example has argued that among manual workers in

> . . . traditional industries a realistic appraisal of alternative structure is lacking even among the most class-conscious workers in the most explosive situations. Whatever the *objective* possibility that they might be the bearers of a new principle of social structure — collectivism — they themselves either do not perceive this or do not know how to translate it into action. (Mann 1973 p 69)

Mann emphasizes the importance of the working class's inability to construct radical alternative conceptions of social structure. He notes that working class culture does contain various 'deviant values', but that they are somewhat vague and simplistic. Moorhouse and Chamberlain have noted,

> According to Mann the 'agencies of political radicalism' are unable to utilize these deviant values because they are forever struggling against their opponents' appeals to emotive, traditional and national symbols to which a 'loyal' response has been inculcated through the schools and mass media. (Moorhouse and Chamberlain 1974 p 387)

Miliband also focuses on the process through which '. . . members of the dominant classes are able, by virtue of their position, for instance as employers, to dissuade members of the subordinate classes, if not from holding, at least from voicing unorthodox views' (Miliband 1969 p 181). We have seen that others have argued that this process actually extends so far as to obstruct their even *developing* genuinely radical views. To support his argument Miliband discusses the reformist nature of even 'radical' political parties in Britain, the role of the Church, of nationalism, of political socialization in general, and the mass media. A broadly similar point has been made by Parkin when he argues that the dominant value system of society derives from the established institutional order — and, not surprisingly, supports it (Parkin 1971).

These then are some of the reasons that have been adduced to explain the lack — so far — of a significant revolutionary working class movement in this country, to explain the

> . . . apparent readiness of the mass of wage workers under capitalism to accept the responsibilities along with the rights of national citizenship and to pursue their objectives through organizations which recognized 'the rules of the game' within both the industrial and political sectors. (Goldthorpe *et al* 1969 p 5)

But does this mean that people are unaware of the work-based deprivations and inequalities mentioned earlier, or that they are indifferent to them?

The point of the arguments described above is that they describe the various subtle societal processes whereby these work-based discontents and resentments are absorbed, deflected and handled such that they rarely give rise to explicit, full class consciousness and political organization. (For a discussion of some of these processes in work organizations, see Salaman 1970.) But it is obvious that despite the 'success' of such societal mechanisms, the extent of acquiescence, resignation, or class consciousness varies from plant to plant, industry to industry, region to region. Despite the factors mentioned above there are some expressions of class consciousness, some dissenting subcultures, some 'radical value systems' as Parkin calls them. There are also, more frequently, 'subordinate value systems' which lack the political class-conscious elements of the radical culture, but which emphasize among other things a 'them and us' view of society. However, as Parkin and others have noted these local, working class cultures are, in the long term, far removed from true class consciousness. Despite the various factors mentioned above it is possible to find examples and occasions of class consciousness of various kinds even though they rarely add up to the sort of total, radical critique described by Mann in his definition of class consciousness.

However, more mundane examples of class consciousness, containing just one or two of the elements of Mann's definition, are not rare. These require explanation and Lockwood's classic study *The Blackcoated Worker* (1958) can serve as a useful starting point. The important feature of Lockwood's analysis of the factors responsible for the development — or lack of development — of class consciousness among 'blackcoated' workers — i.e. clerks — is his emphasis on analysing the actual economic consequences and social experiences in which people were involved because of their location within the productive process, the division of labour. He stresses for example that '. . . the mere fact of "propertylessness" provided no explanation of the actual presence or absence of class consciousness in a group' (Lockwood 1958 p 15). By 'class consciousness' Lockwood means '. . . identification with, or alienation from, the working class' (Lockwood 1958 p 13).

Lockwood argues that different levels of class consciousness displayed by clerks and manual workers, or even variations among clerks themselves over time, are explicable in terms of difference in class position. He distinguishes between various aspects of class position, which can vary independently.

> First, 'market situation', that is to say the economic position narrowly conceived, consisting of source and size of income, degree of job-security, and opportunity for upward occupational mobility. Secondly, 'work situation', the set of social relationships in which the individual is involved at work by virtue of his position in the division of labour. And finally, 'status situation', or the position of the individual in the hierarchy of prestige in the society at large. *The experiences originating in these three spheres may be seen as the principal determinants of class consciousness.* (Lockwood 1958 p 15, my emphasis)

Lockwood then proceeds to explain the class consciousness of clerks in terms of features of, and changes in, these three factors.

Lockwood makes the important point that in order to understand the 'typical sentiments and interests' of a group it is necessary to investigate the social relations prevalent in the work place — the relationships in which the members are involved at work. This point is developed in his 1966 paper, 'Sources of variation in working class images of society'. In this article Lockwood maintains his interest in the development of class consciousness through a consideration of the nature of class imagery, and the relationship between images of society (i.e. of class structure) and aspects of work and *community*. Images of society are related to the development or lack of development of class consciousness, as defined by Lockwood. Class consciousness as defined by Lockwood is not uncommon, and consists of just some of the elements mentioned by Mann and others.

In his exposition of three ideal types of worker, each with a distinctive work situation, and social imagery, Lockwood feels the necessity to include reference to the social milieu within which work occurs. The community structure of the types of worker are important, in Lockwood's analysis, in explaining the workers' social imagery. He writes for example, about the 'privatized' social life on the new estates where the 'privatized' worker, lives. And he notes the importance of occupational communities for the development of the proletarian traditional worker. This inclusion of the outside lives and social contexts of the workers he describes serves to emphasize the importance of non-work factors in the perception, and, therefore, the experience, of work relationships and events.

Lockwood differentiates a number of images of class (based on different industrial and community milieux) which he maintains are variously related to class conscious attitudes. Two of these images of society are especially interesting. The proletarian conception of society is '. . . centred on an awareness of "us" in contradistinction to "them" who are not part of "us" ' (Lockwood 1966 p 199). He further argues that this dichotomous model is related to class consciousness. The work-community background of the proletarian worker results in an image of the class structure of society which in turn is closely related to class conscious attitudes. The privatized worker on the other hand has a pecuniary model of society. Not only does he view his work in terms of the money it pays, but he conceives of class divisions in money terms — and the goods that money buys. This sort of class imagery

> . . . leads to neither class consciousness nor status consciousness but to commodity consciousness . . . the pecuniary universe is one in which inequalities are not expressed through social relationships at all. (Lockwood 1966 p 207)

A number of recent commentators have argued that in fact class images are more complex, variable and 'inconsistent' than Lockwood's early paper suggests (see for example Brown and Brannen 1970a and 1970b). It has also been remarked that the dichotomous view of class relationships apparently maintained by traditional workers in working class communities need not be directly related to class consciousness. In fact it might be inversely related, since such a view of society might lead to an extreme parochialism. Class consciousness, as Westergaard has pointed out, involves a feeling of *class* solidarity, not local, community solidarity.

But from our point of view the most important aspect of Lockwood's analysis is the suggestion that working men can vary in their work orientations and aspirations: in particular Lockwood distinguishes between the involvement of the traditional worker and the 'extrinsic' or instrumental orientation of the privatized worker. This notion of workers' work orientations has been suggested by many other writers and researchers — notably Goldthorpe *et al* (1968), Ingham (1967), Argyris (1968).

If workers have differing orientations towards their work the obvious implication is that what one worker might find entirely unsatisfactory and depriving another might view with relative indifference. In particular it has been suggested that the sort of instrumental orientation to work described by Lockwood (1966) and Goldthorpe *et al* (1968) might serve to reduce the impact of depriving work experiences: workers with an 'instrumental' orientation towards work might develop their 'central life interests' outside of work; or might be prepared to put up with their work in *exchange* for the rewards they particularly value and have been taught to value — money.

There are a number of difficulties with this view. They revolve around the question of the *salience* of the instrumental priorities of the privatized worker. Does he still hope for more satisfying work? Is he really simply denying to himself and the researcher aspirations he knows he cannot fulfil? Or has he in fact established a genuine and strongly held perception and evaluation of work which dominates his selection and experience of his daily work, and which faithfully reflects the values and priorities of capitalist society? If the orientation is not a strongly held one but a begrudging acknowledgement of the options and priorities available, a form of 'adjustment', as Alan Fox puts it, to the world as it is, then this has obvious implications for the development — and display — of class consciousness and industrial action, particularly of the 'hostile outburst' variety. But if this orientation is a strongly held priority in life then it might seem that this would result in the accommodation of the workers into the capitalist work system, which emphasizes the economic exchange involved in the purchase of labour, to the exclusion of other rewards. In fact Fox argues, in Chapter 5, that these two possibilities are not mutually exclusive.

Sennett and Cobb do not regard such attitudes and behaviour as evidence of the incorporation of the working class into the values of their society such that they are prepared, or even willing, to accept the 'costs' of their work, and class position, in exchange for the rewards of consumerism. On the contrary,

   . . . the activities which keep people moving in a class society, which make them seek more money, more possessions, higher status jobs, do not originate in a materialistic desire, or even sensuous appreciation of things, but out of an attempt to restore a psychological deprivation, that the class structure has effected in their lives . . . *the psychological motivation instilled by a class society is to heal a doubt about the self* . . . (Sennett and Cobb 1972 p 171)

But if 'instrumentality' is so deeply held that it '. . . operates like a local anaesthetic' (Daniel 1969) then it is likely that workers' reactions to their work experiences will be in terms of demands for increased quantities of the only reward they value — money. And it might well be that when industrial relations, negotiations and industrial conflict take place in terms of the financial aspects of the employment contract true class consciousness is far away indeed.

It has been argued that the increasing predominance of an 'extrinsic' orientation to work, an emphasis on the financial rewards of work means that the workers concerned *tolerate* the boredom, repetition, danger and the like of their work in exchange for financial rewards, and that they restrict their attempts to improve or change their work situations to demands for more money. Both these consequences obviously involve an incorporation of the worker into the values of the capitalist system. Specifically, 'economism' which is the restriction of trade union activity to struggles over '. . . the modifications of market capacity to secure scarce economic rewards' (Giddens 1973 p 205) involves an encapsulation of industrial conflict, since it not only fails to question the bases of the employment contract, and the 'rights' surrounding it, but actually accepts and deals in the basic value premises of capitalism. An alternative trade union orientation — conflict over control is — as many writers have remarked (Giddens 1973, Fox 1971, Mann 1973) much more political in that it involves a questioning of, and an attempt to gain control over, decision-making in industry. However, managements' right to control is, because of its importance, carefully guarded, and is buttressed by a variety of legitimating processes. (For a contrary view; see Goodrich 1975, and Hyman in this volume.)

Even if it is true that instrumentality is becoming the dominant and salient orientation towards work — and it would seem likely that the employment situation *is* increasingly characterized by what Alan Fox has described as 'low trust' relations, which involve a high degree of economic exchange features such as instrumentality and calculation (Fox 1974) — then this does not necessarily mean that the working class will become (has become) incorporated into the capitalist system. On the contrary, an emphasis on financial rewards is highly volatile. Fox has written:

Insofar as subordinates are — or can be brought to be — strongly committed to the value of a continuously rising material standard of life, managers may hope to strengthen their legitimacy by trying to meet subordinates' aspirations in respect of material rewards, welfare and fringe benefits. Since this is one of the appetites that grow by what they feed upon, it is apt to prove an unstable base for authority. (Fox 1971 p 41)

The same point has been made by other writers: 'economism' is only non-political and non-radical as long as it is satisfied; it also frequently involves disputes over questions of control. Once demands are not met, workers can be extremely militant, and, from the managerial point of view, highly disruptive. Goldthorpe has pointed out that a class society, with the wide disparities in wealth, life-chances and power that such a society involves, might generate discontent among those whose aspirations have broken the bounds of traditional constraints. The result: 'Within a society in which inequality exists as a brute fact — largely without moral legitimation — "disorderly" industrial relations cannot be understood as a particularly pathological development' (Goldthorpe 1974 p 226). From such 'disorderly' industrial relations, from frustrated wage demands, may well develop some of the elements of class consciousness described by Mann. In particular an attempt to discover and maintain 'fair' wage levels might bring into question the whole nature of the employment contract, and this in turn result in an awareness of the more 'political' aspects of work and employment — including a questioning of managerial rights. As Eldridge says, 'Once the cash-nexus becomes of central concern the character of employer-employee relations is affected' (1975 p 311).

Similarly government attempts to restrain or control wage demands and increases transform trade-union events and negotiations into political events. Such government activity as statutory wage control breaks down the apparent separation of industrial and political spheres of action. As Levison remarks: '. . . the [wage] freeze made the central economic issues for working class Americans, the relations of their wages to prices and profits, *political* issues' (Levison 1974 p 269).

In the past such topics were left to the impersonal forces of the 'market'. If a worker's wage gains were eaten up by inflation, the only solution, was to wait until the next contract and demand more money. In politicizing the economy such government action has also politicized instrumentality.

Ironically the very attitudes which have seemed to distract workers from their work deprivations and cause them and their representatives to direct work demands into economic terms might also result, in less favourable economic circumstances, in disruptive industrial activity and a growing awareness of the class reality of their situation – their status as *commodities*. This is one of the core notions of class consciousness.

In conclusion, while the previous section asserted the persistence of class-based inequalities of various sorts at work, this section has considered the ways in which these experiences were perceived by those concerned, and how they relate to the development of class consciousness. The important role of various societal features in the development of a radical political organization was stressed but it was noted that certain elements of the Marxist notion of class consciousness could be discerned quite frequently. In attempting to explain variations in class consciousness (defined in terms of working class identification) recourse was made to Lockwood's three-part distinction of work, market and status situations. However it was noted that it was also necessary to consider the outside-work social context. The relationship between class consciousness and orientation to work (which defined the nature of work experience, employers, colleagues, etc.) was stressed, but the suggestion that instrumentality necessarily implied incorporation and acquiesence was questioned. An instrumental orientation even if it does work 'like an anaesthetic' (which is highly doubtful) could result in a true conception of the workers' position – that they are *commodities*.

7 Work and occupation

For many people work means membership of an occupation. An occupation involves more than just a work title; for in that sense everybody who worked would have an occupation, and such a usage would lose the distinctive and important aspects of the concept. Occupation refers to identity-giving work; work consisting of an acknowledged and recognized body of skills, activities and knowledge which are regarded as having significance for the identity and values of those concerned. To describe a man's work as an occupation suggests that this work carries implications for his identity and attitudes, and, possibly, for his choice of friends and associates (see Salaman 1975). Obviously occupations are not limited only to the middle class; there are also working-class occupations.

Such a definition of occupation raises a number of issues for the sociology of work. Occupations are potential and usually actual 'collectivities'. They involve their members in having some sense of similarity, of colleagueship. This sense of colleagueship, and shared attitudes, can have important implications. For one thing it is obvious that some occupations have a great deal more power than others. This power derives from the members of the occupation gaining collective control over their own work activities. These occupations are called professions.

However, some non-professional, working class occupations also exert this sort of power over their members — skilled trades such as printing, for example. Interestingly these occupations reflect very clearly the ambivalence of the skilled workers' situation — for on the one hand they imply a strong sense of solidarity, and an emphasis on collective action, but on the other these occupations seek to defend, or enhance, their privileged position against other, less advantaged, working class groups. And this leads to a reduction in working class solidarity.

The culture of the professions, however — which emphasizes autonomy, self-regulation, individualism — and which is supported by the power of the collective, professional body, strongly supports middle class ideology. For a thorough discussion of these issues see Terry Johnson's chapter in this volume.

The attitudes, and culture that are shared by the members of occupations — and which play an important part in directing their work activities — can be highly significant socially, and this significance lies in the political implications of professional work, for example, psychiatry, medicine, or science. Another important feature of occupations is that the class-based experiences and events described earlier are not spread evenly among varieties of working class work, but occur, at any one time, unevenly, and frequently on an occupational basis. The implication of this is that the lot of a particular occupation may deteriorate rapidly and dramatically while conditions for most people are less affected. This means that a consciousness of shared, working class destiny is replaced by occupational consciousness, and by attempts to improve the position of one particular occupation. Not surprisingly this sort of activity can be represented simply as stubborn resistance to the inevitable progress of history, technology, etc. And in such a way the *class* — as against occupational — basis of the conflict can be avoided.

Thompson's book (1968) is an attempt to analyse occupational responses to the economic and technological changes of the early industrial revolution. Underlying these changes and their drastic consequences is the fact that the workers concerned found themselves possessing skills and expertise which were no longer marketable. The market for their labour had altered, with devastating consequences for their lives and livelihoods. Thompson gives clear expression to the way in which class events, and the operation of a class-based economic system which evaluates people in terms of the profit that can be made from their labour, actually affects people through their occupation, and how responses to these experiences tend to be in occupational terms, and sometimes to appear retrograde, parochial and, occasionally, fantastic.

Numerous studies describe the plight of modern equivalents to the hand-loom weavers. Tunstall's study of fishermen, for example (1962), describes the dangers and deprivations experienced by men who seem trapped in a cycle of occupational hardship and economic exploitation and an occupational culture which interprets these experiences in such a fatalistic way as to permit the perpetuation of the arrangements.

The culture shared by members of an occupation is also important because such cultures perform an ideological function with reference to inter-occupational relationships and the attempts, by members of an occupation, to advance its interests. Such an enterprise usually takes the form of a description of the nature of the occupational work and of the knowledge and expertise upon which it is based, an analysis of the nature of clients, colleagues and competitors and an argument that the true interests of client and society are best served by practitioners establishing and retaining control over their own occupational practice. In many cases the occupation or profession asserts the need for it to control, select, train and monitor entrants to the occupation, in the public interest. Sometimes as in the case of professionals this control is supported by legislation.

There are many examples in the literature of such ideologies being employed by members of competing occupations to justify and legitimate their expansionist (or defensive) positions. All occupations involve some degree of occupational consciousness, but with some interesting exceptions it is true that 'the degree to which a group has developed a strong occupational consciousness is the degree to which it is capable of increasing its political power and its material rewards' (Krause 1971 p 85).

Members of occupations use ideologies in attempts to increase their power, status and rewards, though some occupations, and some sorts of occupational tasks and work, are better placed than others to develop them. All such ideologies have certain common features:

> An inevitable part of any group action on its own behalf is an ideology which summarizes the meaning of its action and gives reasons why others should support it. Since occupations act politically, either in the strict or the broader sense of this term, they use ideologies . . . occupational ideologies are used by specific

occupational groups to gain the support and action of target groups, such as the occupation's direct clientele . . . other occupational groups with whom the group deals, the government and the general public . . . The 'expertise' of an occupation is often exaggerated for the effect it will have on its publics. (Krause 1971 pp 88–9)

The occupations that have had greatest success in disseminating their occupational ideologies are called professions. A significant feature of this success is that, to an extent, professions have developed a legitimate authority to define the nature of subsystems of society and a category of its members, i.e. clients and the public interest. As Krause has noted, 'To define the public interest as the same as the interests of one's own group is a privilege of power' (Krause 1971 p 98).

A number of recent studies of professions and professionalization have argued, not only that professional cultures, like any occupational culture, serve to represent and advance the interests of the members of the occupation, but also that the particular form of occupational organization known as professionalism (i.e., basically, colleague control rather than client control) is highly advantageous to the practitioners. One advantage is that it insulates the professional from external scrutiny and assessment, and supplies a power basis for client control.

Professions are also important from the point of view of our interest in analysing the relationship between work (and occupations and professions) and society, because of the political implications of professional ideologies and the power of professionals to enforce them. McKinlay has remarked that

> . . . several dominant occupations (especially medicine and law) have come to occupy uniquely powerful positions in western societies from which they monopolistically initiate, direct and regulate widespread social change. Several of the mechanisms which have facilitated these developments [are as follows] . . . the emergence of a mythology concerning professionalism: the removal of certain activities from external observability and evaluation: a process by which professionals have become generalized wise men with an unwarranted mandate to challenge others, through the accordance of an unprecedented degree of trust based on ill-founded claims to altruism: and through the manufacture of artificial needs which render their services absolutely indispensable. (McKinlay 1973 p 77)

McKinlay describes the techniques whereby professionals enlarge their areas of professional activity and control; but it still remains to be demonstrated that the control itself, or the priorities and knowledge held by members of professions, are anything more than 'necessary' working techniques and practices. After all, although it might be noticeable that, say, lawyers appear to be gradually assuming an authority over previously unregulated areas of life, or that social workers are gradually involving themselves in activities previously the responsibility only of the individuals concerned, or that medical men seem to be encroaching into areas of study and research previously the responsibility of social scientists, nevertheless it needs to be shown that such extension of influence and control represents what might be called occupational imperialism.

This is indeed the intention of a number of recent writers some of whose work is discussed by Geoff Esland in Chapters 7 and 8. The starting point for such an analysis is the notion that knowledge (whether professional or academic) is not neutral, or value-free, but can be seen either as a means of legitimating interests, or as a controlling structure in itself. Some writers have argued that scientific knowledge has become a 'new form of legitimating power and privilege' that '. . . permits the extension of an exploitative instrumental rationalization' (Shroyer 1970 p 210). Such a function follows from the way in which such knowledge can be used to disguise the interests that underlie — and are served by — decisions that affect many people's destinies. Frequently such decisions are presented — by the occupation or profession concerned, be it accountants, scientists, planners or whatever — as a possibly unfortunate outcome of an inevitable and inexorable logic or 'technical necessity'. In this way the real nature of such a logic, and its impact on those concerned, is disguised. Knowledge which justifies the instrumental rationality of decisions or which propounds the importance of instrumental effectiveness can be seen to '. . . work against a broader mode of rationalization that would maximize the participation and individuation of affected people' (Shroyer 1970 p 211). People's resistance to such decisions as might affect them is sapped by the high degree of acceptability and authority granted to such criteria. The 'inevitability' of scientific and technological 'progress' thus becomes a self-fulfilling prophecy. See Chapter 2 by Peter Hamilton.

Esland *et al* (1975) supply a number of examples of this political aspect of occupational/professional knowledge and the way it is disseminated within society. Most of them concern those professions such as psychology, medicine and the social services which have achieved some sort of mandate to define the nature of some of society's members and which have socially classifying and theorizing powers. These professions have managed to establish their right, sometimes legally supported, to define what sort of action is necessary within gradually enlarging areas, and have gained monopolistic control over activity in these areas. To define, classify, instruct and theorize about society, its

members and their various needs and problems is to be political, and to
re-create the structures of values and legitimation operative within the
society. Within modern, industrial societies, for example, it has been
argued that '. . . the scientistic image of science has become the dominant legitimating system of advanced industrial society' (Shroyer 1970
p 212). One of the implications is that decisions are presented in terms
of the value-free technical criterion of efficiency and the like, and are
thereby removed from political debate. Laymen become defined as
unequipped to make choices in the relevant spheres of action, which
must be left to the 'qualified experts'.

Conclusion

This chapter has ranged widely over a number of issues in the sociology
of work. The intention has been to show how these various issues are
interconnected aspects of the *politics of work*. By this is meant a
concern for the ways in which work experiences, rewards, activities,
etc., are related to the organization and structure of power and interests
within society. It was argued that the capitalist nature of western
economies was highly significant for the nature of work experience. In
the chapter itself the concept of class was employed to illuminate the
varieties of work rewards, activities, etc., and people's perception of
and reactions to these differences. Some attention was given to the
relationship between work and the development of class consciousness,
and it was argued that the form of work orientation which many
commentators had regarded as indicative of an incorporation of workers into the priorities of the capitalist system could ultimately lead to
a consciousness of the *commodity status* of the worker. An interest in
the politics of work also led to a concern for the ways in which particular occupations and professions develop cultures and ideologies that
define the nature of the occupation, its societal role and importance,
and nature of the work, clients, competitors, etc. Sometimes these
occupational cultures represent occupational response to class-based
deprivations and changes.

It was noted that professions are occupations, the members of which
have established the claim that they must be controlled by their colleagues, and must commit themselves to the professional value system
and the forms of behaviour it requires. Two political implications of
professionalism were discussed — first, that although professionalism
involves the assertion of a right to define the public interest, and of the
altruism of the profession and its members, nevertheless evidence

suggests that such arrangements are also highly compatible with the well-being of the practitioners (see Freidson 1970), and that professional value systems perform an ideological function. Second, the relationship between professionalism and the structure of legitimating and controlling knowledge within society was briefly discussed. It was suggested that those occupations and professions which have established an authoritative mandate to classify and treat society and its members and problems, and those that create knowledge, are in a particularly important position to supply legitimating forms of knowledge.

CHAPTER 2

Peter Hamilton

Social theory and the problematic concept of work

Introduction

The sociologist, in attempting to understand work experiences, classifies and generalizes these experiences so as to relate them to certain collective features of societies. But what is the material which constitutes the reference points or empirical data on which concepts and theories are built?

Let us look at an example of work: work in a mechanized factory, where the demands of the production line determine both the nature of the work and the forms of social relationship among those people involved in the work situation.

PHIL STALLINGS
He is a spot-welder at the Ford assembly plant on the far South Side of Chicago. He is twenty-seven years old: recently married. He works the third shift: 3.30 P.M. to midnight.

I start the automobile, the first welds. From there it goes to another line, where the floor's put on, the roof, the trunk hood, the doors. Then it's put on a frame. There is hundreds of lines.

The welding gun's got a square handle, with a button on the top for high voltage and a button on the bottom for low. The first is to clamp the metal together. The second is to fuse it.

The gun hangs from a ceiling, over tables that ride on a track. It travels in a circle, oblong, like an egg. You stand on a cement platform, maybe six inches from the ground.

I stand in one spot, about two- or three-feet area, all night. The only time a person stops is when the line stops. We do about thirty-two jobs per car, per unit. Forty-eight units an hour, eight hours a day. Thirty-two times forty-eight times eight. Figure it out. That's how many times I push that button.

The noise, oh it's tremendous. You open your mouth and you're liable to get a mouthful of sparks. (Shows his arms.) That's a burn, these are burns. You don't compete against the noise. You go to yell and at the same time you're straining to manoeuvre the gun to where you have to weld.

You got some guys that are uptight, and they're not sociable. It's too rough. You pretty much stay to yourself. You get involved with yourself. You dream, you think of things you've done. I drift back continuously to when I was a kid and what me and my brothers did. The things you love most are the things you drift back into.

Lots of times I worked from the time I started to the time of the break and I never realized I had even worked. When you dream, you reduce the chances of friction with the foreman or with the next guy.

It don't stop. It just goes and goes and goes. I bet there's men who have lived and died out there, never seen the end of that line. And they never will — because it's endless. It's like a serpent. It's just all body, no tail. It can do things to you . . . (Laughs.)

Repetition is such that if you were to think about the job itself, you'd slowly go out of your mind. You'd let your problems build up, you'd get to a point where you'd be at the fellow next to you — his throat. Every time the foreman came by and looked at you, you'd have something to say. You just strike out at anything you can. So if you involve yourself by yourself, you overcome this.

I don't like the pressure, the intimidation. How would you like to go up to someone and say, 'I would like to go to the bathroom.' If the foreman doesn't like you, he'll make you hold it, just ignore you. Should I leave this job to go to the bathroom I risk being fired. The line moves all the time.

I work next to Jim Grayson and he's preoccupied. The guy on my left, he's a Mexican, speaking Spanish, so it's pretty hard to understand him. You just avoid him. Brophy, he's a young fella, he's going to college. He works catty-corner from me. Him and I talk from time to time. If he ain't in the mood, I don't talk. If I ain't in the mood, he knows it.

Oh sure, there's tension here. It's not always obvious, but the whites stay with the whites and the coloureds stay with the coloureds. When you go into Ford, Ford says, "Can you work with other men?" This stops a lot of trouble, 'cause when you're working side by side with a guy, they can't afford to have guys fighting. When two men don't socialize, that means two guys are gonna do more work, know what I mean?

I don't understand how come more guys don't flip. Because you're nothing more than a machine when you hit this type of thing. They give better care to that machine than they will to you. They'll have more respect, give more attention to that machine. And you *know* this. Somehow you get the feeling that the machine is better than you are. (Laughs.)

You really begin to wonder. What price do they put on me? Look at the price they put on the machine. If that machine breaks down, there's somebody out there to fix it right away. If I break down, I'm just pushed over to the other side till another man takes my place. The only thing they have on their mind is to keep that line running.
I'll do the best I can. I believe in an eight-hour pay for an eight-hour day. But I will not try to outreach my limits. If I can't cut it, I just don't do it. I've been there three years and I keep my nose pretty clean. I never cussed anybody or anything like that. But I've had some brushes with foremen. (Terkel 1975 pp 159–60).

This particular account represents many characteristics of work in the mass-production manufacturing industry. A great deal of everyday, commonplace work in our own society is as meaningless, repetitive, unsatisfying, and unfulfilling as this, whether it is in various types of manual or non-manual and clerical occupations. This is not to say that *all* work is of this type, nor that all work is in some sense or another *alienating*. But there is a relationship between the organization of work in industrial societies and certain types of pathological or abnormal experiences and social relationships. We can classify these experiences under various headings. We can describe them in terms which imply that the worker loses his identity and self-respect, that he becomes isolated from his fellow workers, and that he comes to have no commitment to his job, to his occupational role or indeed to other types of social roles which he is obligated to perform. Such classifications, however, tell us little in themselves. It is only when we see them in relation to general structural characteristics of industrial societies that both the normality of work and its bad or pathological effects fall into place, explicable in relation to certain specifically social factors.

In part, the sociological interest in work as a category of both theoretical and empirical importance proceeds directly out of the recognition that many forms of work in modern industrial society have a dehumanizing form, and that this is due both to the structural organization of society, and to particular forms of work organization. This viewpoint may well be put in a slightly less strong form, expressed over-simply as the assumption that the particular forms work takes proceed directly out of the structural characteristics of industrial society, and its key institutional areas. Whatever form of this perspective we prefer, it is convenient to group them under a single heading for classificatory purposes, that of *structural models of work organization*. Such models tend to have their roots in major theoretical viewpoints in sociology, and we can identify structural models rooted in the theories of, for example, Marx, Durkheim, Weber and Parsons. Their key elements are, firstly, that they operate at a high level of theoretical and conceptual sophistication, and secondly that they deal in social-structural factors influencing work experiences and work organization. As a result of these two elements the concepts of work and its cognates which they employ are to be seen as elements in general theories of society and social processes. This perspective in the sociology of work is contrasted with an 'a-theoretical' and non-structural viewpoint or axis which has had some ideological significance in sociological approaches: the *human-relations* or *managerialist model of work*. For the sake of consistency in the rest of this discussion the basic distinction between the two models will be referred to in terms of:

    i *structural models*
    ii *human-relations models*

However, the main objective of this chapter is not to present a full-scale comparison of the structural model and the human-relations model, but rather to focus attention on the various types of structural models in order to discuss their theoretical significance for sociological analyses of work experience and work organization. This type of approach is taken because the structural model has been more theoretically productive than the human relations model, largely because the latter has been excessively concerned with the practice of managerial control of work situations. The structural model, by contrast, has had relatively little impact on managerial practice, but its strengths for the sociologist lie in its power to generate theories which can link the wide diversity of work experiences and situations within an overarching exploration of societal forms.

To return to the account of work in the Chicago car factory. Both the models referred to above can approach that material and make certain types of statement about it. Because of the individuality of the account no theory could use it to support the approach that it takes to the sociology of work. But each model would draw different points out of the account which refer to particular elements in their conceptualization of work and use them as examples of the interests they have in different aspects of work experience. As has been suggested, the structural models will highlight the sources of particular types of experiences as produced by structural features of industrial societies. The human-relations model will be more interested in the effects these types of experiences will have on things like work-performance, efficiency, output, absenteeism and industrial relations in the factory. In the following section, a detailed description of the human-relations model is provided.

1 Work and society in sociological theory

This chapter is, inevitably, the most general in the book. But theoretical abstraction is a very necessary part of the scientific explanation of phenomena — either natural or social — and without an effective mode of conceptualizing the relationship between the varieties of work in a society, and the social structure and culture of that society, there is little or no point in attempting a sociological study of work. However, it is important not to fall into the so-called *fallacy of misplaced concreteness*; that is, mistakenly to treat conceptual schemes as 'reflecting' or in some sense directly representing concrete reality. Abstract conceptual schemes, which help us greatly in constructing theoretical models, should not be construed as direct empirical descriptions of the phenomena they conceptualize. Consequently, when we examine, for example, the structure of work situations in the professions by reference to a theory of social stratification, it is important to remember that no stratification theory can *describe* the actual organization of professional roles in a specific situation, nor indeed can it provide an empirical listing or representation of the total stratification system of the society of which the professions form a part.

Perhaps a more fundamental theoretical problem in relation to a sociological analysis of work is that of competing theoretical world views. Necessarily, the theoretical standpoint which the sociologist adopts determines the questions he will ask of society and the social world, determines what he will identify as relevant empirical data, and to some extent the connections he will draw between his object of study and what he takes to be other relevant social phenomena. In discussing major components of essentially competing structural models, we have to be clear that each of the models provides us with an image of certain societal variables that it stresses in its own particular account. But although some normative or 'prejudiced' factors may enter into the initial selection of a theoretical standpoint and object of study, in the last analysis the basic arbiter between models must be their effectiveness in leading to explanations of observations and empirical data derived from given situations.

In presenting some aspects of a conceptual debate about the interrelationship of work and society I am not attempting to provide an empirical description or account of the social structures of industrial societies, but rather indicating ways in which those social structures may be understood, particularly in relation to work. For if we are to be able to conceptualize and explain why work takes so many diverse forms in industrial societies, and why it has had certain types of social consequences, then we need to be aware of the perspectives which suggest particular theories.

Because of the need to cope with the societal factors which influence and mould the social patterning of work, the range of studies to which reference is made in this chapter, and around which its argument is principally drawn, deal in general with theories of what we might call 'total' social systems. Hence the extended reference to Talcott Parsons' discussion of 'some principal characteristics of industrial society', to Herbert Marcuse's 'Industrialization and capitalism', and to Jurgen Habermas's seminal paper 'Technology and science as "ideology"' (Parsons 1960; Marcuse 1971; Habermas 1971a), which all constitute important elements of a continuing debate about the nature of western industrial society, about its institutional forms, its social structures, its economic systems, value-systems and occupational roles. In particular, the debate focuses on some of the *effects* of industrialization; we have already seen a non-technical account of some of those effects in the description of factory work given earlier. This debate focuses on Marx's conception of *alienation*, on the repressive effects of the organization of work in an industrial, capitalist society. The debate has been conducted essentially between the proponents of various types of structural model, notably amongst the variants of Marxism and by Marxists with representatives of Weberian, Durkheimian and latterly structural — functionalist perspectives. A central element of the debate is the conceptual identification of the major characterizing elements of industrial societies, their weighting as factors influencing work organization and their relationship to specific issues concerning the social class composition of industrial societies and the 'revolutionary' potential of the industrial working class.

Interestingly enough, this debate, which has characterized much general dispute amongst sociologists concerning the comparative utility of different general sociological theories, has no obvious counterpart in the human-relations model referred to earlier. There are good reasons for this: as we shall see, the human-relations model is largely unconcerned with the social world outside of the work situation itself. In that sense it takes the structure of industrial society, whether capitalist or not, as an untheorized given which does not require explanation as a determining factor of work organization. Before looking in greater detail at the debate about industrial society, the human-relations model will be outlined in some detail so as to indicate both the significance and popularity of this approach together with its primary elements.

2 Human relations and industrial sociology

Originating in the 1920s, the human-relations model grew out of a
rather eclectic movement uniting – principally, if not exclusively, in
the USA – sociologists, psychologists, economists and enlightened
managers. They were opposed to certain trends in the understanding
of human working behaviour which stressed the idea that individuals
acted in isolation, and wholly rationally, primarily in order to maximize
their income and to serve their self-interest. Elton Mayo, the central
figure of the human-relations movement, described this viewpoint as
the 'rabble hypothesis' because it assumed that people were unorganized, unconcerned with their social relationships and only interested in
achieving the highest level of personal gain that they could obtain. The
'rabble hypothesis' was also employed a great deal by the proponents
of 'Scientific Management', who saw workers as analogous to machines:
the aim of this form of managerial practice was to increase worker
efficiency by the use of incentive schemes, and in the service of this
aim it almost wholly ignored social and environmental factors in the
work situation.

The human-relations movement developed as a reaction to this
tendency to see worker behaviour as conditioned solely by individualistic and excessively rational orientations. The emphasis of the movement, however, was quite similar to the trends of 'scientific' personnel
management that it was opposing. It was primarily concerned with
identifying the conditions under which workers would be maximally
productive, and with indicating the importance of social factors such
as the cohesiveness of work groups in the creation of such conditions.

The human-relations model grew out of some now very famous
studies of the Hawthorne Works of the General Electric Co. in Chicago
between the years of 1927 and 1932 (Roethlisberger and Dickson
1939). The essential element of this study was the gradual realization
by the researchers that output was determined to a very high degree
by 'informal' group norms, rather than by physical conditions or
incentives. The 'discovery' of informal work groups by the Hawthorne
researchers created an important and continuing trend of empirical
studies in industrial sociology which has consistently emphasized the
importance of group influence over worker behaviour. The driving
force behind the model is its emphasis on the important *adaptive*
aspect of informal work groups which could create a sense of identity
and purpose for workers in a situation where the extreme division of
labour had broken down the bonds of social cohesion.

There is a marked tendency in this model to treat problems in industrial organizations as primarily the result of poor communication, 'bad' management/supervisory practices, and of a low level of group cohesion or of satisfaction in group membership. Very little attention is paid to the conflicts of interest between groups which may relate to their structural positions either in an organization or in the wider society. The emphasis is almost wholly on harmony and equilibrium rather than on conflicts or power differences between management and workers or even the problematic nature of economic rewards.

Having identified the major contrasting model to the structural models which are the main object of study in this chapter, let us return to the debate over the characteristics of industrial societies, and their significance for an understanding of work.

3 The conceptualization of industrial societies

No effective account of the structural and institutional organization of work roles could proceed without a coherent understanding of the economic systems which characterize industrial societies.

In order to begin an examination of this theme it will be useful to examine Talcott Parsons' essay 'Some principal characteristics of industrial societies' because it outlines very clearly some major dimensions of the analytical differentiation of the 'economic' from the 'social'. Parsons outlines a major structural theory of the primary elements of industrial societies. It is important to note that he concentrates on the significance of institutional, valuational, normative and cultural factors in this delineation of what he terms non-economic social structural characteristics.

Without reviewing in depth the major points of Parsons' delineation of major characteristics, some points on his thesis should be made here.

Firstly, Parsons identifies *structural characteristics* of industrial societies and emphasizes how the forms and functions of these structural elements distinguish industrial societies from other types of societies. The importance of Parsons' emphasis on structural factors is that he takes industrial societies to be differentiated quite clearly from other types of society in terms of the social institutions, social roles, stratification systems, and power structures which they contain.

Secondly, Parsons emphasizes in his analysis that the distinctive structural characteristics of industrial societies are a consequence of their differentiation onto a more complex level. He emphasizes that this process involves not simply the evolution of organizations specifically devoted to productive activity, but also the emergence of precisely defined occupational roles, and the limitation of the scope of some institutional areas (e.g. the family) in the development of qualitatively new institutional sectors.

Thirdly, Parsons isolates the legal system as an important determinant of the institutional framework of industrialized societies. He stresses that industrialization requires a legal system which defines the rights and obligations of individuals and enterprises in ways which *conflict* with traditional bases of social solidarity, and so can begin to institutionalize values of *universalism* in relation to economic activity, and *specificity* in relation to constraints on the development of economic institutions such as *contract*.

Fourthly, Parsons' schematic account deals with general aspects of the social structures of industrial societies. It is not an exhaustive description of those structures, nor is it a theory of their complex internal operation. It is rather a suggestion of how such societies might be viewed as operating social systems, with important indications of the types of structural variations which they could exhibit — as for example in the role governments may play in the encouragement of industrialization.

4 Major dimensions of the structural model

Having considered Parsons' essay as a relatively straightforward example of the type of structural theory which portrays work relationships as specifically produced by characteristics of the wider social system, let us now turn to an examination of some of the sources of the structural model in the history of sociology itself. For it is not accidental that we can locate Parsons within a recognizable tradition of structural theories, a point which takes us some little way towards a major theme of this chapter, which is that the ways we conceptualize work and work relationships within sociology are very closely linked to the historical emergence of sociology. When the major early works which established sociology were being produced — from Marx to Durkheim, roughly speaking, a period covering the mid-nineteenth century to the early years of the twentieth — the whole of European society was subject to major strains created by industrialization whose principal effect was felt in the changing work environment. Societies which before 1800 were largely composed of various types of agricultural workers, peasants, self-employed artisans and craftsmen were very rapidly transformed into industrial societies where the factory and its work rhythms were the norm, progressively influencing all areas of even non-industrial work.

Sociology too was a product, in some senses, of industrialization — or at least a reaction to the social changes attendant upon it.

As has been indicated, perhaps most interestingly in the work of Robert Nisbet (Nisbet 1968), the emergence of sociology was connected to a widespread concern in the early- and mid-nineteenth century with the social, political, cultural and economic effects of the movement from a non-industrial society to a rapidly evolving industrialized society (the term 'pre-industrial' is misleading when applied to pre-nineteenth century Europe, for various reasons).

Similarly, at much the same time sociological and economic ideas about the social phenomenon of *alienation* began to have some currency. Adam Ferguson and Adam Smith both saw that the advance of the division of labour brought with it both the benefits of greater wealth and the curse of alienation. Ferguson, whose work Marx much admired, predicted that the extension of the division of labour would alienate man from his community, his labour and himself, and that it would further increase the uneven distribution of wealth to the detriment of society. Smith recognized the darker side of the division of labour; its potential dehumanization of the worker. Men confined to one or two simple operations would lose the need to use their minds and become, as he put it, 'as stupid and ignorant as it is possible for (men) to become'.

These concerns were broadened and extended into political aims for an extended franchise and more importantly for the creation of working conditions which were not subject to the Malthusian constraints of 'misery, vice and famine'. Many European intellectuals, both radical and conservative, were concerned with the human consequences of industrialization and in particular with the creation of an industrial working class whose members, in the main, were forced to exist at a subsistence level. The early French socialists, and Saint-Simon in particular, began to see the interrelationship between the industrial, capitalist, socio-economic system on the one hand and the character of industrial work on the other, and to recognize that this interrelationship was producing effects quite at variance with values of human dignity and human fulfilment.

The work of the young Marx takes over precisely this concern with the human effects of work, but sets it very firmly in a structural context. Marx's *Economic and Philosophical Manuscripts* (1844), his first attempt at analysing capitalist society, was focused on the failure of classical political economy (e.g. the work of economists such as Smith, Ricardo, Malthus, Senior, Say) to deal effectively with the relationship between capital, labour and private property. In that early work Marx began a philosophical and a theoretical concern with the processes by which the capitalist socio-economic system repressed and dehumanized its labour force. Developed into the concept of alienation, this concern was to animate all of the major components of Marx's work. The analysis of alienation was to remain central to Marx's mature theory of capitalist development. We will return to devote more detail to the concept of alienation later.

The economic, political and sociological analyses engaged in by men such as Comte and Marx — whatever their ideological diversity — were first and foremost concerned with an explanation of the total or global features of industrial society, from which could be deduced reasons for the principal 'bad' social effects of industrial capitalism: impoverishment of the working class, exploitation, poor living conditions, lack of political democracy, and so on. The understandings and explanations of these social effects which could be generated from general theories of industrial society in themselves produced both the characteristic concerns of much early sociology and the major axes of the continuing debate about the nature of industrial society.

Three main axes are relevant in discussion of the relationship between social theory and what we might want to term the 'sociology of work'. Each of these major axes proceeds directly out of the concerns of the early sociologists — Marx, Weber, Durkheim — with the consequences of industrialization and the social structures of capitalist societies. In turn, each of the major axes has generated a tradition of theoretical enquiry into the conceptualization of modern society. I want to indicate some of the dimensions along which these theoretical resources create and situate an effective sociological analysis of the complex interrelationship between forms, institutions, and organizations of work roles on the one hand, and major institutional and structural features of industrial societies on the other.

The history of the debate about the relationship between work and industrial society has been focused on a debate about and with the Marxian conceptions of industrial, capitalist society. The debate with Marx has crystallized very many of the major theoretical issues within sociology, and not simply in relation to the consequences industrialization has for industrial workers. Probably more than in any other major sub-area of sociology, the sociology of work touches very directly on theoretical issues which are central to sociology as a whole, precisely in relation to the theoretical understanding of industrial societies. To an important extent Marx, Weber, and Durkheim have provided crucial elements of modern social theory. In the case of Marx, very many versions now exist of his 'theory of capitalist society', some concentrating on developing and extending the basic Marxian concepts in order to deal more effectively with modern forms of capitalism which have eluded Marx's direct prognostications, and some more directly involved in correcting erroneous and 'ideological' representations of the original theory in order to construct a more subtle and sophisticated version of what Marx 'really said'. Although the same level of extension, exegesis and reinterpretation has not been applied to the work of Weber and Durkheim, their theories about the nature and forms of capitalist industrial society have been modified and absorbed into a much wider strand of sociological theorizing. In particular, the work of Talcott Parsons merits close attention in terms of the extension of Weberian and Durkheimian concepts into a wider and more comprehensive theory of modern industrial-capitalist societies.

It is clear that one of the principal emphases of the sociology of work has been work in its *political* aspects, in both a specific and a general sense. The debate with Marx centres quite importantly on this political aspect. Marx was most interested in providing an analysis of the socio-economic system of capitalism because of a variety of political goals that he espoused. Some of these were quite specific, in the sense of being concerned with the creation of socialist political parties and trades union organizations. Others were more long term and general, concerned with the creation of a new type of political society, which would emerge directly out of the struggle to transform the existing conditions of industrialism, within which the social and institutional structures of capitalism held sway. For Marx, certain social and political consequences followed the organization of society in terms of capitalist rationality. The most important of these was the *alienation* of the worker, firstly from the value of the product he had created, thence from full and effective social relationships with both his fellow workers and his employer, and from his own labour and finally from direct involvement in the political and cultural ordering of the society in which he lived. In referring to alienation Marx was describing the estrangement of men from the product of their labour, the dehumanization of their working conditions and their status as workers. All of these followed immediately from the mode of production and the social relations of production extant in a capitalist industrial society. But they also followed, in their direct forms as alienation of the worker, the laws of a particular conceptual orientation which Marx employed in his analysis of capitalism. This orientation — the labour theory of value — stressed in particular that it is only possible to understand men's economic and social relations if one reckons the value of their various products in terms of the labour, or more properly labour-time, which those products require. Thus Marx builds the whole of his mature theory of capitalism (crystallized most effectively, though only in part, in *Capital*) on the basic assumption that capitalism *requires* the capitalist to expropriate some portion of the labour time of the worker, and hence of the value of the product he has created, as his profit. To Marx this logic of capitalist appropriation provides the mainspring of social organization in capitalist society, for it determines the essential nature of work in that society. We will return to a more detailed analysis of this point at a later stage. The main theme to be drawn from this is, however, that the Marxian conceptualization of society requires the understanding that capitalist society contains within itself the seeds of its own demise. The alienation of the worker in both a physical sense and a political-cultural sense itself produces a situation in which working class and bourgeoisie are in basic and irreducible conflict. Marx predicted that this conflict would only be resolved by a radical transformation of capitalist society, in which the producers of wealth themselves came to own the means of production. Although this 'revolution', in itself, might not be violent, it would in all senses of the term be a revolutionary situation – and thus directly and centrally a political situation – in which the main forms of capitalist society would be swept away. This is one strand of the directly political connotations of the sociology of work. For it follows that if one adopts the Marxist perspective, then 'work' in capitalist industrial society must manifest forms which are directly alienative of the worker and which thus provide a direct explanation – in political terms – of relationships between workers and employing organizations. A great deal of attention is devoted (particularly by humanist sociologists of work and will be found in later chapters of this book) to aspects of this argument that the relationship between workers and employing organizations can best be understood in terms of the relative political power of the groups involved in the situation.

The Weberian and Durkheimian responses to the Marxian analysis of capitalism do not have the same global implications as Marx's theories. To some extent, both Weber and Durkheim are more sociological (in the present-day sense of the term) than Marx in their analysis of modern society, precisely in the way in which they devote attention not only to economic factors, but to more diverse social and cultural factors as well. Marx devoted a relatively small amount of attention to institutional, normative and cultural factors, as compared to Weber and Durkheim and more recent sociological theorists as, for example, Parsons. Marx was not in any sense an economic determinist, although his theoretical concerns were very much with the economic factors characterizing capitalist socio-economic systems. This emphasis on non-economic factors was consciously applied by both Weber and Durkheim in an attempt to create more inclusive and effective theories of industrial society which could act as a counter to Marxism.

Both Weber and Durkheim were concerned with particular types of consequences of industrial–capitalist society. In this sense, their work parallels that of Marx and continues the concern of intellectuals and scholars in the early part of the nineteenth century with the effects of the new *industrialism*. Marx's interest in the social-structural causes of alienation, and its manifestations in the form of reification, fetishization of the commodity, and material exploitation and expropriation, were paralleled by the interests of Weber in the process of rationalization, the development of bureaucratic organization and the increasing incidence of a purely technical rationality in economic and political affairs. Indeed, Weber's picture of capitalism is no more rosy than Marx's although Weber does draw some very different conclusions from it. Again, Durkheim emphasized the disruptive effects of industrial society, the consequences a complex division of labour and an increasingly urban society would have for relationships between individuals. Indeed Durkheim's classic study, *Suicide*, deals centrally with the emergence of *anomie*, the normlessness produced by the disintegration of moral order and of cohesive value systems within complex industrial societies (Durkheim 1952). This analysis itself was based on a conceptual scheme and sociological methodology worked out somewhat earlier to deal with an explanation of how social order and integration was, in itself, possible in a complex industrial society. Durkheim's famous distinction between *mechanical* and *organic solidarity*, as it appears in *The Division of Labour in Society*, provides the basis of the analysis of anomie, to the extent that the existence of anomie points to the imperfect relationship between the norms and values of the new society and its social forms (Durkheim 1933). The consequence of this imperfect relationship is a situation in which some individuals find themselves unrelated to the social order within which they live, unable to connect their social relationships together in a meaningful group context because they cannot identify with a social group which manifests their interests or creates a common purpose to which they could subscribe.

Durkheim himself believed that anomie would never be resolved in modern societies without the creation of new, occupationally-oriented social groups to which individuals could relate themselves. Only within such groups — and Durkheim envisaged them as modern types of the medieval guild organizations – could workers find a locus of meaningful values and normative orientations which could connect them into the value system of the wider society.

What connects the three 'fathers' of sociology, and what makes them more than simply interesting for a discussion of the sociology of work, is that their concerns with the nature of work and of work organization in industrial society were very closely connected both to the structure of their major sociological theories, *and* to some fundamental distinctions in theoretical orientations to the 'sociology of work' since their time. Let us now look in a little more detail at the major concerns of Marx, Weber, and Durkheim in order to draw out the implications of their work.

5 Marx

As indicated earlier, one of the most significant aspects of Marxian theory is its avowedly political emphasis, both in the sense of seeing industrial organization as exhibiting the form of a political structure of power relationships, and as the source of an essentially political concern with the study of industrial organization *as a means of changing it*. In that sense, Marxian theory is much more concerned with the directly political implications of work than the human-relations inspired approach to the sociology of work.

It is unnecessary to review the major elements of Marxian theory in this chapter. However, in presenting a Marx who can legitimately be described as contributing a fundamental orientation to the sociology of work, it is necessary to examine some of his mature theory in order to determine its influence on subsequent sociological concerns.

In the previous section I mentioned the significance of Marx's employment of a *labour theory of value*. In this section I will be dealing with the concept of alienation in greater theoretical detail in relation to the labour theory of value. In part, we can see his employment of this theory as the continuation of a humanistic tradition in European thought. This is particularly noticeable in Marx's usage of the concept of alienation – *Entfremdung* (Mandel 1971). Marx employs the concept of alienation to describe, initially in essentially philosophical and anthropocentric terms, what he takes to be the essence of human existence, and how that essential existence is deformed and mutilated by social organization, the division of labour and its repressive consequences. The concept of alienation, then, was initially derived from a set of humanistic assumptions about the deformation of man's

— or rather more specifically men's — essential humanity by the forms of production which societies had historically employed (Schmidt 1969). Marx's concept of alienation stresses the disparity between man's 'species-being', the fact that he can only actualize and realize himself through his work, and the social conditions which prevent man's use of all his abilities and skills in his work and thus alienate him from the source of his essential humanity. It was Marx's belief that the conditions which produced alienation stunted the ability of men to express themselves fully in their work, because in all societies where there was a division between owners and producers of wealth, workers had no control over the products which their labours created. Instead of being an exemplification of men's skills and attributes, the creation of some product and its consequent expropriation by capitalist, feudal lord or guild master is merely a means of the worker's subsistence. Instead of being able to create a product which reproduces his individuality and humanity, the capitalist mode of production and its social relations create a situation in which the worker's labour is expended in return for his subsistence, and nothing more. Indeed, something is *taken away* from the worker, and thereby the process and condition of alienation is crystallized: for in producing a commodity, or so Marx argued, the worker is putting something of himself into what he has created — his labour. In a capitalist society, the entrepreneur who employs the worker pays him a wage for the time he spends in his factory. During his work period the worker expends so much labour time producing commodities. The entrepreneur sets his wage rates so that he pays only for a certain proportion of that labour time, and thus only for a certain proportion of the value created by that labour. The excess labour time, and consequently the *surplus value* created during it, therefore comes into the hands of the capitalist. This is what is conventionally termed as profit. Marx argued that all wages would run at about the subsistence level, or at least that there would be a historical tendency for wages to gravitate to that level. Consequently workers, whatever the value of the products they produced — a value determined by the amount of labour time expended on the creation of the commodity and the skills and abilities of its producer — would merely be paid enough to ensure their subsistence and no more. Out of the surplus value, which the capitalist exploits from that labour of his workers, comes the accumulation of capital and its concentration in the hands of a minority. This is the logic and basis of capitalism.

In coming to employ a labour theory of value to describe the workings of the capitalist system, Marx was exemplifying the social and institutional processes which alienated the worker, cut him off from his essential humanity and reduced him to the level of a mere animal because he existed around or even below the subsistence level. Alongside this technical analysis of the economic processes which alienated the worker and turned him into a mere commodity to be bought and sold on the labour market, Marx argued that the very same economic processes were developing the social relations of capitalist production to a point at which only three socio-economic classes would continue to exist; *proletariat, entrepreneurs* and *rentiers*, the two latter groups combining to form a relatively unified *bourgeoisie*. The relations and necessary conflicts between these groups would determine the future of capitalist society:

> Intrinsically, it is not a question of the higher or lower degree of development of the social antagonisms that result from the natural laws of capitalist production. It is a question of these laws themselves, of these tendencies working with iron necessity towards inevitable results. (Marx 1930 p 12)

Although there is substantial debate about the predictions Marx made concerning the 'bursting asunder of the capitalist integument' and of the essential structure of the new socialist society lying in the womb of the old capitalist society, there is little doubt that Marx attached considerable importance to the political organization of the proletariat. Marx saw the development of trade-union organization as a necessary pre-requisite for the creation of a working-class consciousness which would recognize correctly the opposition between the interests of proletariat and bourgeoisie, and attempt to create an increased level of class conflict in order to hasten the demise of alienation and the capitalist socio-economic institutions which are its source (Lukacs 1970).

Apart from its influence on stratification theory, the Marxian model of the structure of capitalist society and the economic processes which are its basis has popularized the notion that the primary determinants of social action are economic factors, or even that social action is essentially economic action in the sense of being conditioned by pre-existing, macro-societal economic structures. As we shall see when discussing Weber and Durkheim and the argument about capitalist rationality, it is not necessary to accede to this 'economism' in the sociological analysis of work. However, it is important to note that much recent work in industrial sociology, and sociologically-orientated industrial-relations studies, employs in one form or another a variant of the Marxian model. This is not to say that this has been necessarily unfortunate for the development of industrial sociology. Rather, it has meant that a particular emphasis has been placed upon specific sectors of industrial organization. In this emphasis, alienation plays an important role. The humanistic quality Marx assigned to work — the idea that man actualizes and realizes himself chiefly through his work — is a potent source of concern with the social conditions which increase alienation. These conditions, which Marx identified as the social relations of production in capitalist society, produce a situation in which men are denied the full use of their skills and faculties and as a result lose their sense of self and identity. Men are unable to express themselves through their labour because that labour itself has become a commodity, and is thus no longer a part of themselves but something bought and sold on the market (Marx 1930 pp 43–58). It is in that sense that the material alienation of labour power corresponds to a social, psychological and ultimately biological alienation of men from the essential qualities of their human nature.

This concern with the alienative effects of work in capitalist society has formed a central core in much previous industrial sociology and it remains a potent theme in much contemporary literature. Recent examples of this approach are Beynon (1975), Wedderburn (1974) and Beynon and Blackburn (1972). Eldridge (1971) provides a full and detailed analysis of the concepts of work and alienation in Marx's writing and can be seen as an extension of some of the ideas developed in the preceding passages of this chapter.

Much has been made of the observation that Max Weber's sociology can be plausibly portrayed as dominated by a debate with the 'ghost of Marx'. To the extent that he wished to enquire much further into many of the issues Marx had raised over the social system of capitalism, Weber certainly posed much of his work in an oppositional framework which denied the economic determinism he (perhaps wrongly) saw as vested in Marxian theory. But it is also true that a great deal of Weber's contribution to sociology went into areas which had been barely touched or totally ignored by Marxian theory, and this is particularly true of his treatment of organizational forms such as the 'rational–legal' bureaucracy. Thus whilst Weber does not directly address the problem of alienation as conceptualized by Marx, he certainly developed some important ideas about the social consequences of both capitalism and socialism for work relationships, particularly through his discussion of the cultural process of *rationalization* (of which capitalism is only one amongst many exemplifications). Let us now move on to examine Weber's work in more detail.

6 Weber

Weber's major contributions to the sociology of work lie along three dimensions, one theoretical and the other two substantive. They are:

1 The methodology of *verstehen*, and its crucially important logical premise that actors' subjective intentions form a significant basis for their social action. In that sense, Weber was very importantly and diametrically opposed to the Marxian idea that consciousness is primarily determined by objective economic conditions.
2 A concern, at the civilizational level, with the phenomenon of *rationalization* (the replacement of traditional and value-oriented social and political institutions with instrumental institutions) and its effects — particularly those which influenced the emergence of a rational capitalism and the extension of bureaucratic organization.
3 A description of stratification systems in capitalist society which, taken together with the two other elements above, led Weber into very different conclusions from Marx about the future of both capitalist, *market*, economies and socialist, *planned*, economies.

The picture Weber draws of capitalist society, and of work within it, has some resemblances to that of Marx. Although Weber did not deal with the topic of alienation (a conceptual theme which is of comparatively recent origin, emanating from the rediscovery of some of the early writings of Marx and from Hegelian interpretations of Marx's 'critical theory' of capitalism) he did concentrate on what he took to be an important repressive effect of the advance of capitalistic rationality — bureaucracy.

Weber's *verstehende* (interpretative) methodology of social action stresses the significance of individual voluntarism, the freedom of individuals to act in terms of values and concepts which they conceive to be significant and important in any social situation. In particular, Weber saw history as having no intrinsic meaning and as not exhibiting any necessary laws of social development. And this methodological premise was his principle point of departure from Marx, whom he saw as developing a materialist philosophy of history which was, to Weber, quite untenable, especially in its assertions about dialectical change.

Within the Marxian analysis of social development, individuals are held to have little free choice as to their social action: they are ultimately determined in their actions by socio-economic forces and their class-situation. The 'laws' of historical materialism seem to suggest that individual action can at best only retard or accelerate an immanent social transformation. Weber felt, and his analysis of the relationship between the attitudinal consequences of ascetic Protestantism and the values of capitalism attests to this, that the individual's choice of *ultimate values* is far more important in many circumstances to the creation of new social institutions than specifically 'material' or economic factors. Thus, Weber saw the emergence of capitalism in its distinctively modern forms as exhibiting a complex of ideal and material interests, some of which had no relation to economic factors. This is most clearly expressed in his famous work on the Protestant ethic. Capitalism was not produced purely by economic factors, Weber argued, and it is important to recognize the social and historical significance of the role of individuals, who by subscribing to certain types of ultimate values, influenced the direction of social change without being subject to directly economic motivations.

Weber's concern with the repressive and inhuman effects of capitalism was concentrated on its influence on social institutions and their transformation into instruments of the developing formal and substantive rationality of capitalism. This formal rationality Weber isolated as the basis of capitalism, and he felt that its spread heightened the equation of maximum productivity with maximum efficiency such that the development of capitalism inevitably resulted in a greater degree of formal rational organization at all levels of social organization. Rational legal bureaucracy, in that sense, was the corollary of capitalist development and its burgeoning demands for a higher and more far-reaching level of instrumental social organization in all areas of social life. Weber, as a liberal, saw this extension of organizational rationality as degrading individual voluntarism, removing the freedom of the individual to act in terms of his own definition of the situation, and replacing this freedom with rules and constraints. The assumption that an individual's actions are in principle calculable opens them up to control by a purely technical rationality which takes no account of the ultimate values to which that individual might hold.

It is important to note that Weber saw the Marxian 'solution' to capitalism as a worsening of this creeping bureaucracy. Socialism, Weber said, would only bring a greater amount of organization, for the abolition of private ownership of the means of production, and the limitation and transformation of the market institutions, meant an ever greater erosion of individual voluntarism arising from the inevitable replacement of private ownership by bureaucratic management.

When we come to the third dimension of Weber's theoretical relevance for the sociology of work, his analysis of stratification, it is possible to discern an integration of some Marxian elements into the Weberian framework. Weber employed the Marxian conceptions of class

and class struggle and accepted in part the premise that economic factors determine peoples' life chances to an important degree. It has been
argued that Weber and Marx shared an interest in the same fundamental
human issues, specifically a concern with the human consequences of
the emerging industrial system (Lowith 1970). Where Marx saw capitalism as alienating workers in both a social-psychological and material
sense from their natural humanity and from the value created by their
own work, Weber saw the advance of bureaucracy as bringing with it an
extension of the worst consequences of capitalism and particularly what
he termed 'the iron cage of modern industrial labour'. Socialization of
the means of production would not in fact abolish alienation but
extend it, by destroying what remnants of individualism still remained
(Weber 1968 p 139).

But where Weber disagreed with Marx on the future development of
capitalism and the social consequences of socialism he certainly
employed a concept of class which drew closely on Marx. However,
his conception of the class system of capitalist society was rather
wider than that of Marx, and he did not accept the idea that classes
are wholly to be defined by economic factors. Weber distinguished
three major types of classes: *property* classes, *professional* classes, and
social classes. (In one recent translation 'professional' has been rendered
as 'commercial' classes; I have decided to adopt the more helpful
'professional' because it seems closer to Weber's original meaning; cf.
Mommsen 1974 p 60.) Although it is very complex, Weber's analysis
of class is strongly related to differences in values and social action
which proceed out of income, occupation and property differences.
In that sense it is a rather wider and more explicit analysis of class
than that of Marx, and it deals rather more closely with influences on
social action which are based on occupational groups.

In particular, Weber's concept of professional class is most closely
concerned with the antagonisms between occupational groups. This
class includes entrepreneurs as well as professionals and workers. Weber
takes the basic class character of this professional sector to be the
degree of participation its members have in entrepreneurial management, and the extent to which they can influence either government
or organized pressure groups to adopt policies which are conducive to
the maintenance of established entrepreneurial positions. Weber further
subdivides this class into 'positively' and 'negatively' privileged classes:
into the former fall the executives, managers, and those with specific
and marketable professional skills (accountants, solicitors, scientists,
doctors, artists, etc.) and into the latter fall the bulk of the industrial —
skilled, semi-skilled and unskilled — workers who can merely sell their

working capacity. This is a valuable qualification, in that it takes into account a distinctive feature of developed capitalism – the distinction between the owners and the managers of commercial enterprises, for it is often the latter who monopolize the decision-making process. It also serves to indicate that workers are negatively privileged in the sense of being deprived of participation in managerial decisions.

Weber's other two class groups, *property* and *social* classes are less interesting for our purposes: the former contain groups whose social positions are determined primarily by their positive privilege in owning or controlling a great deal of property or their negative privilege in having no property at all in the economic sense – slaves, paupers, etc. This is not to say that *property* is an insignificant determinant of work relationships: indeed it could be argued that in some contexts it is undoubtedly the most significant – as e.g. has been shown by Newby (1977) and Bell, Newby *et al* (1978) in relation to capitalist arable farming in terms of the work relationships of farmers and farm workers. However, my concern here is to isolate some crucial elements of Weber's theory of capitalist development rather than to provide a comprehensive exposition of their content. *Social* classes included for Weber all types of class in which 'individual and generational mobility' was easy and usual (Weber 1968 p 302). They were composed of four social categories:

i the whole of the working class;
ii petty bourgeoisie; e.g. small shopkeepers, etc.;
iii propertyless intelligentsia and specialists: technicians, civil servants, various types of clerical workers;
iv classes which had a privileged position deriving from property *or* exucation.

Although Weber went into a great deal of detail on class structures, he did not employ the idea that classes were all-important in determining social action. Such action, he felt, was not determined by economic interests alone, even in situations where economic interests are to the fore. Actors are influenced by a great number of non-economic factors, Weber said, which cut right across class-based stratification – factors like tradition, religion, law, cultural values, etc. These factors are just as important as the instrumental types of social conduct created by capitalist industrialism.

In Weber's developed theory of capitalism, which identifies it as the economic ramification of the extension of institutional areas of formal, technical, rationality in western society, the *market* is the key functional mechanism of capitalism. The market is the basis of both the rationality of capitalism and its essential dynamic quest for economic expansion. Indeed Weber thought that only through a market-based system could a maximum amount of formal or instrumental rationality be achieved, and maximum productivity and efficiency result. In that sense, economic efficiency, because it depends on the existence of markets determining prices as the equilibration of supply and demand, is embodied in its purest and most technically rational form in capitalism. Because socialism would involve a planned economy, and thus would avoid the institution of the market, it would be a less rational and less efficient economic system.

However, Weber's conception of the formal-instrumental rationality necessary to capitalism has been critically opposed as confusing the formal rationality of capitalism, and its concept of reason, with the *historical substantive* rationality, and social factors which characterize capitalism. It is to that debate which we now turn.

In Herbert Marcuse's essay, 'Industrialization and capitalism' (1971) and Jurgen Habermas' essay, 'Technology and science as "ideology" ' (1971), the issue of the interdependence of socio-economic structures, with specific and alienating forms of work organization, modes of political control, and the productive functions of science and technology is discussed in relation to the problematic conceptualization of capitalist rationality in the work of Max Weber.

There are two ways of approaching this issue, both of which proceed from variants of the Marxist critique of Weber. They are best expressed in essays written by two representatives of the Frankfurt 'school' of German sociology, Herbert Marcuse and Jurgen Habermas. The fact that these two sociologists have important links with the Frankfurt school does not, however, mean that they share the same approach, for each represents a different generation of scholars and thus puts forward an analysis of Weber founded on rather different principles, despite the fact that the two essays were written within a few years of each other. Indeed Habermas' essay is a direct reply to Marcuse, and questions his use of the concepts of 'instrumental' and 'substantive' rationality in relation to a discussion of Weber. Habermas makes the radical point (for a Marxist scholar) that modern societies are increasingly developing institutional sub-systems of purposive-rational action which are replacing the Marxian 'motor' of economic progress — the forces and (social) relations of production — with the reliance of productive forces on scientific and technological *knowledge* rather than simply *capital* and *labour.* Both these writers take as their stepping-off point Max Weber's delineation of the formal components of capitalist rationality. Marcuse argues that Weber's apparently 'value-free' conceptualization of the formal elements of rationality, which he identified as embodied in the institution of private enterprise, the concept of the abstract legal person, 'free' wage-labour, and bureaucracy, is itself simply an expression of certain historical tendencies and social forces in the development of capitalism. Far from deducing the technical necessity of capitalist social relations from the abstract concept of reason, Marcuse argues, Weber has simply confused the idea of reason with the values and interests of a specific social group — the bourgeois, capitalist, middle class. Marcuse goes on to argue that, in effect, the framework of substantive rationality within which modern capitalist society operates is a distinct and repressive form of political domination. At the same time, capitalist rationality has harnessed science and technology to its structure of domination: as Marcuse says,

> ... science, by virtue of its own method and concepts, has protected and promoted a universe in which the domination of nature has remained linked to the domination of man — a link which tends to be fatal to this universe as a whole. (Marcuse 1964 p 166)

The reasons for this subordination of science and technology to the repressive and alienating structure of capitalist society are embodied in the possibilities of technical *control* over both things and men which science affords. In Marcuse's view, the alienating and dehumanizing character of work in modern, advanced industrial societies is determined very significantly by the *control* function which science and technology have acquired in such societies. This control function has been created out of the social processes of *rationalization* of which Weber was so aware, and which inspired his interest in conceptualizing the emergence of a specifically capitalist rationality. As Weber recognized, rationalization implied the mathematization of many aspects of social life, their subordination to a calculability which would render them subject to purely technical criteria of profit and loss, gain and efficiency. The clearest example of this is the development of capital accounting, a method of book-keeping which accurately calculates the economic record of a business enterprise and its members. Capital accounting, as Weber showed, has only appeared as a form of economic calculation in the capitalist societies of the western world. It is thus an important element in the development of capitalist rationality. But, as Weber recognized, capital accounting is not merely an abstract reckoning of money values; because it represents the social relationships involved in business enterprises, 'capital accounting in its formally most rational shape thus presupposes the *battle of man with man*' (Weber 1968 p 93).

In noting the destructive effects of capitalist rationality which appear in Weber's conceptualization of capitalism, Marcuse points to the substantive inhumanity and destructive irrationality which lies behind the formal rationality: even in the case of capital accounting, 'inhumanity is hidden in the rationality of the balance sheet' (Marcuse 1971 p 140). This substantive irrationality lying behind the facade of formal rationality is nowhere more obvious, says Marcuse, than in the emergence of what Weber called *rational-legal authority* and its institutional form of *bureaucracy.* For Weber's argument that industrialization is inseparable from bureaucratic control is part and parcel of his more general thesis that capitalist rationality generates the need for more detailed techniques of control and thus organizations to mobilize expert knowledge. But at the same time, Weber indicates that bureaucratic administration is founded upon an essentially irrational charismatic force, and that it is no more than one way in which charismatic authority may be routinized. Hence the organizational and institutional consequence of capitalist rationality — bureaucracy — is in itself an apparently 'rational' administrative apparatus concealing from direct view a system of political domination. In the light of this, it is not surprising that Marcuse asserts that *'the concept of technical reason* is perhaps itself *ideology.'* For Marcuse, technique itself is essentially domination and control over nature, things, and, of course, men. He is thus led to state the view that science and technology, so central to the economic structures and the work patterns of industrial societies, exhibit a rationality which is historically specific and that in principle they could be turned away from their current goals of the control of man and nature. By changing the direction of values and methodology of science and technology, Marcuse says, their role in the alienation and dehumanization of work could be abolished. But would they still be science and technology in any rational or useful form?

Habermas takes up Marcuse's argument that scientific-technological progress is both a productive force and an ideology. Habermas stresses that Weber, in using the concept of 'rationalization', was most interested in the effects of science and technology on the institutional structures of modernizing societies. And indeed Habermas suggests that his own fundamental distinction between *purposive–rational action* and *communicative action* describes the process that Weber was attempting to deal with in his analysis of rationalization. In a developing industrial society, subsystems of purposive-rational action characterized by instrumental norms will come to control the institutional and cultural framework. Marx's analysis of the capitalist society of the nineteenth century demonstrates this domination of the institutional framework of society by the relations of capitalist production. Habermas argues that since Marx's time two important developments in advanced capitalist societies (state economic intervention, and a greater interdependence of scientific research and technology) have led to science/ technology becoming the major productive force. The chief consequence of this change, for Habermas, is that two of the key concepts of Marx's analysis of capitalism, *class struggle* and *ideology* are no longer powerful elements of an understanding of capitalism. Habermas argues that, as a result, the model of forces and relations of production in the classical Marxian theory would need to be replaced with a model which distinguishes the societal significance of sub-systems of purposive-rational action and communicative action, and allocates a decisive significance to the role of scientized technology in both the extension of the productive facilities of industrial societies and the creation of a legitimating ideology which supports the predominance of instrumental values and norms.

Habermas sees two parallel processes of rationalization as possible elements of an advanced industrial society: the scientific-technical progress which transforms social institutions into subsystems of purposive-rational (or instrumental) action, and the rationalization of communicative action. This latter, he suggests, would involve the removal of restrictions on public control of and discussion about the directions of societal development, an 'emancipation' which would permit the genuine democratic control of the major areas of life subject to technical criteria of control.

The association of Marxian analysis of the alienative effects of capitalism with the Weberian model of an unfolding 'rationality' which characterizes modern society may thus be seen to have led, in the work of Marcuse and perhaps to a greater extent Habermas, to a profoundly pessimistic view of the nature of work. Whilst for Marcuse the developing *formal* rationality of capitalism merely exacerbates the repressive power of its *substantive* irrationality — a situation preventing, in ever more powerful systems of *control*, any possible move towards substantively rational and thus unrepressive systems of social relations — for Habermas it is the systematization of rational knowledge seeking processes themselves which makes capitalism so invincible and alienation both more subtle and more inevitable. For both of them there is the recognition that modern capitalist society no longer exhibits the ruthless fact of overt exploitation, for the alienation of worker by capitalist employer has ceased to exist in any but the smallest of enterprises. The characteristics of work are thus mediated by the power of large bureaucratically run organizations, directed by technically

sophisticated teams of professional managers whose productive
resources are founded on the fruits of a complex, scientifically based
technology.

But if the partial synthesis of Marx and Weber leads to such a model
of work in modern society as this – the 'technological alienation' which
Marcuse and Habermas identify – can we look to the other 'founding
father' of sociology, Emile Durkheim, for a different approach to the
conceptualization of work in modern society? Although it is conventional to characterize Durkheim as being overly concerned with stability
and order in society, it is nevertheless true that he identified several
key points of strain and conflict in the work relationships of capitalist
society which parallel both Marx's thesis of alienation and Weber's
concern with the effects of bureaucratization.

7 Durkheim

For our purposes, Durkheim's major work of importance is *The Division
of Labour in Society*, first published in 1893. Durkheim's aim in this
study was the demonstration of a significant sociological relationship
between the extension of the division of labour in industrial societies
and the forms of social solidarity, morality and law which they
exhibited. In particular he wanted to explore the sources of social
solidarity in a complex industrial society, and indicate what causes
the division of labour to deviate into those abnormal forms which
create the ills of capitalism.

In that latter respect, Durkheim was at least as concerned with the
human effects of capitalism as Weber or Marx. He was interested in
discovering how industrial societies hold themselves together, bearing
in mind both their complexity and the apparent individual autonomy
of their members. Durkheim contrasted the situation in pre-industrial
societies with that obtaining in industrial societies – where the former
are held together by common ideas and sentiments, shared norms and
values (the *'conscience commune'*) the latter do not seem to be capable
of such a 'mechanical' or simple level of integration. Rather, their very
complexity and specialization, their ramification into diverse institutional spheres seems to work against the very possibility of integration
itself. This theme of the disintegrative effects of industrial complexity
was a very potent one at the time Durkheim was writing, and appeared
as a central issue in the work of Comte, Spencer and Toennies (Lukes
1973a pp 140–7).

The concept of the *conscience commune*, often referred to as the '*conscience collective*' and translated as 'collective consciousness', was used by Durkheim to refer to collective beliefs and sentiments such as the value systems of morality and religion. Durkheim tended to think of such collective beliefs and sentiments as forming a distinctive system, a basis of values, attitudes and ideas which constituted the bedrock upon which social solidarity was founded.

Durkheim took the view that solidarity in industrial societies is constructed out of a different institutional and moral framework than that persisting in the *conscience commune* of pre-industrial societies. The division of labour, by which he meant occupational specialization, 'is more and more filling the role that was once filled by the *conscience commune*; it is this that mainly holds together social aggregates of the advanced type' (Durkheim 1933 p 173). Thus it is that the division of labour creates a condition in which social cohesion can be reconciled with the processes of individuation which characterize industrial-capitalist societies. This complex process of dynamic equilibrium, in which social solidarity is not eroded by a significant degree of social differentiation but, on the contrary, is ensured by it, was referred to by Durkheim under the well-known heading of *organic solidarity*, and it is unnecessary here to expand on the concept. However, let us examine the 'abnormal forms' of industrial society which Durkheim isolated where the division of labour deviated 'from its natural course' and which he examined in the third section of *The Division of Labour.*

Durkheim identified three major repressive effects of capitalism and industrial organization.

i anomie
ii inequality
iii inadequate organization

7.1 Anomie

In his account of anomie, Durkheim was concerned with the absence of rules or norms governing relations between social functions, which crystallized in industrial conflicts and commercial crises. Both economic anarchy and industrial conflict were a consequence of the rapidity of industrialization. With the emergence of a market economy:

> . . . production becomes unchecked and unregulated; it can only proceed by taking risks, and in the course of doing so, it is inevitable that calculations will go wrong, sometimes in one direction, sometimes in the other. Hence the crises that periodically disturb economic functions.

As the market extends, large-scale industry appears. It has the

effect of transforming the relations between employers and workers.
A greater fatigue of the nervous system, combined with the conta-
gious influence of large agglomerations of men, increases the needs
of the workers. Machines replace men; manufacturing replaces
small workshops. The worker is regimented, separated from his
family throughout the day; his life is ever more separate from that
of his employer, etc. These new conditions of industrial life naturally
require a new organization; but since these transformations have
been accomplished with an extreme rapidity, the interests in conflict
have not yet had time to achieve equilibrium. (Durkheim 1933 p 362)

Indeed, Durkheim was very concerned with identifying types of
work situation which could make work meaningful to the worker, by
means of increasing his understanding of the total production process
in which he is engaged.

. . . normally, the operation of each special function requires that
the individual does not become narrowly enclosed within it, but
rather maintains constant relations with adjoining functions, and
takes note of their requirements, the changes they undergo, etc. The
division of labour presupposes that the worker, far from remaining
bent over his job, does not lose sight of his collaborators and inter-
acts with them. Thus he is not a machine repeating movements
without knowing their meaning, but he knows they lead somewhere,
towards an end that he perceives more or less distinctly. He feels
that he is serving something. (Durkheim 1933 p 372)

Unfortunately for his theoretical understanding of industrial society,
Durkheim defined the anomic consequences of capitalism as abnormal,
as a deviation from the ideal circumstances of organic solidarity. The
worst features of capitalism — vicious competition, class conflict,
degrading and meaningless work — all appeared to Durkheim as merely
pathological effects of a temporary lack of suitable institutional and
organizational controls.

7.2 Inequality

However, Durkheim did isolate social *inequality* as an important and
widespread danger to organic solidarity, in two forms: as an inefficient
distribution of individuals in social roles, and as a lack of equivalence
in the exchange of goods and services for labour. Solidarity could be
lost in a class society because the distribution of social functions did
not correspond to the distribution of natural skills. In such a situation,
only constraint will bind individuals to tasks which they perceive as
too low for their ability. Class conflict is a natural consequence of such

a situation. Solidarity would also suffer where the price of an object bears no relation to its labour cost or its service. This could lead to a situation of exploitation of one group by another, where

> . . . one social class is obliged, in order to live, to offer its services at any price, while the other can do without them, thanks to the resources at its disposal, which are not however necessarily due to any social superiority, the second unjustly dominates the first. In other words, there cannot be rich and poor at birth without there being unjust contract. (Durkheim 1933 p 384)

Durkheim conceived of industrial society as, ideally, a meritocracy; and he believed that it was developing towards that end. Such a meritocratic society would, he felt, create an exact reciprocity between social needs and the production and distribution of goods and services. As has been pointed out, his efforts in this respect are unconvincing, and raise more difficulties than they resolve (cf Lukes 1973a p 177).

7.3 Inadequate work organization

Solidarity disappears, Durkheim argued, in any organization of commercial enterprise when there is insufficient co-ordination between the functional activities of workers, and when workers have insufficient work to occupy them. Durkheim believed that such a situation could be avoided by more careful work organization, greater involvement of the worker in his enterprise, improvements which would achieve both greater skill on the part of the worker and the development of a higher level of functional co-ordination and solidarity.

Many of Durkheim's ideas about the conditions which result in a lack of organic solidarity have been taken up by researchers concerned with increasing productivity and work satisfaction. Indirectly, Durkheim's theories encourages some of the principles of the human-relations approach to the study of work. In particular, the studies pioneered by the American sociologist Elton Mayo in developing the human-relations model, including the famous Hawthorne studies, have some similarity to Durkheim's idea that anomie could only be combated by the creation of occupational groups which would give the worker a sense of kindredness and common purpose with his fellow workers. This idea, fostered by Mayo during his tenure at the Harvard Business School, and generalized as the function of the 'informal work-group', has since been popularized into various tenets of personnel management.

Durkheim's view that social solidarity could be created in industrial societies chiefly by the formation of 'professional' occupational groups constituting moral communities has received a recent extension in the work of Paul Halmos (1970). Halmos has argued that the 'professional service ethic' emanating from the medical profession and social work is in the process of penetrating the value systems of all occupational groups in industrial societies. 'Personal service' professions have become the leaders in a process which is creating a new moral uniformity in all industrial societies (Johnson 1972 p 13).

Durkheim's vision of modern industrial society as having an 'ideal' form which can only be subverted by abnormal processes of class conflict, anomie, or exploitative working conditions, much as in the same way the health of a body is degraded by illness or disease, produced a radical disjuncture in his social theory. On the one side there is a model of 'perfect' social solidarity which the division of labour generates within a complex, capitalist industrial society; on the other side a group of concepts relating to abnormal social processes which work, unless they are restrained, so as to reduce the amount of solidarity obtaining. Because these processes are viewed as pathological — the consequence of insufficient differentiation of the social system or of obstacles to the creation of a true organic solidarity — Durkheim was unable to develop a critical theory of capitalist social relations. In other words he could not see how the pathological forms of work relationship produced by unrestrained economic competition were generated by the very form of social order — organic solidarity — which he identified as the pinnacle of societal evolution.

Conclusion

The primary objective of the preceding discussion of Marx, Weber and Durkheim has been to situate their distinctive theoretical positions in relation to the sociological category of *work*. What has been demonstrated is the centrality of this category to the founding fathers of sociology, although it is quite true that none of them provides an effective sociological definition of work — Marx perhaps comes closest to this in his use of 'labour', although even here it is possible to identify shifting meanings. Despite the range of approaches to the explanation of modern society which appears in their writings, it is clear that each of the founding fathers was profoundly impressed with the need to comprehend and illuminate the pathological and dehumanizing aspects of work relationships in a developing capitalist society. Sociology is a child of industrialization, for so many of its earliest and strongest ideas are concerned with the problems faced by all forms of social groupings in the transition from traditional, largely agrarian and mercantilist societies, to urbanized, industrial, capitalist societies. Hence the concern with economically defined class in Marx, and its consequences of fetishization of the commodity, alienation and ideology. Hence also Weber's lifelong concerns with rationalization, the repressive effects of bureaucratization on human freedom; and Durkheim's worries about the social pathology of anomic social relationships generated by too rapid processes of socio-economic change. Each in his own way grasped the category of work as the locus of change and, in most cases, worsened social relationships, but each presented the link between these relationships and the form of the wider society in a different way according to the dictates of the model of their contemporary society which they favoured.

It is because the founding fathers dealt in distinctive ways with the pathological consequences of industrial capitalism for working relationships that we can treat work as a central sociological category of theoretical importance today. As I have indicated, the critical question of how 'work' is to be dealt with revolves around a distinction between two types of theoretical model, one a highly articulated form of theory dealing with *structural* models of the society — work relationship and the other a less well-conceptualized and more pragmatic form which I have referred to as the *human-relations* model. It is my contention that the former offers the best opportunity for the sociologist to develop an effective analysis of work relationships because it requires him to focus his attention on the ways in which those relationships are structured by the wider social system. Yet one important qualification is necessary.

As in so much modern sociology, the sociology of work is dominated by a basic distinction between essentially Marxist interpretations and theories, and non-Marxist approaches. Quite clearly, the power and persuasive force of the Marxian approach derives from two factors. Firstly the consistent emphasis in Marx's work on the dehumanizing and repressive effects of work in capitalist society, and secondly the difficulty of analysing work sociologically without explicit and continual reference to an economic theory which makes sense of the economic nexus of work. Marxism, of course, involves a fusion of sociological and economic theory in a way which is, I believe, quite unique but not thereby necessarily superior to all other sociological attempts at understanding the variety of types of work, work organizations, and work relationships in industrial societies. There is, however, considerable scope for the expansion of non-Marxist approaches to the sociology of work rooted in structural models, although there is little evidence as yet of attempts to create such research initiatives.

CHAPTER 3

David R. Weeks

Industrial development
and occupational structure

1 Industrial society or industrial societies?

When we come to talk about the nature of industrial society we immediately encounter a problem of definition. When do societies stop being pre-industrial and when, if ever, do they develop into a post-industrial phase? Any rigid demarcation is liable to be misleading and unhelpful for the general reason that we are not talking about strictly distinct stages. Industrialization is a process of societal change, fuelled by a variety of physical and social conditions, and analysed by looking at a selection of strategically significant phenomena. Common measures of the degree of industrialization are: gross national product per head, disposable income per head, educational achievement of the population, the degree of urbanization and the nature of private consumption patterns.

One major attempt at explaining the process of industrialization on a world-wide scale has been made by Kerr, Dunlop, Harbison and Myers in their book *Industrialism and Industrial Man*, first published in 1960.

Their major thesis is that all industrial societies display common structural features which will become increasingly dominant as time goes on, replacing and superseding the distinctions we commonly use today to describe different cultural, social and political systems. The time-scale during which such a transformation will take place is necessarily an extended one and such changes as they suggest will take many generations to materialize.

The basic driving force behind such changes, however, remains a consistent one for they suggest the existence of a 'logic of industrialization' which underlies industrial development. It is in terms of this 'logic' that they describe the current industrial development of what we might call underdeveloped or pre-industrial societies and it is the continued influence of the 'logic' which will increasingly create a uniformity of structure amongst already industrial societies. In the introduction to their book they describe how they moved away from a concern with particular societies and their specific modes of development, to a more general orientation.

> Instead of ideologies and dominant personalities, we became increasingly attentive to the inherent nature of the particular industrializing system and the basic strategy and forces at work within it. (Kerr *et al* 1973 p 36)

We can now turn to an account of the logic of industrialization which Kerr *et al* spell out under four main headings. The following arguments draw out what the authors term the 'universals' of industrialization, the 'imperatives intrinsic to the process' or 'the prerequisites and the concomitants of industrial evolution' (p 42).

2 The logic of industrialization

2.1 Changes in the industrial work force

Under this heading Kerr *et al* (1973) stress that the industrial process breaks down or makes redundant traditional crafts and skills and replaces them with a more complex system employing new and more efficient technology. The source and continuing need of such a new system is scientific and technological knowledge, radically different in content and style from traditional productive knowledge. The new industrial system required a wide range of high-level skills and professional competency broadly distributed throughout the working population. Thus the old occupational structure is transformed by the emergence of a more differentiated and specialized work force without which the industrial process could not function.

This change in the nature of work also introduces a new dynamic into the situation, as many technological skills have a transitory element almost built into them, and with the development of new technology a continual process of retraining will be necessary. It is, of course, debatable how important such skill-turnover is, but it is certainly fairly disruptive in the earlier stages of industrialization with the shift from rural to urban work roles, and the process of industrial development, or 'progress', will always require some adjustment of work skills and performance.

It is this element of change which defines another aspect of the new industrial work force and that is a significant increase in occupational, geographical and social mobility. Thus, not only must workers expect to change jobs, through retraining, but they may well have to cope with associated geographical shifts.

A typical pattern is a continuing reduction in the proportion of the labour force employed in agricultural work and a shift towards industrial jobs mainly based in an urban environment. At a later stage of industrial development, a further occupational shift occurs with an increasing proportion of the work force moving into non-industrial or 'service' jobs, mainly of a clerical or white-collar variety. Clearly each stage of development is likely to involve both occupational and geographical mobility.

In addition, however, Kerr *et al* see a significant increase in social mobility, i.e. greater movement of the population up and down the occupational hierarchy. This emphasis on 'achievement' has important consequences for the family unit. Kerr *et al* argue that, 'there is no place for the extended family; it is on balance an impediment to requisite mobility'. The requirement of industrialization is the nuclear family, small and mobile.

Not only does an industrial system require large numbers of workers with specialized technological and managerial skills but it also depends on a higher level of general education amongst the wider population. As might be imagined, education performs not only the function of disseminating useful knowledge for the productive system, it may also mean the population is subject to greater social control, in particular by means of mass communication. Education itself, of course, also acts as an agent of social control.

In general terms the new industrial work system may be described by the terms: 'differentiated', 'hierarchical', 'regulated' and 'controlled'. This situation Kerr *et al* argue arises despite the cultural origins of the society in question. For them any resistance on the part of the work force to these changes is likely to be ineffective and short-lived; the problem is not so much one of continually coping with labour discontent but rather one of providing effective management to direct the industrial process.

2.2 The increasing scale of society

The second set of factors considered as crucial to the 'logic' are those connected with the increasing scale of society. In particular the rise of large-scale organizations is significant and the associated phenomenon of what Kerr *et al* term 'urban dominance', which grows in importance as the proportion of the population employed in agriculture shrinks.

The administration of an increasingly complex society also requires a substantial extension of the range and scale of government activity. Not only does such a growth aid the co-ordination of the expanding occupational structure but it also, of course, represents an addition to that structure in terms of governmental bureaucracy. The extent to which governmental activity may be involved in the direct ownership and control of industrial undertakings will vary depending on whether a society was at the forefront of industrialization or a relatively late starter. The former development was more dependent on private initiative, the latter on public initiative.

This last point does not necessarily mean that individual freedom is directly threatened by industrialization and Kerr *et al* argue that in point of fact the range of human choice is likely to be increased, at least to the extent that industrial society provides desirable options.

In more general terms Kerr *et al* see the need for the emergence of a 'web of rules' to govern the operations of the work-place and provide a framework of co-ordination in terms of the conditions of work. Within this 'web' they include such issues as compensation, discipline, lay-offs, transfers and promotions, grievances, norms of output, pace and performance.

2.3 Consensus in society

Under this heading Kerr *et al* argue that the factors we have been considering above generate an influential and self-perpetuating consensus in society, an image of what industrial society is, and should be, like. Most important is the acceptance of science and technological knowledge as a guiding principle in industrial development and the promotion of technical change. As a necessary corollary, education is accorded a high value and the resulting 'output' is efficiently utilized in the context of an open society where occupational, geographical and social mobility are encouraged.

To employ all these factors effectively there needs to exist an ethic of commitment to hard work reinforced by the sanction of carrot or stick, according to political taste. Despite this difference Kerr *et al* argue that: 'Regardless of means, industrialization entails a pace of work and an exercise of personal responsibility seldom known in economic activity in traditional societies' (Kerr *et al* 1973 p 54).

2.4   The scope of the industrial society

Fourthly, and finally, in terms of their major themes Kerr *et al* argue that 'the industrial society is world-wide'. The seed of industrialization once sown develops in a comparatively benign environment stimulated by the spectacle of surrounding more developed growth. Each new seedling is fertilized by the technological pollen of more mature plants, a process that promotes not only growth but also similarity.

It is in terms of all these factors we have mentioned that Kerr *et al* believe we can discern a process of industrial development which transforms any society, no matter what its cultural heritage, into a modern industrial unit.

For societies which have already achieved industrialization Kerr *et al* argue that the development options which may have been apparent at the start of their industrialization have now largely been forgotten or abandoned. They suggest that, 'the age of utopias is past' and 'an age of realism has taken its place', the process of industrialization is seen to have a built-in pragmatic principle rejecting the unworkable and leaving in its place a realistic form of industrial organization and administration. They consider that the conflict of ideologies is blunted and fades between societies as does also the conflict potential within societies.

A major unifying force, as earlier, is seen to be technology both in determining the organization of work and the self-image of the worker, 'the occupation takes the place of the class'. The need for mobility in the labour market continues, a reflection of the dynamic character of the society.

With the spread of international trade and the associated technology, the consumption patterns and needs of industrial societies are said to converge and with improved transportation, knowledge of, and demand for, new products spreads quickly, 'people may not be willing to settle for much less in their own system than the standards and performance of competing systems' (Kerr *et al* 1972 p 269).

Education continues to play a central role in the provision of suitably qualified personnel for the industrial system and by increasing the proportion of the working population with high-level skills it is argued that the income differentials in the occupational structure will diminish at the same time as eliminating the most disagreeable occupations and raising the income of those at the bottom of the pay scale.

When we come to consider future developments Kerr *et al* suggest that the kind of future men appear to be choosing and pressing for may be termed 'pluralistic industrialism'. By this they mean:

. . . an industrial society which is governed neither by one all-powerful elite (the monistic model) nor by the impersonal interaction of innumerable small groups with relatively equal and fractionalized power (the atomistic model in economic theory). The complexity of the fully developed industrial society requires, in the name of efficiency and initiative, a degree of decentralization of control, particularly in the consumer goods and service trades industries; but it also requires a large measure of central control by the state and conduct of many operations by large-scale organizations. (Kerr *et al* 1973 p 270)

The key term is clearly 'pluralism'. It is within this framework that may be seen to develop a truly open society. Individual liberty is safeguarded by the web of rules which define the social life for all members of society. With the establishment of 'a new economic equality' as a result of changes in the opportunities for education, the state takes on the role of umpire to make sure that none of the pluralist partners becomes too powerful and thus enabled to change the rules to its own advantage. In such a manner social conflict will be reduced to peaceful competition and the defining worth of a man will be his occupational contribution. 'Education, occupation, occupational organization will all be drawn together to structure the life-line and the economic interests of many if not most employees' (p 275).

In a postscript Kerr *et al* reflect on their original speculations eleven years after their first appearance and generally endorse their earlier views. They still stress that 'the iron hand of technology tends to create relative uniformity in job structure, compensation differentials and technical training' (p 292). When they talk about the concept of 'pluralistic industrialism', however, they adopt a more cautious tone and speak of several possible forms emerging; from market socialism (or state capitalism) through social capitalism to forms of state syndicalism.

It is by no means easy to decide whether we should consider industrial societies of the capitalist and socialist types as variants on a common form or as distinct and separate social systems. Initially it seems clear that the degree of similarity which one perceives between capitalist and socialist societies depends on the level of analysis which one employs and the range of social indicators which are taken to be significant. There is also the problem of knowing when one is making a fair comparison, i.e. that one is comparing societies at the same phase of the industrialization process. To compound these already substantial difficulties there also remains the problem of securing reliable and relevant statistical and other evidence on which to base any conclusion.

One particularly useful scheme of analysis is suggested in Dalton's book 1974) *Economic Systems and Society*. Dalton notes that in many obvious ways capitalist and socialist societies share a common industrial form but he stresses the importance of seeing the situation in an historical context. Given that stipulation, he appears to draw out five major dimensions of comparison. Firstly, there exists the similarity of technology — the same product requires basically the same kind of technological knowledge and machinery, and also often the same form of bureaucratic organization, no matter where it is produced. Secondly, we need to consider the goals of the industrial system as revealed in policy decisions affecting the operation of the productive system. In general terms material affluence, social welfare and national defence appear to be common goals but the means of their achievement differ substantially when we contrast the socialist command economy with the capitalist market economy. This relates to a third point concerning the nature of decision-making in the two societies. With no productive capital in private hands socialist societies are typified by central planning decisions where capital investment plans are not directly related to the influence of market forces. In this way, and also fourthly, the financing arrangements of the two systems differ both in terms of the providers and benefactors of such financing. Finally we should consider the other end of the industrial process and note the different forms of labour control that are evident and in particular the different roles of trade unions.

In the next part of this chapter we shall consider some of the evidence on these points as they are reflected in the occupational structure but first we should be clear about the issues of the controversy we have been discussing. The major objection to all theories that have postulated the notion of industrial convergence has been that such ideas pay insufficient attention to the guiding political ideology behind industrialization.

By talking about a 'logic' of industrialization there is always present the possibility of reifying aspects of the industrialization process, i.e. making the social changes involved appear necessary and immutable when they are in fact contingent on cultural conditions and political decisions. This likelihood is increased when the range of what are considered relevant variables is also circumscribed by an implicit or explicit allegiance to some form of economic determinism. In a notable critique of the convergence thesis, which has been partially accepted by Kerr *et al.* Goldthorpe (1971) argues that it is impossible to talk convincingly about the nature of the industrial system without taking into consideration the principles and procedures lying behind the allocation of productive capacity and the distribution of industrial rewards. In other words you cannot separate the industrial system from the social stratification system within which it operates. To speak of the industrial system as if it were an independent allocator of scarce social resources is to impose a false uniformity onto all industrial societies. A similar point is made by Smelser and Lipset (1966) with regard to societies at an early stage of industrial development when they note that the distribution of political power, and its supporting ideology, directly influences the allocation of economic resources (p 26).

From what has been said so far it is clear that the question of the nature of industrial societies is by no means an easy one to formulate, let alone to answer. One way of resolving some of the difficulties, however, has been suggested by Bell when he draws the distinction between convergence and internationalization. He writes:

> Further, one has to make a distinction between convergence and internationalization. One may have an internationalization of style, in painting or music or architecture, so that a 'modern' artist may paint the same way in France, England, Japan and Mexico. And there may be an internationalization of scientific knowledge and technological process, but *societies*, as specific historical entities represent distinct *institutionalized* combinations which are difficult to match directly to each other. On different dimensions (technology, architecture) they may resemble each other, or draw from a common fund of knowledge or style, yet on other dimensions (values, political systems, traditions) — and the ways these become formulated, say, in educational systems — they may differ. If there is a meaning to the idea of convergence it is that societies resemble each other somewhat along the same dimensions, or they may confront a *similar core of problems*. But this in no way guarantees a *common or like response*. The response will be relative to the different political and cultural organizations of the specific society. (Bell 1974 p 114)

So far we have painted a broad picture of the nature of industrial society, to set the scene as it were for the consideration of more specific issues. We have necessarily departed from a strict concern with occupational structure in order to locate such evidence as we shall be considering on that topic in its proper perspective. We can now turn to a study of some of the relevant empirical evidence.

3 The world of work: historical and international comparisons

3.1 Dimensions of comparison

In any social science exercise that attempts a wide-ranging historical or international comparison, a major problem arises regarding the availability and comparability of empirical data. With such an all-inclusive topic as industrialization the problems are indeed formidable. Given these difficulties the exact figures presented in the following statistics should not be accepted as totally accurate, rather they should be seen as indicating the trend of change or development.

When considering the nature of changes in the occupational structure there are a number of general features which need to be borne in mind. These have been summarized by Moore (1966). Firstly, with regard to the demand for labour by the industrial process this may be seen as a reflection of the demand for goods and services as that is represented either by a central planning decision or by market forces. Secondly, the particular skills required will vary according to the 'factor mix' between capital and labour, in other words the level of technology will largely determine the variety of occupational roles. The nature and utilization of technology is also, of course, subject to political control and, therefore, a number of technological options are available to achieve an industrial society. This will in turn affect the particular mix and complexity of occupational roles.

On the other side of the coin, the supply of labour will be affected by other factors. The upper limit on industrial development may be set by the demographic structure of the society, only a certain proportion of the population will be available for work, although traditional ideas on this may change, as has occurred with the large increase in the proportion of women who are engaged in full-time employment. A society may, of course, add to its workforce, or in fact reduce its size, through immigration or emigration and this must be regarded as another significant factor in determining occupational structure. Finally we must not forget the role of education and training in making available specialized skills of an intellectual, technical or craft nature.

Bearing these general points in mind we can now consider how well Kerr *et al*'s description of the changing nature of the occupational structure during the industrialization process fits with the available evidence. The problem of how we should conduct the comparison is, of course, a major concern and any strategy is likely to be in some way misleading. For the purposes of this chapter we shall restrict our comparison to the societies of Soviet Russia, the USA and Great Britain, with some additional evidence from Western European societies. The occupational structure of Great Britain will be considered separately in the next section of the chapter and we shall restrict our present comparison mostly to the USSR and the USA. The historical span

Figure 1 Civilian employment by sector

Source: **Labour Force Statistics, 1961–72, O.E.C.D. pp. 38–9.**

of our evidence will be mainly within the twentieth century.

To begin with, let us look at the very general changes in the shape of the occupational structure of some industrial societies. According to Kerr *et al* they should all show signs of changes in the same direction over time. In particular, we would expect to see a steady decline in the proportion of the population engaged in agriculture and a steady increase in the population employed in the industrial sector. At a later stage, Bell suggests that the major growth sector will be that devoted to service trades, particularly of a white-collar kind.

A comparative chart for sixteen countries over the period 1961–72 is given in Figure 1. Although this is a comparatively short and recent time-span we can see clear evidence of a declining agricultural sector, more fully advanced in some societies than others, and the growing influence of the 'other activities' sector which we can loosely equate with service trades.

For further evidence we can refer to Table 1 (on p 85) which provides us with additional comparative data.

The evidence with regard to the USSR is rather more difficult to obtain but according to Smirnov, 47 per cent of the work force was employed in agriculture in 1939 which had been reduced to 31 per cent by 1959. The proportion of the population employed in this sector remains substantial, however, and Lane estimates that 20 per cent of the work force were working on collective farms in 1971.

At the other end of the scale, the increase in service trades has been substantial. Using the figures of Osipov as a basis we can calculate that service workers constituted 16 per cent of the work force in 1913 and 32 per cent in 1963. According to Garnsey (1975) the sectoral distribution of employment in the USSR in 1960 was 39 per cent in the primary sector, 32 per cent in the secondary sector and 29 per cent in the tertiary sector.

Of particular note has been the rapid increase in engineering and technical personnel, a growth of 516 per cent between 1932–61 according to Lane (1971) which compares with a growth of 325 per cent for manual workers. This has led to a relatively high percentage of the working population in these categories when compared with Western societies. Of special significance is the way in which Osipov (1966) accounts for this change:

> From the point of view of training, the above changes in the occupational composition of personnel warrant the following conclusions. First, changes in specialized occupations eliminate many of the old occupations, in particular those involving arduous physical labour, and increase rapidly the new occupations combining elements of

manual and mental activity. Second, uniformity of scientific and technical principles in the operator's knowledge, experience and skill are characteristic of the newer occupations, which leads to the use of common basic principles in their occupational training. Third, the extension of the breadth of occupations in socialist production becomes a distinctive feature of occupational specialization to an increasing extent. The operator's work depends more and more on modern equipment, which will demand ever higher skills and educational standards from the worker, until highly skilled

Table 1 Civilian labour force by main sectors of economic activity

Country	Year	Agriculture[1]	Industry[2]	Other
1 Australia	1976	6.4	33.2	60.4
2 Austria	1976	12.4	40.1	47.5
3 Belgium	1976	3.4	39.0	57.6
4 Canada	1976	5.9	29.7	64.4
5 Denmark	1976	9.3	31.4	59.3
6 Finland	1976	13.9	34.7	51.4
7 France	1976	10.8	38.1	51.1
8 Germany	1976	7.1	45.1	47.8
9 Greece	1976	(34.3)	(29.0)	(36.7)
10 Iceland	1976	15.1	37.6	47.3
11 Ireland	1976	23.8	29.8	46.4
12 Italy	1976	15.5	43.5	41.0
13 Japan	1976	12.2	35.8	52.0
14 Luxembourg	1976	61.	46.3	47.6
15 Netherlands	1976	65.	33.7	59.8
16 New Zealand	1976	11.8	34.2	54.0
17 Norway	1976	9.4	331.	57.5
18 Portugal	1976	27.1	36.3	36.6
19 Spain	1976	21.5	37.1	41.4
20 Sweden	1976	6.2	35.4	58.4
21 Switzerland	1976	82.	43.9	47.9
22 Turkey	1976	63.1	15.5	21.4
23 United Kingdom	1976	2.7	40.0	57.3
24 United States	1976	3.8	28.7	67.5
25 Yugoslavia	1976	47.3	21.1	31.6

[1] includes forestry and fishing
[2] according to the definition used in OECD, *Labour Force Statistics:* mining, manufacturing, construction and utilities (electricity, gas and water)
Figures within brackets are estimates by the OECD Secretariat.
Source: OECD, *Basic Statistics: International Comparisons, 1978*

labour becomes the only kind of labour in communist society. (Osipov 1966 p 47)

It could hardly have been better put by an advocate of the logic of industrialization. On the other hand it gives rise to the interesting, but troublesome conclusion for convergence theorists that on one measure, overall sectoral distribution of the labour force, the USSR appears relatively under-industrialized, whilst on another measure, percentage of the work force employed in skilled, professional or semi-professional jobs, the USSR appears as more advanced than some western societies (Garnsey 1975).

By way of comparison, Bell (1974) notes that in the USA the proportion of the population engaged in agriculture, forestry and fishing was 15 per cent in 1947, 5 per cent in 1968 and a projected 3 per cent in 1980. For the same years the populations of the work-force in the service sector are 49 per cent, 64 per cent and a projected 68 per cent (see Table 2—3). (Bell 1974, p 132).

Another significant development expected as a consequence of the logic of industrialization is a rise in the white-collar sector of the employed population, a movement we have already marginally touched on in mentioning the increase in technically qualified personnel in the Soviet Union. On a more general basis, Bell notes that white-collar workers accounted for 42 per cent of the USA workforce in 1960 and should account for nearly 51 per cent in 1980 (Tables 2—4 and 2—5 on Bell, 1974, pp 134 and 135). The statistics for the USSR are construc-ted on a slightly different basis but Semyonov estimates that by 1980 the 'intelligentsia and employees' will account for between 30 and 35 per cent of the working population.

Within this white-collar group we might expect the numbers of employees working for government bureaucracy to increase, in keeping with the predicted extended role of government as industrialization progresses. The figures for the USA support this rather vague and uncertain measure of government influence and Bell records that the combined federal, state and local government employees accounted for 11 per cent of the workforce in 1947, 14 per cent in 1968 with nearly 17 per cent predicted for 1980 (Table 2—3, Bell, 1974, p. 132). Interestingly the burden of administration would appear to be shifting slightly away from the federal administration and towards state and local authorities, a move perhaps associated with the decentralization predicted by Kerr *et al.* For the Soviet Union, from the figures that are available, Garnsey (1975) suggests that, contrary to common opinion, the USSR has a much smaller proportion of its workforce employed in public administration than occurs in most Western societies.

Next we can turn to the question of mobility which Kerr *et al* suggest will increase and continue at a high level with the extension of industrialization. For the Soviet Union, Shubkin in Osipov (1966) writes as follows:

> The establishment of the social relations of socialism led to most important changes in Soviet society and to its extremely high level of social mobility. This process is still actively under way. The high rate of economic growth, technical progress, the tremendous increasing demands of the national economy for skilled workers, the enhancement of the role of science, and the high degree of social homogeneity have all created the basis for a free choice of profession according to inclination, given young people confidence in the morrow, and made possible the selection of new vocations not traditional in the particular family. (Shubkin 1966 p 86)

The establishment of many new and novel jobs would seem to imply a high rate of occupational mobility and with the fairly rapid decrease in agricultural work we may expect a corresponding degree of geographical mobility. This point must not be accepted without caution, however, for Russian sociologists themselves are quick to point out that a significant cultural gulf still separates rural and urban communities in the Soviet Union. In terms of social mobility Semyonov provides the following information:

> Approximately 80—90 per cent of the socialist intelligentsia, including engineers, technicians, agrotechnicians, teachers, doctors, scientists, artists, cultural workers and so on, are people who came from the working class or the peasantry. (Semyonov 1966 p 130)

For the USA, Bell (1974) notes that in 1949 out of a total of 87 million who were employed at least at sometime during the year 43 million entered or re-entered the labour force. In terms of geographical mobility between 1955 and 1960 more than half of the population changed residences of which about 40 per cent moved to different states or countries. In terms of social mobility he remarks that intergenerational moves of occupation show 'a continuing movement of upward class mobility into salaried, technical and professional employments' (p 314, fn 26).

Of the other features of industrialization that Kerr *et al* mention, the main items are: compensation, discipline, lay-offs, transfers and promotions, grievances, norms of output, pace and performance. Many of these cannot easily be subjected to empirical test due to lack of data and even where some evidence is available there are serious difficulties to be faced in ensuring comparability.

One issue that we can touch on briefly is the area of compensation which we can investigate in terms of income differentials. Kerr *et al* suggest that such differentials should reduce as industrialization progresses. In general terms income differentials seem less steep in socialist societies than in capitalist societies particularly if comparing manual workers with administrative staff. In capitalist societies of Western Europe and the USA changes in differentials display no overall trend and for the most part have been fairly stable for the last 25 or 30 years. In socialist societies the trends are more difficult to discern but there is some evidence of the introduction of incentive payments into wages which has led to a widening of differentials (Parkin 1971).

One general point we can draw out, however, is the way in which the distribution of income is not determined independently of political decisions which in a fundamental way regulate the nature of material and social inequalities in the society concerned. We shall return to this point when we consider the situation in Great Britain.

The only other issue we can usefully raise is the question of whether occupational prestige is perceived similarly in capitalist and socialist societies. Do occupations occupy the same position in the hierarchy in each type of society? The evidence here is far from clear, some researchers claiming to have established evidence for the existence of a common scale (Inkeles and Rossi 1956) whilst others dispute this view and claim that socialist industrial systems display a distinct and different set of (Socialist) values (Wesolowski 1969).

In summary we can usefully refer back to Bell's distinction between convergence and internationalization. Along many dimensions of occupational structure, as we have seen, there is some reason to accept the argument in favour of a growing internationalization. Many social analysts from differing political perspectives stress the overriding importance of technology in transforming the industrial occupational structure and in this respect societies are undoubtedly becoming more alike. However in a detailed analysis of Soviet development and its relevance to the convergence debate Elizabeth Garnsey (1975) has raised a number of important points. She shows that the occupational structure in the USSR has been moulded by policy decisions made at the political centre. This has resulted in, for example, a very low proportion of the workforce being employed in sales and 'commercial' activities and a relatively high proportion working in production when compared to western societies. She further argues that such developments have been mirrored by other Soviet bloc countries in eastern Europe. The general point is that there are more paths of industrial development, in terms of occupational structure, than many convergence theorists suggest.

It is when we turn to the social mechanisms controlling these changes and to the specific consequences of such changes that major questions of interpretation arise. As we have noted above issues which directly affect and represent social stratification in its broader sense, factors such as income distribution and occupational prestige, are much less easily contained within the notion of internationalization. In a way these are aspects of the convergence thesis and current evidence must declare the thesis in these respects unvalidated and likely to remain so.

To grasp some of the general points made so far in a more familiar context we can now turn to a consideration of the occupational structure of our own society.

4 The occupational structure of Great Britain

In this brief account of the occupational structure of Great Britain we will be concerned with many of the same variables that we have considered in relation to our wider comparative survey. The aim is not only to show how Britain fits into any pattern of industrial development but also to provide a general statistical backdrop against which may be compared many issues to be discussed in later chapters.

As with any statistical comparison the data do not always present themselves in the form we may require and where this is the case some secondary analysis has been carried out on the figures. The comparability of the data also presents a difficulty in that figures are drawn from a variety of sources but as we are mainly concerned with the trend of change this is unlikely to cause major distortions. In this respect we shall use the terms 'working population', 'economically-active population' and 'occupational structure' and 'workforce' interchangeably although the first two terms refer to different methods of data collection and the latter two terms are simply general ones to cover both of the others.

To be clear what we mean by the term 'occupation' we can refer to the definition used since the 1951 Census of Population:

The occupation of any person is the kind of work which he or she performs, due regard being paid to the conditions under which it is performed; and those alone determine the particular group in an occupation classification to which the person is assigned. (Quoted in Gould and Kolb 1964 p 474)

In general terms an occupation is simply the job a person does.

We can start our analysis by plotting the growth in terms of absolute numbers of the working population since 1841. Although the earlier figures are probably less reliable and any detailed analysis would need to take account of the occasional changes in classification of industry and occupation (such as occurred in 1911), the overall trend is clear. The figures, taken from Census returns excepting those for 1972 and 1977 are represented in Figure 2.

In terms of the proportions employed in each sector of industry the changes have followed very closely the trends we observed earlier. If we divide occupations into primary (agricultural), secondary (manufacturing, productive) and tertiary (services) the general trend of development is represented in Table 2 below.

Table 2 Percentages of the total work force of Great Britain, for selected years, in each occupational sector.

Sectors	1881	1901	1951	1976
Primary	13%	9%	5%	2.7%
Secondary	50%	47%	49%	40.0%
Tertiary	37%	44%	46%	57.3%

Source: Figures for 1881, 1901 and 1951 from Bain (1970) Table 2.4, p15. Figures for 1976 taken from Table 1, p 85, this chapter.

The growth in the tertiary sector has been particularly rapid since the end of the Second World War (Lewis 1973).

Another significant change, closely associated with the growth of the tertiary sector, has been the rise in white-collar jobs. In 1911 such jobs accounted for only 18 per cent of the working population but this had grown to nearly 43 per cent by 1971 (Price and Bain 1976). In comparison manual workers as a proportion of employees had dropped from 74.6 per cent to 54.7 per cent, the difference between the combined white-collar and manual workers' figures and the total number of workers being made up of employers and proprietors who also diminished proportionately from 6.7 per cent to 2.6 per cent.

Within the white-collar group the greatest growth was attained by clerks who increased from 4.5 per cent to 13.2 per cent of the working population in 1966. However, in terms of rate of growth the most important occupations are undoubtedly those of scientists, engineers, draughtsmen and laboratory assistants and Bain, Bacon and Pimlott (1972) note that, 'if these growth-rates continue, the occupational composition of the future white-collar labour force will be consider-

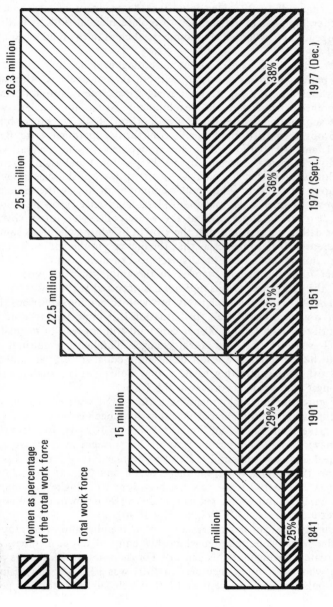

Figure 2. Total work force of Great Britain for selected years showing the changing proportion of women as a percentage of that total

Women as percentage of the total work force

Total work force

7 million — 1841 — 25%

15 million — 1901 — 29%

22.5 million — 1951 — 31%

25.5 million — 1972 (Sept.) — 36%

26.3 million — 1977 (Dec.) — 38%

Source: Adapted from British Labour Statistics: Historical Abstracts, 1886-1968, and OECD Labour Force Statistics, May 1978

ably changed' (p 99). One important determinant of such changes is
the development of technology to replace manual skills as well as the
emergence of new labour requirements, such as in the field of computers
(Hall 1969).

We should be careful about accepting evidence of a white-collar
occupation explosion, however, without further analysis. Although the
gross increase must be regarded as significant there is an important sex
differential included in the development. As we noted above, women
have substantially increased as a proportion of the workforce but they
have not been distributed equally over the occupational range. Between
1911 and 1971 the proportion of women among manual workers
hardly changed (between 26 and 29 per cent) and Bain, Bacon and
Pimlott suggest that in general terms their level of skill has in fact been
reduced. In terms of white-collar employment during the same period,
however, women have made considerable advances growing from 29.8
per cent to 46.2 per cent of the white-collar workforce. Given this
information we can interpret the growth of white-collar jobs somewhat
differently. It becomes clear that the increase in the white-collar sector
arises not so much from the displacement of men from manual jobs but
rather from the overall increase in the employment of women. Moreover the major part of this increase has occurred at the lower end of the
white-collar range with relatively few women gaining senior positions in
their organizations. Given this situation it is important to note that a
majority of men (about 60 per cent) are still engaged in manual work,
which suggests that any social changes, familial and cultural, which
might be expected as a result of a 'white-collar society' are still a good
way off. It is interesting to note that Bell records a similar situation
amongst white-collar workers in the USA.

Figures for unemployment have fluctuated widely throughout this
century and are problematic since they have been collected on a varying
basis (see Bain, Bacon and Pimlott 1972, pp 102–4). The data that we
do have, however, indicate a rate of 2.5 per cent in 1900, an all-time
high of 22.1 per cent in 1932 and an average rate of around 2 per cent
in the 1960s (adapted from Bain, Bacon and Pimlott 1972 Table 4.8
p 119). In the 1970s the rate has been somewhat higher reaching 5 per
cent in 1976 and over 6 per cent in 1978 (Department of Employment
Gazette 1978, vol. LXXXVI, no. 9, p 1090).

Finally we can consider trade union membership. The proportion
of the working population which has enjoyed union membership has
fluctuated throughout this century. For the total workforce the proportion who were union members in 1901 was 12.6 per cent, rising to a
high-point of 45.2 per cent in 1920, which fell away to 22.6 per cent

in 1933. From then until 1948 the proportion steadily increased with only minor fluctuations when it again reached 45.2 per cent. Since that time and throughout the 1960s the figure remained in the low 40s, but possible indications of a new period of growth were to be seen in 1970 when the density of union membership reached 47.7 per cent and by 1974 the figure had reached 50 per cent (Price and Bain 1976, p 340). These gross figures disguise the important sex differential that exists in union membership. A majority of male workers have been union members since 1946 (nearly 57 per cent in 1974), whereas the largest proportion of women workers to belong to a union was 37 per cent achieved in 1974 (from Bain, Bacon and Pimlott 1972 Table 4–12, pp 123–4 and Price and Bain 1976 p 349).

The general growth of white-collar jobs did not initially lead to a rapid growth in white-collar union membership. However, Price and Bain note that:

> Between 1964 and 1970 total white-collar union membership increased by 33.8 per cent, an increase over a six-year period which was greater than that recorded in the previous sixteen years; and in the four years to the end of 1974, a further 671,000 members were added, an increase of 18.7 per cent. This rapid increase outstripped the steady rate of growth of white-collar employment, and consequently white-collar union density rose by 5.6 percentage points to 35.2 per cent in 1970, and by another 4.2 percentage points to 39.4 per cent in 1974. By 1974, 36 per cent of all union members were white-collar employees compared with 26 per cent ten years earlier, and with 21 per cent in 1948. (Price and Bain 1976 p 345).

Before leaving the statistics on union membership we should be clear what they represent. We have employed a fairly strict definition of what constitutes a trade union and have excluded organizations which represent occupational groups and perform many of the functions of trades unions but which do not declare themselves as such. Thus some professional associations are not included. It should be clear, therefore, that our statistics on union membership do not provide a valid *general* index of the degree of collective activity undertaken by workers in contemporary British society, although they give an indication of changes in such activity.

In terms of wage differentials it is very difficult to give a brief and accurate account of the state of affairs. In very broad terms, however, we compare in the following table the average weekly earnings of full-time manual and non-manual men, 21 years and over, excluding those whose pay was affected by absence.

Table 3 Earnings of full-time manual and non-manual male workers

	April 1972		April 1977	
	Non-manual	*Manual*	*Non-manual*	*Manual*
Average weekly earnings	£43.5	£32.8	£88.9	£71.5
Non-manual average weekly earnings as a % of manual average weekly earnings	133	100	124	100
Average number of hours worked per week	38.7	46	38.7	45.7
Average hourly earnings, including overtime pay and overtime hours	110.7p	71.3p	227.2p	156.5p
Non-manual average hourly earnings as a % of manual average hourly earnings	155	100	145	100

Source: Department of Employment Gazette, September 1978, adapted from Table 126, p 1110

From the above table we can see that there has been a minor narrowing of the difference in average earnings between the two groups in the period considered. To put these figures in a longer historical perspective we can refer to Chart 1 which plots broad changes in average earnings since 1948. From this we can see that, excepting the relative improvement for manual youths and boys, the groups moved approximately in parallel up to 1970. Since that date women's earnings have risen relative to those of men, as have manual workers' earnings relative to those of non-manual workers. Also the relative improvement of manual youths and boys has been continued.

Although income distribution in the way we have described it is an important element in indicating social and material inequality in Great Britain it represents only the most visible tip of an iceberg of further inequalities. If we consider any of the other major social indicators associated with industrial society further aspects of substantial inequality are revealed. The various contributing factors have been assessed and their combined influence plotted by Field (1974) in a most useful review of all major research in this area since 1945. It is only by considering the interrelated nature of these factors that we can understand what Field calls the 'cycle of inequality'.

In his analysis Field (1974) shows that social class or socio-economic

Chart 1 Trends in average earnings: all industries covered: October 1948–77

£s

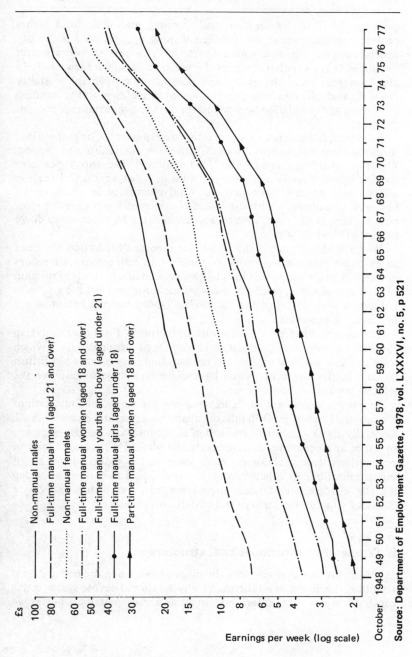

Non-manual males

Full-time manual men (aged 21 and over)

Non-manual females

Full-time manual women (aged 18 and over)

Full-time manual youths and boys (aged under 21)

Full-time manual girls (aged under 18)

Part-time manual women (aged 18 and over)

Earnings per week (log scale)

October 1948 49 50 51 52 53 54 55 56 57 58 59 60 61 62 63 64 65 66 67 68 69 70 71 72 73 74 75 76 77

Source: Department of Employment Gazette, 1978, vol. LXXXVI, no. 5, p 521

grouping (defined by occupational prestige and skill, from higher professional occupations to unskilled manual occupations) is the key variable in determining a wide range of life-chances. 'Almost wherever one looks it is clear that those in the lower social classes are relatively disadvantaged. From the most basic consideration of infant mortality rates, through the educational achievement of children, to the standard of housing the correlation between lower class and disadvantage remains the same.

Such inequalities that exist are either determined by, or perpetuated through, basic inequalities in the distribution of wealth and income. Wealth is strikingly unequally distributed with the top 1 per cent owning approximately a quarter of total personal wealth and the top 10 per cent owning three-quarters. What redistribution has occurred has only spread the wealth out a little more evenly amongst the most wealthy top 10 per cent, with no appreciable gain by those lower down the scale (Field 1974 p 58).

We have already noted the trends for income distribution but need to be aware that a narrow concern simply with cash remuneration does not reflect other important inequalities associated with work. Provision of holidays, sick-pay, pensions and allowances for time-off are gradually reduced as one descends the social class ladder, but the extent of job insecurity is increased.

The combined effect of these various factors is, Field argues, to trap those in the lowest social classes into a 'cycle of inequality' from which they can find no easy escape; the changes that have occurred in British society in the last thirty years have done very little to improve the relative position of these groups.

From this assortment of figures and comparisons some indication of the general trends in Britain's occupational structure can be gained. Generally speaking, Britain has followed the international development of other advanced capitalist societies and plotted a course, at least in occupational terms, consistent with some of the tenets of a logic of industrialization. In other respects, however, especially when considering the distribution of occupational rewards, the British experience does not support the logic of industrialization thesis.

5 Women in the occupational structure

In this section we shall consider the place of women in the occupational structure. There are several reasons why we should devote space to this topic. Firstly, work is often thought of as a male preserve whereas we have already seen that women have been a large and growing proportion of the labour force for many years, particularly in those significant areas of service occupations and white-collar work. Secondly, the characteristics of female occupational patterns are in many ways distinctive and important. Thirdly, in terms of future development women are likely to be increasingly significant, for example, with the implementation of Section 1 of the Equal Pay Act 1970, in December 1975. Before we begin the statistical account of the position of women in employment we must be clear on a point of definition. Where the term 'female' is used this refers to all females in employment, the term 'woman', however, refers only to those females aged 18 and above, this is a standard distinction in all Government statistics on female employment.

As we have seen, women form an increasingly large proportion of the labour force and females accounted for 38 per cent of all employees in 1977. In 1971 the overall economic activity rate for females was nearly 43 per cent, compared with 61 per cent for the whole population, the female activity rate in 1921 was nearly 34 per cent (figures from *Women and Work*, Manpower Paper No. 9 1974 pp 5 and 6, and Bain, Bacon and Pimlott 1972 Table 4.7, p 118). It was a similar state of affairs in the USA that led Franklin D. Roosevelt to say, 'Don't talk to me about manpower any more because the manpower question has been solved by womanpower' (quoted in Glennerster *et al* 1966).

This increase in the employment of women has been largely a result of the increasing proportion of married women now working. In 1931 only 10 per cent of married women worked, in 1951 nearly 22 per cent and in 1971 over 42 per cent. In 1971, 62 per cent of all female employees were married. As might be expected the greatest increase in the proportion of women employed was amongst those aged between 35—54 so that for married females the activity rate was only 36 per cent for those aged 25—29, 59 per cent for those aged 45—49, in 1971 (Manpower Paper No. 9, 1974 p 8). The activity rates also increased as the woman's educational qualifications increased.

A characteristic peculiar to female employment is the high proportion of part-time employment (less than 30 hours a week). For all women workers this has been a steadily increasing trend over the last decade or so. In 1963 about 37 per cent of all women employees worked part-time and this had risen to over 45 per cent by 1972. Amongst younger female workers (15—19 years) the proportion was very much lower at only 2 per cent in 1966. This is reflected in the fact that in 1966 more than 80 per cent of all part-time female workers were married, and more than 80 per cent of part-timers were 35 or over (*Department of Employment Gazette* 1973, vol. LXXXI, no. 11, pp 1090– 1). The proportion of men engaged in part-time work was less than 5 per cent.

The incidence of part-time employees in the total female labour force varies from industry to industry. In 1971 around 39 per cent of female employees worked part-time in the service industries compared with only 20 per cent in manufacturing industries.

This general pattern of economic activity amongst women is clearly a reflection of family commitments. Thus in 1966 less than 20 per cent of married females in households with children under 5 were at work, and in 1971, 58 per cent of married females with no dependent children, but only 30 per cent of those with two dependent children, worked more than 30 hours per week (Manpower Paper No. 9, 1974 p 5). As one might expect the incidence of part-time working increases amongst married women, in relation to full-time employment, as the number of children in the family increases (*Department of Employment Gazette* 1973, vol. LXXXI, no. 11, p 1092). In her survey of married women workers, Viola Klein (1965) supports this view when she notes that her outstanding impression is 'that women's lives, today, as much as ever, are dominated by their role — actual or expected — as wives and mothers' (Klein 1965 p 76).

In terms of their range of employment women have historically found it difficult to gain admittance to, and acceptance in, some jobs and it has sometimes taken a major national crisis, such as war, to provide women with wider occupational opportunities (Williams 1965). In 1971 over half of all female employees were in jobs in three major service industries, namely the distributive trades (17.1 per cent), professional and scientific services (23.1 per cent) and miscellaneous services (such as catering, laundries, etc.) (11.7 per cent). All service industries employed over two-thirds of all female employees (Manpower Paper No. 9, 1974 p 16). In some service-industry groups, women outnumbered men:

> These were the professional and scientific services, which include teachers, nursing and social work, the 'miscellaneous' group, which includes workers in hotels, restaurants and pubs, laundries and hairdressing, and which had the highest proportion of part-time workers in the whole census, the distributive trades, and insurance, banking and similar services. In only one of the manufacturing-industry groups, clothing and footwear, was there a preponderance of women over men employees, (Economic Progress Report No. 56, 1974 pp 2–3)

In terms of occupational groups we have already noted that in 1971 females represented 29 per cent of manual workers but 46.2 per cent of non-manual workers.

In terms of hours worked full-time men and women manual workers in 1971 had very nearly the same normal basic weekly hours although in terms of actual hours worked men worked longer due to their over-time employment. Amongst non-manual workers women worked very similar hours to men.

With regard to earnings the situation is typically complex. The period prior to the implementation of the Equal Pay Act showed a trend towards equality of remuneration. As we noted above, the difference in the amount of overtime worked accounts for a proportion of the sex differential in total earnings amongst manual workers. There still exists, however, a substantial differential in median hourly earnings, which excludes overtime pay.

Increasingly, however, moves towards equal pay have been evident particularly where wages are determined by national agreement. In 1973 amongst non-manual workers the median female hourly rate of all industries was about 55 per cent of the male rate, but this reflects the large proportion of women at the lower end of the white-collar groups (mainly clerks). The moves towards equal pay in this area are more difficult to assess as this kind of employment is more rarely subject to earnings determined by national agreement. What evidence there is suggests that the larger the firm the more equal the pay is likely to be (*Department of Employment Gazette*, 1973, vol. LXXXII, no. 8, p 694). With regard to pension schemes and sickness pay when com-pared with their male counterparts, female manual workers were substantially worse off with respect to both sick pay and pensions in 1970. For non-manual workers, women were marginally worse off in terms of sick pay but substantially worse off in respect of pensions. (Manpower Paper No. 9, 1974 p 35).

At the upper end of the occupational range discrimination against women is difficult to demonstrate conclusively but the survey con-ducted by Fogarty *et al* (1971) *Women in Top Jobs* found evidence of such discrimination in all areas they investigated (business, the BBC and the administrative class of the Civil Service).

Reasons often given to justify this state of affairs usually include reference to higher job turnover and poorer record with regard to absence from work. Both these allegations are valid to some degree although the difference between men and women in this respect is often not as great as is sometimes assumed (Manpower Paper No. 9, 1974 pp 37–40).

Where women do occupy positions of authority at work it is often in jobs which can be seen as an extension of their traditional domestic 'caring' role. Such occupations as nursing and social work would be an example. It is in such jobs that women may often have authority or power over other women and children but rarely over men. It is in the light of such observations that many feminist writers have argued that a sexual stratification process operates in modern industrial society.

To summarize this section we can quote from Klein who conducted a survey amongst employers of married women. Although her remarks refer only to married women workers we must bear in mind that this means a substantial majority of all female employees (over 60 per cent).

> One is left with the general impression that in most firms the employment of married women is accepted as a necessary expedient to trade over a period of labour shortage. Few managements, other than those traditionally employing female labour in large numbers, have yet accepted the idea that married women workers have come to stay. Adjustments to fit them into the existing labour force are therefore mostly made *ad hoc* and are not part of a long-term labour policy. It will presumably need a longer period of full employment and industrial expansion before employers can be persuaded to regard married women as a substantial and useful part of their usual personnel, for whom working conditions will have to be created which will enable them to pull their full weight. (Klein 1965 p 135)

6 Mobility in industrial society

The issue of population mobility is a large and complex one and in this brief discussion we can do no more than scratch the surface of a much wider debate. It is important as an issue, however, as we have briefly seen already, being a major tenet in the logic of industrialism thesis, and in more parochial terms with regard to occupational change in our own society. In this section we shall consider the problem on two levels. Firstly we shall look at some of the major findings on *social* mobility for non-socialist industrial societies, and in particular the USA, and secondly we shall be concerned with occupational mobility in Great Britain in recent years.

6.1 Social mobility in industrial societies

In the following discussion the argument will concern only non-socialist societies, some evidence on social mobility in the USSR was presented earlier in this chapter, but generally the evidence from socialist societies is fairly limited and hard to assess in comparable terms.

Let us firstly be clear about the terms we are using. Social mobility has been defined as 'the movement of individuals, families and groups from one social position to another' (Goldhamer 1968 p 429). Social position has typically been assessed in terms of the occupation held by males, and usually males who are the heads of households. Occupations have normally been grouped into manual or non-manual categories with a move from manual to non-manual being described as upward mobility and a move in the other direction, downward mobility. Measurements of the changes have included calculations of intergenerational mobility, a comparison of father's and son's occupations, and intragenerational mobility, changes by an individual in his own lifetime. In particular the grading of occupational 'prestige' simply in terms of manual or non-manual categories may be seriously misleading, for example, will a skilled manual craftsman always rank lower than a minor, but white-collar, clerk? Much recent work has been devoted to constructing a more satisfactory approach to occupational grading and occupational prestige (see Goldthorpe and Hope 1972 and 1974), but the findings we shall be reporting rely on the more traditional techniques.

The opportunities for upward social mobility have traditionally been regarded as resulting from three main factors. Firstly, the technical changes which have created novel occupational positions and also lessened the likelihood of a son being able to directly inherit his father's job. Secondly, immigration, which, particularly in the USA, tended to push up the scale the lower sections of the indigenous population and, thirdly, the lower fertility rate of those in higher occupational positions often meant that those groups could not adequately fill the vacant positions from their own offspring thus providing opportunities for those from lower down the scale (Blau and Duncan 1961).

Given these assumptions, which have not gone unchallenged, the estimation of social mobility involves several steps, a comparison of some starting point with a later achievement, an analysis of the means of mobility (i.e. the key determining factors), an account of the mobility process (i.e. the extent to which, and how, career developments reveal patterns), and finally the consequences of mobility. To date, most research has concentrated on the first stage, with only scant regard being paid to the others. The methodological problems and costs involved are certainly major reasons for this state of affairs (Lipset and Bendix 1967).

Constraints on the measurable extent of mobility will include

changes in the number of available occupational vacancies, the actual
degree of differential fertility between occupational groups, changes
in rank accorded to occupations, changes in the number of inheritable
status-positions, and changes in legal restrictions pertaining to potential
opportunities (Lipset and Bendix 1967). On the other side of the coin
sociologists usually make the assumption that higher positions are in
fact sought after.

In terms of the major determinants of personal mobility Blau and
Duncan suggest that for intergenerational mobility the key factors are,
father's occupation and education and son's education and first job.
The nexus for these factors is of course the family and the influence of
the family in determining occupational choice will be considered in
the next chapter. For some sections of the population an additional
important inhibiting factor will be their race.

As one might expect, the changes in social mobility have reflected
to some degree the changes in the overall occupational structure,
especially with regard to the expansion of service and white-collar
jobs. It is, however, an invalid procedure to assume automatically that
two trends do in fact correspond with each other.

The major findings on social mobility of the intergenerational
variety suggest that manual to non-manual shifts have been of a similar
magnitude in many societies (Lipset and Bendix 1967) although the
probability of someone achieving mobility is inversely proportional
to the distance they travel up the scale according to Blau and Duncan,
reporting on the USA. Thus the major mobility 'flows' occur between
adjacent categories although Blau and Duncan (1967) suggest that
major obstacles to mobility are the changes from agricultural to blue-
collar jobs and from these to white-collar employment. Lipset and
Bendix note that the basis of recruitment to professions and other elite
groups varies greatly from one society to another. In summarizing the
trend of the extent of social mobility Goldhamer (1968) suggests that
there has been no great change in the USA over the last two decades
and the overall degree of upward mobility has been relatively large and
outweighed downward mobility. He also suggests that the extent of
social mobility is probably no greater in the USA than Europe.

Given the equivocal state of the evidence our conclusion on social
mobility as a reflection of occupational changes and the emergence of
an 'open' society must be uncertain. The mobility that does occur is
mainly short-range and least evident where admissions to positions of
power and influence are involved. As an important defining feature of
industrial societies the issue of mobility remains an unresolved one.

6.2   Occupational mobility in Great Britain

A national survey on occupational mobility in Great Britain was carried out in 1963 and investigated the changes that had occurred during the preceding ten years. The survey, which involved nearly 20,000 respondents, dealt only with the geographical and occupational moves that people had undertaken and no attempt was made to convert this into a full assessment of social mobility. In this chapter, however, we are mainly concerned with the occupational structure so the findings of the survey (Harris and Clausen 1966) are worth considering in some detail.

We can begin by looking at the geographical mobility reported. In 1963, 48 per cent of the sample were living at the same address as ten years earlier and 69 per cent were at the same address as five years before. Of those that had moved within the ten years, 64 per cent had remained in the same town and only 21 per cent had moved more than 10 miles. Where people had moved from one region to another the major trend had been to London and the South East. As might be expected the greater number of moves had been by those under 30 and also by those with higher educational qualifications. Of all those who had moved within the ten years, the desire for improved housing or, alternatively, redevelopment or notice to quit had been the major reason for 56 per cent of the sample moving; work reasons accounted for only 17 per cent. Interestingly, those who had moved for work reasons tended to be better educated. When respondents were asked what would encourage them to move, a majority (51 per cent) said 'nothing at all', 29 per cent said 'improved pay, promotion and prospects' and 9 per cent said 'better housing'.

If we now turn to the occupational status of respondents we note that:

> The distribution in 1963 is similar to 1953; the largest difference is the decrease in skilled manual workers, the increase being mainly among clerical and office workers (particularly women), and among the unskilled. The proportions in the professional, managerial, and both partly skilled groups (manual and non-manual) have remained more or less the same. (Harris and Clausen 1966 p 50)

We can get a clearer picture of the situation if we consider the mobility displayed by each of five occupational categories, taking the combined total for both sexes. In the first group (professional and administrative workers), 93 per cent of those who had been in this group at the beginning of the ten year period were there at the end. Only 3 per cent had slipped down one category, 3 per cent had fallen 2 or 3 categories and only 1 per cent had dropped more than 3 categories. In the second group, managerial and minor professional workers, 86 per cent had remained in this category; the main moves had been down to clerical and skilled non-manual work. Only 1 per cent had risen into the highest category. In the third category, skilled manual workers, 77 per cent had remained in this group and the number of moves down were double the number of those in an upward direction. The two lowest groups, the partly-skilled (both manual and non-manual), and the unskilled showed the biggest movement in an upward direction. Amongst partly skilled manual workers, 12 per cent had risen to skilled manual work and 8 per cent to non-manual work. Only 4 per cent had reached managerial status and 7 per cent had dropped to unskilled work. Amongst the partly-skilled non-manual workers, 16 per cent had changed to skilled or partly-skilled manual work, 6 per cent had risen to skilled non-manual, 4 per cent to managerial and 9 per cent had fallen into unskilled jobs. Those in the unskilled group could only remain where they were or move upwards. In fact 20 per cent rose to partly-skilled work, 9 per cent to skilled manual and 2 per cent to skilled non-manual work. Less than ½ per cent reached managerial status. In general then we can detect some degree of mobility but as we noted earlier in a more general context, most change was of only a minor kind with very restricted access to the top groups.

As far as changing jobs is concerned 56 per cent of those men who had been employed throughout the ten years had only had one job, 18 per cent had had two, and 11 per cent, three jobs. About 10 per cent had been employed in 10 or more jobs. With regard to length of time in a job 36 per cent of jobs for men lasted less than one year (38 per cent for women), and 64 per cent lasted under three years (60 per cent for women). Length of time in a job was positively correlated with the job's occupational status and the educational qualifications of the worker. The two most frequent reasons for changing jobs (about 17 per cent of the total each) were redundancy and voluntary change to take a better job. The group most affected by redundancy were manual workers, the degree of skill not seeming to be significant. Nearly two-thirds of all workers had a job to go to when they left their previous employment, but the proportions ranged from 89 per cent for professional and administrative workers to 53 per cent for unskilled workers. The changes in terms of industrial classification varied considerably with mining, quarrying and professional and scientific services retaining 80 per cent of employees over the ten years while manufacturers and processors of food, drink and tobacco only managed to retain 56 per cent. The lowest retention figure was in public administration and defence 46 per cent, but this included substantial numbers of men discharged after National Service.

From this survey, therefore, we can see that the changes in occupations in Britain, for the period 1953–63, were similar to those for other industrial societies. The rearrangement of jobs corresponded to the overall redistribution of work amongst the main economic sectors but the overall rate of mobility was not high. That mobility which did occur was relatively short-range both in terms of occupational status and geographical location.

The 1972 survey by the Social Mobility Group at Nuffield College, Oxford, into occupational mobility in England and Wales presents more recent evidence. Although the full results of this survey are not yet available it is already clear that patterns of intergenerational mobility may be very complex. A variety of general theories have been subjected to test and none have clearly demonstrated their validity (see Goldthorpe and Llewellyn, 1977a).

What has become reasonably clear is that with the major changes in the occupational structure upward mobility by many is compatible with intergenerational stability by those at the top of the hierarchy.

> During a period in which demand for professional, administrative and managerial personnel rises quite sharply, a large measure of intergenerational stability at the higher levels of the class structure can, of course, coexist with much upward mobility into these levels; and further, any control over access so as to favour men of not greatly dissimilar social origins will be difficult to maintain at all strictly. In other words, strategies of exclusion become at the same time less necessary and less viable. (Goldthorpe and Llewellyn 1977a p 281)

A fuller analysis of this trend with a discussion of its relevance to the class structure may be found in Goldthorpe and Llewellyn 1977b and Goldthorpe, Payne and Llewellyn 1978.

Conclusion

In this chapter we have provided a reasoned approach to the topic of occupational structure in industrial societies by outlining a theoretical model of the industrialization process and then comparing the propositions of that model with the empirical evidence in both a comparative and domestic context.

It is worthwhile, however, making a few points about the limitations of the approaches we have been discussing and have used. With regard to the 'logic of industrialization' the evidence we have considered certainly fails to settle the issue one way or another. This is unsurprising for a number of reasons. Firstly, the issue is in a sense unresolvable for our consideration of it has merely been a 'snap-shot' glance at one particular instant whereas the whole topic concerns a highly complex and ongoing societal process. Secondly, the evidence we would require for even a complete 'snap-shot' picture is not available and, thirdly, we have been predominantly concerned with occupational structure which represents only one aspect of the problem. We have seen, however, that it is a faulty logical and sociological procedure to leap from the identification of international trends simply concerning occupational structure to generalizations about the social structure of whole societies. In this way we have perhaps also given a useful perspective to the notion of work in society.

The other major limitation we should point out refers to the method of presentation we have ourselves employed, especially when discussing the British occupational structure. The analysis we have given is predominantly a statistical one, a list of 'facts'. In themselves, however, 'facts' tell us little about the nature of our society. The number of available 'facts' is endless, what is important are the social processes, meanings, and consequences that underlie them. In passing, for example, we have mentioned that the distribution of occupational opportunities and rewards is closely connected with wider aspects of the social stratification system. We have implicitly suggested that power over such scarce social resources is unequally distributed in a patterned way. The basis of such power may be revealed in different forms. For most workers the most important aspects revolve about the class-based nature of our society where low skill and prestige rankings are reflected in generally poorer life-chances. Others bear the additional problems of a low power position based on racial or sexual factors. The 'facts' when viewed in such a light take on new dimensions of meaning and significance to challenge any over-simplified approach by the social scientist. Thus our 'facts' *explain* very little. They simply reflect a particular way of looking, a way which has in many instances proved convenient and useful. The major virtue of such an approach is that it may help us to decide where to go on to, where next to look.

CHAPTER 4

Mary Anne Speakman

Occupational choice and placement

Introduction

Previous chapters in this book have already outlined the nature of the occupational structure within different types of political organization and shown how the predominant mode of work organization has moved through agrarian, industrial and, according to some writers, post-industrial phases (as described in Chapter 3). Chapter 1 has also shown that the division of labour has resulted in the unequal distribution of work rewards, from working conditions and material remuneration to the intrinsic satisfaction and meaning to be gained from working. For at least some degree of stability to be attained, certain factors must be operating to result in adequate staffing within the occupational structure to satisfy the requirements of an industrial society and to ensure that all jobs, pleasant or unpleasant, high or low paid, remain filled. In this chapter, therefore, we turn to the issue of how people come to be placed in jobs and to the question of how much choice people have over their own individual position in the occupational structure. We shall be concerned with the situation within capitalist societies: most of the material discussed relates to Britain and the United States.

One of the principal factors operating in the maintenance of a stable system is the relationship between a person's social class background and his occupational position and achievement. Very crudely this relationship can be stated thus: most children from working class homes enter manual occupations and most children from middle class homes enter non-manual occupations. The relationship is obviously not as simple as that, however, and the chapter will be concerned with extracting and discussing some of the variables that cause this situation to persist. The statement implies that the family acts as a mediator in perpetuating differential access to certain sorts of work – one way in which it does this is via its role as the socializing agent of children into different value structures, work orientations and class images. Another way is evident in its relationship to educational opportunity. The type of education received and level of certification achieved often determine the range of jobs available to the individual and the family's social class position is very closely linked to entry into education. Class-based differential opportunities are perpetuated by the differential emphasis placed by parents and teachers on the value of education for children in different social strata and strengthened by the different cultures of high and low streams within comprehensive schools, grammar and secondary modern schools, reflected in the different curricula, the 'labelling' of children as suitable for different levels of education by teachers, counsellors, careers advisors, etc. Although individual abilities, aspirations and motivation need to be taken into account they are themselves affected (encouraged or dampened down) by the positions that the individual occupies in the educational system.

The availability of certain sorts of work is thus related both institutionally and culturally to stratification and this relationship to a large extent determines how individuals come to decide on their future work careers and how an initial commitment to a particular type of work is formed. When talking about an individual's career we shall be referring to the concept of career in two different ways. Careers can be seen in a subjective sense by reference to a process of a series of adjustments to the demands of social institutions, formal organizations and informal social relationships – the interpretation of events and consequent behaviour of particular individuals in specific contexts is the subjective aspect. On the other hand, one can stress the objective nature of careers by viewing them as patterned progressions of social statuses or positions. This brings out the influence of social structure in influencing behaviour and shows how personal adjustment is limited by conditions outside the individual's control.

In a broad sense, careers can be seen as including all aspects of an individual's life:

> . . . subjectively career is the moving perspective in which a person sees his life as a whole, and interprets his attributes, actions and the things which happen to him . . . objectively it is a series of statuses and clearly defined offices . . . typical sequences of position, responsibility and even of adventure. (Hughes 1937 pp 409–10)

In the more specific occupational usage, career can be viewed as the movement from . . .

. . . one position to another in an occupational system made by any individual who works in that system. Furthermore, it includes the notion of 'career contingency', those factors on which mobility from one position to another depends. Career contingencies include both objective facts of social structure and changes in the perspectives, motivations and desires of the individual. (Becker 1963 p 24)

In discussing the entry into the occupational structure, this chapter is thus concerned with careers in the latter sense — the choice of an occupational career and movement into that career which *objectively* may be constrained by external structural factors (e.g. economic conditions, degree of qualifications, etc.) and *subjectively* is perceived within the context of individual aspirations, orientations and imagery. This is not to say, however, that the individual's experience in his occupational career will not have an effect on his career in the broader sense or on certain aspects of it (e.g. a carry-over effect on leisure activities). The concept is, however, also used in the broader sense, by using it to link the progression through statuses held in the family, in school and *then* in an occupation. We are concerned with a time-scale that goes beyond just working careers and with showing how the individual's career before entering work affects both that entry and the likelihood of subsequent adjustment.

Theories of occupational choice and placement have covered a wide range of explanations, those deriving from psychology and social psychology tending to place more emphasis on the *choice* of occupation from all those available, that choice being one that is most consonant with one's self-perception and that will best satisfy one's ambitions and aspirations, and those deriving from sociology tending to be more concerned with how that choice is limited by structural factors, how ambitions and aspirations are themselves socially structured, and with how placement is effected. One problem that arises when examining processes of occupational choice is that of the use of the word 'choice' itself, as it has been used in different ways and, in different contexts, can mean different things. The problem hinges on how far choice can be 'free' within the structure of society and furthermore subjectively perceived as such by the individual. This is one of the basic areas of disagreement between the individual-ambition model of occupational choice (Ginzberg, Super, Musgrave) and the structure-opportunity model (Keil *et al*, Roberts) as discussed in Sections 1 and 2 respectively. How far can an individual make an informed and desired choice that will fulfil his ambitions and self-concept or does a stratified society effectively limit choice by setting up boundaries that operate through the family, educational system and occupational structure?

Most of the research on this area referred to in this chapter is concerned with school-leavers and entry into their first job. This is partly because initial commitment to a particular job and the experience arising from that have significant effects on general work orientations and on later career prospects and career development. Also, there is rather more relevant material on specific factors affecting first job choice than on factors affecting a change in later working life.

The next section examines the theories of occupational choice that have derived from developmental psychology (the individual-ambition model), followed by a discussion of the structure-opportunity model implicit in sociological research. Section 3 then takes a closer look at some of the factors that influence the process of choice of work and placement, in particular the influence of the family and of education. Section 4 examines the influence of sex and race on occupational opportunities.

1 Developmental theories of occupational choice

For a long time, the most influential perspective in the area of occupational choice and placement was that deriving from diffferential psychology and typified by the 'square pegs-square holes' type of theory. The developmental theories first appeared during the 1950s and, within the psychological framework, have subsequently largely replaced the former orthodoxy by providing a more comprehensive attempt to integrate the various areas of knowledge about careers, job attitudes, ambitions and placement. These theories attempt to explain human behaviour and attitudes in terms of maturation of the individual's innate capacities and some researchers within this field have felt that our understanding of job entry and occupational choice would increase by being treated in this way — notably Eli Ginzberg and his colleagues, and Donald Super. Since much of the relevant sociological research has taken the form of a dialogue with, or a criticism of, these psychological theories it seems appropriate to start by considering in more detail the work of these two researchers.

1.1 Maturational stages of occupational choice

Ginzberg's initial research in 1951, set out in his book *Occupational Choice* (1951), was concerned to identify the stages through which young people's occupational choices develop: 'the key to the study of occupational choice appears to lie in an appraisal of the way in which the individual, as he matures, reaches decisions with respect to his eventual occupation' (Ginzberg 1951 p 29), for 'an individual never reaches the ultimate decision at a single moment in time, but through a series of decisions over a period of many years; the cumulative impact is the determining factor' (Ginzberg 1951 p 27).

Ginzberg developed a framework within which to order his data that showed the factors likely to influence this decision-making. This three-part scheme comprises 'the self' (capacities, interests, goals and values and the individual's time perspective, e.g. his cognizance of the length of training process), 'reality' (socio-economic familial factors, evaluation of the work world, education and life plan which includes plans for marriage) and 'key persons' (parents, teachers, etc.) who may have a significant influence on the individual.

Three main stages in the evolution of occupational choice determination were isolated. These are related to the more general maturation of the individual and influenced by the factors outlined above and changes in these factors over time. The age ranges suggested are, however, only rough approximations and the successive stages are supposed to merge smoothly into each other. The 'fantasy' period covers the years 6 to 11 and is characterized by the playing out of adult roles without the awareness of the means and ends appropriate to acting such a role for real. The 'tentative' choice stage covers the period of adolescence (11 to 17) and can be subdivided into four stages: the interest, capacity, value and transition stages. Basically, this typifies the gradual maturation of the self-concept and the growing awareness of external and internal factors as influencing the objective choice of career. Thus choice is firstly based on an individual's interests; secondly, it is realized that capacities must be taken into account and, thirdly, the individual must begin to evaluate possible occupations in the light of his interests and capacities, his goals and personal values. Fourthly, the transition stage is reached at the time when the individual is about to leave school and enter college or work and is, to quote Ginzberg, a period of 'restrained suspense about the future' (Ginzberg 1951 p 75). This is characterized by a shift from subjective considerations to a greater awareness of external reality.

Finally, the period of 'realistic' choice is reached — for Ginzberg, this typifies the situation for the new college student at about 18 years. This covers the opportunity for exploration (pursuing certain study subjects, discussion with key persons, attending careers conferences), followed by crystallization of ideas, a period of assessment of all the factors influencing the occupational choice under consideration. Lastly comes the stage of specification, the final narrowing down of possibilities leading to the final decision.

Thus, the decision to enter a certain sort of work would seem to be a gradual process based on the maturation of self and the gathering of more and more specific information and experience related to occupations that will give the self the maximum fulfilment. But it should be noted that this conclusion was based on a study of a 'definitely privileged group' of children, adolescents and college students in terms of economic position, family support and status in the community (Ginzberg 1951 pp 41–3). This group was deliberately chosen in the research design so that 'the external environment interfered as little as possible with their freedom to pursue any occupation' (Ginzberg 1951 p 41). Ginzberg himself notes that there may be problems in applying this theory to lower-income groups, but in a series of subsequent research projects, building upon the conclusion of the work summarized above, he still insists that his general theory can be adapted to take account of these cases. But especially in view of the fact that school-leavers from these lower-income groups may well have to enter work before even entering the 'realistic' stage, it is questionable as to how successful the research has been in supplying the 'general' theory that was intended.

1.2 'The psychology of careers' — Donald Super

Super's research is also concerned with the developmental process of career choice and is described in his book *The Psychology of Careers* (1957), subsequent research being based on this work. However, his conclusions have again been found to correspond most closely with high educational and subsequently occupational achievements. Nevertheless, his work has found favour with practitioners in the careers-guidance field with his emphasis on vocational development and maturity. The desire to relate a long-term developmental process with effective long-term guidance is especially prevalent in the USA (cf. Gutsch and Alcorn 1970): careers guidance in Britain has been, at least until recently, more pragmatic and less related to theory.

Super suggested that occupational choices develop through similar stages to those suggested by Ginzberg (although he uses slightly different labels to denote these stages), but placed more emphasis on social environment in structuring the individual's conception of his interests, abilities and capacities. He suggests that individuals need to carry out various developmental tasks at given stages of vocational development before they can proceed to the next stage (e.g. self-exploration in the home via role-playing, more formal exploration at school, in part-time work, etc.), eventually leading to a set of vocational aspirations (Super

1957 pp 80–100). A related concept is that of vocational maturity which can be scored to assess how adequately the individual is coping with his developmental tasks. Further, vocational development is seen as leading to a situation of 'integrative vocational adjustment' which refers to 'the accomplishment of a task with the greatest degree of long-term satisfaction to the individuals' (Roberts 1975 p 136). Thus, a self-concept emerges from the interaction between the individual's capacities and his social environment.

However, in contrast to Ginzberg, Super does not suggest that ambitions are firmly crystallized at the time of initially entering employment, but accepts that ambitions may change after starting work and that careers may change direction. So the self-concept continues to develop through 'the early stages of a young person's career until an occupational role fully consistent with the individual's self-concept [is] discovered' (Roberts 1968 p 141). This longer-term developmental perspective is allowed for by the addition of establishment, maintenance and decline stages to the earlier growth and exploration stages which roughly correspond to Ginzberg's fantasy, tentative and realistic stages in terms of age. The stages of exploration and establishment are seen as crucial to vocational development, for it is in these periods that the vocational tasks are carried out — crystallizing a vocational preference, specifying it, implementing it, stabilizing in the chosen vocation, consolidating status and advancing in the occupation. Figure 1 gives a diagrammatic view of how Super (1968) sees the main developmental stages as compared with Ginzberg.

The developmental theories have offered much in the way of providing and maintaining an occupational ideology for those engaged in vocational guidance, especially in the USA. Realization that job choice may be a salient issue facing individuals, education and the economy has arisen more recently in Britain and the development of a more comprehensive and enlightened system of careers counselling that does more than simply allocate people in jobs has found much credence in the developmental stages approach.

However, although the theory's assimilation into the careers guidance movement may be 'comprehensible in terms of professionals' needs' (Roberts 1975 p 138), it may not be so comprehensible in terms of the supporting evidence. The emphasis on occupational choice as the central process of vocational development may be misplaced. The importance of the self-concept in terms of choosing an occupation that coincides with one's aspirations, need for self-actualization and self-fulfilment would seem to be far from the actual situation where educational qualifications, family background and the local job

Figure 1   The main stages of vocational development described by Super and Ginzberg

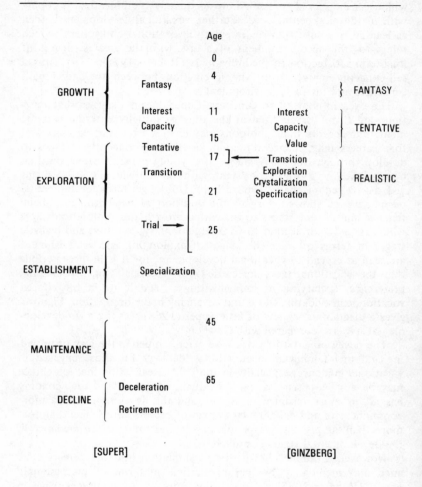

Source: Super in Hopson and Hayes 1968 p. 21.

opportunity structure are the limiting factors for most school-leavers. 'The developmental theory of occupational choice typically resembles reality in the case only of those more privileged individuals who are able to make genuine career decisions' (Roberts 1975 p 139).

Two questions arise from this: firstly, are the theories valid and, secondly, are they workable in practical counselling terms or merely a legitimation for the professional status of those engaged in careers guidance work? The first question is given some attention here. In an earlier paper, Roberts (1968) describes research that he undertook in order to test the premises of the developmental theories against data on the occupational behaviour and attitudes of young people in Britain. The tenets of the psychological theories were found inadequate (and led Roberts to propose the opportunity-structure model discussed in Section 2). This raises the problem of the cross-cultural validity of the theories – the developmental theories were primarily developed in America and it may be that they are more easily applicable in that society than in Britain.

Another study, conducted by Hayes (1971), also throws doubt on the theories under consideration. Hayes suggests that the developmental theories assume a causal relationship between the self-concept and occupational choice:

> The individual chooses an occupation (i.e. a work role and its associated non-work roles) which is congruent with his self-concept and his preferred global life style. It is assumed that the self-concept, when crystallized, *causes* some occupations to appear more attractive than others. (Hayes 1971 p 40)

In a review of the relevant literature, Hayes found little evidence to support his assertion and in his own study found that,

> . . . while the school-leaver may possess comprehensive self-concepts of himself as a pupil, sportsman, son, sibling, etc., there is room for serious doubt as to whether his occupational self-concept is crystallized or comprehensive. The evidence suggests that occupational choice is made on the basis of an incomplete or partial self-concept, one which focuses largely on the Economic Man, and that it is only when the individual experiences work at first hand that he begins to crystallize his occupational self-concept in psycho-social terms. (Hayes 1971 p 40)

That is, material factors were more commonly given as reasons for choosing an occupation than the psycho-social factors of choosing work as reinforcing the self-concept by providing creativity, social interaction and identity.

1.3 The individual-ambition model in sociological research

Nevertheless, what has been termed the 'individual-ambition' model
(Newman 1968) has found a place in sociological research, primarily
in the work of Musgrave (1967), who has proposed that these theories
may be profitably restated in sociological terms. He suggests that the
notion of development can be used in conjunction with the concepts
of socialization and role theory. The individual is seen as moving
through a sequence of roles in the home, the school and the occupational setting. Each role-playing location is seen as part of the process
of socialization in that the future range of roles becomes apparent and
the individual's ambitions and self-image are gradually formed.

Musgrave isolates three types of role socialization — primary, secondary and tertiary — and links these to stages of occupational maturation:

Stage 1   Pre-work socialization   The three main agents of socialization
at this stage — family, school and peer groups — provide experiences for
the child which not only shape his abilities but also his self-concept of
his own abilities, which both influence his later choice of career. The
pathway of roles available to the child, and hence his choice of occupation, is narrowed by the experiences he undergoes at the hand of these
three agents. This period provides the primary socialization necessary
for induction into the economic behaviour characterized by the second
stage and provides opportunities for occupational role rehearsal through
play activities, i.e. anticipatory socialization.

Stage 2   Entry to the labour force   This stage is characterized by
secondary socialization. From the occupational role map built up
through role rehearsal and observation of the behaviour of role models
(mainly parents, teachers, older siblings), the young person has to
choose a particular occupation from those available. Vocational guidance and trial work periods during vacations may be an important
influence at this stage in socializing the individual into choosing work
and in matching his choice to the selection process of industry and local
opportunities.

Stage 3   Socialization in the job   Here the individual undergoes a process of tertiary socialization during which he has to learn the role
behaviour particular to one occupation. As he becomes socialized into
his occupational role the self-concept that he constructs must meet the
demands of new role models, e.g. managers, work-mates. Prior anticipatory socialization may prove crucial in the successful adjustment

to this process, but where the individual fails to meet the role prescription of the job or decides to reject them, either early or later on in working life, he may proceed to

Stage 4   Job change   The inclusion of this stage means that despite the prominence given to the first choice of occupation, the framework can be applied to all choices of occupation that an individual makes throughout working life.

In terms of the development of the individual's ambitions and self-concepts, the similarity between Musgrave's theory and the developmental theories is clear, though Musgrave does give more attention to structural considerations and allows, as does Super, for changes in occupation after initial entry into employment. But Musgrave's work still fails to take account of many factors, such as the differential evaluation of occupations between social groups, and is still too individualistic in its approach, given the social structure within which occupational choice is confined.

2 The structure-opportunity model

In the individual-ambition model, ambition is important in defining occupational choice, whereas in the alternative model proposed — structure-opportunity — ambition is seen as being adapted to the occupation that the individual finds himself able to enter, i.e. the occupational structure and the opportunities it presents determine ambition.

In this sense, Musgrave's thesis can be seen as giving inadequate attention to social structure, to the opportunities available and to the differential access to certain positions. Furthermore it involves a basic theoretical weakness in attempting to explain social behaviour in terms of an oversimplified model by assuming a value consensus. Socialization into work roles is seen as positively functional in terms of society's needs but this ignores the significance and extent of variation, conflict and the differential meanings placed on work by different groups. It assumes that work and wanting to work are given the same values by everyone. The adjustment of self-concept to the demands of managers and work-mates is not as self-evident when issues such as these are raised. Thus the theory cannot adequately account for the extent and direction of occupational choice (see Coulson *et al* 1967). Also, from the evidence so far collected by research, it is doubtful that young people have as comprehensive role maps, information and knowledge about the world of work as Musgrave suggests.

Nevertheless Musgrave's suggestion that occupational choice is a process is theoretically fruitful. It may also be the case that the individual-ambition model may be applicable to some school-leavers if only to the 'privileged minority' researched by the developmental psychologists. For example, Sherlock and Cohen (1966), in a study of dentist trainees, found that the decision to enter dentistry was quite purposive and based on a rational compromise between the desired rewards and ease of access – a minimax strategy. Many of the students would have ideally preferred to be doctors but felt that dentistry, while offering similar financial and personal satisfaction rewards, would offer a greater chance of success in terms of access to a professional occupation. This neatly illustrates the integration of self-concept with exploration and specification.

There must be, however, certain factors that would lead to such a decision: factors that are common (though of differing degrees) to all young people approaching work. Keil *et al* (1966) have drawn attention to the formulation of a set of attitudes towards work and the experience of work and have isolated some of the variables involved in the process of moving from school to work that may influence choice of a particular kind of employment. Although their paper does not quantify the relative significance of the factors listed below, it should be theoretically possible to measure the comparative weighting of each variable by application of factor analysis:

  i family: economic level, social class, sibling pressure, family tradition, degree of parental aspiration;
 ii neighbourhood: type of residential area, residential stability;
iii school: type, area, attitude of teachers, school culture;
 iv peer group: ages, occupation if any, social background, activities;
  v formal institutions: Careers Service, access to industrial visits, part-time work;
 vi general work situation: availability of employment, national economic situation.

It has already been seen that Roberts (1968 and 1975) has criticized the developmental theories as ignoring the importance of factors such as these. The level of the occupational hierarchy entered depends largely upon educational achievement, which is closely related to family background: whatever the individual's self-concept may be and however ambitious he may be, he cannot enter a level for which he is unqualified.

The individual may simply have to take whatever work is available. Roberts considers that what is important is to account for (a) occupational role allocation – the way in which school-leavers are differentiated and placed in various roles within the occupational system – and (b) occupational socialization – how the individual is induced to accept a new role as a worker in a specific occupation to which he has been allocated. Roberts's study (1968), which set out to test some of the hypotheses raised by Ginzberg and Super, certainly found little evidence to support their contention that occupational *choice* is the key factor determining entry into employment. Furthermore,

> . . . when in employment, individuals' career movements are most easily explicable in terms of the opportunities their existing occupations open up. Individuals climb career 'ladders' only when they are sufficiently lucky to enter occupations in which progressive careers are available. (Roberts 1975 p 140)

The 'climates of expectation' available within particular educational institutions are internalized by their pupils and the qualifications achieved determine the openness of choice of employment and the possibility of career progression.

Combining three sources of evidence (occupational accessibility; the relationship between education and vocational aspirations; and occupational socialization), Roberts suggests a theory in which the key concept is that of 'opportunity structure'. 'Careers can be regarded as developing into patterns dictated by the opportunity structures to which individuals are exposed, first in education and subsequently in employment, whilst individuals' ambitions, in turn, can be treated as reflecting the influence of the structures through which they pass' (Roberts 1975 p 142). It can be seen that for the majority of early school-leavers their opportunity structures are limited. Although Veness (1962) has suggested three directions of choice (tradition-directed, such as following in father's footsteps; inner-directed, relating to abilities and interests; other-directed, relating to external factors such as monetary return), it is likely that even such a limited three-dimensional choice is not the case for many adolescents. Maizels (1970), employing these three categories in a study of adolescent needs and the transition from school to work, found that the desire to use abilities and interests in working life was more important than the desire for status or personal security or the wish to follow family patterns, but as many as one in three of the boys and girls in the sample did not realize their first job preferences, especially in the area of skilled non-manual and intermediate occupations.

Apart from the opportunity structure influenced by the home, school, etc., the importance of including the general work situation has also been stressed by Blau *et al* (1956). They call 'attention to the importance of taking labour-market information into account . . . because a person can obviously choose only among the alternatives known to him' (Blau *et al* 1956 p 535). Thus in a situation of high unemployment, for example, the range of options open to the individual will be very limited or even non-existent and government attitudes to unemployment will obviously be important in such a situation. Further, 'the process of selection [by employers] . . . must be taken into account in order to explain why people end up in different occupations' (Blau *et al* 1956 pp 532–3). This is a point taken up by Blackburn and Mann in relation to unskilled labour and the workers' lack of knowledge of 'the employer's use of mystifying selection techniques' in the internal labour market (Blackburn and Mann 1973 pp 37–8).

Thus, to summarize, the individual-ambition model can be criticized on at least two fronts. Firstly, despite the widespread belief in the operation of free occupational choice, choice is in fact constrained by variables such as home, school and the general work situation (the ways in which home and school actually influence the process will be discussed in the next section on social class) resulting in the fact that different groups of school-leavers possess different ease of access to various types of employment and different forms of occupational imagery.

Secondly, it can be seen that ambitions are largely determined by the occupational opportunities available. For example, ambition tends to be consistent with the current job. Carter (1962) found that the majority of respondents in his study possessed ambitions in line with their current jobs and where jobs were changed, ambitions were adjusted accordingly rather than the changes being planned in order to realize ambitions. Veness (1962) also found that even where school-leavers had failed to enter their preferred employment, they were rarely dissatisfied, i.e. their ambitions had adjusted. To a large extent, young people's ambitions appear to be based on realistic vocational aspirations: upon the occupations they can *expect* to enter. The opportunity-structure model thus sees ambitions as an anticipation of careers that the individual is likely to enter rather than determinants of patterns that careers follow, and indeed, the word 'ambition' is itself likely to have different connotations for different social groups.

3 Social class and occupational choice

The two models discussed above are, perhaps, not really alternatives.

Sociologists tend to be interested in how *types* of people tend to enter certain *types* of work. Psychologists tend to address the slightly different problem of how an individual comes to enter one from amongst the range of jobs available, and the developmental theorists have approached the occupational choice/placement problem from this particular angle. Thus it could be that the psychological base of these theories provides a complement rather than an alternative to the sociological perspective. It has also been suggested that the two models may represent the occupational choice factors operating from different social groups (Newman 1968). Thus the individual-ambition model may be more relevant to the middle class, whereas the structure-opportunity model may be more applicable to the working class. To see whether this may be the case it is necessary to examine in more detail aspects of the stratification system that may influence the situation and support the two approaches. The main factors under consideration are the family, the education system and class cultures.

Many writers have assigned the family a central place in the continued functioning of a class-based society and in determining the orientations and position of its children, by virtue of the differential access to resources in a stratified system with a hierarchy of occupational roles and statuses. For example,

> The same individual who has a role in the occupational system is also a member of the family unit . . . if the status of the parents is hierarchically differentiated, there will inevitably be an element of differential access to opportunity. (Parsons 1948 pp 269–70)

The family into which an individual is born provides the initial ascriptive element, locating him in the social structure and forming the base from which subsequent achievement can take place. The level of this base is associated with the range of opportunities made available to the individual, derived from the position of the family within the social structure. Thus a child born into the middle class acquires a different set of life chances to the child born into the home of a manual worker, not only in terms of material comforts and facilities that are likely to increase the middle class child's opportunities of achievement within the educational and occupational structures, but also in terms of orientations towards education and work. Further, the range of local opportunities in the community of which the family is a part may have a determining influence: what Thomas and Wetherell (1974) have called the 'area-employment environment'. For example, a child born into a family in a mining community grows up in an environment of more limited options than a child born in a large industrial city.

The primary agent of socialization is the family, within which the child begins to inculcate the norms and values of the social group into which he is born. Emphasis on different values varies between social groups and the social class of the family gives some indication of the values that are likely to be emphasized during the process of socialization within the family. It is highly probable that the values transmitted by the family will influence both occupational choice and entry and career development — the child who is exposed to strong achievement values is more likely to have more ambitious career plans and expectations than the child brought up in a more ascriptive environment.

Certainly, Carter's studies (1962 and 1966) suggested that 'the home is fundamental: its general atmosphere orientates children towards particular levels of employment, and the school-leavers' attitudes towards work are affected by the outlook of other people at home who are employed' (Carter 1962 p 88). However, although the family is important in fostering this general orientation, Carter found that working class parents were unable to offer specific, informed advice on the job market. More recently, Thomas and Wetherell (1974) found that the father's socio-economic status and income, and also his behaviour and view of life and employment, were quite influential in determining his son's attitudes to work, although again specific advice was minimal for those in the lower socio-economic end of the sample and this is quite explicable in the sense that the nature of any parental advice is presumably a function of the limited but realistic occupational world view of the parents. Ashton and Field (1975) suggest that the most important and all-pervasive factor influencing relationships between parents and children is the work situation of the parents, for this carries over in a variety of ways into the family situation. This can be seen in, for example, different methods of control, attitudes towards problem-solving, verbal versus physical methods of communication and relates to the security of the parents' work, level of income, autonomy in the work situation, etc.

The importance of the work situation of parents in passing on to their children a particular view of their class situation is discussed by Mackenzie (1975) who points out that 'the scanty evidence available suggests that manual workers are more likely to view their class situation as relatively fixed while non-manual employees see the class structure as a ladder that an individual may climb up or down according to his own abilities and ambitions' (Mackenzie 1975 p 177), images of society that are likely to be generationally transmitted to their children and thus affect their attitudes towards work. Referring to research by Kohn (1969), Mackenzie goes on to show that these class images are related to different value systems:

> In particular he [Kohn] found manual workers to be committed to
> a value system stressing conformity to external authority while non-
> manual workers were far more concerned to exercise (and to see
> their children exercise) *self-direction.* And these differences in values
> were linked to three aspects of work situation — aspects which differ
> radically between manual and non-manual occupations. These are:
> the extent to which individuals are closely supervised at work . . .
> the degree to which work tasks allow for a variety of approaches;
> the extent to which work tasks require initiative, thought and
> independent judgement. (Mackenzie 1975 p 181)

Lockwood (1966) is also concerned to show that different work situations experienced within the working class and the middle class result
in different conceptions of the class structure and in different images
of power and prestige (dichotomous/conflict versus hierarchical/status
models for example). (The implication of this for the differential
meanings placed on work by different social groups is considered in
Alan Fox's chapter.

Such different images of society are transmitted to children initially
through family socialization patterns as the following quotation from
Ashton (1974) indicates:

> For the majority of young people the frame of reference acquired
> within the family of orientation and confirmed by their experiences
> at school and work is carried over and utilized in their family of
> procreation. At one extreme are the unskilled workers who at work
> have a very limited range of discretion in the performance of their
> tasks and are subject to imperative modes of control. When they
> establish their own families they are likely to use such modes of
> control, and to allow their children only limited discretion for as
> they have not been exposed to other forms of interaction these are
> the only terms within which they know how to operate. In compa-
> rison with the careerless the skilled workers have a greater degree of
> autonomy at work, but only within a clearly delineated framework
> of rules that define their role in the work situation. In their families
> they are likely to allow their children some discretion within clearly
> defined limits, and to emphasize the learning of rules rather than
> learning the manipulation of rules for it is within this framework
> they have had to operate. Finally, there are the middle class workers
> whose work is characterized by open systems of communication,
> relatively high levels of autonomy, and inter-personal forms of
> control. These are also the predominant patterns of communication
> and control which they experienced at home and school and which
> they in turn will use in their family of procreation. (Ashton 1974
> p 185—6)

The position of the family in the social structure is also highly relevant in terms of its influence on access to education (especially secondary), certification and attitudes towards education – and it has already been mentioned that the level of education attained usually determines the level of the occupational hierarchy entered. It has often been shown that children from working class homes tend to enter secondary modern schools or the lower streams of comprehensive schools whereas middle class children tend to enter grammar schools and the higher streams of comprehensives, even when measured ability is similar[1]. Elder (1965) and Abramson (1971) among others have shown that the level of educational attainment in terms of school-leaving age and formal qualifications achieved differs markedly between secondary modern and grammar schools and between upper and lower streams in comprehensives, thus effectively lowering the opportunities for further and higher education for working class children as well as the range of available jobs. If post-school qualifications are obtained prior to entry into work, entry into the occupational system is likely to be at a higher level in the occupational hierarchy. Thus the type of education obtained is closely linked to the timing of entry into the occupational structure and the extent of educational qualification will influence the level of entry.

Figure 2 and Table 1 give some indication of the relationship between social class background, type of school attended and destination on leaving school. Figure 2 derives its data from the General Household Survey which takes only a 5 per cent sample and, therefore, its representativeness for the whole population can be questioned. However, it does indicate clear differences between the type of secondary school attended for children from different socio-economic groups and this pattern has been found in several other researches (cf. Liversidge 1962 and Abramson 1971). Table 1 does not use the same source as Figure 2 and, therefore, is not strictly comparable but does show that the likelihood of pursuing further education is less with a secondary modern school background than with a grammar, and particularly direct grant or independent, school background. A movement directly into employment is the more likely occurrence.

[1] The social class origins of pupils in secondary modern and grammar schools corresponds to the lower and upper streams of comprehensive schools. The effects of streaming would so far appear to be similar on the whole to the more explicit selective system (e.g. see Ford 1969 and Pedley 1969). Not all comprehensive schools are streamed, but there is little research to show in what ways this may be affecting occupational aspirations.

Figure 2 School attended by socio-economic group of father,[1] 1972

England and Wales

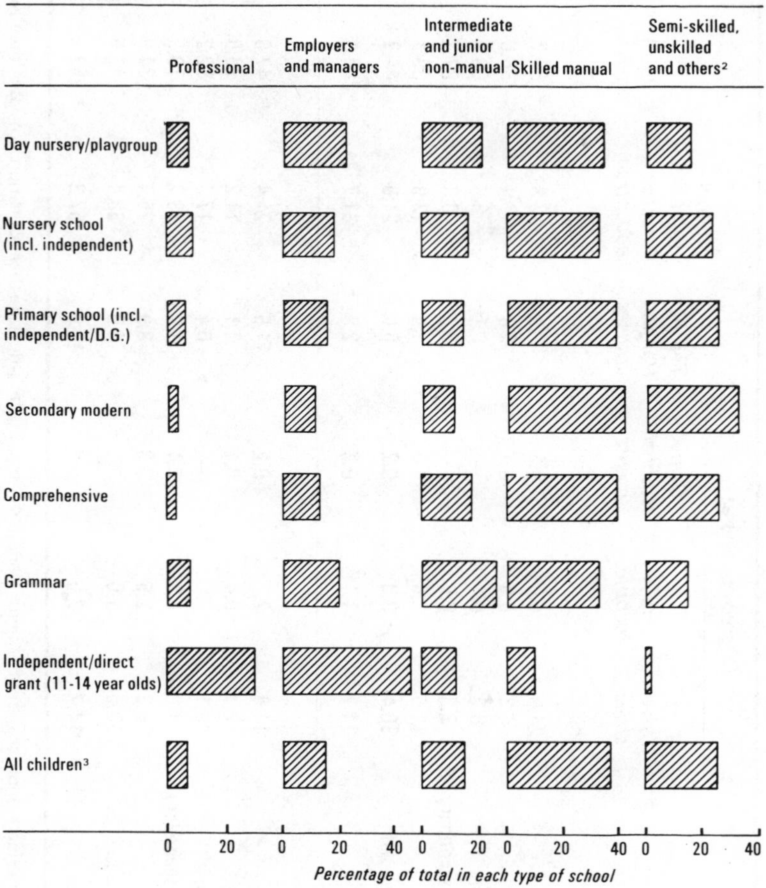
Professional
Employers and managers
Intermediate and junior non-manual
Skilled manual
Semi-skilled, unskilled and others²
Day nursery/playgroup
Nursery school (incl. independent)
Primary school (incl. independent/D.G.)
Secondary modern
Comprehensive
Grammar
Independent/direct grant (11-14 year olds)
All children³
0 20 0 20 40 0 20 0 20 40 0 20 40
Percentage of total in each type of school

[1] Head of household is taken where no father present

[2] Includes those not in, nor looking for, paid employment (including retired/disabled) Armed forces excluded

[3] Aged less than 15 – excluding those 'not yet started'

Source: *Social Trends,* no. 5 1974 p. 150.

Table 1 Destination of school leavers: by type of school, and by sex, 1974/75

England and Wales

Percentages and numbers

| | Degree courses at | | | Teacher training courses | Other full-time further education | Employ-ment[1] | Total sample size (= 100%) (thousands) |
	Univer-sities	Poly-technics	Other establish-ments				
Boys (percentages):							
Grammar	24.5	4.0	0.3	2.8	12.8	55.7	28.0
Comprehensive	4.3	0.9	0.1	0.8	7.4	86.6	222.5
Secondary modern	0.2	0.1	–	0.1	9.3	90.4	67.6
Other maintained secondary	2.8	0.9	–	0.8	8.3	87.2	12.3
Direct grant	41.5	3.6	0.3	1.5	13.9	39.3	7.9
Independent recognised	30.4	3.0	0.2	0.6	21.6	44.2	15.5
Total boys (thousands)	24.7	4.1	0.3	2.9	31.7	289.9	353.7
Girls (percentages):							
Grammar	14.8	2.2	0.2	11.5	24.4	47.0	29.8
Comprehensive	2.7	0.4	0.1	3.1	14.2	79.5	212.5
Secondary modern	0.1	–	–	0.4	17.3	82.2	64.3
Other maintained secondary	1.2	0.3	0.1	1.9	18.2	78.3	11.0
Direct grant	28.3	2.5	0.3	8.9	25.4	34.8	8.1
Independent recognised	13.5	1.0	0.2	4.6	38.4	42.5	12.5
Total girls (thousands)	14.2	2.0	0.3	11.9	57.3	252.5	338.1

1 Includes those entering temporary employment, pending entry into full-time further education not later than September-October 1976, and those who left for others reasons and whose destinations were not known.

Source: Statistics of Education, Volume 2, School Leavers, CSE and GCE, *Department of Education and Science*

The relationship between the extent and ease of mobility and forms of educational systems is summarized by Turner (1961) who suggests that sponsored mobility, characterized by a controlled selection process, is the main form of social ascent in Britain. The United States, in contrast, is characterized by contest mobility which is seen as a more open system likened to a sporting event in which many compete equally for a few recognized prizes. The effects of the two systems in relation to occupational ambitions is summarized as follows:

> Researches in the United States consistently show that the general level of occupational aspiration reported by high-school students is quite unrealistic in relation to the actual distribution of job opportunities. Comparative study in England shows much less in the way of 'phantasy' aspiration, and specifically shows a reduction in aspiration among those not selected following the 'eleven-plus' examination. (Turner 1961 pp 129–30)

The effects of such a selective system are apparent not just in objective data on attainment and aspiration but also in the declining interest in school life as a meaningful experience shown by low-stream pupils, the 'deep-seated apathy' noted by Crowther (Central Advisory Council for Education 1959 p 391): an attitude that is often heightened by the 'labelling' of pupils as 'dull' or 'non-academic' by teachers who do not share the same kinds of cultural and linguistic experience as those they teach. In fact, Douglas (1971) showed that this process may be at work even in the primary school, especially where primary schools are streamed: it is suggested that 'children acquire, early in their years at school, attitudes to learning that are related to their later success or failure' (Douglas 1971 p 190). And the channelling of children becomes more explicit as their educational career progresses – the type of school or stream directing the child towards certain sectors of the occupational structure.

This implies that the education system offers differential access to skills and qualifications for children from different class backgrounds, thus affecting the range of occupations open to choose from on leaving school and setting up barriers to choice for a great many. But it is not just in terms of the formal requirements necessary to enter certain kinds of work that the stratified system is apparent; it is also reflected in the orientations to work that arise through the socializing influence of the school and which can often be seen to correspond with the orientations that are developing concurrently through the influence of the family.

Ashton (1973) has argued that 'young people acquire different frames of reference that direct them toward different types of occupation, their experience of which reinforces the frame of reference originally acquired at school. In this way their school experience is functional in preparing them for the world of work' (Ashton 1973 p 147). In a study of working class adolescents, he determined from a 'societal perspective' two educational channels, one leading through the lower streams of secondary modern and comprehensive schools resulting in 'careerless' occupations and the other leading through the higher streams of secondary modern schools and the middle streams of comprehensives resulting in 'working class careers'. The different scholastic positions thus act as feeder channels into semi-or unskilled work or skilled work respectively.

From an 'experiential perspective', these channels lead to different frames of reference. That of children in the lower streams is primarily concerned with the concrete, the here and now, with no short or long-term planning. That of children in higher streams is more positive and more planned, being influenced by their awareness of their superior position in the school, encouragement by teachers, etc. In another paper, Ashton (1974) extends this analysis to a discussion of the factors influencing middle class adolescents. Through the achievement orientation of the family socialization patterns, these young people come to see themselves as 'capable of making a middle class career and become aware of the relationship between this and successful school performance . . . their experience of school serves not only to validate the frame of reference acquired within the family, it also serves to confirm the values and standards of the home' (Ashton 1974 p 178). These young people are allocated to higher educational channels within the school, giving more opportunities for certification and come to see themselves as the 'cream of their age group' in the light of the favourable and supporting behaviour of teachers and school culture. Their commitment to middle class occupations is further reinforced by acquiring a specific orientation to work — educational tasks are seen as providing long-term rewards in terms of successful entry into work, and immediate satisfaction is secondary. Once in the world of work, the young people are further committed to a specific occupation, through their investment in learning non-transferable and relatively complex tasks in a lengthy training process and in the cultural expectations of employers that their young workers will not change jobs frequently but will strive towards success. These underlying attitudes and orientations within the school and work situation (resulting in differing ambitions and destinations) have been termed 'the hidden curriculum'.

Thus, for all three groups, the individuals, through their experience at home, in the school and at work, are making a series of 'side-bets'

Table 2 Elements involved in commitment to and involvement in work

Occupational channel	Factors in choice	Nature of skills	Commitment	Job outcomes	Involvement
Careerless	Immediate rewards	Easily learnt	To occupational channel	Known and fixed. Job identity irrelevant	Low throughout
Working class career	Short term prospects and immediate rewards	Object centred. Long training required. Not transferable	To specific occupation in channel	Known short term rewards. Job identity becomes an important part of self conceptions	Initially high to moderate. May decrease later in career
Middle class career	Long term prospects and immediate rewards	Person centred. Long training required. Not initially transferable but may become so later	To specific occupation or profession	Known short term rewards, but indeterminate long term rewards. Success in job becomes increasingly important part of self	Initially moderate to high. Increases with success in career

Source: Ashton 1974 p 181

that function to commit them to different sorts of work. Table 2 out-lines some of the factors involved in the process of commitment for the three channels. The 'careerless', 'working class career' and 'middle class career' groups are, however, ideal types and there are bound to be exceptions. Some children from working class homes do move into middle-class jobs and vice versa and there is marriage across these lines so there is some mobility present. Studies like that of Jackson and Marsden (1962) have shown that a 'sunken middle-class' wife of a manual worker can have an important effect in raising her children's educational and occupational aspirations and achievements. Ashton's analysis has helped clarify the field, but its limitations should be noted.

Lane (1972) has also postulated a frame of reference approach whereby individuals come to enter different jobs on the basis of dif-ferent educational experiences. Here he takes individuals' 'models of the world' from which over time individuals are able to determine what is or is not possible and which are 'distillations of experience of society, constructed and modified over time' (Lane 1972 p 257). Income is seen to be especially important for this in that working class people may perceive the economic world as unstable and unpredictable and thus tend to see long-term investments in education as irrelevant and opt for a near horizon and immediate pay-offs, whereas if the world is seen as stable and predictable, people are more likely to defer immed-iate gratification in favour of long-term investment, a situation more likely to be found among middle class families. Such a model is passed on to children and in the light of the above, opting out of the school system at an early age is seen as quite rational for working class children. Similarly, staying on at school and opting for a career involv-ing a lengthy training process can be seen as quite rational for middle class children, indeed maybe even more so, as the middle class adoles-cent and his family are likely to have more adequate information as to the possibilities within the job market and its potential.

The notion of making 'side-bets' which serve to commit the indivi-dual to certain channels within the educational and occupational systems brings us back to the difference in emphasis between the individual-ambition and the structure-opportunity models and the whole issue of choice of work.

Haystead (1971) has attempted to isolate the stages at which action may be taken in formulating a choice. Using the example of the econ-omist's tree[2], in which the nodes represent choice points and the branches channels through the social structure, she suggests that at each node, a certain choice may be adopted leading to movement along one of the branches. Movement may be purposive or haphazard depending on the awareness of the individual as to whether choice exists or as to the effects of certain choices. We can see that movement from primary to secondary school, choice of curriculum, transition to a GCE stream, and the decision to leave school or to continue with further education may represent such nodes. Developing this further, Haystead proposes that the awareness context of the individual is built up from social experiences and will largely determine what choices are made as well as the eventual outcome in terms of occupation. This formulation is developed from the work of Glaser and Strauss (1964) and is summarized in Table 3 below.

An 'open' awareness context would represent a situation where the individual and others involved were fully aware that he faced a choice between alternatives and possessed full information. This is rarely the case, although it might represent the situation as Ginzberg sees it as the culmination of his developmental stages. The situation for most individuals would probably fall within the 'partial' awareness context where knowledge on some but not all of the four categories is lacking. Evidence of the lack of information held by most working class children would suggest a movement towards a 'closed' awareness context. Social class may influence the type of awareness context by determining the age at which choice must be made, academic achievement, familial emphasis on 'career' or 'secure job', etc.

Table 3 Awareness contexts and process of choice

	'Open' awareness context	'Closed' awareness context	'Partial' awareness context		
1 Awareness of choice	+	−	+	+	−
2 Knowledge of job requirements	+	−	−	−	+
3 Knowledge of job characteristics	+	−	−	−	+
4 Knowledge of characteristics of individual	+	−	−	+	+

+ represents knowledge   − represents no knowlege
Source: Haystead 1971 p 85

[2] The economist's tree refers to an instance of the lexicographic paradigm whereby once the decision to move along one branch (A) has been made, one then only has the choice of movement along sub-branches (A_1; A_2; etc.). The further one progresses along A, the harder it is to move back to the A node and proceed up the trunk to branch B or C, etc.

If one correlates the stages of vocational development, as postulated by Ginzberg and Super, with these nodes, one could hypothesize that the middle-class adolescent is able to pass through these stages in a truly developmental way. Given the 'fit' between home and school cultures, values, knowledge and support, then a meaningful choice leading to self-fulfilment and actualization is possible. If one allows for the confines of the current labour market, then the decision to enter a specific occupation reaches as near as possible a 'free' choice. Nonetheless, it should be noted that this greater degree of freedom of choice is itself determined by the structure of society and of occupations that give rise to this variation between opportunities for different social groups. However, for the remainder — the working class adolescents — the situation is very different. As we have seen, the links between home and school are less congruent, and the working class adolescent acquires an orientation towards work bearing less resemblance to the ambition model of the developmental psychologists. Given the early school leaving age of most working class young people, the point at which they have to decide on their working career is reached even before Ginzberg's 'realistic' stage is arrived at. Even if this were not the case though, it is doubtful whether the structural limitations to achieving an ideal integration between individual and work would be surmountable in a class-based society.

4 Stratification by sex and race: implications for occupational choice

The implications of stratification by class for occupational choice and placement have been discussed at some length. It is important to note, however, that society is further stratified along two other dimensions that also have an effect on differential opportunity. That is, there are systems of stratification by sex and by race which are different from familiar forms of stratification by economic, political or status group position, although they interact with these other stratification systems.

There is plenty of evidence to show that girls do at least as well as boys in terms of intellectual ability and examination achievement during their school careers (see, for example, Douglas 1967, Oakley 1972). However, there is an inconsistent relationship between their abilities and performance before leaving school and their subsequent employment. Weeks (in the preceding chapter) has noted that, despite the increasing employment of girls and women, they tend to be concentrated in three major service industries (the distributive trades, professional and scientific services and miscellaneous services), in the lower ranks of the professions, or, where they do occupy positions of authority, this is usually in work which can be seen as an extension of the traditional female 'caring' role, such as nursing, primary school teaching or social work.

There are, of course, some differences between working class and middle class girls. Working class girls are likely to become more immediately aware of the different expectations and roles of men and women. They see their parents working in sex-typed jobs and are exposed to a pattern of early marriage and traditional feminine behaviour that is not questioned by parents who rarely have the time or energy to devote to their daughters' education and who usually have little faith in the usefulness of a long academic career. Middle class girls may well find it easier to concentrate on studying and achieving at school, as social and educational aspirations are very much a part of middle class life. Whilst further and higher education is a far more realistic goal, such training still tends to be sex-typed — compare, for instance, the numbers of girls and boys entering teacher training colleges in Table 1. Conflicts between work and femininity may still be faced if attempts are made to enter the predominantly male arena of higher education.

Nonetheless, there are similarities between the upbringing of middle and working class girls and boys that cut across the boundaries of class. Once again, the family can be seen to play a fundamental part in training children to be 'acceptable'; a large part of this is its influence on sex role stereotyping and the learning of gender identity. Girls are trained in the 'traditional' aspects of female roles by helping their mothers in the home, becoming involved in 'affective' relationships, and learning to be concerned with nurturance and responsibility. Boys, on the other hand, are more likely to be encouraged towards achievement and self-reliance and to concentrate on 'relational' activities. The focusing of attention on 'appropriate' toys, activities and household tasks for each sex is backed up by the sex-typed images portrayed in reading primers, comics, magazines, advertisements and films. These factors all involve a rehearsal for future adult male and female work roles.

Just as awareness of class differentials, originally learnt in the home, is fostered by schooling, so the initial preparation for sex-typed jobs is supported by different educational experiences.

School does not give equal opportunities to girls and boys whatever (formal) egalitarian ideology it may seem to represent. The way forward is far more clear-cut for boys who still face a life of continuous working. Whatever level of job they are steered towards, they look unambivalently towards a working future. Girls, however, are still schooled with the marriage market in mind, although this may not be acknowledged consciously. This inevitability in their lives provides as much excuse within the school, as for the girls themselves, for their ultimate under-achievement. The belief that a girl finds her deepest and truest satisfaction in a husband and children is very prevalent . . . , despite discussions about sexual equality and women's increasing presence in the work-force. (Sharpe 1976 p 130)

The secondary school in particular plays an important part in directing children towards pre-determined directions. Subjects can be broadly classified into 'girls' subjects and 'boys' subjects. Girls' subjects concentrate around the 'arts', cookery, needlework, typing and commerce. Boys' subjects are scientific, involving problem-solving and analysis, as well as practical skills such as woodwork and metal work. Boys do take and succeed in arts subjects, the schools implicitly implying that boys are capable at working at anything. Girls also, but less often, take science subjects and their academic success as measured by 'O' and 'A' Level passes is increasing from year to year, but so far this has had little effect on changing the sexual division of scientific labour or the conventional stereotype. This overt division between boys and girls in the school is reinforced by a 'hidden curriculum' embodied in the domestication and pacifying procedures operating through control and disciplinary channels and in the transmission of dominant societal values which include the behaviours thought appropriate to each sex. The 'domestication' imposed on pupils is more effective on girls as it coincides with on-going familial experience and has important consequences for later adult roles.

The result of these sorts of factors is that girls are faced with a far narrower range of career choices than are boys. Sharpe's study of schoolgirls found that office work was the most popular choice of job, which reflects the enormous increase in the demand for office-workers in this century and the 'respectability' of such work. The next popular jobs were teachers, nurses, shop assistants and bank clerks, followed by receptionists, telephonists, air-hostesses, hairdressers and children's nurses or nannies; professional choices such as doctor or lawyer were rare. All these chosen jobs were confined to the realms of 'women's work' — there was very little venturing into male or even neutral occupational territory (Sharpe 1976 pp 160–1). The schools and Careers Service do little to provide information on alternative occupations.

It is important to note that, because housework and childcare are not social activities, it is extremely difficult for women simultaneously to care for children and participate fully at work. Whilst marriage and childrearing are no longer assumed to be incompatible with a working life, the lack of childcare provision adds a further complicating factor, and is reflected in the large number of female part-time workers. Girls no longer have to choose between work or marriage but many have decided to add a career to their domestic role. For women returning to work after a period of child-rearing there are further problems – the attitudes of employers, the lack of up-to-date knowledge about the pre-marriage career, and the fact that the types of work that many women are engaged in are those most likely to change due to new technology, thus requiring further training which is often unavailable (Seear 1968).

In addition to the myth of freedom of occupational choice, there is the myth that a woman's place is at home looking after her husband and children. This 'helps to validate the continued cheap reproduction of workers and, therefore, the maintenance of capitalist business and industry' (Sharpe 1976 p 183).

When we turn to the issue of stratification by race, it should be noted that we are not necessarily referring to black immigrants, but to all those who do not comprise the indigenous population. Whilst the examples used in the following paragraphs refer to West Indians and Asians, many of the factors influencing the educational and occupational experiences hold true for other immigrants. Immigrant labour is most often used to fill jobs vacated by the indigenous workforce. As Braham notes:

> The presence of immigrant workers in modern sectors of industry . . . does not detract from the principle that immigrants are concentrated in 'suitable' jobs; that is, unskilled or semi-skilled manual jobs (or skilled ones not involving authority over indigenous workers) which have difficulty attracting labour. (Braham 1975 p 128)

This results in the development of a dual, non-competitive labour market in terms of pay, hours and conditions of work. 'As far as employers are concerned, granting normal promotion and making vocational training easily available to immigrant workers will greatly diminish the benefits of a large amount of cheap labour' (Braham 1975 p 131).

For second-generation immigrant children, family and school experience once again can be seen to operate on depressing career expectations and opportunities. Sharpe noted that for West Indian girls opportunities were limited by social and material deprivation that were often shared by the indigenous white working class community, but this was aggravated by prejudice and discrimination within schools, by language problems, and by culture-based intelligence tests that put many black children into ESN schools. In most schools today, the distribution of black children is such that most are at the bottom and their numbers decrease as they move up towards the higher forms. An assumption that black children are less able has often been implicit in school organization. The children themselves often recognize that they are schooled in low-level employment; some have begun to reject what is offered especially in areas of high unemployment. This probably occurs more in male than female youth, since girls are usually more able to obtain 'better' work than boys, e.g. in offices or in nursing (though usually State Enrolled rather than State Registered). A large number of black unemployed youths refuse even to register with employment agencies and support themselves by drawing strength from the life of their community.

For Asian youths, the situation is little different — work is usually found in factories and industries where they undertake the nightwork, awkward shifts and menial tasks. Some East African Asians have been able to find higher level work or have set up their own small businesses or shops, stemming from the acquisition of craft skills before emigration to Britain. The opportunities for Indians are slightly wider ranging, especially for the upper castes, and children are given positive parental encouragement to seek professional careers. For Asian women, the problems are particularly acute. Traditionally they have occupied a subordinate position in the community and Moslem women in particular have been kept in strict *purdah* away from men who are not relatives. The attempt to preserve this practice in Britain has made 'life almost intolerable for some girls at school, who have to mix and do lessons with boys, while at the same time any rumour that they have been seen talking to boys may result in their being removed from school' (Sharpe 1976 p 271). Young Asian girls who have attended school in Britain are increasingly being allowed to work, at least until marriage, but this has caused many parents to worry about the possible consequences of this for their daughters' marriage prospects as marriage is highly respected and its sanctity unquestioned. Pre-marriage contact with males is often seen as 'tainting' the girl's purity as marriage is based on a contract rather than on romantic love.

The lack of opportunities for varied work choices and careers is thus particularly apparent in the immigrant population in that the values and backgrounds of the non-indigenous community and family, coupled with prejudice and discrimination in schools and employers' needs for cheap labour all combine to produce a situation of particular constraint in terms of occupational choice and placement.

Conclusion

Throughout this chapter, it has been suggested that in any analysis of the problem of occupational choice and placement, one must bear in mind the objective criteria of the labour market, employment trends and the occupational structure, and the skills and qualifications required to enter that structure. Further, the subjective dimensions of class images of work, orientations and attitudes to work have been seen as equally important. Blackburn and Mann (1973) have suggested that the subjective dimension may be experienced as one of constraint in that the actual job choice may not be a meaningful experience especially for people near the lower end of the stratification system. The objective job situation may further be experienced as an extension of constraint in that the individual has extremely limited control over the labour market (both globally and within firms) and lacks knowledge concerning vacancies and the selection criteria of firms. Also, if initial (and later) job placement is unsatisfactory, this is likely to militate further against effective later choices in terms of career development and acceptance into the job market. In other words, relating this to the 'tree analogy' introduced earlier, once an individual has embarked along a career branch that proves unattractive or unsuitable, it becomes even more difficult to step onto another branch than it was before.

This would appear to be supported by the structure-opportunity model discussed above. Social class has been seen to play a determining role in affecting the reality of occupational choice and placement. This is largely operative through the social placement and ascriptive functions of the family and in the socialization patterns that orient young people towards certain categories of work and towards internalizing certain class-based images of work. The family also offers differing access to educational opportunity and to educational certification, the possession or lack of which determines the occupational opportunities open to the individual. Further, the influence of the school tends to reinforce the frame of reference or climate of expectation towards work originally acquired within the individual's home and community.

In view of this, it has been suggested that the emphasis of the developmental theories on individual ambitions and self-fulfilment is unrealistic.

> The notion that young people possess freedom of occupational choice and that they can select careers for themselves upon the basis of their own preferences is a pure myth. It is not choice but opportunity that governs the manner in which many young people make their entry into employment. (Roberts 1971 p 145)

In this sense, the situation facing the majority of young people about to enter the world of work is one of constraint, in which they have to reconcile their dreams and aspirations with the existing opportunities.

CHAPTER 5

Alan Fox

The meaning of work

Introduction: the meaning of 'meaning'

At first sight the very title of this chapter may seem obscure. What are we speaking of when we refer to 'the meaning of work'? We are helped to get the sense of what this question is about, and how modern society comes to be concerned with it, by an article by Peter Berger (1964).

Many valuable points are established in Berger's piece, but the one with which we shall lead into this chapter has been more explicitly stated by another writer.

> The question of the meaning of work, of how it is experienced, is primarily a cultural problem; and cultures differ enormously in the way work is interpreted in their value-scheme . . . Neither the basic physiological drive of hunger, nor the basic equipment of production – man's brain and eyes and hands – instruct him in what meaning, what pattern, he shall give to work, any more than the basic drive of sex, and its genital equipment, tell him what meaning, what pattern, he shall give to love. (Riesman 1955 pp 177–8)

We can draw our first proposition from this passage of Riesman's. It is this: that in being concerned with work meanings we cannot confine ourselves to research and analysis into the experience of the *individual* alone (or even a number of individuals), crucial though this is as one level of enquiry. For man is at once a creator and a creature of *society*. The human individual is a widely (though not infinitely) variable organism who moulds, and is in turn moulded by, social groupings of very different kinds with very different structures and values. Through his membership of these social groupings the individual helps to shape them, but he is also shaped *by* them. And here we find a second level of research and analysis emerging. This is the *social* level; the level of social organization which is manifested in so many diverse forms and varieties and which embodies and transmits work meanings that are both the product and the moulder of man's thought and activity. The unit of study therefore has to be, not man as such, but man-in-society. In a very real sense the individual *learns* what to want from work, and what meaning it is to have in his life.

Since what people learn to want is a social fact of great importance there will be a variety of institutions and dominant groups eager to do the teaching. They seek to ensure that built into the structure, design, and conduct of work and work organizations are meanings which serve *their* interests, purposes and values. It has long been the case in our society, however, as in others, that dominant groups have not been able to monopolize the propagation of values and meanings. Rival values and meanings exist as a potential challenge to the prevailing order in the sense that, like any other ideas, they can be used as a resource by those seeking to change that order.

It soon becomes apparent, however, that we need more yet than simply a study of personal meanings and another of socio-cultural meanings; we need also to explore the relationships and interaction between the two. This further area of enquiry emerges as soon as we ask questions like: how many people in our society can be said to enjoy even an approximation to a free choice of the work meanings they live by? What are the constraints, influences and organizational pressures which cause an individual to live by one set of meanings rather than another? How are people affected by the meanings they live by, and what are the consequences for the social groupings or classes of which they are members? Are any structural regularities observable in our answers to these questions? How is the situation changing, and what are the possibilities for the future? These are the questions we shall be trying to answer in this chapter. But first must come an elaboration of the distinction with which we began.

1 Personal and social meanings

On one level of enquiry, then, we can ask the individual what part work plays in his own life; what significance it has for him personally. Here the first approximation to an answer may well involve him in stressing one or other of the two great alternative meanings which will soon emerge as central to our discussion. Does he feel it to be of central importance to his personality development and life fulfilment or does he, on the other hand, see it as little more than a tiresome necessity in acquiring the resources for survival or for what he may define as the real living which begins when work ends? We can further ask him, not simply what *is*, but what he considers *ought* to be the situation in these respects. As we shall see, people differ widely in the personal meanings and aspirations they invest in their labour.

On another level of enquiry there is, as we have seen, a very different kind of question to be asked. We can seek to elucidate social or cultural meanings. Social meaning will be defined here, for convenience, as that currently embodied in the existing design, organization and institutional and legal context of work. What we are recognizing here is that the design of work and its associated institutions cannot help but express certain values and preferences as against others.

The values and preferences implicit in the design and organization of work can be said to derive from the meaning of work that has been brought to bear by dominant groups and interests with the power to initiate and uphold that design and organization. It is in the sense that work organizations are a form of *social structure* that we shall refer to this meaning which informs and shapes them as the *social* meaning of work currently prevailing. We can briefly anticipate later discussion by recognizing that the emphasis brought to bear upon work design by dominant groups in most countries of the modern world is exclusively 'instrumental'; it is an emphasis on the practical *outcome* of work, as against the value of the *work experience itself* for those who do it. In other words, work is designed exclusively in the light of such criteria as profits, output, fulfilment of 'production norms', or effective performance, not in the light of that profoundly different rival conception that work should ideally provide a humane, balanced, and fulfilling life for those engaged in it, thereby concerning itself with 'human' as against purely 'market', 'economic', or 'performance' requirements.

This same emphasis is also powerfully transmitted by a wide variety of influential sources in the processes of socialization and social communication. It has thereby gained a predominant acceptance in the sense that probably most people regard it as 'reasonable' and 'only to be expected' that socially organized work should be designed in this way. Many, perhaps most, accept the message in the further sense that *they themselves* take an instrumental view of work. They value it largely for its practical outcome in terms of the weekly pay packet or monthly salary cheque, and see it as having no central significance for their personal life, development and growth. Of course the very nature of the practical outcome which *they* seek to enlarge (pay, security, benefits) frequently brings them into conflict with the owners and controllers of work organizations, for whom success in practical outcome is measured in terms of profits, output, or effective performance.

This social meaning can be said to have a further type of existence in addition to its manifestation in the design of work. It exists as an element in the communication and culture of the society in question, being expressed in the symbols of a common language accessible to all through books, records, journals and all the other media of transmission, storage and retrieval. A similar shared reality is likewise enjoyed, however, by those rival meanings which, though not 'social' in the sense used here of being the dominant influence shaping the present design and organization of work, enter into the culture and become capable of moving the hearts and minds of men. The established social meaning and such competing meanings as enter into a society's cultural resources may become issues of contention between conflicting classes, or sections of classes, who if given the opportunity may mobilize power to support their own conception of how work should be designed and organized. Inspiring these power struggles, of course, are the issues with which we are familiar, such as financial rewards and other conditions of employment, job security, discipline, control and similar aspects of managerial prerogative.

We must remind ourselves here, of course, that societies vary in the degree to which their dominant groups or classes actively exploit their power to prevent rival work meanings being effectively disseminated and propagated. Totalitarian patterns of rule, whether of 'Left' or 'Right', do not offer the same scope for open and organized dissent as do democratic patterns, where those who might dearly love to try a few active and comprehensive measures of thought-control may be restrained by an awareness (a) that traditions and institutions embodying certain 'liberal freedoms' command a strength of attachment within their society which could generate serious political difficulties and risks were they to be too vigorously attacked, and (b) that the existing patterns of socialization and communication have so far proved adequate to subserve the orthodoxy of work organization, to which rival meanings constitute as yet no threat serious enough to require running the political risks referred to.

It does not follow, however, that dominant groups within totalitarian regimes feel completely free to impose whatever work meanings might best serve their objectives and interests. There are limits to the degree to which discontent at the grass roots can be suppressed or controlled, and even in the Soviet Union those in positions of rule have considered it judicious to relax some of the more draconian measures introduced under Stalin whereby, for example, absenteeism, lateness and voluntary quitting became criminal offences punishable by imprisonment (Conquest 1967, McAuley 1969, Osipov 1966). Other regulations which remain are not necessarily enforced by enterprise managements, who in their struggle to fulfil or exceed production targets have to grapple with the shopfloor realities of morale, goodwill and cooperativeness.

2 Dominant social meanings and power

As a consequence of an accumulation of minor modifications resulting from trade union demands and political pressures it is impossible to describe the world of work as being shaped and regulated by a unitary, homogeneous, and consistent social meaning in terms of its values, objectives, and priorities. It takes its shape from a variety of pressures, and for this reason is a patchwork of diverse values and purposes displaying many contradictions and inconsistencies. Nevertheless, as our discussion has implied, it is possible to think of a certain social meaning as being prevalent or dominant. It would be surprising if this were not so. The power and influence required to have one's preferred social meaning embodied in the design and organization of work are not equally distributed among the various interested groups. It is for this reason that we have to talk of 'dominant' groups or classes which, through their superior power, are equipped to ensure that it is *their* values and objectives, expressed in terms of the predominant social meaning of work, which on the whole prevail in the relevant organizations and institutions. Thus, for example, while the full rigour of 'labour as a commodity' has been ameliorated, its central meaning persists in the arrangement whereby the minority with control over economic resources (private or public) may grant or withhold the access to employment of the rest, who because they have no control over economic resources must put their labour power at the minority's disposal.

Dominant groups or classes are also likely to agree, therefore, on what general approach to work should be encouraged, fostered and promoted among the members of society, for it is plainly to their advantage that this should match the general approach they embody in their construction and administration of work arrangements. Fortunately for them they benefit from the same inequalities of control in the field of communication and socialization as in the design and organization of work. They are thus in a privileged position to influence people's conceptions of work and what they aspire to get from it.

Their influence on popular assumptions about work is important to them. Were it to be the case that the values and expectations currently prevalent and active throughout the wider society conflicted with those by which owners and controllers shaped and designed work and its organization, the men of power would obviously face difficulties. As yet, however, few such difficulties arise to any degree that need seriously worry them. Here and there, as we shall be noting later, can be seen ominous symptoms that may herald major problems for them, but this is still problematical. For the most part, the meaning of work predominantly disseminated and propagated accords well with that which informs the institutions of work themselves.

It is important, however, to reiterate our earlier point that this is not a closed system. The advantage enjoyed by dominant groups or classes falls well short of being total, though in societies where the state asserts full control over socialization and communications the advantage may be very nearly so. In what are usually called 'the Western democracies', however, rival opinions and values have their say and wield some effect, thereby generating contradictions and tensions when their influence on people and events conflicts with that predominant in established institutions and communications.

Quite apart from these considerations, it would be a mistake to suppose that the effects of socialization and communication agencies are exerted uniformly and to the same effect upon all members of society. Many factors mediate between the individual and the agencies concerned, and these to varying degrees reinforce, mitigate or counter their effects upon him. One set of factors of special importance includes family, class and educational background. As we shall see in more detail later, it is possible to generalize — but no more than generalize — here. In the working class, low expectations and aspirations with respect to intrinsic rewards tend to strengthen the individual's receptivity to the widely-propagated message that only the extrinsic rewards of work are really important (even to the extent that he may forego a measure of the former for the sake of the latter). In the middle class, on the other hand, the tendency is, as we shall see, for the individual to learn a more complex set of orientations to work. Other mediating factors may include the individual's position in the life-cycle (Goldthorpe *et al* 1968 pp 147–8). They suggest (though are not supported by Ingham's 1970 evidence) that the younger married wage-earner with dependent children may seek to maximize his pay packet, whereas the older man whose children have grown up may prefer a more relaxed life on lower earnings. Also relevant may be local community structure and values. Some researchers and theorists have found it useful, for example, to set up a model of the 'traditional' working class community of the sort seen as typical of older industries such as coal-mining, shipbuilding, docking and cotton manufacture. Lockwood (1966) presents such a model alongside two others which he suggests as useful for analysing other types of situation – the 'deferential' working class pattern and the so-called 'privatized' worker. The point to note for our present argument is his inference that 'the work and community relationships by which they are differentiated from one another may also generate very different forms of social consciousness' – consciousness which includes attitudes to work and the work situation.

His paper is an example of a type of sociological – and social-psychological – exploration discussed elsewhere in this book. It selects as significant – if we take the 'traditional' model as an example – such variables as (a) concentration of the workers concerned in solidary occupational communities which are in some degree isolated from the wider society, (b) a considerable measure of job involvement and expressive attachment to primary groups, (c) closely knit cliques of friends, workmates, neighbours and relatives, and (d) a stress on mutual aid, public conviviality and conformity to locally-prevailing standards, attitudes and expectations and aspirations. As a consequence of these and other factors, says Lockwood, 'workers in such environments are as unlikely to change their pattern of consumption as they are their political loyalties, because in both cases they are encapsulated in social systems which provide them with few alternative conceptions of what is possible, desirable, and legitimate'. Or, to put it in other terms, membership of these 'highly connected and cohesive kin networks and relatively stable and undifferentiated working class communities lead to the placing of definite limits on the level and the type of consumer behaviour' (Ingham 1970 p 58).

The significance for our discussion is apparent. However, attention has been drawn to the ways in which the bonds, values and expectations of these tightly-knit, inward-looking communities are being undermined by the influence of transport, communications and the media – television, it is said, becomes a window on the world and the way other people live as well as a vehicle for extolling the delights of 'consumerism' and affluence. Such developments have fostered considerable debate and controversy about another of Lockwood's models – the 'privatized', earnings-maximizing worker – a model seen by some as useful for understanding the 'new working class' of the housing estate and the later-developing light-engineering, electrical, mass-production and process industries. Here we find ourselves noting the possible implications for our discussion of geographical, residential and social mobility. The essential characteristics of the privatized worker include (a) residence, as a result of, say, geographical mobility due to rehousing, in an urban environment that in no sense can be called a 'community' in the full sense of that word, (b) freedom, therefore, from community pressure to conform to traditional local standards, attitudes, expectations and aspirations, (c) the replacement of communal sociability with a socially-isolated, home-centred existence in which aspirations focus on rising material standards for the family and children, (d) increased susceptibility to a message of competitive acquisition increasingly propagated not only by advertising but also by many other agencies of public communication and (e) an attitude to work which, to a greater degree than the 'traditional' worker, sees it as almost wholly instrumental; as a necessary evil to be undertaken solely for its extrinsic meaning in maximizing earnings.

Like all concepts, models and theoretical frameworks, this construction *selects* certain characteristics and variables as being of special significance and as calling for special emphasis. Again, like all of its kind, it is liable for this reason to criticism of two kinds. One kind of objection would be that, descriptively and analytically, the selection is less useful for understanding and explaining the relevant phenomena than some different selection would be. This would express a belief by the critic that the model fails to alert the observer to certain aspects of reality deemed (by the critic) to be analytically significant. Such criticism may or may not be combined with that of a second kind. Because the interpretation of social reality is highly controversial, no model in this field can be 'neutral'. By drawing attention to some characteristics and variables and ignoring or playing down others, it encourages a certain way of perceiving, interpreting and acting in the world. If these perceptions, interpretations and actions are disputed then the model itself will be controversial. Models that encourage acceptance of orthodox, conventional views in a way which supports the *status quo* are therefore no less 'biased' in this sense than models that generate or support criticisms of it.

The models of the industrial worker that we have just noted come under criticisms of both kinds. That of the 'traditional' proletarian and his community has been described as a somewhat romanticized and idealized version which fails to register, for example, that, among older working class communities, orientations to work might be just as instrumental as those of the contrasted stereotype, the privatized worker of modern times. The latter model, in turn, has been criticized as encouraging a view of the modern wage-earner as irredeemably materialist and socially quiescent, thereby distracting attention from the potentiality for more radical and challenging aspirations among rank and file work groups. We can hardly explore such disagreements here, but they illustrate the controversial nature of interpretations and perspectives in this field (Bulmer 1975).

Some aspects of the relevance of *social* mobility for our discussion are noted by Ingham (1970 pp 130—6). One of the important post-war debates in this field, however, has concerned the degree to which relative affluence for some sections of manual wage-earners has carried them towards middle-classness ('embourgeoisement'). Such a movement might have implications for their attitudes towards work and their employer as well as for other dimensions of experience. The research of Goldthorpe and his colleagues, however, has brought a convincing scepticism to bear on the notion that rising material standards and 'consumption-mindedness' necessarily signify a movement towards a middle-class way of life (Goldthorpe *et al*, 1968, 1968a, 1969).

3 Relative deprivation and privilege

Our concern in the last few pages has been to register the fact that the values and messages projected by public communication and socialization agencies do not bear uniformly and to the same effect upon all members of society, but are mediated and refracted for the individual by the experience and values offered by family, class, education, community and other variables.

We turn now, however, to enlarge, in broader and more generalized terms, on the practical implications of the predominant social meaning of work ('instrumentalism' as we shall call it) for occupational strata at different levels of the status hierarchy. We shall examine these implications in terms of the sharp differences in experience of work and life that they produce, and in terms of the contrasting adaptations made by people at the different occupational levels. We shall find ourselves, for simplicity, referring to the relatively deprived 'majority' and the relatively privileged 'minority'. This is an acceptable language provided we remember that there is no such sharp cut-off as a too-literal usage might imply, but rather a graduation of differences, with a certain amount of overlap in the middle ranges which makes categorization specially debatable at certain points.

We begin by examining some evidence. If we look for systematic enquiry into what the practical implications are, for the majority of employees, of the instrumental approach to the design of work, we can find one example in the research of Davis, Canter and Hoffman (Davis and Taylor 1972). It must be borne in mind that they examine only *industrial* work in manufacturing companies, and there are of course many other kinds. Nevertheless there is good reason for believing that much industrial work-design manifests in extreme form the same attitudes, values and assumptions that inform, though sometimes less obviously, the design, organization and conduct of other types of work.

Davis and his colleagues, then, offer empirical evidence of the criteria normally applied in the case of lower-level industrial jobs; evidence based on the practice of 24 manufacturing companies in the United States. They use this evidence to advance the hypothesis that management works predominantly to an excessively narrow instrumental conception in the design process — a conception taking those forms collectively known as 'scientific management'. It is, they assert (as do many other critics), a conception so narrow that, in seeking to minimize the *immediate* costs of performing the required operations, management's work-design creates discontents and frustrations which push up longer-term costs in the form of high labour-turnover, increased absenteeism, poor quality, reduced productivity and other such manifestations. Management then proceeds to divert resources towards attempts to revive employee morale and strengthen employee identification with the company through personnel and 'human relations' strategies which seek, usually unsuccessfully, to make good the damage caused by management's own work design. Their own view is not that management should move away from instrumentalism as such, but that it should take into consideration the *total* costs of its present approach and design work accordingly. Their expectation is clearly that were it to do so, it would probably find management objectives better served by back-tracking somewhat from the pure orthodoxies of scientific management and introducing a larger measure of discretion into lower-level jobs. This approach has become a fashionable talking-point under such titles as 'job enrichment' and 'the autonomous work group'.

A further point to be stressed, however, is implicit rather than explicit in their analysis. Any management that is concerned to design and operate a work organization for some wholly instrumental purpose not fully shared by the rank and file labour force, be it profit, expansion and growth, a surplus for the public funds, or fulfilment of a production norm in a planned society, will be involved in asserting *control* in the sense of inducing, constraining, and pressuring people to do what they would not otherwise choose to do and to accept arrangements and policies they would not otherwise choose to accept. Its approach to the design process will therefore be shaped by its sense of what type and degree of control is required if its purpose is to be adequately pursued. The less confident it is that rank and file members fully share its purpose, the more detailed and assertive is likely to be the control it attempts to impose on their behaviour (Fox 1974). Because top managers lack confidence in their employees' commitment, they maintain control structures through which they seek to constrain the rank and file into the desired patterns of behaviour. The combination of low-discretion roles and control structures which seek a close regulation of their occupants' performance and behaviour constitutes a framework of constraints far more restrictive than that set up for higher-discretion employees and occupations. Top managers and administrators tend to see their own objectives as being incompatible with a high degree of job autonomy, wide influence over top decision-making and substantial freedom for self-development among the rank and file. The two great alternative work meanings are seen as mutually exclusive so far as the majority are concerned.

The *ownership* of resources is not *by itself* decisive in shaping the design of work and work organization. Private ownership of the means of production, coupled with an advancing technology, a stratified society and the principle of unlimited private gains, have produced extreme division of labour and the hierarchical inegalitarian control structures with which we are familiar. But public ownership can and does produce the same kinds of structure where power is heavily concentrated, where the aim is to produce goods or services on a large scale at minimum cost, and where for one reason or another those in authority doubt whether they can rely on rank and file members behaving in full practical identification with them and with their purposes and values. Thus while a transfer from private to public ownership is a *necessary* condition for moving away from the design of work and work organizations characteristic of private enterprise capitalism, it is not a *sufficient* condition. Controllers of public property may, and in fact often do, decide to maintain the same structures of control, thereby prompting the emergence of the term 'state capitalism' (Lane 1971 pp 43–4). Lenin and other Soviet leaders, for example, were enthusiastic supporters of scientific management methods and the same parallels persist today. Some brands of socialism and communism have always embodied a 'longing for order, discipline, and capable leadership' and a conviction that socialism 'can only succeed if it produces wealth more efficiently than capitalism' (Haber 1964 pp 150–5). Lenin's advice in a pamphlet to the Bolsheviks in post-revolutionary Russia was hailed by an American journal as being fit for publication 'in any of our efficiency magazines with some changes of phraseology, for it is devoted to urging increase of production, speeding up processes, iron discipline during work, careful accounting, business devices, the Taylor system of scientific management and the like . . .' (Haber 1964 p 152). Printed also in New York, it ran to two translations and five editions.

Small wonder, therefore, that contemporary observers are apt to

argue that along many dimensions 'the USSR is not dramatically unlike
Western industrial societies' (Lane 1971 p 69), and these dimensions
certainly include the design and organization of work. Such considerations inevitably detract from the convenience of concepts like 'capitalism', 'socialism' and 'communism', for they indicate that each of these
concepts covers a spectrum of meanings and that the user must specify
those meanings to which he wishes to draw our attention. This specification is all the more necessary when 'capitalist' countries like the USA
and 'communist' countries like the USSR are alike in some respects
and sharply different in others. Both are highly stratified societies, but
Lane argues a 'really significant difference' in that the USSR has no
'private-propertied class possessing great concentrations of wealth'
(Lane 1971 p 69). Both show similar work structures in terms of division of labour, hierarchical control and wide inequalities of status and
rewards (as Lane also emphasizes), but the existence in the USA of an
independently-organized trade union movement gives its members a
more effective check on management policies and decisions — a major
feature in the context of the 'liberal freedoms'.

With these considerations in mind we return to the Davis, Canter,
and Hoffman research, remembering that their conclusions, which now
follow, are valid for many other countries besides western Europe and
America.

1. Current job design practices are consistent with the principles of
rationalization or scientific management. *They minimize the dependence of the organization on the individual.* [Italics are added for
emphasis, since this expresses an important aspect of power and
control. A.F.] At the same time they minimize the contribution of
the individual to the work of the organization, i.e. its production
process.
2. Current principles of job design reflect the mass-production
precepts of specialization of jobs and repetitiveness of work.
3. Job design practices minimize the effects of the individual's
actions on the organization in regard to absenteeism, turnover, etc.,
by specifying jobs requiring short training time and having low skill
requirements. Current practices also minimize the effects of 'labor
scarcity' whether due to high labour costs or unavailability of
individuals or skills, and permit minimum hiring rates of pay.
4. Management . . . by adhering to the very narrow and limited
criteria of minimizing immediate cost or maximizing immediate
productivity . . . designs jobs based entirely on the principles of
specialization, repetitiveness, low skill content and minimum impact
of the worker on the production process. Management then frequently spends large sums of money and prodigious effort on many

programs that attempt to: (a) counteract the effects of job designs;
(b) provide satisfactions, necessarily outside the job, which the job
cannot provide; and (c) build up the satisfaction and importance of
the individual which the job has diminished. (Davis and Taylor 1972
pp 80—1)

Generations of the working class, subjected to this pattern of work
experience, have made a 'realistic' adaptation to it by relinquishing, or
by never bothering to take seriously, aspirations towards intrinsic
satisfactions. Much evidence points to there having always been a
tendency for major sections of lower-level employees to see their
work in purely instrumental or 'extrinsic' terms, meaning by this that
they see it only as a means to the consumption of goods and services
outside work (or some other extrinsic reward) and that the work itself
has no intrinsic meaning and satisfaction for them. This is probably
the predominant meaning attached to work by most of those in the
lower strata of the occupational hierarchy and by some groups in the
middle — certainly in the lower-middle class, and perhaps even higher.
Some skilled groups in the upper-working class, however, clearly find
a certain degree of intrinsic meaning, substantially less than those in
the higher middle class occupations but in some cases more than those
performing routine clerical tasks, many of whose work situations have
become transformed by rationalization and mechanization into 'white-
collar factories'.

For the most part, then, work for the majority is little more than
an irksome precondition for the real business of living. Most people in
our society accept, in the main, a personal meaning in their work which
accords well (i.e. is 'congruent') with the social meaning embodied in
the present design of work and the predominant meaning projected by
public communications. This puts the emphasis, not on what work does
or could do for the human personality, but on what it achieves in terms
of some practical outcome. The congruence thus resides in the fact that
both the social meaning and the personal meaning stress the instrumental, not the intrinsic, value of work. Private employers, managers and
senior administrators in governmental and other public services do not,
in other words, design their organizations to serve the ends of the
human personalities employed in them.

We have spoken so far, however, only of the majority. What of the
minority? Here, in the higher strata of the occupational hierarchy, we
find privilege, as we shall see in more detail later. In this context,
privilege lies in the availability not only of (usually superior) extrinsic
rewards but also of intrinsic satisfactions and experiences of a kind
widely regarded in our culture as nourishing and enriching to the

human personality. These stem essentially from the greater discretion, challenge and autonomy vested in higher job roles. To say of these kinds of work that they nourish and enrich the human personality is of course to imply a certain *theory* or *conception* of human personality. This conception sees such work activities as making available to those undertaking them not only extrinsic returns, but also:

> . . . enriching experiences through which men can meet challenges and overcome obstacles, develop their aptitudes and abilities, and enjoy the satisfactions of achievment. In the course of these experiences men undergo psychological growth, realise themselves, and reach due stature as full mature and autonomous moral agents. Perhaps the central notion here can be expressed in the language of decision-making, choice and responsibility. Men make themselves through their own choices – by taking decisions and accepting responsibility for what they choose. This is the process of self-determination and growth. A work situation which offers no – or only the most trivial – opportunities for choice, decision, and the acceptance of responsibility is therefore one which offers no opportunities for growth. (Fox 1971 p 4–5)

This conception comes in religious and in secular (liberal humanist) forms. Probably a high proportion of people in most societies have never heard of it. Many of those who have would dismiss it as having no practical relevance to the world of work; others accept it only up to the point where it does not impede the pursuit of economic values. Among the latter, some positively urge its fuller application to work in the conviction that this will *aid* the pursuit of economic values, but do not seek to press it to the point where it threatens those values.

It can usefully be explored further by applying an analysis of work which distinguishes two sets of component elements found in every job – the *prescribed* and the *discretionary* elements (Jaques 1967). The former specify precisely how the job occupant should discharge certain functions – as when a train-driver is instructed to 'keep below the speeds, as shown on a speedometer, specified for each curve on a railway'. The latter grant the job-occupant freedom of discretion within those prescribed terms – as when he is told to 'use the best method in the circumstances', thereby being given freedom to decide what is 'best'. By definition, therefore, jobs with only a negligible degree of discretion offer only a negligible opportunity for those activities of choice and decision-making that are said to be bound up with the process of self-determination and psychological growth. As we ascend the occupational status hierarchy we find a general tendency for the discretionary element in work to increase correspondingly, with obvious implications for the potential meaning available for people to find in it. Whereas most of those in lower occupational strata, with their relatively highly-prescribed, low-discretion jobs yielding little intrinsic meaning, feel constrained to adapt to their situation by focusing on the instrumental rewards, those in the higher strata are privileged to respond to an altogether deeper conception which sees work as among the central sources of significance in life (Fox 1974). Their job situation offers them the potential that work can promote the enlargement and fulfilment of their own personality.

The analysis points, therefore, to a major dimension of inequality. The owners and controllers who administer private and public property in the resources and facilities of production bring an instrumental approach to their task, and their practical interpretation and enforcement of this approach affords the majority of rank and file little scope for self-actualization through work. For them, instrumentalism and self-actualization bear a strong — though well short of absolute — tendency to be mutually exclusive. The minority in higher-status occupations (including, of course, the controllers) are fortunate in that, so far as their own roles are concerned, instrumentalism and self-actualization tend to be compatible rather than mutually exclusive.

The argument can be taken further. Freedom is considered a crucial value in our society, and a recent study argues that the notions of autonomy and self-development are among those central to this concept. In other words, one part of the answer to the question: 'When is a person free?' is that he is free 'in so far as his actions . . . result from decisions and choices which he makes as a free agent, rather than as the instrument or object of another's will . . . His autonomy consists precisely in this self-determined deciding and choosing.' A further part of the answer is that a person is free when he is able to 'realize his potentialities, that is, to make out of himself the best of what he has it in him to be . . .' (Lukes 1973b pp 127–30). It is clear that the productive system allocates these freedoms and opportunities with profound inequality.

It would be a mistake, however (as the preceding argument shows), to suppose that upper-level jobs are necessarily consciously designed to embody this rival conception, although a number of them are, for some people are lucky enough to be able to design their own jobs. But probably most upper-level jobs are so designed simply because it is believed by their designers that the work concerned could not be performed effectively if the intrinsically-significant features were removed from the job definition. What we are recognizing here, in other words, is simply that even a wholly instrumental approach to the design of work results in upper-level jobs being shaped in ways which incidentally afford their occupants some intrinsic meaning.

This point is sufficiently important to call for emphasis. It can be put another way by pointing out, first, that the reason why the owner of a factory usually employs many people whose work roles are closely circumscribed, embody little discretion, and offer their occupants little opportunity for intrinsic satisfaction, is that he sees this pattern of low-discretion jobs and managerial control as the most profitable — an instrumental orientation. But he will also employ some people — managerial controllers, technical specialists and other groups — whose roles embody much greater discretion. His reason is not that he wishes to offer these groups an intrinsic meaning which he is withholding from the rank and file. It is simply that for the same instrumental purpose as prompts him to hire low-discretion employees, he decides he needs a few high-discretion employees to plan, control, supervise and coordinate them. For those who occupy these roles it is their good luck which secures them their intrinsic satisfaction, not the owner's intention. Should it serve his purpose for any reason to change managerial roles in a way that reduces their intrinsic satisfaction he would seek to do so, though they may of course be powerful enough to stop him.

Similarly, those setting up a university normally endow the requisite academic roles with a considerable degree of discretion — not because they have as their object the personality enrichment of the individuals concerned, but because they define the tasks to be done as being such as to require this type of job specification. The objects are to conduct successfully the higher education of adult men and women, and to pursue original writing and research. Those who design university work structures believe, for the most part, that the kind of performance required for these roles can only be secured under conditions which grant the occupants considerable freedom and discretion. Once again, the approach to the problem of work design is instrumental in nature but results in the creation of work roles which afford their occupants intrinsic satisfaction.

The privilege enjoyed by many at higher occupational levels is therefore that, within an economic system designed largely to pursue only the instrumental returns from work, they have the opportunity to enjoy also the intrinsic returns. But Goldthorpe and his colleagues (1968) point out that no direct and immediate relationship exists between the 'objective' nature of a job situation and the orientations and attitudes of its occupant, in the sense that the former predictably 'determines' the latter. We have already noted, and will explore more closely later, the fact that people learn orientations to work from a diversity of sources besides the work situation itself, and their experience of the job and response to it is no mere mechanical response to certain objective features of it but the result of how they perceive those features and the meaning they give them in the light of their more widely-acquired orientations. The orientations themselves may, of course, undergo change, under the influence either of work experience itself or of factors external to it.

Reasons such as these show why we can only generalize about class experience. These contingencies still permit us to say, however, that most people at higher occupational levels value the intrinsic returns from work and have come to expect them, just as most people at lower levels learn to do without them, either because the job makes it difficult to extract any intrinsic meaning whatever from their work, or because it offers so little that they are prepared to trade it for the attraction of a fatter pay packet, which is likely to loom larger for those on lower incomes. This may be the appropriate point at which to note that those workers who relinquish a modicum of intrinsic satisfaction for the sake of higher earnings in, say, a mass-production plant are not necessarily confirming the picture of working-class material greed so beloved by those newspapers favoured by the comfortably-off. They may simply want to provide their wives and children with some of the comforts and pleasures so long taken for granted by the middle and upper classes. Of the workers, for example, who every workday converge upon the car-assembly plants in Oxford from surrounding villages, some have worked on the land and enjoyed it but, unlike the doctor, the lawyer, the scientist, the manager and the don, found that the job which gave them at least some intrinsic satisfaction did not also give them the standard of life to which they and their dependents now aspire.

A further point becomes relevant at this juncture to the question of those factors *external* to the work situation which can shape people's orientations and aspirations towards it. We are right to accept the arguments of those who point out that we must explore far beyond the factory gates in order to understand why the people within them behave as they do. But cautions are necessary. Since we have noted that the basic shape, nature and structure of work organizations are predominantly determined by the property-owning and property-controlling class, it might be easy to infer that, in accepting the importance of factors *external* to the organization, we are moving away from the emphasis on work behaviour and attitudes as being in certain basic respects 'class-determined'. This is not so, as can be seen by reminding ourselves of two points already made. First, such socialization and communication influences as bear upon people in the meaning they vest in work serve predominantly the values and objectives of owners and controllers of economic resources. The same class factor emerges albeit in different form. Second, the effects of family, education and community (or other residential) factors in mediating these influences on the individual are themselves powerfully derivative of class forces (Mackenzie 1974 pp 243–4). The orientations and aspirations which the individual finds prevalent in family, school, relatives, friends and other groups to which he looks for clues on how to live are themselves strongly shaped by work experience of past as well as present generations, and this experience will have been derived from the same class-stratified division of labour as he is himself entering or about to enter. The school-leaver from a working-class home may indeed have 'prior orientations' to work of an instrumental kind before he even reaches his routine, heavily-subordinated, low-discretion job, but it could still be the case that they stem from responses by earlier generations to a similarly class-differentiated work design imposed by a similarly class-differentiated power structure. Thus while our theoretical framework makes it useful to distinguish between prior orientations and those which result from experience in the actual work situation, we must remain aware of the extent to which the same basic forces mould both.

4 Instrumentalism and rationality in work

So far we have been concerned to establish a certain theoretical structuring in order to make better sociological sense of a wide variety of ideas and empirical data. We turn now to examine some aspects of social meaning that are specially worth noting.

We may usefully begin by registering a point that has been common to all societies and must remain so. In order simply that people may eat and survive the elements, some of them, at least, must undertake activities that we normally think of as work. All socially-received meanings must therefore include the notion that some work has to be done — by someone — simply to provide whatever standards of material, cultural and spiritual sustenance are demanded. Whatever other meanings may develop to supplement this basic instrumental one, they can never oust it altogether. This does not necessarily mean, however, that work is highly regarded. To make a contribution to this indispensable social function is not necessarily the route to respected status. In many societies throughout human history, those dominant groups who have succeeded in inducing their fellows to regard them as being of the highest elite status have not necessarily been found among those who worked. For one example among many, we need only remind ourselves of that society often held up as the pinnacle of cultural and civilized glory, the Athens of the fifth century BC, where work was defined as the activity of slaves. Leisure was a badge of status; a notion which has proved popular among many elites and aristocracies. But since such dominant groups usually expect to eat well and live comfortably, they normally guard carefully the privilege of not working for one's living. They usually ensure that those *outside* the elite who aspire to live without work are accorded the lowest status and obliged to suffer penalties. In Tudor and Elizabethan Britain, for example, few were more anxious than the leisured classes to 'correct', with violence if necessary, 'sturdy beggars' and 'vagrants', and the application of the Poor Law during these and the subsequent centuries of industrialization has left deep marks on Britain's social history and class relations. Some of these characteristics persist into our own time. Rich men may, if they choose, live in idleness indefinitely on inherited unearned income without incurring the institutionalized humiliations which attend a poor man's efforts to live indefinitely, say, on unearned income from state agencies. We explain such differences, of course, by reference to the rights of property and inheritance, but these only heighten the significance of the differences rather than reduce it. Evidence of class attitudes on these matters emerges from a recent national survey. Middle class discussion of 'scroungers on the Welfare State' usually assumes them to be working class. Yet the survey revealed that about half the professional and managerial people registered as unemployed and drawing benefit were, on their own admission, not really seeking jobs. Two thirds of non-manual workers of 55 and over did not intend to work again or to search intensively for another job, in contrast to only one third of manual workers. Moreover, the non-manuals were also much more likely to be doing part-time work while continuing to draw benefits. Yet they were subject to much less pressure by employment service officials to find a job than were manual workers (Daniel 1974 pp 26–8, 32, 146).

Though some dominant social groups may regard work as indispensable only for lower social groups, indispensable for most people it has necessarily remained, from the earliest hunting and food-gathering tribes to the advanced industrial societies of today. And this simple proposition leads on to a further consideration relevant to the social meaning of work. The mere statement of the historical transition just enunciated is itself enough to conjure up notions of how the forms of work have changed. Our minds turn readily to the dramatic changes of the last two centuries alone. There is a danger, however, that it may conjure up too much. So deeply embedded in our culture is the idea of 'progress' that, whatever the subject of our concern, we turn quickly to the assumption that we can trace a more or less continuous linear 'development' in human affairs with respect to the subject in question. This is especially likely to be so with technology, the development of economic resources, and work. The layman may well suppose it safe to assume a steady increase throughout human history in what might be called 'economic rationality' in the design and organization of work. The concept of rationality, as used here, has two aspects. There is, first, the separation of work as a segmentalized, instrumental activity in its own right, sharply distinct from other activities and relationships such as those bound up with the family, friends, leisure pastimes, social ritual or the religious life. And second, there is the further instrumental emphasis on designing the *content* of work solely with a view to maximizing effectiveness of performance, efficiency, profits or some related criterion assimilable within the general category of economic ends.

With some sense of the meaning of this concept, we can proceed now to the proposition that any notion of a linear trend during human history towards increasing rationality of work must be rejected, as Udy's work has demonstrated (Udy 1970). Udy distinguishes three broad stages of social development, with a movement from 'primitive' societies, marked by food-gathering, hunting and fishing, to 'traditional' societies which demonstrate, in their fullest form, settled communities, sedentary agriculture, centralized forms of government and complex stratification systems; followed by the further movement, with which we are familiar, from traditional to modern industrial societies. Udy argues that forms of work organization in traditional society (the second stage) are not *more* economically rational and efficient than those of primitive society (the first) but *less*, becoming bound up with kinship practices, ritual, political custom and religious rites, and consequently showing a tendency to 'become bogged down in a morass of excess manpower, overly elaborate authority systems, and socially complex role requirements that tend to detract from work performance *per se*' (Udy 1970 p 57).

Here, then, in traditional societies (which, along with primitive societies, still exist today), we find social meanings of work which, unlike our own predominant meaning, do not emphasize its instrumental function, but regard it as inseparable from a wide range of other human activities and relationships.

Along with industrialization, however, and the accompanying thrust towards expansion, growth, output, and profits, has come the growing emphasis on economic rationality as defined earlier, whereby work is seen as a totally specialized and segmentalized activity which must be sharply segregated from other spheres of human experience and human need, and which must be designed solely with instrumental purposes in view. We are familiar with the consequences in terms of that increasing specialization and sub-division of labour which has left many if not most working members of modern industrial society with fragmented tasks that, by widespread agreement, carry no central significance for their lives and offer only the means to enjoyment of life outside work.

5 Rationality and its apologists

It is around this issue that much of the debate on what should be the social meaning of work has come to revolve. Many commentators have urged that we must accept the existing situation philosophically since the disadvantages are outweighed by the benefits even for the rank and file at the base of the organizational and occupational hierarchy. The self-interested motives of some of those at the top of the hierarchy who argue that 'all is for the best' are not difficult to discern. But the same perspective is often advanced, implicitly or explicitly, by theorists with no immediate personal axe to grind. Robert Dubin, a leading American industrial sociologist, has argued that although the 'vast majority' of industrial workers are unable to enjoy personal development and fulfilment in their work situation, this does not matter, since they neither expect nor demand it in that sphere of life. They seek and find it instead outside work: in the family, in leisure pursuits, in spare-time occupations, in non-work relationships. He supports the proposition 'that the problem of creating an industrial civilization is essentially a problem of social invention and creativity in the non-work aspects of life' (Dubin 1962 p 265). Karl Mannheim, too, notes, and does not challenge, the idea that since

> . . . mechanization of industry and its schematized routines deny creative outlets and personal initiative to the many [leisure] becomes increasingly the place for personality development and self-expression . . . For the majority leisure instead of work has become the road to civilization. (Mannheim 1951 p 269)

David Riesman pressed the same view in a well-known work (Riesman 1950), though he subsequently shifted his ground (Weiss and Riesman 1963).

For those who find this position acceptable certain advantages follow. What was described earlier as the dominant social meaning in industrial societies, namely that work must be designed and organized so as to maximize output, efficiency, effective performance, or profit, becomes easy to support. Even the university academic who may derive profound intrinsic satisfaction from his own occupation need feel no uncomfortable sense of privilege or stirring of guilt, since the millions labouring in factories, mills, mines, shops, building sites and offices do not want such central involvement in their work and find their deeper life meanings without difficulty elsewhere. No ethical problems arise as a consequence of work being designed so as to exclude these deeper life meanings for the majority. We need focus only on the practical issue of compensating for such work by enlarging the amount of, and facilities for, leisure and spare-time activities. No concern need be felt, therefore, with that rival conception of work which has long inspired condemnations of industrialism and visions of a wholly different economic and social order. This is the view of work as it is for a privileged few — a process of self-discovery, self-development and self-fulfilment.

6 Work as self-development

From this view, which might be called 'holistic' as against segmental (Parker 1971), we cannot in fact compartmentalize the individual's life as modern work rationality seeks to do. The human personality is a unity and should be respected as such; if we require that the individual behave as a responsible moral agent in his or her role as citizen, husband, wife, father, mother or friend, the social purpose must be to design work and work organizations in such a way, it is said, as to permit and evoke behaviour as a responsible moral agent there too — a condition obviously not realized, it would be claimed, in much if not most, lower-level work in industry, business and commerce.

Such has become the prominence of 'self-development', 'self-realization' or 'self-actualization' as a talking-point in modern discussions and experiments on work design that we may usefully explore the notion a little further at this stage. The first point is that the concept itself is a vague one. Exactly what aspects of the 'self' are to be 'developed', 'realized', 'actualized'? Historically we can trace, within the Western tradition, three different versions of the conception of work as self-development: the Puritan, the Greek and the Romantic. The exact nature of the relationship between Protestantism and the rise of capitalism (Weber 1930, Tawney 1938, Birnbaum 1953) is complex and not yet entirely clear, but certainly in Britain's Victorian middle classes, where the Puritan tradition was strong, 'the religious theory of work was a commonplace . . .' (Houghton 1957 p 247—48). Within this theory, the idea of self-enhancement was bound up with other virtues of work.

> The arraignment of idleness, the value of work for the development of the individual, and the sense of a mission both to serve society in one's particular calling and to further the larger destinies of the human race, were almost as much the ideals of business as of Protestantism. [The Christian had to work] with the sense of having a purpose or mission . . . to which he was dedicated: the service of God in his secular calling. And by doing so, he also served himself because he developed his god-given talent . . . (Houghton 1957 p 244)

There is space here only for passing reference to a few of the numerous ways in which social practice fell short of precept. Victorian Britain was the arch-arena for the preaching of doctrines urging the specialization of work in separation from such other dimensions of human experience and human need as family life, religion, friendship, aesthetic and spiritual experience, and the whole world of ethics. Mercifully, of course, doctrine failed to determine reality; history reveals some businessmen bringing religious conscience, friendship, common decency, and even aesthetic sensitivity into their work activities. Yet it also reveals the brutal philistinism of many who did not, and who imposed this segmentalist experience upon themselves as well as upon others. Puritan earnestness shaped the middle class scene sufficiently to provoke a reaction by some towards the Greek ideal. Convinced that this and other current forces were producing 'incomplete and mutilated men', they sought 'a complete and harmonious development of one's nature, in which body and soul, reason and emotion and imagination, should find their integral places in a fully realized personality' (Houghton 1957 p 287). In the event, however, the conception of self-development which became established in our culture and has come down with increasing strength to our own day was not the Greek but the Romantic idea. John Stuart Mill, among others, urged, not a striving for harmoniousness within the personality in the sense of conformity to some standard 'balance', but,

> . . . freedom for the individual to go his own way and live his own life; freedom, in short, to cultivate and call forth all that was unique in himself, within the limits imposed by the rights and interests of others. Development meant the development of his special capacities

for intellectual, moral, and aesthetic life, not their harmonious flowering in a balanced personality. (Houghton 1957 p 290)

Such ideas became included among the stock notions of the Western liberal tradition, which sees the 'common good' as 'founded on personality, and postulates free scope for the development of personality in each member of the community' (Hobhouse 1911 p 130). It must be noted, also, that this brand of humanism lies at the heart of Marx's thought. Central to Marx's work is a conception of man as a creature with individual potentialities that should be given scope for full realization through productive labour, but which can only be realized within a society that has eliminated the gross inequalities represented by class domination, economic exploitation, and the division of labour they produced.

Certainly from the point of view of self-realization in work, the inequalities were as apparent, for those who cared to see, in his day as in our own. It was all very well for the Victorian manufacturer, professional man, author or poet to proclaim the gospel of work and relish the deep satisfactions to be derived from it in terms of spiritual redemption, practical accomplishment, personal fulfilment or simply the vanquishment of *ennui* and *accidie*. Then, as now, these rewards were far more elusive for the rank and file. One researcher who has examined numerous autobiographical writings by nineteenth-century working people has concluded that for the working class, work was mostly

> . . . taken as given, like life itself, to be endured rather than enjoyed; most were probably glad to have it at all, and to expect to derive satisfaction or happiness from it was an irrelevant consideration . . . It is true and predictable that this attitude varies with different types of occupation and work-task, and that skilled workers were able to derive notably more satisfaction from their work than semi-skilled and unskilled . . . But these were the minority of workers in the nineteenth century, as now; the factory hands and workers in sweated trades, the domestic servants, farm workers, navvies and labourers did not, if their writings are to be trusted, either think very much about their work or derive a sense of fulfilment from it. Work was a means to an end, not an end in itself, and the end was survival in a hostile world which often seemed to deny even this modest ambition. (Burnett 1974 p 15)

7 Nineteenth- and twentieth-century meanings

Here, then, within nineteenth-century British industrialism, could be found three contrasting social meanings of work. For those at the apex of the social pyramid, both the material necessity to work and the inner compulsion to work were marks of inferior status. We are familiar with the implications of the first — that leisure was a prerequisite for the true gentleman. The implications of the second, too, have probably been as far-reaching: the strand in Britain's culture which disparages professionalism and glorifies the cult of the amateur appears to have its roots in aristocratic disdain for middle-class, Puritan, dedicated earnestness (Moore 1973 pp 488–90). Many sometime Puritans succumbed to this example. Important aspects of Britain's economic and social history can only be fully explained by the fact that aristocratic modes, values and meanings retained a powerful glamour for aspiring sections of the middle class. The remarkably persistent imprint left by the landed aristocracy on British ideas and aspirations revealed itself not least in the entrepreneur who began as a Calvinistic gospeller of work and ended as an ennobled landowner living on his country estate, with sons at one of the new public schools acquiring expectations of inherited wealth and a contempt for 'trade'.

Beneath these levels, among the middle classes, the Victorian gospel of work waxed in all its self-tormenting complexities. Alongside its dominant extrinsic significance in terms of wealth, status and power, there lay available, as we have seen, its intrinsic significance in terms of self-enhancement, whether seen in Puritan, Greek, or Romantic definition. Many at these occupational levels could experience both, in some degree, as their personal meanings. For the working classes, there was principally only the extrinsic meaning available, and that at not much above subsistence level for many. Work design excluded for all but a minority of skilled men the possibility of intrinsic meanings, and the struggle for survival absorbed too much energy to allow aspirations in that direction.

When we compare this situation with the present, it could be argued that the similarities are as significant and interesting as the differences. The conspicuousness of aristocracy and its values has become severely muted, yet, as we noted earlier, certain of its characteristics have persisted. The 'work-shy' rich are still treated with markedly more respect than the 'work-shy' poor: the gentlemanly status of 'leisure' (as distinct from poverty-stricken 'idleness') can hardly be said to have lost the power to move the hearts of men, though there are important differences of emphasis in this respect as between Britain and, say, America.

It is still the case that the prevailing personal meaning of work among the lower occupational strata sees it as a necessary evil for the purposes of earning one's living, supporting one's family, financing one's pleasures. For the most part, members of these strata lack any real moral involvement in, and personal identification with their work; tend to separate it sharply from leisure and family life, and value it largely in instrumental terms, though of course at a much higher material level than their early counterparts.

Among professionals, top managers, administrators, and kindred groups, the same differences from the general working-class pattern still reveal themselves. They share, of course, with other strata, an ever-keen concern with extrinsic rewards, but many among them invest a personal involvement in and identification with their work which permits no sharp segmentalized cut-off from family, leisure and other dimensions of human existence. Their job situations enable them, then, to draw, usually in generous measure, upon both the social meanings of work that have figured most prominently in our discussion.

8 Empirical data: job satisfaction

It is time now, having developed some central *qualitative* categories and propositions, to elaborate and support them with *quantitative* data. How do these different meanings reveal themselves quantitatively in terms of the personal meanings which individuals derive from their work situations? Here we turn to the empirical evidence of attitude surveys and questionnaires.

Research in this field is beset by pitfalls. The replies people give, for example, to structured questionnaire surveys can give us much useful information, but the surveys have to be carefully and imaginatively devised if they are to illuminate the complex, many-layered, and sometimes apparently contradictory body of attitudes we bring to work in general and our own job in particular. Crude 'sponge' questions, for example, as to whether people are 'satisfied' in their work, soak up too much diffuse and undifferentiated information to be useful. Satisfied with what? Pay, security, status, workmates, the work itself, future prospects, having a job at all? Daniel (1969) stresses the difference between satisfaction *with* a job and satisfaction *in* a job, and there are other traps for the unwary (Blauner 1967a).

Certain findings, however, emerge so consistently from a number of countries that they must be given considerable weight. Prominent among them is one that supports our previous discussion: that

. . . workers at the lower skill and socio-economic levels regard their work more frequently as merely a way to earn a living and in general recognize fewer extra-financial meanings in their work than do workers of higher skill and socio-economic levels. [Extra-financial meanings] become more and more important as we ascend the occupational and skill ladders. (Nosow and Form 1962 pp 53—4)

This evidence comes from America, as do the findings of Morse and Weiss that for those in middle class occupations work means having something interesting to do and being able to enjoy a sense of accomplishment — life without work being seen as less purposeful, stimulating, and challenging — whereas for the person in a working class occupation work is simply synonymous with activity — directed activity occupying his time, his mind and his hands, the alternative to which is to lie around bored and restless (Morse and Weiss 1955). Hyman's research revealed upper social classes emphasizing the importance, in choosing one's life's work, of the congeniality of the work in terms of one's personality, interests, and qualifications, whereas lower social classes were more likely to stress direct economic considerations such as pay and security (Hyman 1967). Centers, likewise, found middle class respondents, asked a similar question, emphasizing 'self-expression', while working class respondents emphasized 'security' (Hyman 1967).

In Britain, research by Goldthorpe and his colleagues into a sample of relatively well-paid manual wage earners indicated 'the generally low level of [intrinsic] satisfaction that they derived directly from their work-tasks and roles. Only a minority appeared to find the work they performed inherently rewarding . . .' (Goldthorpe *et al* 1969 p 54—5). The instrumental aspect was 'very strongly emphasized by *all* groups of workers within our sample . . . considerations of pay and security appear most powerful in binding men to their present jobs' (Goldthorpe *et al* 1968 pp 37—8). It was their view that

> . . . in the conditions of modern British society, the tendency will increase for industrial workers, *particularly unskilled or semi-skilled men*, to define their work in a largely instrumental manner . . . The more traditional modes of working-class life are now steadily being eroded both by such factors as urban redevelopment and greater geographical mobility . . . [Moreover] models of new standards and styles of living will become both more evident and more compelling. (Goldthorpe *et al* 1968 pp 174—5)

Kolaja's research in Yugoslavia, where work organizations are structured to provide a degree of employees' self-management (the degree achieved being disputed), indicates that there, as elsewhere, can still be found systematic differences, particularly between, on the one side, unskilled and semi-skilled workers, and on the other, skilled and white-collar workers and management, in terms not only of satisfaction with pay and conditions but also of their identification with the enterprise and their interest in company affairs. The lower strata (the majority) 'seemed to feel that the factory was not "their factory", but rather afforded an opportunity to earn a living which could be exchanged for another and better opportunity as soon as one appeared in the future' (quoted in Emery and Thorsrud 1969 pp 40—1). Similar indications emerge from research into industrial democracy in Norway (Emery and Thorsrud 1969). The scene appears little different within the Soviet Union in these respects. An inquiry by American researchers into attitudes among ex-Soviet citizens indicated

> . . . the greater relative importance to the manual worker of pay, and secondarily of working conditions (discipline), as contrasted with the non-manual's concentration on the intrinsic qualities of the job . . . Interesting work dominated the desires of the intelligentsia, [who tended to] take a decent standard of living for granted. (Inkeles and Bauer 1959 p 118)

The same inquiry confirms findings mentioned earlier by indicating that Americans in the higher status jobs were more likely than the manual groups to choose jobs which permitted 'self-expression' and 'interesting experience' (Inkeles and Bauer 1959 p 118). Finally, two Soviet sociologists, after research on groups of their own nationals, conclude that

> . . . attitude to work depends on the content and character of work . . . The general tendency is for occupations in which the work is more complicated and subject to technical progress to be associated with high indices of attitude to work, and greater interest in the job . . . The tendency . . . arises from the actual opportunities that the job affords for creative work and initiative. (Zdravomyslov and Yadov 1966 pp 109, 119)

What emerges from this diverse and geographically wide-ranging evidence confirms our earlier discussion in demonstrating that personal meanings in work do not differ randomly as between individuals. The lower we direct our attention within the occupational status scale, the more likely we are to find people deriving little conscious meaning from their work apart from the pay and security it offers. Conversely the higher we look the more likely we are to find people seeing work not only in terms of these extrinsic rewards but also as a medium for self-expression, interest, challenge, personal fulfilment, and other 'extra-financial' or non-monetary meanings. Personal meanings in work, in other words, are to a marked degree correlated with social stratification, for occupation is closely related to social class. How the individual looks at work depends to a considerable extent upon his or her location in that complex social layering that we think of as the class structure.

9 Personal meanings: a closer focus

Before we pursue the significance of this, however, we must bring a closer focus to bear on those personal meanings that extend beyond seeing work solely in terms of its cash rewards. The need to do so derives from the fact that simply to postulate a division between work as a purely instrumental activity and work as a process of self-actualization falls well short of explicating the full range of meanings which may enter into work.

In expounding these meanings we are indicating the range of what is possible. No generalizations of any value can be made. We cannot even fall back on the proposition that the extent to which individuals or groups draw upon these meanings can be easily discovered by empirical investigation in each case. The reason for this is that while some of the meanings an individual draws from work may be apparent to him, others may not. The former can be called 'manifest' meanings — though even here it is one of the difficulties of empirical research that the individual is not always reliable in reporting his own motivations; what he believes or likes to believe about the place of work in his life does not necessarily tally with the facts. Difficulties are compounded when we turn to 'latent' meanings; those of which the individual remains wholly or largely unaware until he is deprived of them. The difference between manifest and latent meanings may be illuminated by an analogy with the meaning and significance of breathable air for human life. Asked what was most important to us, we might well reply in terms of money, work, sex, music, books, gardening, sport or whatever. Threatened with deprivation of air, we would re-arrange our priorities fairly rapidly. This is not to suggest that latent work meanings necessarily have this degree of significance, but simply to call attention to their 'taken for granted' quality. By definition the individual is rarely in a position to report these and assess their relative importance in his life. It is for such reasons that we cannot judge with any confidence just how significant are the meanings we are about to examine, though we do know that all of them have to appear in the total list of possibilities. For the same reasons the order of their appearance cannot indicate their relative importance.

As we turn to examining them it would be well to maintain a sense of the manifold variety of human labours covered by the category of 'work'. So much academic and popular attention has focused on the manual worker in mass-production industry that we sometimes need to remind ourselves of the wide diversity of work roles in our kind of society. It is useful to bear in mind, therefore, not only 'the man on the assembly line' but also prison officers, journalists, public-school masters, farm workers, monks, computer programmers, lorry drivers and pig farmers.

First, then, it is clear that work provides the individual with opportunities to relate himself to society. As Morse and Weiss indicate, 'If men work only for money, there is no way of explaining the degree of dislocation and deprivation which retirement, even on an adequate salary, appears to bring to the formerly employed' (Nosow and Form 1962 p 29). Work can serve for the individual as an organizing principle in the sense of gearing him into society and enabling him to view himself as making a useful contribution by providing goods and services.

> The operator assembles cars or machines; the farmer grows food; the physician reduces pain . . .; the teacher broadens the intellectual horizons of his students; the policeman protects citizens against law-breakers . . . The unemployed man, by contrast, . . . has seen the clock go round but he has nothing to show for the hours that have passed. (Sofer 1970 p 86)

This meaning is likely to be specially important in a society whose culture contains a general expectation that its members will perform useful work. An American writer argues that a 'man's closest link to his society is his job or profession . . . The health of the individual in a society and the health of the society depend on how they are linked to each other. And the most significant link is in the work relationship' (Levenstein 1964 p 20).

Giving special strength to such meanings as these, in some societies, (e.g. those of Western Europe and the USA), may be surviving impulses of the Protestant Ethic (or a secularized and modified form of it) which venerates the pursuit of individual salvation through hard work, thrift, and competitive struggle. A notable talking point in North America of recent years, however, has been the growing allegation that this ethic is weakening — and indeed, among some sections of the young, being flatly rejected. (For this debate, see Levenstein 1964, Chapter 2; Whyte 1960 Chapters 1 and 2; and *Work in America* 1973 pp 10–13, 43–51). Given the concern among many weighty men of affairs that it be held as strongly and widely as possible, the charge has naturally occasioned some grief. In Britain, middle class anxieties and moral harangues of a kind familiar for at least two centuries have always had a different basis — the head-shaking conviction, not that the Protestant Ethic is losing its grip on the lower orders, but that it never had such a grip in the first place. Appropriate envy is directed at counterparts in, for example, Western Germany, where it is supposed that the workers know how to work. It is revealing both of the Protestant gospel of work and of Britain's class relations that, after the cosmic-scale horrors of the Nazi regime, Germans earned themselves a partial reluctant forgiveness among many British middle class observers simply through their reputation for sustained hard work and obedience in achieving not only recovery but economic supremacy in Western Europe.

The second personal meaning we must note here is that work may serve sociability needs by providing the individual with opportunities for interaction with others. The workplace has always been, for some, a place to meet people, converse, and perhaps form friendships, as for example when married women previously tied to home and children welcome the chance to move into a wider world. If the work itself is experienced as intrinsically satisfying and personally involving by its practitioners, the situation can also, given certain conditions, offer membership of an 'occupational community' which lends further kinds of satisfaction. Since they make no sharp segmentalized distinction between the worlds of work and non-work they find friendships among those who follow the same occupation and derive support, identity, and self-respect from participation in this community (Salaman 1974).

When membership of a work group means not only a sharing of sociability, values, and collective pride, but also participation in a shared and integrated purpose, the returns can be specially rich. Mannheim refers to 'joy in co-operation, the sense of team membership, response to discipline, pride in skilful mastery of tasks . . .' (Mannheim 1951 p 267). Such a combination can be found exceptionally in industry, science, and the armed services.

Third, comes the role of work in enabling the individual to sustain status and self-respect. This has several aspects.

> The job is a key element in wider social status. With a few exceptions a man's occupation is a more reliable single guide to his place in a society's hierarchy of prestige than any other indicator. We rank people largely by virtue of their occupations and tend to categorize people by occupation in dealing with them. (Sofer 1970 pp 90—1)

Within the smaller and more immediate world of friends, acquaintances, and personal involvement in associations and clubs, the loss of a job can bring a sense of humiliation and consequent withdrawal to avoid embarrassment. Research has produced reports indicating that

> . . . the release from the discipline of regular work was accompanied by family tension and emotional disturbance; that economic distress was sometimes the crucial last straw in breaking up a marriage; that the children of unemployed persons are susceptible to loss of prestige among schoolfellows; that the unemployed father may lose his authority over his children and esteem and leadership within the family (especially if the wife takes a job); that the children of an unemployed man lose a sense of security and tend to become resentful towards their parents, nervous and anti-social and that their school performance deteriorates. (Sofer 1970 p 89)

Any attempt at 'total social accounting' would have to include these consequences whenever political and economic leaders contemplate a deliberate creation of unemployment to 'cool an over-heated economy' or 'restore a little flexibility to the labour market'. Such effects are not confined to manual wage-earners. Examples of managers declared redundant also bear witness to the stigma effects — the shame which sometimes prompts attempts to conceal the loss of a job; the behaviour of friends who edge away as if fearing to be tainted by failure or misfortune. Here one becomes aware of the 'dark side of the moon' — the less attractive face of the self-actualization ethic, with its emphasis on individual striving for excellence, achievement and recognition. The striving may, of course, bring the sweet smell of individual and personal success. But the sour smell of failure is likewise individual and personal; the failed middle class professional cannot efface himself in the crowd as can the rank-and-file shop-floor operative, who is protected by the very anonymity which makes his work so much less personally meaningful to him.

Next comes the significance of work in terms of personal identity.

> Occupational roles provide opportunities to define oneself to oneself and to others, to enter into a stable set of relations with colleagues or clients and to acquire an ideology that explains one's place in the world. A variety of identification possibilities go with an occupation — with persons, skills, institutional position, occupational ideology, employing organization, functions in society and so on. (Sofer 1970 p 92)

Jobs differ profoundly, of course, in what they offer along these dimensions, but even in the humblest activities prestige may attach to the worker who distinguishes himself in strength, dexterity, or whatever else is valued, and the recipient may derive meaning from this reputation.

The fifth possible meaning is more important for many people than it may at first seem. 'Work roles structure the passage of time . . . through . . . requiring that one must be at a particular place or carry out a particular activity at a particular time' (Sofer 1970 p 93). The significance here is of work providing a routine that wards off boredom, structures one's life, passes the time, offers something to do. 'Even the people who dislike their work as dangerous, unpleasant or monotonous often recognize the value of the work routine to them and cannot imagine how they would fill the day if they were to retire' (Friedmann and Havighurst 1954 p 190).

This role of work merges into the next – the value of meaningful activity in helping to distract the individual from private worries, fears, disappointments, depression and emotional disturbance. The professional, for example, who commits himself totally to work can be reacting to, as well as causing, the failure of his marriage. Loneliness, isolation and fear of death are also known to lend work this kind of meaning.

A seventh significant factor in work is its importance in providing scope for the satisfaction of 'achievement', usually defined in terms of a struggle towards high standards that are recognized as such by some valued group, large or small. Clearly, as with some other meanings, jobs differ widely in what they offer along this dimension and there need be little surprise that achievment motivation in contemporary Western society is considered to be particularly associated with middle class values, opportunities and education – a link we shall be exploring more fully later.

Finally, it is a fact of observation that people may derive meaning from a job situation in which the work itself is humble and repetitive or in some way disagreeable, trying, or dangerous, if they are conscious of contributing to some transcendent cause with which they feel able to identify. The cause may be – as in the case of some medical practitioners, social workers and other so-called 'helping' professions – the physical, mental, familial or environmental well-being of other people, where the service is usually immediate and direct. Sometimes the cause is embodied, more indirectly so far as lower participants are concerned, in an organization to which they feel proud to contribute, in this way even low-status employees in humble roles within high-morale hospitals, research teams, military units and perhaps some business establishments, can come to value this personal identification with the organization in a way that becomes central to their life. Indeed, Soviet sociologists assert that their workers' identification with the needs of Soviet society and with the building of communism enables them to turn even what may be intrinsically uninteresting work into something that is significant and meaningful for them (Naumova 1966 p 268). More easily verifiable for the Western observer is evidence coming from Israeli kibbutz industries which indicates that, within such of these egalitarian self-governing work organizations as are still fired by high moral purpose, people accept dull, disagreeable work for the sake of that purpose, though devices such as job rotation may be used to reduce the strain. (A useful introduction to the kibbutzim and the changes overtaking them can be found in Hunnius *et al* 1973).

Identification also emerges as having some significance in enhancing the meaning of work for employees in small as against large establishments. Research by Ingham, which included both, revealed that in small firms (numbering less than 100),

> . . . workers are to some extent *morally* involved in the enterprise in so far as their involvement is based, at least in part, on identification. This is to say, these workers are not merely attached to their organization by the cash nexus — but are, in effect, committed. (Ingham 1970 p 53)

As before, we must beware of assuming that smallness and the associated characteristics described by Ingham *cause* the identification in some automatic deterministic way — he suggests that the majority were in any case *predisposed* to the pattern of work and work relationships to be found in small firms — greater informality, fewer bureaucratic rules, personalized relations with the owner, close work-group relations, wider variety of tasks and more job rotation. To gain these kinds of work experience they were prepared to accept a level of pay far lower than was obtainable in large establishments (over 3000), where, by contrast, men seeking to maximize pay were ready to accept impersonality, bureaucratic regulation, anonymity and a faster pace of work. There is some evidence, then, for a degree of self-selection into different types of job situation by people with differing priorities in terms of work orientation and meaning. A key notion, as we have observed already, is that of *congruence* (or incongruence) between employee orientations and aspirations on the one hand, and job structure and rewards on the other.

10 Social stratification and the 'cycle of inequality'

In explaining more fully the personal meanings that may enter into work we have been concerned with *possibilities*, not measured *probabilities*. As we have noted, attempts to identify and measure the incidence of many of the meanings would face considerable difficulties. Some of the contributions made by work to our material, social, emotional, and perhaps even spiritual economy are apparent to us, but others we may be unaware of until we are deprived of them or observe the damage suffered by our fellows when all or some of these contributions are withdrawn.

Provisionally, then, we must return to the quantitative proposition quoted earlier from Friedmann and Havighurst that, in terms of the simple and basic distinction between economic (financial) meanings and non-economic (extra-financial) meanings,

> . . . skilled craft and white-collar groups stressed the extra-financial meanings of work to a much greater extent than did the workers in heavy industry, thus bearing out our hypothesis that these meanings of work become more and more important as we ascend the occupational and skill ladders. (Nosow and Form 1962 p 54).

We are reminded, thereby, that in returning to measured probabilities along this dimension we are confronted with the significance of social stratification. This remains no less salient when we inquire into the degree of *job satisfaction* expressed by those carrying out different types of work. Immediately apparent are marked occupational differences closely related to occupational status and class. Inkeles and Bauer collected a number of surveys covering five countries (USA, USSR, Germany, Sweden, and Norway). All reveal a general tendency towards a systematic decline in the proportion satisfied as one descends the occupational status scale (Inkeles and Bauer 1959 pp 102—7). Blauner offers a similar summary of evidence. 'When a scale of relative job satisfaction is formed, based on general occupational categories, the resulting rank order is almost identical with the most commonly used occupational status classification . . .' (Blauner 1967a p 475).

Apologists for the *status quo*, including some academics, have sought to disarm what might prove to be inconvenient reactions to this data. A favourite means for this purpose has been the findings by Dubin mentioned earlier. The controversial aspect of his study is not his assertion that 60 per cent of his sample of industrial workers 'did not see their jobs and work places as central life interests for themselves'; nor is it his conclusion that factory work 'may now very well be viewed by industrial workers as a means to an end — a way of acquiring income for life in the community' (Dubin 1962 p 254). Plenty of other evidence and opinion supports him on this score, as our preceding pages have shown. What renders him vulnerable to criticism is the message conveyed by his presentation that what *is*, must be taken as *given*: must be accepted as a datum calling for no political or ethical appraisal. A class-correlated dimension in inequality in a major sphere of life is presented as if it were a fact of existence beyond the reach — or indeed the need — of reform. Instead of seeing the workers' refusal to regard work as a 'central life interest' as itself a consequence of, and a form of adaptation to, their class-determined work situation, Dubin chooses to regard it as a *justification* of that situation; as an indication that all is for the best in the best of all industrial workers' worlds.

Here we need only remind ourselves of the general truth that if the individual is to maintain average mental health and happiness, he must, on the practical level of everyday life, make 'realistic' assumptions, operate with 'realistic' aspirations and make 'realistic' adaptations. Workers who see no reasonable prospect of securing a job which affords them intrinsic satisfaction, self-fulfilment and comparable related meanings — or who find that to secure such satisfaction they must pay a price in material rewards which seems to them (or their wives) excessive — are likely to moderate their aspirations accordingly, make the best of life as they find it, and emphasize such meanings as are within their reach — which as Dubin and many others have shown will probably be limited to financial rewards and perhaps certain additional meanings of subsidiary priority. After several years habituation to this situation their adaptation to it may well become an established and structured element in their personality and attitude to life and work. As we have seen, however, in many if not most cases people do not need personal experience of work to develop an established set of orientations and expectations towards it. Educational experience and other prior forms of conditioning are known to be potent in this respect. This leads on to considerations so crucial that they must be examined more closely. Even before this is done, however, we can note a point of relevance for the kind of apologetics based on Dubin's research. Once we bear in mind people's remarkable facility for adapting themselves to making the best of, or at least enduring, almost any set of circumstances, it becomes a highly dubious procedure to take a given pattern of adaptation to a given set of circumstances and offer the fact of the former as a reason for being complacent about the latter.

When we examine the prior conditioning factors that help to shape people's expectations and orientations towards work and its place in their life, we become especially aware of those tendencies towards self-perpetuation of the social system that are notable in most societies for most of the time, though it is vital not to so emphasize them as to obscure the dynamics of change with which they co-exist.

A brief account of the so-called 'cycle of inequality' must begin with the now established fact that the educational system is biased against the children of lower socio-economic classes. Secondary modern schools (or the equivalent streams in comprehensive schools) contain a higher than average proportion of children from blue-collar groups; whereas grammar, direct grant and independent schools contain higher than average proportions of children from professional homes. Moreover, children from poorer homes are more likely to leave school early. This gap, which cannot be explained simply by differences in measured intelligence, continues widening when we move on to further education. For example, the 'proportion of children with measured intelligence between 115 and 129 who entered full-time higher education is 34 per cent for middle class children and only 15 per cent for those from manual working class homes' (Field 1974 p 20). Since further education and the qualifications it makes available greatly affect the type of work for which recipients are groomed, trained and prepared, we can already, even from these few facts, detect relevant tendencies thrown up by the system of social stratification. One is for middle class children to pass through an educational sequence which alerts them to, and equips them for, expectations of a 'career' offering a meaningful work experience as well as superior extrinsic rewards. This set of expectations and understandings as to what constitutes a significant career choice is likely to be reinforced by family, relatives and friends. Equipped with the appropriate conception and personal meanings of work, along with the qualifications required to pursue them, middle class children move on to their careers in management, administration, science or the professions. In due course they transmit to their own children the same educational advantages and superior aspirations, and the cycle at this level is complete. Meanwhile, at another level, a very different set of tendencies is working itself out. The child of low socio-economic class and status, handicapped by home and social background in terms of both aspiration and achievement, may be passively accepting the educational label of being among the hewers of wood and drawers of water — accepting the destiny, in other words, of being led 'inevitably towards the lower-level jobs — usually in manual work, whether skilled or unskilled'. Many in these categories 'do not mind much what jobs they get, are not particularly bothered'. Work 'would have to offer a considerable degree of intrinsic interest if it were to kindle any sparks. The point here is that, so far from kindling any sparks, the work of many children is such that it dampens down even more their outlook upon and enjoyment of life: it confirms them in their view that "you can't expect much out of work — you just have to do it" ' (Carter 1966 pp 110, 166). These responses may well be reinforced by home and social milieux; parents and relatives have learned this lesson themselves in their time. Continued experience of work into adulthood further consolidates the whole stance, which in due course is transmitted, along with the same educational handicaps and disadvantages, to the next generation. (For a fuller account, which notes a wider range of trends than is relevant here, see Carter 1966, and Willis 1977).

Between the two extremes can be found strata of upper working class and lower middle class families where children pursue a course compounded of elements of both. School performance tends to be superior to that in the lowest socio-economic classes, but inferior to that in the classes above. They become committed to working class occupations, but occupations that enable them to 'make something of themselves'. They are more likely to move into skilled jobs, where they 'take pride in the mastery of their skills and the fairly autonomous exercise of them and thereby develop a high level of involvement in their work' (Ashton 1974 p 183).

This account points to the importance, for many if not most people, of powerful, self-reinforcing circles of circumstance, relatively favourable for the minority, relatively unfavourable for the majority. Yet, as we have felt it necessary to emphasize, these circles are far from being closed — ideas and aspirations can and do break their way in and introduce their own dynamic towards change.

11 'Work as it might be': latent aspirations

Considerable potential for such change lies latent within the aspirational patterns of the majority at present confined to intrinsically unrewarding work. People speculate about the world as it might be — or might have been. They can be invited to say, for example, what they would have aspired to had circumstances, opportunities, and their own knowledge and judgement been different.

> Over the last two decades, one of the most reliable single indicators of job dissatisfaction has been the response to the question: 'What type of work would you try to get into if you could start all over again?' . . . This question, some researchers feel, is a particularly sensitive indicator because it causes respondents to take into account the intrinsic factors of the job and the very personal question of self-esteem. (*Work in America* 1973. See also Blauner 1967a pp 475–6)

Applied to occupational groups at different levels of the status ranking, the question reveals a systematic decline, as we descend the scale, in the percentage who would choose similar work again. University professors, company lawyers, scientists and journalists, for example, all show percentages of over 80; skilled printers 52, skilled steelworkers and carworkers 41, unskilled steelworkers 21, unskilled carworkers 16.

Here is evidence of the multi-layered nature of people's attitudes towards work. On one level, members of relatively disadvantaged strata adapt to what they regard as inevitable or unchangeable, making the best of circumstances and offering appropriate behaviour and responses (including responses to sociologists' questionnaires). In this process of adaptation they bring into play, consciously or unconsciously, certain familiar psychological mechanisms. A common pattern 'is to lower aspirations or rationalize skin-deep levels of satisfaction into major justifications of one's work' (Fox 1971 p 14). In the words of Argyris,

> We could argue that the workers are saying (1) 'I must enjoy it in order to live with myself' (thereby reducing the potentiality of dissonance); (2) 'I must enjoy it or else I have to go through the extremely difficult task of finding another job' (thereby again reducing the probability of his own unhappiness and discomfort); and (3) 'One way to live with the job is to enjoy it'. (Argyris 1964 p 70)

Yet implicit in these mechanisms is the existence of another level of awareness which acknowledges and responds positively to values and life-styles very different from those the individual normally works to; which he normally keeps under control for everyday purposes of realistic adjustment to life as he finds it; but which may occasionally, at times of special stimulus, tension, or frustration, erupt into the workaday world and thereby bring an impact to bear on events.

12 Control and alienation

When people indicate in some way or another their awareness of a gap between work as it is and work as it might be, we are driven to ask what it is they lack. The answers offered by research are, of course, complex. But Blauner, along with others, has argued that the most fundamental elements can be grouped under the single crucial category of *control* (Blauner 1967a pp 478–81). This covers a wide range of phenomena, prominent among them (a) control over the use of one's time and physical movement, which is essentially control over the pace of the work process, (b) control over the environment, both technical and social, and (c) control in terms of freedom from hierarchical authority.

These dimensions are, of course, closely interrelated: a top business executive scores high, an unskilled worker low, on all. As the examples suggest, they are also closely related to status. In support of his proposition that the 'relationship between occupational status and control is particularly marked', Blauner quotes another specialist, Edward Gross, to the effect that the (status) 'hierarchy is a direct reflection of freedom from control'. He concludes that it 'is possible to generalize on the basis of the evidence that the greater the degree of control that a worker has (either in a single dimension or as a total composite) the greater his job satisfaction'.

Since the purpose here is simply to indicate links between the study of work meanings and the study of other aspects of work, this crucial aspect of control will not be pursued further. Instead its importance for another major theme relevant to work meanings, alienation, will be briefly noted.

The concept of alienation has been so widely applied that some commentators doubt whether it remains open to salvage as a useful analytical tool. Even in the hands of Marx, who did most to develop its application to work, to man's personal experience, and to his relations with others, it took a variety of expressions that cannot be explored here. (For an exposition, along with a general survey and discussion, see Ollman 1971.) We shall limit ourselves to that usage of the concept that is specially relevant to control structures within work organizations.

Marx saw the individual as needing to realize his essential nature through productive labour, and as requiring, for this process, life within a society in which he enjoyed freedom from domination and exploitation by others for their own purposes (Meszaros 1970, Ollman 1971). Capitalism represented precisely this domination and exploitation by the propertied of the propertyless for the purpose of private profit. We can supplement this exposition by recalling that managers of state property, too, may similarly seek to dominate their rank and file by imposing a division of labour, a pattern of decision-making, and a structure of control which in no way differ from those of the private sector.

If men realize their full and essential selves only through freedom from control in their productive labour, then the greater the domination imposed on them in the work situation the more they are blocked, cut off, or estranged from their essential nature; in other words, the more they are (along one of Marx's dimensions) alienated. It does not follow, as is often assumed, that the alienated condition necessarily expresses itself in terms of frustration. To the extent that men are constrained to adapt to a context in which work offers only instrumental, extrinsic satisfactions and rewards, they may not actively aspire to the kind of self-actualization through work that Marx had in mind. And to the extent that men do not actively aspire to self-actualization, they submit to its absence without necessarily manifesting active and overt dissatisfaction. To be sure, they may, as we have seen, entertain latent desires towards fulfilment in work which can, on occasion, break through the normal behaviour of everyday routine. Such outbursts rarely, however, emerge as revolts against their condition of alienation as such, but rather lend reinforcing energy to grievances of an extrinsic kind. When men strike for higher pay, the passion of their campaign may sometimes be strengthened by resentment against intrinsic deprivations as well, though these may never be articulated, if only because in our society men are expected to strike for financial rewards but not for psychic rewards.

Such considerations do not, however, gainsay the proposition to which they are appended. Alienation, besides being describable in terms of objective class and property relations, is also describable in terms of a state of mind, a set of attitudes, and a style of behaviour with which the individual responds to the objective characteristics of his work situation; these add up to an orientation which, in stressing only the extrinsic rewards and instrumental significance of work, lacks the moral involvement, personal commitment, and identification that are usually evoked by the consciousness and enjoyment of intrinsic rewards. But it is an orientation not necessarily associated with active discontent and frustration. Thus men may be alienated yet express 'satisfaction' with their lot and remain firmly attached to their work situation.

For all that men themselves, however, may accept unprotestingly their alienated state, it can still bring problems for management, in the form of rank-and-file indifference towards organizational fortunes, managerial objectives and indeed all matters ranging beyond simple shop-floor equations of pay, effort and security. Such problems become greatly compounded if discontent with the lack of intrinsic satisfaction starts to break through, or if the scale of financial compensation for this lack comes to be seen as inadequate. Strikes, high labour turnover, absenteeism, a high sickness rate, managerial difficulties in recruiting labour and a variety of other problems may follow.

In these circumstances management may conclude that the marginal costs of extreme division of labour, rigorous control and other characteristics of scientific management have begun to outweigh the marginal benefits, thus calling for a slight reversal of the historic thrust in this direction in the hope of winning back some of the employee commitment hitherto so readily sacrificed. This is the context within which currently fashionable ideas of 'job enrichment' and the 'autonomous work group' take their rise (Davis and Taylor 1972). Despite much accompanying publicity about 'treating workers as ends rather than as means', 'giving employees opportunities for self-realization', and the like, such strategies remain unmistakably in the instrumental category. The purpose remains the service of management's instrumental ends; all that has changed is management's calculation of how best to achieve them. It will be recalled that the pursuit of efficiency, effective performance or profit does not *necessarily* require jobs to be designed so as to exclude intrinsic satisfactions; if they did then intrinsically-satisfying work would be rare indeed. The language of 'job enrichment' specialists may sometimes seem to echo the language of Marx, William Morris, Thomas Carlyle, and others who have thundered against industrialism and its values, but whereas the language of the latter spoke of a new social vision, that of the former speaks of a new 'enlightened' strategy to be applied within the parameters and cost assessments of a calculative managerial rationality which can be, and usually is, applied to publicly-owned as well as privately-owned means of production.

13 Stratification and the design of work

Our analysis has assembled for us a pattern of personal work meanings that correlates closely with the structure of social stratification. We must now consider the nature of this relationship. We begin with what might be called the 'received interpretation' offered by many economic historians and some sociologists. It is the one likely to be preferred by the relatively well-favoured members of society, for reasons which will become apparent. This conventional view sees the existing design of work and job patterns, personal growth and fulfilment, and all the associated class and status differences, as having been 'created' by the scientific, technological and organizational advances of the continuing Industrial Revolution. According to such a view, this technological and organizational thrust, developing in response to what was 'necessary' or 'appropriate' to the 'demands' of the prevailing economic conditions, is in itself neutral. As such, the work designs and job arrangements 'required' by this technology have been simply responses to the unavaoidable exigencies of industrialization; responses to that constant search for increasing efficiency and productivity which (as commonly pointed out) has benefited us all, though of course (as less commonly pointed out) in widely differing degrees. The consequences we have examined concerning work meanings, job satisfaction and alienation are thus the irresistible 'needs' of our kind of industrial system. It is accepted as inevitable, though regretable, that so many people should find themselves with intrinsically unrewarding work, but the benefits of the system accrue to all and in any case it is not essential that work be a central life interest so long as leisure, family and other non-work activities can serve the same function.

From this view, then, industrialization through technological and organizational development is seen as a practical necessity for social advance; a process which in itself has no political or ideological implications (Dickson 1974). The forms of work and work organization with which we are familiar are dictated by the technology that emerges in response to society's economic needs, aspirations, and pressures. It is within the context of this whole perspective that we find frequent use of such phrases as 'the impact of technology on society' and 'the social consequences of technology'.

Frequently, too, the nature of class and status divisions is seen as a product of these economic and technological 'necessities'. Some sociologists, for example, have analysed social stratification as a 'functional necessity' for all societies. Especially such a complex social system as modern industrial society (East or West) must, it is said, recruit, train, allocate and reward appropriately a great diversity of talents, skills and aptitudes in order to fill the wide range of necessary jobs, some of which are more important, difficult or taxing than others. 'Social inequality is thus an unconsciously evolved device by which societies insure that the most important positions are conscientiously filled by the most qualified persons' (Davis and Moore 1967 p 48).

The received view just briefly sketched has been powerfully challenged (Habermas 1971a). One kind of challenge turns the conventional approach on its head by arguing in effect that the technology and patterns of work organization developed in capitalist society are as much the *effects* as the *causes* of the shape of that society. This type of critique begins by pointing out that industrialization took its rise within a society already deeply stratified in terms of hierarchical and authoritarian class relations of a dominative and exploitative kind. It would seem naive to suppose that, within such a context, technological and organizational innovations are likely to proceed wholly as independent and autonomous forces. More plausible is the supposition that, given the existence of dominant groups or classes dependent for their superior status and material privilege upon their power over subordinate classes, the technology and organizational work patterns developed by the dominant groups are likely to be those that reinforce, can be adapted to, or at least are not incompatible with, the existing hierarchical structure of social control. For example, there is no reason to be surprised that when the early entrepreneur developed his business structure it did not occur to him to establish it on a basis of equality in power, rewards, and status; to institute 'workers' self-management'; to contemplate methods of production which gave major powers of decision-making to those from whom he sought to extract an economic surplus. On the contrary, it was to be expected that the general social relationships between, on the one hand, the propertied, employing and managing classes and, on the other, the propertyless, employed and managed classes would be carried over into the technology and organization of work. The strategic choices made by dominant groups with respect to work technology and organization, in other words, were and are shaped, not only by a concern for efficiency, profit, or whatever, but also by the assumption that they must embody and express the forms of discipline, regimentation and command which uphold the position of the dominant groups themselves. This is not to suggest that these technological choices derive from careful and conscious calculation. Social development is more complex and subtle than that. Rather is it the case that the individual employer, administrator, or top manager is unaware of, or does not seriously consider, any alternative to the hierarchical, authoritarian modes that have evolved and which confront him as 'the going method' when he comes to shape his own structure. Yet it remains true that the going methods evolved as they did because they pursued efficiency or profits through control structures which upheld the status and privileges of dominant groups; it remains true also that such structures persist and are followed often without question for precisely the same reasons. No calculated deliberate decisions were required to maintain this continuity, yet with each business generation these structural forms embodying class relations and class ascendancy become further reinforced, not only in law and usage, but also in people's minds as the obvious and natural way to get things done.

In this way, then, technology and organizational work patterns take on the shape, values and assumptions central to the class structure, and consolidate that structure by sustaining and promoting the interests of the upper strata. To see technology and the social organization built round it as politically neutral is therefore fallacious. Moreover, the very definition of technology as neutral has an ideological, politically biased effect. By representing the patterns of work design and organization with which we are familiar as inevitable necessities of technological development, it offers a legitimating and justifying gloss on what is an essentially political distribution of rewards, status, and other scarce values (Dickson 1974).

This basic challenge to the conventional view comes in various versions. One version would concede that, while those dominant groups pursuing the industrialization process for profit, status, power or related interests have indeed fostered technological and organizational patterns which both expressed and reinforced prevalent structures of hierarchy, privilege and authoritarian control, other consequences must also be noted. First, its advantages have not been monopolized by the dominant groups. Lower strata also have benefited. Second, the industrialization process, while upholding the essential features of the class structure, has also modified it in ways which have softened some of its harsher features. The use of hard, brutalizing manual labour has decreased; the use of middle-strata occupations in the white-collar administrative, professional, technical, and upper manual-work groups has increased. And third, it has stimulated into existence trade-union and political labour movements which, by mobilizing the rank and file, have modified power relations and thereby obliged employers, managers, and administrators to adjust and adapt their behaviour in certain respects to rank-and-file preferences.

Yet the significance of the critical challenge to the received perspective remains. Throughout this chapter the links between, on the one hand, social stratification and, on the other, work meanings, job satisfaction, intrinsic rewards and alienation have become apparent. These links have brought us to the crucial debate as to whether class and status structures are to be seen as the 'effects' of a 'neutral' technology, or whether (or how far) they must be seen as 'causes', in that dominant groups have fostered a preferred (and thereby politically significant) technology and organization which, in sustaining strongly hierarchical patterns of control and division of labour, have generated the work meanings and responses now dominant.

Important implications attach to one's choice between these rival accounts. The first implies what might be called a relatively bland view of society, whereby work meanings and experiences bearing overtones of deprivation, disadvantage, and personality impoverishment are simply the unfortunate and unavoidable consequences of a collective 'social' pursuit of material progress and rising standards of living; consequences which, however, can be fully compensated (by those very rising standards) outside the job situation. It hardly needs emphasizing that such a view is likely to commend itself to those who benefit most from the present system, who will naturally be disposed to encourage its propagation. Understandable also is the fact that they are likely to experience discomfort when presented with the second perspective, which offers a sharper-edged interpretation by drawing attention to the class interests which shape work design — and thereby work meanings and experience. From such a perspective the whole shape and nature of the productive system appears as deeply political, and the businessman's cry of 'Let's keep political interference and doctrinaire ideologies out of business' is regarded as serving an ideological purpose by implying that the design and conduct of business is a purely technical and politically neutral matter.

Conclusion: dynamics of change

We conclude this chapter by pulling together certain major propositions that have emerged, indicating some of the profoundly important and difficult questions which they throw up, and pointing to certain dynamics of potential and actual change that are relevant to these questions.

We have seen that the owners and controllers who administer private and public property in the resources and facilities of production bring an instrumental approach to their task, and that their practical interpretation and enforcement of this approach affords the majority rank and file little scope for self-actualization in work. The minority in higher status occupations are fortunate in that, so far as their own roles are concerned, instrumentalism and self-actualization tend to be compatible rather than mutually exclusive.

For those who consider this one of the most profound of social inequalities, major queries arise to be asked and are beginning to receive answers which carry differing degrees of conviction. How far does the nature and abundance of modern goods and services really require the denial of self-actualization in work for the majority? A few innovators among the controllers, strongly encouraged by some consultants and academics, are concluding from their own experience that a fully effective instrumentalism, in the circumstances of today, may in some situations require a few minor withdrawals from the full application of scientific-management orthodoxy. Confronted with individual or collective behaviour suggestive of that state of alienation that we have defined in terms of a largely instrumental approach to work and an indifference to the wider objectives and values of higher management, management may introduce job enrichment and greater autonomy for the work group. We saw that these tendencies remain limited, however, by the constraints of economic and productive rationality. Although the academics involved often work to a concept of human personality akin to the one outlined in Section 3 *Relative deprivation and privilege*, as do for example Argyris (1964) and Herzberg (1968), they usually go no further than to argue that the self-actualization concept could be applied a good deal more to work design than it is now, without sacrificing economic values.

Similar possibilities of change lie with those managerial decisions to modify technology or organization that are in no sense prompted by special problems of employee behaviour but which stem from technical advance; a change of method, product, or quality; or a general search for increased output, lower costs, or whatever. These may enlarge or reduce the discretionary element in work, the proliferation of rules, and the rigour of control from above. As with the modifications mentioned earlier, they may fulfil or deny, reduce or enlarge people's expectations of work and the meaning they find in it. But certainly among the possibilities is that technological or organizational change pursued by management for instrumental reasons may, as an unintended consequence, create jobs offering somewhat greater intrinsic satisfactions.

Other contributors to the debate (Dickson 1974, Schumacher 1973) offer a more radical approach by urging the adoption of a different type of technology and organization which operates on a smaller and more humane scale (taking into account also, perhaps, ecological and environmental considerations). Those supporting such an approach differ according to whether or not they assert that their preferred productive system is capable of offering a range of goods and services and a level of costs and prices that are comparable with those offered by our present arrangements. Some would argue that, freed from the preconceptions and hitherto unexamined assumptions rooted in past and present patterns of class control, we could devise a productive system which offered a measure of self-actualization for everyone who wanted it but nevertheless maintained a comparable level of productive diversity and efficiency. It is, perhaps, excusable to return a certain scepticism to this argument – a scepticism (as against cynicism) which calls for a fuller elucidation than it has so far received.

Others are ready to concede that a significant and perhaps major sacrifice of productive efficiency, scope and abundance would have to be made, but may argue that this would make for a saner society and is in any case unavoidable since our planet's resources cannot support

economic growth at the present rates. In so far as we were to have the
ability to choose our type of productive system we would have to face
this issue in all its complexities. Some of us may declare ourselves quite
prepared, for example, to forgo the delights of electric tooth-brushes,
colour television, and a new mass-produced car every three years,
should it be shown that the present long and complex chain of extreme
division of labour, large-scale hierarchical organization and advanced
sophisticated technology was incompatible at certain strategic points
with self-actualization in work for all concerned. We may hesitate,
however, if told that the same structures are necessary for producing
the precision-radiography plant that can cure cancer.

Others, of course, in making an informed choice with some knowledge of consequences and alternatives, might well want to retain the
whole range of our present abundance, electric tooth-brushes and all,
even at the cost of forgoing self-actualization for themselves as well
as others. Here we draw attention to man's needs and aspirations as a
consumer. Just because the design of work has hitherto largely ignored
man's needs as a *producer*, that is no justification, when we try to
adjust the balance of concern, for rushing to the equally unacceptable
opposite extreme of ignoring man's needs as a consumer. Should the
aspiration towards self-actualization gain ground, the extent to which
it is believed to conflict with productive abundance might well determine the level of stress and strain that resulted.

These considerations are not to be taken, however, as attempts to
pre-judge the crucial question raised earlier — how far does our present
productive range and output require the denial of self-actualization in
work for the majority? We shall need to be far more alert to this question in future, for if we demand self-actualization for ourselves we
cannot, in equity, deny it to others. A social policy as well as a personal
preference is involved, and an informed choice of policy must rest on
judgements that are as reliable as we can make them.

Our discussion has brought us back, then, to the issue of personal
meanings in work and whether any changes can be detected. How far
will people's rising aspirations become, or remain, focused on instrumental meanings in work and how far will they shift towards intrinsic
meanings? The factors making for the former are compelling. The
multifarious pressures, inducements, and appeals of 'consumerism' (of
which mass advertising is only the most obvious example) are influential in reinforcing the instrumental emphasis on financial rewards. But
of equal importance, those with the greatest power to design work
and work organizations — themselves usually enjoying intrinsic as well
as greatly superior extrinsic rewards — are likely to have little personal

or professional interest in promoting intrinsic values in work for others except insofar as such a policy contributes to efficiency or profits. Governments are likely to support such priorities.

It is currently virtually impossible, therefore, for anyone seeking to contribute to public policy in this field, to reject the criteria of economic growth and technological advance and continue to be regarded as a 'responsible' participant by those wielding power and influence. A recent report commissioned by Britain's Department of Employment (Wilson 1973) contains a preface by the then Secretary of State. He emphasized a point made in the Department's *Code of Industrial Relations Practice* to the effect that 'managements, recognizing the need of employees to achieve a sense of satisfaction in their jobs, should provide for it *so far as is practicable*' (italics added). He meant, of course, so far as it is seen as compatible with efficiency or profits. He continued, 'People are then more likely to . . . feel committed to their jobs and willing to accept greater responsibility. This is one important way in which people can use their talents and energies more effectively and the country make the most of their use' (Wilson 1973 p iii). The instrumental overtones are apparent. They are equally so in the report that follows. Its author displays keen sensitivity to the intrinsic values in work, but conveys the sense that they must be pursued only in so far as they promote, or are at least compatible with, full economic viability measured in terms of 'total accounting'. This, he believes, gives some scope for improvement in the quality of working life. 'There have been quite convincing demonstrations . . . that modern work systems can be devised to meet the needs of a competitive economy while at the same time affording a range of jobs which are at the least comparatively satisfying and progressive for most of the people available to do them' (Wilson 1973 p 44). Underlying the note of hope here is a sense of the economic limits which he clearly believes must moderate our expectations. Others would draw those limits a good deal tighter. Strauss, for example, emphasizes the range of jobs which it would be 'prohibitively expensive' to redesign for purposes of self-actualization (Strauss 1963 p 48).

In so far as it is argued that members of lower occupational strata must continue to be denied intrinsic satisfactions for the sake of economic benefits accruing to 'society as a whole' support is sought from the Dubin arguments. For most industrial employees, we are reminded, work is largely an instrumental activity that plays no central part in their life and personal fulfilment. Why, it is argued, should we not accept this preferential emphasis on the financial rewards as the expression of a free choice, thereby not only respecting their right to choose but also conferring economic benefits upon 'society as a whole' at the same time? It is surely a perfectly legitimate preference for people to accept a sacrifice of personal fulfilment in work in order to dervice larger economic resources for pursuing personal fulfilment outside work. This, it has been said, may disappoint some academics, but they must learn not to impose their own value judgements on others (Strauss 1963 pp 47—52). Indeed, the fact that so many people do not aspire to self-actualization in work

> . . . may be a fortunate thing . . . Should we say, 'Thank God for the number of people who have made an apparent adjustment to routine jobs. Would that there were more'? Perhaps . . . it would be best to devote our resources to ever-shortening the work week and helping people to enjoy their leisure more fully. (Strauss 1963 pp 55—6)

Our previous discussion suggests three points that can be brought to bear on this position. First, any notion that the members of a society, or the participants in an organization of work, collectively choose the social meaning embodied in the productive system and its social relations must be rejected. Employees are not consulted about the ends and means of the organizations in which they work, which represent for the most part the strategic choices of those vested with control over private and public property. Second, even were people to be presented, in our *existing* social context, with the chance to choose between, on the one hand, self-actualization in work at a lower level of material standards and, on the other, higher material standards at the cost of self-actualization, their choice could by no means be described as a free and informed one. Some would feel constrained by sheer economic need to choose the latter; others would be similarly constrained by family background and other early conditioning, or as a consequence of public communications which urge or assume the supreme importance of 'consumerism' and the materialist values it embodies. Many in the lower occupational strata would simply not have the sorts of experience, aspiration or opportunities necessary for judging the respective merits and demerits of the two ways of life. Few of us yet have what is necessary for making a judgement, of the kind referred to earlier, as to how far our present productive output of goods and services is really dependent upon existing beliefs and assumptions concerning the design of work and work organization. The third and final point relates to the implicit acceptance of profound inequality contained in the position we are examining. When a comparison is drawn between (a) the type of productive system currently operating in which efficiency and material abundance are pursued at the expense of employee self-actualization in the lower ranks, and (b) one that cultivates the latter at the expense of the former, it becomes clear that it is the higher occupational strata who benefit most from the choice currently made, for as we have seen the higher strata enjoy both superior material rewards *and* opportunities for self-actualization. When Strauss thanks his Maker and declares it fortunate that so many in the lower ranks manage to adjust to their lot, we may fairly ask: fortunate for whom? It can scarcely be denied that those faring best from existing choices are those in the upper ranks, who of course have most say in the choosing. It is perhaps worth noting in this context that Barrington Moore, in his conclusions to a massive work of painstaking scholarship tracing the diverse paths pursued by different countries towards 'modernization' (parliamentary democracy, fascism, communism), comments that,

> . . . there is no evidence that the mass of the population anywhere has wanted an industrial society, and plenty of evidence that they did not. All forms of industrialization so far has been revolutions from above, the work of a ruthless minority (Moore 1973 p 506)

It is noticeable that those who would dismiss such observations with the argument that 'the mass of the population' did not know what was good for them, and enjoyed industrialization once they got it, are often quick, as Strauss is, to disparage philosophies and ideologies which challenge the *status quo* on the ground that people must be left 'free' to choose their own values and not have other people's preferences forced down their throat.

In returning to our present theme it has to be recognized, however, that Strauss's perspective may well prove to be the one that prevails. It is by no means impossible that in general people will remain adapted to the system of finding their meaningful life outside work, especially if working hours are reduced and leisure facilities (themselves becoming profitable mass industries) are increased. The quality of such a civilization is a large question which cannot be touched on here.

There remain, though, other possibilities. How far *homo sapiens* can continue to predicate his society on the pursuit of rising material affluence has itself become a keenly debated moral and ecological question and the answer could impose major constraints on the issue we are considering. But also significant are small signs here and there in advanced industrial societies of a decline in 'willingness to take on meaningless work in authoritarian settings that offers only extrinsic rewards' (*Work in America* 1973 p 47). Worth recalling here is the fact that the rising standards of living promoted by industrialization, in freeing numbers of people from the preoccupying toil required for sheer survival, have left them with the time and energy to develop a consciousness of themselves as unique individuals with a right to live, grow and make something of their time on earth. This is, in fact, among the factors creating the modern 'problem of work'. In the past, as in many parts of the world still today, most people struggled simply to survive. They existed anonymously, accepted fate, and died having experienced little or no consciousness of an individualized personality with its own aspirations. For growing numbers this is no longer true. The change would seem, on the face of it, to constitute a fruitful soil, in the long run at least, for that conception, meaning or ideology of work which stresses its potential significance for self-realization.

America and Scandinavian countries already demonstrate minor symptoms, and in France and other Western countries the whole debate is far more vigorous than in Britain. A recent American survey, covering a national sample of over 1500 people, and conducted jointly by the US Department of Labor and the Survey Research Center of the University of Michigan, found that:

> Although the respondents' need for economic security and personal health and safety were paramount, there was ample indication that daily satisfaction, or the reverse, in one's job was substantially connected with the so-called intrinsic factors in work situations. (Wilson 1973 p 15)

The gathering debate could itself contribute to a quickening of aspirations in this field. The influence of international agencies in stimulating the debate may not be negligible. The Director-General of the International Labour Office, in his Report to the International Labour Conference of 1972, argued that:

> Job satisfaction and the humanization of work must now rank high on the agenda of social policy. Should not the ILO play a much larger role in the identification of opportunities and the promotion of policies and practices, for humanizing man's life at work? Our constitutional mandate in the matter is clear . . . We have hardly yet begun to discharge this injunction . . . (Jenks 1972 p 37)

The Michigan survey report concludes by noting that 'The health of the economy is still measured solely in terms of the efficiency with which it can produce large quantities of consumer goods' — and that considerable progress has been made in this direction. But it stresses a second basic need — 'self-fulfilment of individuals through their work' — which has barely begun to be recognized. We must conclude our discussion of future possibilities, therefore, with the observation that the situation remains open.

One last point remains to be made. It has been argued in the preceding pages that the existing design of work and work organizations rests on a given distribution of power in society, and that power superiority has lain, and still lies, with those whose interests or objectives led them to impose a wholly instrumental criterion. We have noted, also, that in so far as they come to believe their interests or objectives will be served by marginal changes in some jobs towards less fragmented and less unsatisfying tasks, they will offer these changes unbidden. It would be sentimental and misleading, however, to conclude without registering the probability that they will strongly resist, both at the practical organizational level and at the ideological level, any proposed changes which seek employee self-actualization *at the expense* of economic values. In other words, since the present predominant social meaning in work is upheld by power, any fundamental change to a different meaning would require a major challenge to existing power dispositions in society; a challenge which could hardly be limited to work design alone, but would extend to all the associated structures, values and relationships which we find ourselves noting in this and other chapters of this book.

CHAPTER 6

Janet Woollacott

Dirty and deviant work

> Now the delegation of dirty work to someone else is common among
> humans. Many cleanliness taboos, and perhaps, even many moral
> scruples, depend for their practice upon success in delegating the
> tabooed activity to someone else. (Hughes 1958 p 52)

The importance of work in the determination of the sub-cultures in
which people live, the images which people have of themselves and the
weltanschauung or world-vision through which people construct their
version of social reality and the specific social relationships in which
they are involved, have been heavily stressed in the sociology of work. It
is important, however, to see this discussion in relation to occupations
and activities which are frequently seen as external to the 'normal' world
of work. Criminal occupations, the work of concentration camp guards,
of prostitutes, blue-movie makers and many others are rarely seen as
having much in common with work in factories or offices.

However, although differences between occupations and occupational
cultures exist and must be discussed, there are also shared characteristics
in most forms of work in capitalist societies which are worth examining.
Sociologists have, therefore, approached quite wide-ranging activities
and attempted to understand them in terms of a specific conceptual
framework. This comment on the organization of crime indicates the
way in which criminal 'work' can be analysed along very similar lines
to more legitimate forms of work. Professional criminals can then be
studied like any other occupational group.

> . . . we can study not only why people take up this occupation, as
> criminologists have traditionally done but also how the occupational
> tasks are divided up and interrelated, how working groups and
> communities and other groups are alike. We can study the social
> organization of professional crime because it is a socially ordered

activity. Professional criminals follow the rules and customs of their work much as other workers do. It is said that there is 'honour among thieves'; in fact the mutual expectations among criminals go far beyond mere honour, and cover all the understandings and agreements necessary to their co-operative activity. (McIntosh 1971 p 98)

Of course, differences, for example in the relationship of an occupation with the overall authority structure in a society, can be crucial to the understanding of that occupation. As McIntosh points out, the curious feature of the criminal world she outlines above is the 'willingness to disobey some of the rules of the state and yet to abide by the custom of their own group' (McIntosh 1971 p 98). Any examination of deviant and dirty work clearly has to take into account both *continuities* and *discontinuities* with more 'legitimate' or more 'normal' occupations.

The way in which particular kinds of work are seen as 'dirty' or 'deviant', and the distinction of that kind of work from that which is 'clean' and 'normal', is of considerable significance in understanding not only the real problems faced by people engaged in 'dirty' work but also the place of specific kinds of work in a capitalist society and in the legitimating ideology of the class structure of that society. Interactionist studies have tended to concentrate on the former area, a logical consequence of the assumptions of many interactionists that work roles and the meanings attached to work are important in the definition and maintenance of a person's self-image. Such assumptions have been questioned within the interactionist tradition. Dubin, for example, in a study of American manual workers, suggests that 'the central life interests' of the workers lay outside of work (Dubin 1962 p 247). However, a great deal of research in the sociology of work has been concerned with the professions or with those occupations undergoing a process of professionalization, and in this approach, identification and commitment of self and work has been heavily emphasized. To some extent the notion of 'dirty work' is related to this kind of approach in its focus on the problems and reactions of people to doing work which they or others regard as 'dirty'. Interactionist studies of deviance have centred similarly on the reactions of people within certain groups to being labelled 'deviant'.

Hughes argues that 'dirty work' is defined in the process of social interaction, and those who do dirty work, so defined, may experience difficulties in interaction and may have to learn to adjust to carrying a certain social stigma (Hughes 1958). He also argues somewhat paradoxically that all occupations contain a form of dirty work, and that it constitutes a part of any job:

Now every occupation is not one but several activities; some of them
are the dirty work of that trade. It may be dirty in one of several
ways. It may be simply physically disgusting. It may be a symbol of
degradation, something that wounds one's dignity. Finally, it may be
dirty work in that it in some way goes counter to the more heroic
of our moral conceptions. Dirty work of some kind is found in all
occupations. It is hard to imagine an occupation in which one does
not appear, in certain repeated contingencies, to be practically
compelled to play a role, of which he thinks he ought to be a little
ashamed. Insofar as an occupation carries with it a self-conception, a
notion of personal dignity, it is likely that at some point one will feel
he is having to do something that is *infra dignitate.* (Hughes 1958
p 50)

The last sentence is indicative of the central Hughesian conception of
'dirty work'. It is not so much physically dirty work as work which
involves a personal sense of degradation on the part of its practitioners.

The examples which Hughes uses to illustrate the notion of 'dirty
work' are quite illuminating. In his discussion, janitors, prison guards
and hospital attendants all feel in some sense contaminated by 'dirty
work'. On the face of it, there are several occupations which spring to
mind as either physically more dirty or more publicly disapproved of
than the work of, say, janitors. Yet janitors are extremely important in
the presentation of Hughes's argument. Using the work of one of his
graduate students, Hughes examines the bitterness with which janitors
view the 'dirty work' of their profession. Apparently, the revulsion
with which janitors react to garbage collection is not merely physical
but is aggravated by the way in which it represents for them their
relationship with their tenants. The part that garbage collection plays
in the janitor's job is seen by the janitors as reinforcing the tenant's
low opinion. Garbage collection is Hughes's archetypal 'dirty work'.
Garbage collection is not only physically dirty but it carries with it a
formidable barrier to the acquisition of desired higher social status on
the part of janitors. Janitors are, therefore, understandably sensitive
about the collection of rubbish since, despite their higher incomes, it
implies servant status in their power relationship with white-collar
tenants. It is noticeable that janitors 'serve' upper class tenants with
much less resentment and internal conflict. At the same time, and
somewhat ironically, the information about their tenants, which janitors
can derive from the garbage, provides basis for their power position in
refusing or 'managing' tenant demands.

Hughes assumes that delegation of dirty work to others is an integral
part of occupational mobility. He argues, for example, that nurses have

delegated work to attendants and cleaning staff, in an attempt to increase the prestige of their occupation. He also considers, however, that certain high-status occupations intimately involve dirty work, and that in cases like these, 'the dirty work is somewhat integrated into the whole, and into the prestige-bearing role of the person who does it' (Hughes 1958 p 52). Medicine, for example, is seen as involving a 'deeply satisfying definition of role' despite the handling of the human body which Hughes sees as constituting the dirty work of the medical profession. It could, of course, be argued that doctors do delegate much dirty work to those of lower status, and over time have rid themselves of their tasks in this respect. However, Hughes locates his idea of dirty work within the social relationships of work, in what he calls 'the social drama of work', in the crucial relationships with that category of persons with whom people at work regularly come into contact: janitor and tenant; doctor and patient; musician and audience. The central problem for people in such occupations, according to Hughes, is 'the maintenance of a certain freedom and social distance from those people most crucially and intimately concerned with one's work' (Hughes 1958 p 53).

Definitions of work like 'dirty work' are obviously related to the power of particular groups to project such definitions and maintain them over time, and this is an area of discussion which Hughes largely ignores. He concentrates instead on groups which accentuate and react to such definitions. Gold's research on janitors indicates that janitors believe their tenants' view of them. None of the janitors interviewed by Gold rejected the tenants' definition of the occupational group but took instead the attitude that he personally is 'different and better' (Gold 1952). Janitors accept labels or definitions from above, a key factor in their vulnerability to degradation (Garfinkel 1956). Hughes recognizes that 'dirty work' tends to be identified and then repudiated by *aspirants to professional status* but goes no further. It is arguable, however, that professional status is closely linked to the power of the members of an occupation to define their work for those people with whom they come into contact. If we compare the situation of janitors with that of doctors, this becomes much clearer. The 'deeply satisfying definition of role' which doctors enjoy is effectively based on occupational power (Hughes 1958 p 52). Johnson's proposition that 'professionalism arises where the tensions inherent in the producer-consumer relationship are controlled by means of an institutional framework based upon occupational authority' (Johnson 1972 p 51) indicates some of the processes involved in professionalization. Struggles over managing tensions in the doctor/patient relationship permeate doctors' and patients' actions in most historical documentation of the occupation

(Freidson 1962). However, doctors acquired control and professional status in the expansion of middle class bureaucracy in the second half of the nineteenth century; and in the setting up of occupational associations, they not only acquired control over occupational behaviour but also over consumer or non-occupational behaviour. In this situation, the relationship between 'professional' and 'client' is initiated by the client and terminated by the professional. Moreover, the professional controls the image of his work to which his clients and others respond. Tensions still exist within the relationship between doctor and patient but potentially 'difficult' situations are 'managed' via the ideology of diagnostic competence. Diagnostic and therapeutic ideologies are particularly influential in our society. For example, in a similar way to the medical profession, American funeral directors attempt to propagate a particular image of their work, in which the 'dirty work' of embalming is placed firmly in the background, and aesthetic and service considerations in the forefront, although their control is much less effective than that pertaining to medicine (Haberstein 1962).

The treatment of 'dirty work' in Hughes's discussion is not unlike certain interactionist approaches to deviance which stress the importance of 'labelling'. Hughes argues that the labelling of dirty work has consequences for the way in which those doing it are treated by others, and seen by themselves. The dirty work of some occupations is integrated into a satisfying role image, in other occupations it is not. Those workers in non-powerful and non-prestigious occupations face problems of 'adjustment', to use interactionist terminology. The interactionist approach to deviance follows much the same lines. In *Outsiders*, for example, Becker argues that 'deviance is not a quality that lies in behaviour itself, but in the interaction between the person who commits an act and those who respond to it' (Becker 1963 p 14). The book is explicitly concerned with the effects of labelling on deviant careers. Hence Becker describes the career of the dance musician, whose view of his work is not shared by other people. Dance musicians have conceptions of themselves which differ from and, therefore, conflict with the non-musicians for whom they work, and vice versa.

Labelling is particularly important in the interactionist perspective in terms of what Goffman calls 'social stigma' and its consequences for the self. Being labelled as a 'prostitute' or a 'criminal', as 'deviant' or 'dirty', involves a similar kind of stigma as physical disability and may initiate a similar kind of moral career. Joining a stigmatized group, then, involves overcoming the 'normal' response to stigma and accepting its members in ordinary human terms. Initiates may well be surprised that they do not find members of the group repellent or strange. A girl's

description of her entry into prostitution and into meeting her first
madam indicates her implicit 'normal' assumptions about what a madam
should be like:

> When I turned into Fourth Street my courage again failed me, and I
> was about to beat a retreat when Mamie came out of a restaurant
> across the street and warmly greeted me. The porter who came to
> the door in response to our ring said that Miss Laura was in her room
> and we were shown in. I saw a woman comely and middle-aged, who
> bore no resemblance to the horrible creature of my imagination.
> She greeted me in a soft well-bred voice, everything about her so
> eloquently spoke of her potentialities for motherhood that instinc-
> tively I looked around for the children who should have been cling-
> ing to her skirts. (Goffman 1963 p 53)

The major problem for those who are engaged in stigmatized work
of this kind seems to be in dealing with people outside the stigmatized
group. A professional criminal recounts with some bitterness the
embarrassments and difficulties of dealing with non-criminals:

> I remember a man coming to see me, a straight man he was, and he
> looked along that row of books over there on the shelves and said:
> 'You know it's really amazing you should read books like this, I'm
> staggered I am. I should have thought you would read paperback
> thrillers, things with lurid covers, books like that. And here you are
> with Claud Cockburn, Hugh Klare, Simone de Beauvoir and Laurence
> Durrell.'
> You know he didn't see this as an insulting remark at all: in fact, I
> think he thought he was being honest in telling me how mistaken he
> was. And that's exactly the sort of patronizing you get from straight
> people if you're a criminal. 'Fancy that!' they say. 'In some ways
> you're just like a human being!' I'm not kidding it makes me want to
> choke the bleeding life out of them. (Parker and Allerton 1962 p 111)

The group which shares social stigma, however, provides emotional
support and a counterview of the 'normal' world.

It is not only criminal groups and the most obviously stigmatized
occupational groups, which provide support for their members. Poets,
artists and musicians all provide evidence to suggest that interaction
with people outside the occupational group may be difficult. Indeed,
artists are often preoccupied with the problems of necessary interaction
with audiences. Auden points to the way in which poets may lack the
respect and attention which they desire from audiences:

> The ideal audience the poet imagines consists of the beautiful who
> go to bed with him, the powerful who invite him to dinner and tell

him secrets of state, and his fellow poets. The actual audience he
gets consists of myopic school-teachers, pimply young men who eat
in cafeterias and his fellow poets. This means that, in fact, he writes
for his fellow poets. (Auden quoted in Abbott 1948 p 176)

Artists and poets, like members of other stigmatized occupations, tend
to turn to other artists and poets for understanding, practical help and
emotional support and in so doing they often *reject* the values and
mores of people outside their own occupational group. In Allerton's
case, he declares that it is the opinion of other criminals and their
friendship which matter to him, rather than his relationships with
people who are straight. It is clear that occupational groups can provide
security for their members to a lesser or a greater degree. Allerton is
involved in a socially ordered world, which provides workable definitions of self and situation.

Early studies of prostitution suggested that East End prostitutes
derived considerable security, both personal and practical, from the
group with which they work. Would-be reformers of prostitutes were
often disturbed by the lack of concern about the 'normal' condemnation of prostitutes in those they were intending to reform. Only comparatively few of the *16,000* women interviewed in Merrick's (1890 p 5
quoted in Pearson 1972) study reported that their entry into prostitution conformed with the sex campaigner's view in terms of being
'betrayed by gentlemen'. The occupational culture of prostitution was
often blamed for the reluctance of many prostitutes to be converted
by reformers to the 'normal' view of their work. Indeed, when Rolph
(1955) broaches the question of leaving prostitution, in a much later
research project, the strength of the supportive culture of prostitution
is stressed in opposition to the explicitly reformist position of the
research.

Clearly, however, those working in stigmatized occupations have
to adjust to interacting with people who have a view of them which
they don't share, and one way of avoiding a certain degree of ambivalence is to embrace the world-vision of the occupational group.

The legitimization of otherwise stigmatized actions as 'work' is quite
common amongst occupational groups labelled as deviant or dirty.
Allerton, for example, is quick to deny allegations that he does not
work for his living. He argues that

Most crime – unless it's the senseless petty thieving sort – is quite
hard work. . .
    Planning a job, working out all the details of the best way to do
it – and then carrying it out; under a lot of nervous strain and

tension — and then having to run around afterwards, if it's goods, fencing the stuff, getting a good price for it, delivering it to the fence, and so on — all this needs a lot of thinking and effort and concentration. It certainly is 'work', don't kid yourself about that. (Parker and Allerton 1962 p 86)

Justifications of large-scale criminal organization in America as 'business' follow similar lines. As Capone is reported to have said, 'There was too much overhead in my business anyhow, paying off all the time. . . They ought to make it legitimate' (Ness and Fraley 1967). Male prostitutes have also been known to reject the label of 'homosexual' since they are more concerned with earning money or hustling (Reiss 1964). Working as a male prostitute is, in their eyes, not to be confused with being homosexual:

No matter how many queers a guy goes with, if he goes for money, that don't make him queer. You're still straight. It's when you start going for free with other young guys, that you start growing wings. (Reiss 1964 p 184)

To some extent, it can be argued that this kind of 'adjustment' provides a balance between the 'normal' acceptable viewpoint and that of the 'outsider' group. The work and money motive is acceptable in the 'normal' world, if the action necessary to acquire it is not. Indeed, deviant groups which 'work' have a claim on 'normality' in a capitalist 'utilitarian culture' which other groups may not have. It has been claimed, for example, that the kind of drug use which has been labelled deviant is hedonistic, whereas drug use for health purposes or for relaxation from work is not condemned (Young 1971).

On the other hand certain occupations or roles are seen as deviant precisely because of their non-utilitarian character. The influence of the Protestant ethic in capitalist societies, the idea that work is good for its own sake, runs counter to the work of the poet or the artist, which stresses sensuous pleasure in words or paint or music and which is rarely routinized. R.N. Wilson argues that the poet's role is deviant in American society:

Americans do things and go places. The poet does things and goes places too, only he does unusual things and goes to uncharted places. This in itself may make him an object of suspicion. But he is guilty of a worse crime and one which sets his role more incontrovertibly against the American temper: his efforts have no obvious utility. In this respect he is more deviant than the gangster, whose role at least has an objective utility for himself in that it may make him rich before it makes him dead. (Wilson 1964 p 17)

Artists and poets experience particular problems of interaction because of their ambivalent position. However, artists can turn to the Renaissance creative view of work as a legitimation of their activities and it is largely in terms of 'creativity', 'genius' and 'originality' that they present their own work. Members of art occupations, indeed, legitimate their work in very different ways to those groups involved in deviant or dirty work, which can still point to the 'personal' or 'social' utility of their activities.

Although the importance of labelling in particular empirical situations cannot be ignored, and the labelling perspective can be quite illuminating about particular aspects of people's reactions to labelling, labelling does not in itself constitute an adequate theory of why deviance occurs or concomitantly why dirty work is identified and repudiated. Many of the ideas of the interactionists, and particularly those who are concerned with the effects of labelling or social reaction, pose certain problems. Ideologically, the stress of labelling theory on injustice, scapegoating and stigmatizing is obviously sympathetic to the underdog and this was perhaps an understandable reaction in deviance studies away from the 'pathology' approach of identifying criminal and deviant types which preceded it. Nevertheless, the vision early interactionists seemed to have of people reacting to labelling is one in which adjustment seems to be the only possibility and 'making out' became the focal point of interactionist theoretical expertise (Gouldner 1971). The preoccupation of theorists like Becker, Goffman and others with the way in which being labelled by another group of people can change a person's conception of self and lead to a situation where there is a progressive commitment to deviance often assumed that labels fall from the sky in an arbitrary manner and then set in motion an excessively deterministic social psychological trigger mechanism.

Moreover, Becker's account of deviance is not at all clear in that he presents two models of deviance in a parallel but somewhat contradictory way. It has been argued that these constitute common-sense and sociological models of deviance and that Becker seems to confuse the relationships between the two (Pollner 1974). The common-sense model is one in which deviance is seen as inhering in the act. However, Becker at other times proposes that:

> Social groups create deviance by making the rules whose infraction constitutes deviance, and by applying those rules to particular people and labelling them as outsiders. From this point of view deviance is *not* a quality of the act the person commits, but rather a consequence of the application by others of rules and sanctions to an 'offender'. The deviant is one to whom that label has successfully been applied;

deviant behaviour is behaviour people so label. (Becker 1963 p 9)

The double model of rule-breaking and labelling is present in this statement, although Becker tends to concentrate on the labelling perspective. In one way Becker is right to avoid a purely 'labelling' approach in that such an approach notably fails to take into account 'the idiom of common-sense possibilities which informs and infuses common-sense talk about deviance' (Pollner 1974 p 33). But Becker's own typology confuses the two models of deviance and violates the definition of deviance based on labelling. The whole idea of a 'real' deviant becomes implausible in the labelling schemes and 'mistakes' in identification of deviance are impossible.

Table 1

	Obedient behaviour	Rule-breaking behaviour
Perceived as deviant	falsely accused	pure deviant
Not perceived as deviant	conforming	secret deviant

Source: Becker (1963 p 20)

If deviant behaviour is that so labelled, the category of 'secret deviance' is an impossibility and the category 'falsely accused' poses great difficulty. The typology is not, as it purports to be, a conception of the phenomenon of deviance based on labelling, but involves an understanding of deviance in which deviance is seen as objective and real, and in which labelling is of only secondary importance. Becker himself recognizes in later work the difficulties of reserving the title of deviance solely for rule-breaking behaviour which is so labelled.

There are also certain practical problems to the labelling definition. Becker's argument implies that most actions have no social meaning until a labelling process has taken place, and this can be somewhat misleading. While it is possible to show that the same action can be treated as deviant or non-deviant depending on the label applied to it, acts do possess meanings dependent on the social context which are not arbitrary and of which most people are aware. Killing, for example, may be legitimate in war-time but not when working for 'Murder Incorporated', but most people are aware of the differences between the two actions in terms of their social meaning within the authority structure of their society. Hughes in a rather similar way to Becker seems to see definitions of dirty work emerging in the course of social interaction at work rather than in a wider historical context. The stress in interactionist studies always tends to be on the immediate 'fore-

ground' of social life. One route out of this concentration on labelling
in creating a self-conscious commitment to particular kinds of work is
to examine and distinguish the different social processes involved:

1 how particular kinds of action come to be labelled deviant,
   criminal or dirty;
2 what happens to people when such labels are applied.

If we examine the work of the SS, particularly in the concentration
camps, some of the problems of the labelling perspective emerge and it
is also possible to show the analytic distinctions between dirty work,
deviance and crime in a practical situation where they overlap.

The SS who manned the concentration camps and carried out the
Nazi 'final solution' to the 'Jewish problem' have been said to have
carried out 'the most colossal and dramatic piece of social dirty work
the world has ever known' (Hughes 1958 p 23). They are particularly
interesting in relation to the arguments discussed here because of the
rapid and extreme changes in the 'labelling' of the work they carried
out. Within Nazi Germany they constituted an elite corps doing
important, necessary, if 'dirty', work. The internal propaganda of the
SS, if not their general reputation in Germany and outside, laid stress
on their racial supremacy, their 'heroism' and their 'hardness'. After the
war they were seen as criminals and 'deviants', and the kindliest thing
that was said of them was that they were pathologically disturbed and,
therefore, not entirely responsible for their actions.

Hughes suggests that the 'final solution' represents dirty work that
'got out of hand', that the work of the SS was different from the work
of, say, ordinary prison guards only in the matter of degree and that
this, to a large extent, explains why the 'good people' of Germany
could countenance at least partial knowledge of what went on within
the concentration camps. He argues, therefore, that most Germans
wanted a 'solution to the Jewish problem', even though most of them
would have shrunk from the actions of the SS, and that, in this sense,
the SS were a pariah group carrying out the will of the German people.
Hughes seems unaware that this was precisely how the SS legitimated
its actions in its internal propaganda. Even during the war and at the
height of their power, the SS enjoyed a somewhat unsavoury reputation.
Bettelheim records the satisfaction with which prisoners at Buchenwald
learnt that the soldiers of the Death's Head units of the Gestapo borrow-
ed uniforms from other units when they visited the nearby town of
Weimar, because 'nice girls' there refused to have anything to do with
them (Bettelheim 1961).

Leaders of the SS recognized their unpopularity; indeed, it must have been difficult to avoid doing so, but they did rationalize what they did as necessary 'dirty work' for which Germany would eventually be grateful:

> Heydrich came up to me, and looking over my left shoulder, said solemnly, 'Abroad they take us for bloodhounds, don't they?' and then: 'It is almost too difficult for some people but we must be hard as granite. Otherwise our Führer's work will come to nothing. Later people will thank us for what we have taken upon ourselves.' (Carl Jakob Burckhardt quoted in Bucheim 1968 p 339)
> I know that many people in Germany shrink when they see our black tunic; we recognize this and do not expect to be beloved by too many people. But all who have Germany at heart will and must respect us. . . . (Himmler quoted in Bucheim 1968 p 390)

Similarly, members of the SS who supervised the extermination camps justified their actions afterwards in terms of obedience and efficiency. The commander of Auschwitz, Hoess, described what he did as work carrying out an extermination programme, the reasons for which seemed to him to be 'right' (Hoess 1961):

> But from the very beginning I was so absorbed, I might say obsessed with the task that every fresh difficulty only increased my zeal. I was determined that nothing should get me down. My pride would not allow it. I lived only for my work. (Hoess 1961 p 122)

Outside the SS, other National Socialists attempted to remain politically neutral and to concentrate instead on their 'work'. Albert Speer in a memorandum to Hitler said that:

> The task which I have to fulfil is an unpolitical one. I felt comfortable in my work so long as my person and also my work were valued solely according to my specialist achievement. (Fest 1972 p 299)

Within the SS, duty, obedience and work replaced consciousness of wrongdoing. Himmler's speeches typically bewail the weight of responsibility involved in carrying out the order to annihilate the Jews, emphasizing how repugnant the work was to the nature of Germanic man, but at the same time, he stresses the *duty* of National Socialists to perform their historic task.

While the notion of 'dirty work' tells us something about the *legitimation* of the work of the SS, particularly within the camps, it tells us little more since Hughes, like many interactionists, rarely deals with the organization of power in societies, which is precisely what makes categories like 'dirty work' and 'deviance' understandable in a broader context. Within the *weltanschauung* of Nazi Germany, the actions of the SS could be construed as 'dirty work'. Many Nazis and upper echelon members of the SS describe their physical disgust as watching the torture and murder of the Jews and the effort required to maintain 'efficiency' in these circumstances. Himmler's speeches constantly refer to the problem.

Himmler's own squeamishness is well documented despite his readiness to commit murder under his orders (Fest 1972 p 185). However, there is also evidence that many Germans at the time regarded the actions of the SS as criminal rather than 'dirty work' and that far from carrying out the will of the German people, the SS was constructed expressly to carry out the will of the Führer and the Nazi party. Hitler claimed the right to remould the German state entirely according to his own judgement and, revealingly, he once called the German people his 'instrument'. This relationship is symbolized for the SS in the oath of allegiance which was given to Hitler rather than the German state, and which indicated the special loyalty owed to the Führer by members of the party and the SS.

Moreover, many of the orders emanating from Hitler were never brought into line with the existing legal system, even by subsequent legal interpretation (Bucheim 1968). Hitler's 1939 instructions on euthanasia and his order for the murder of the Jews certainly belonged in this category. Hitler's own attitude to the law was contemptuous. He once told Hans Frank, 'Here I stand with my bayonets, there you stand with your law. We'll see which counts for more!' (Fest 1972). Within Hitler's state the actions of the SS were legitimated. At the same time, changes in the labelling of the actions of the SS from 'criminal' to 'dirty work' and back to 'criminal' again correspond to changes in the power structure of German society. Labelling was not arbitrary. Nazi Germany effectively brought a stop to the previous legal system and made hitherto criminal and deviant acts 'normal' and to a large extent 'acceptable' both within the SS and outside it. After the war, this was reversed. As Goebbels realized, changes in the interpretation of Nazi policies and actions was always possible given the failure of the Nazi party to retain power. 'We shall go down in history,' he remarked, 'as the greatest statesmen of all time, or as the greatest criminals' (Fest 1972 p 158).

Bracher points to the transformation of the structure of government whereby the police and the SS state developed alongside and were interconnected with the normal court and state bureaucracy. Bucheim argued that Hitler basically despised the law, regarding legal regulations as 'no better than politically inept limitations upon his freedom of

decision and action' (Bucheim 1968 p 131). He suggests that the legal
activity of the regime, in particular the Nuremberg laws on race, were
freaks in a state that was otherwise committed to illegal action:

> ... the Nuremberg racial laws are an astonishing phenomenon.
> Although the historical evidence is not conclusive, it would seem
> that, in so far as discrimination against the Jews was concerned, the
> Nuremberg laws were calculated to bring to an end the previous legal
> uncertainty, which had provided a fruitful field for terrorism of all
> descriptions: at least the laws produced a norm giving the victims
> certain possibilities of protecting themselves. *The factual content of
> the racial laws was of course evil*; in comparison to the previously
> existing situation, however, it was at least measurable evil and all
> experience of existence under totalitarian tyranny shows that this
> is more tolerable than sheer unpredictable arbitrary action. The
> purpose of Stuckart's and Globke's famous objections was to codify
> the restrictions placed upon the Jews with even greater precision and
> to lay down as many practical details as possible, in order to give
> them some security in such rights as were left to them. Persecution
> of the Jews with complete social ostracism and ultimate genocide
> as its aim was, of course, general National Socialist policy, and so the
> breathing space gained by the Nuremberg laws was short-lived. Illegal
> measures became the rule once more and finally culminated in mass
> murder. (Bucheim 1968 p 132)

Bucheim regarded the Nuremberg laws largely in terms of their relationship to the proven 'criminality' of the SS, in that they could not
provide legal justification for the actions of SS guards in Auschwitz,
for example. He sees the laws, therefore, as providing a 'break' in the
chain of non-official terrorism. However, this argument to some extent
neglects the important role played by the 'regular' legislation of the
regime in providing legitimation not only for the Nuremberg 'restrictions' and 'control' of the Jews but also for *further* actions against the
Jews.

It was precisely the meshing and interlinking of the SS state or the
'Führer executive' with the normal German state bureaucracy which
both screened and legitimated terror and violence. The Nuremberg laws
are particularly important because they illustrate so well the encroachment of the SS on norms of justice and law, which continued outwardly
to exist, while in reality serving as a facade for the absolute power of
the Leader. As Bracher points out, 'the basic law of the Third Reich'
was the 'omnipotent power of the Führer':

> The creation of the system of terror and extermination and the
> functioning of the police and the SS *apparatchiks* operating that

system rested on this over-turning of all legal and moral norms by a totalitarian leader principle which did not tolerate adherence to laws, penal code or constitution but reserved to itself complete freedom of action and decision-making: political power was merely the executive of the leader's will. (Bracher 1973 p 435)

Nevertheless, the appearance of legality was very important in maintaining the illusion of morality and legality. The many changes in the organization of government which took place under Hitler served at one and the same time to pervert the normal bureaucratic and legal system and to invest the rapidly expanding SS with the appearance of regularity and legitimacy. The SS had originated as Hitler's personal guard and saw itself as a party police. The changes in the position of the SS *vis-à-vis* the police is but one example of the process described above. Himmler, as police president of Bavaria, managed to gain control over the entire political police of Bavaria and later over the political police in all German states. This personal union of the centralized Gestapo and Himmler's SS gave official independence to the domestic terror machine. Himmler's titles *Reichsführer* SS and *Chef der deutschen Polizei* indicated both the centralization of the police which had previously been under the control of individual states and the transfer of the police from administrative to SS control (Bracher 1973). In June 1936 Himmler divided the police into two main departments: the Order Police and the Security Police, the latter under the administration of Heydrich who as SS Group Leader was also chief of the Security Service of the SS in charge of intelligence and ideological control. The criminal police also became part of the Gestapo, that is of the SS (see Appendix).

The final goal of the reorganization was the existence of SS departments for all political areas and the integration of the police into the SS and SS army, that is, 'a ruling system with its own bureaucracy and coercive apparatus, with the police as the most important wedge' (Bracher 1973 p 439).

The rise of the SS and both its pseudo-legal and its extra-legal ideology, combined with a rule of terror in which even Hans Frank recognized that 'it is not too much to say that the individual citizen has lost all rights in Law' and 'when any citizen can be consigned to a concentration camp for any length of time and without any possibility of redress' (Bucheim 1968 pp 198–9), certainly produced a quiescent population. However, the recruitment of the SS also indicates the success of the Nazi regime in inculcating large numbers of men with the racist precepts of National Socialism. Many studies of the SS have attempted to show that it was largely composed of 'psychopaths' and 'sadists' and that this explains the actions of the Death's Head units of the SS in the concentration camps. There is evidence to show that a small number of the SS concentration camp guards could be so described (Dicks 1972). Yet it would be difficult to talk about all members of the SS or even of all the SS concentration camp guards in these terms. Clearly, the SS selectively recruited those who were likely to respond to its demands for 'hardness', 'obedience', 'efficiency', 'comradeship' and 'racial superiority' (Bucheim 1968). The training of the SS was that of a total institution and the stress was on 'hardness', only relieved by a form of 'camaraderie', which meant that the SS protected many of its members who did not conform entirely to the rules. There are many examples of such indulgence, both personal and general. The rule forbidding sexual intercourse with other races, for example, was rarely enforced in the concentration camps and the legal officers of the SS agreed that there should be no statutory or severe punishment for disobedience to this ruling. The focal point of SS propaganda was obedience to the will of the Führer and acceptance of this reversed former concepts of order and value. The killing of the Jews was not seen as murder but the crime of murder still existed. Himmler's decision on the unauthorized shooting of Jews is interesting in this context:

> Motive is the deciding factor in the question whether and if so, what, punishment should be imposed for unauthorized shooting of Jews: If the motive is purely political there should be no punishment unless such is necessary for the maintenance of discipline. In the latter case, depending on the situation, judicial punishment can be imposed under Paras 90 or 149 of the Code of Military Law, or alternatively disciplinary action can be taken. If the motive is selfish, sadistic or sexual, judicial punishment should be imposed for murder or manslaughter as the case may be. (Bucheim 1968 p 363)

In reality camaraderie within the SS meant that punishment was rarely imposed for unauthorized killings of Jews, even when the motivation was clearly not political.

It could be pointed out that there were many members of the SS who did not relish their role in 'the final solution' and consistently evaded orders or attempted to get out of the Death's Head units of the SS (Bucheim 1968), yet for the most part the SS accepted its taught duties. According to Bucheim the remarkable feature of the mass murder of the camps was that they were performed by people who in the ordinary course of events were 'decent citizens', who in normal circumstances would have been unlikely to commit a crime but whose sense of right and wrong had been obliterated by ideology (Bucheim 1968 p 363). Observers at the post-war trials repeatedly remarked how 'ordinary' men like Hoess and Eichman appeared to be. Few such men thought their 'orders' were wrong. They accepted the necessity for providing a 'final solution' to the 'enemy behind the wire'.

Hoess's autobiography provides a great deal of evidence on the sense of guilt which pervaded the SS. He describes his unease, when he is first trained at Dachau by Eicke for concentration camp duties:

> It was clear to me that I was not suited to this sort of service since in my heart I disagreed with Eicke's insistence that life within the concentration camps be organized in this particular way. My sympathies lay too much with the prisoners, for I had myself lived their life for too long and had personal experience of their needs.
>
> I should have gone to Eicke or the *Reichsführer* SS then, and explained that I was not suitable to concentration camp service, because I felt too much sympathy for the prisoners. I was unable to find the courage to do this. (Hoess 1961 p 86)

He also indicates the general nature of this feeling among concentration camp guards in a report to Himmler on the *Rapportführer* at Auschwitz:

> P was always there at executions; he generally did his killing with a shot in the nape of the neck. I have often watched him and I could never see the slightest sign of emotion. As he carried on his fearful job, he was calm and relaxed, unhurried and expressionless. Even when he was on duty in the gas chambers, I could never detect a trace of sadism. His face was always impassive and emotionless. Psychologically he had become so callous that he could go on killing uninterruptedly without a thought in his head. Of all those who actually had to do with the killing P *was the only one who never once took me quietly aside and poured out his heart over this fearful business.* (Bucheim 1968 p 374)

Nevertheless, the general acceptance of the 'rightness' of the final solution and the duty of SS officers to obey singleheartedly the Führer is revealed particularly in the reactions of SS officers to their trials as criminals after the war. Very few SS officers admitted guilt. Even Hoess, whose autobiography was written at the instigation of officers concerned in his trial, admitted only that the policy of extermination was mistaken and to a large extent absolves himself of responsibility, in stating that 'unknowingly I was a cog in the wheel of the extermination machine created by the Third Reich. The machine has been smashed to pieces, the engine is broken and I, too, must now be destroyed' (Hoess 1961 p 205). Many SS officers also legitimated their own work by blaming the worst excesses of the camps on the Capos:

> They [the Jews] were mainly persecuted by members of their own

race, their foremen or room seniors. Eschen, their block senior, distinguished himself in this respect . . . This block senior used every possible means, no matter how low, to terrorize the other prisoners, not only physically but, above all, mentally. He kept the screws on the whole time . . . He goaded them into acts of violence against one another, or against the Capos, so as to have an excuse to report them for punishment . . . He was the 'devil' incarnate. He showed a repulsive zeal towards the members of the SS, but was ready to inflict any kind of iniquity on his fellow prisoners and members of his own race. (Hoess 1961 p 144)

The 'normality' of many SS officers and their conviction that their part in the 'final solution' was dirty work rather than crime can only be understood in terms of the National Socialist *weltanschauung*. Changes in the labelling of the activities of concentration camp guards with the defeat of Nazi Germany were largely rejected by the SS guards on trial.

Obviously, this discussion of the role of the SS has been so brief that it has only been possible to raise some of the issues involved. Nevertheless, it is hoped that the necessity of linking the analysis of 'dirty work' and of 'labelling' to the changing power structure of German society, inherent in the Nazi seizure of power, has been made plain. Moreover, it should also be clear that recruitment into stigmatized occupations like that of the Death's Head units of the SS may involve active choice on the part of the recruit or reaction to other pressures. In this latter process, labelling does not provide an adequate account of the motivation of recruits, but requires considerable elaboration and development.

One of the main problems of dealing with the idea of 'dirty work' is the very disparate examples which can be used as illustration. 'Dirty work' in this chapter has varied from the work of janitors to that of prostitutes to that of the SS guards in concentration camps. Obviously these diverse occupations cannot be equated with one kind of formally defined 'dirty' or 'deviant' work, although they may have some characteristics in common. In itself the notion of 'dirty work' has little theoretical and explanatory force. Analysis of the social structural context of work which is called 'dirty' is crucial. The interactionist perspective, within which studies of dirty work and deviance developed, has always tended to neglect wider issues relating to class and power. Hughes's account of the dirty work of the SS makes no attempt to look at the all-important changes in the organization of German society which allowed what would previously have been criminal acts to be interpreted as dirty work. Similarly, studies of deviance have often ignored processes of social change and the possibility that 'deviant' acts may initiate social change and thereby become 'normal'. On the other hand, the interactionist tradition has always stressed the continuities between activities labelled as 'deviant' or 'dirty' and those which are seen as 'normal'. Much of Hughes's research points to common modes of adjustment and adaptation in very different forms of work. For example, he indicates the very similar ways in which men attempt to control their work situation in the case of janitors, jazz players and doctors (Hughes 1958). In the fifties, this represented a considerable advance in the sociological treatment of stigmatized work and actions in demystifying a whole area of activity which had previously been explained only in terms of the innate characteristics of the people involved. In looking at the discontinuities between dirty and normal work, however, interactionists, as had already been noted, were primarily concerned with the personal consequences of doing dirty work and generally failed to examine the manipulative and ideological elements involved when one group effectively labels another group's work as 'deviant' and 'dirty'.

It is partly because of this focus on the 'exotic' treated as 'normal' that interactionists also disregarded the way in which manual labour as a whole has been seen as 'dirty work' within particular capitalist industrial societies. The relationship of definitions of dirty work to the development of the middle class is well worth exploring. Orwell's classic account of his childhood indoctrination into the belief that 'the lower classes smell' indicates both the general association of the working class and dirt, and the middle class repudiation of dirty work:

> It may not matter if the average middle class person is brought up to believe that the working classes are ignorant, lazy, drunken, boorish and dishonest; it is when he is brought up to believe that they were dirty. Very early in life you acquired the idea that there was something subtly repulsive about a working class body: you would not get nearer to it than you could help. You watched a great sweaty navvy walking down the road with his pick over his shoulder; you looked at his discoloured shirt and his corduroy trousers stiff with the dirt of a decade; you thought of those nests and layers of greasy rags below, and, under all, the unwashed body, brown all over (that was how I used to imagine it) with its strong bacon-like reek . . . Even 'lower class' people whom you knew to be quite clean — servants for instance — were faintly unappetising. The smell of their sweat, the very texture of their skins, were mysteriously different from yours.
>
> But the essential thing is that middle class people *believe* that the working class are dirty . . . and what is worse that they are somehow *inherently* dirty. (Orwell 1962 pp 112–14)

The expansion of the middle class during the nineteenth century and afterwards involved the adoption of a mode of life in which the rejection of manual labour played an important part in reinforcing and legitimating the newly acquired status of the middle classes. The influence of the Protestant ethic is also evident in the identification of cleanliness, thrift, work and financial success. The idea of 'dirty work' has played an interesting part in middle class ideology in English capitalism.

It is worth noting that the designation of dirty work or deviance often operates to support other kinds of work or activities. It underwrites with moral approval 'clean' work and 'clean' activities generally, hence the labelling of prostitution as 'dirty' gives marriage a peculiar status. The labelling, prosecution and conviction of SS concentration camp guards and other Nazis did much to reinforce and legitimate the powerful position of the Allies after Germany's surrender. The identification of manual work and dirty work obviously supports and legitimates professional and white-collar work, and the status of the people who do that work, in an important way. However, the impact of doing the 'dirty' work of manual labour has been considerably decreased by the strength of the occupational cultures of many working class groups and the success of such groups in projecting their own construction of reality. Mining communities, for example, accept that they do physically dirty work but also regard their work as central productive activity (Dennis *et al* 1956). Similarly in Beynon's account of working for Ford (Beynon 1975), the disapproval of the workers is directed not at the lowest status jobs or the most physically dirty jobs but at the role of supervisor. The dislike and ambivalence which focus on the supervisor's job indicate the clash of work divisions embodied within it as well as the idea of betrayal of the working class group.

Conflicting views of the meaning of work are always a possibility given the conflicting groups within the occupational structure of any society and those conflicting views are often structured in dominance. This is an area which Hughes fails to explore because it requires that concepts like 'deviance' and 'dirty work' should be systematically related to the analysis of class and power.

The discussion of 'dirty work', 'deviant work' and 'criminal work' in this chapter also raises questions about the kind of theoretical explanation implied by the treatment of crime and deviance as forms of work. In the first place, all crime and deviance cannot be treated as work. In the second place, the discovery that criminals treat theft and the SS treat killing as work may illuminate certain aspects of criminal and SS life without necessarily providing an explanation of either phenomena. Indeed, the stress on the continuities between 'normal' work and, say, 'criminal' work may obscure the crucial differences. Hirst, for example, points out that the distinguishing feature of the criminal seeking illicit gain lies in his relationship to the means of production, which is very different from that of the labourer:

> The thief in capitalist society appropriates material products and means of exchange; in the act of theft he neither produces commodities nor services, nor engages in commerce nor financial speculation. He is consequently neither a productive or unproductive labourer, nor is he a capitalist, rather he is strictly parasitic on the labour and wealth of society. The thief steals from the members of all social classes and from all social institutions. (Hirst 1972 p 49)

Notions such as deviant and dirty work can only acquire some theoretical relevance if they are located in a theoretical framework in which both work and deviance are specified in relation to the mode of production, class conflict, the state and its ideological hegemony. The inadequacies of the idea of 'dirty work' incorporated within the interactionist perspective is indicated by its parallel treatment of the work of janitors, the SS and manual workers generally. This involves a reductionism *ad absurdam* of very different social phenomena — but only if the interactionist view is accepted uncritically.

Appendix

The administrative divisions of the political police after 1938 give some indication of the scope of their activities (Bracher 1973 pp 438–9):

II–A	Communism and other Marxist groups
II–B	churches, sects, émigrés, Jews, camps
II–C	reaction, opposition, Austrian affairs
II–D	protective custody, concentration camps
II–E	economic, agrarian and socio-political affairs and organization
II–G	supervision of broadcasting
II–H	party affairs, groupings and auxiliary organization
II–J	foreign political police
II–Ber.	situation reports
II–P	press
II–S	fights against homosexuality and abortion
III	intelligence

CHAPTER 7

Geoff Esland

Professions and professionalism

This and the following chapter, *Diagnosis and therapy*, deal primarily with professional work and various aspects of professional organization. This chapter considers professions in general — their modes of practice, their ideologies and the means by which they regulate their clients; and the following one looks at the particular group of professions which has become known as the 'personal service' professions. These are the occupations which specialize in the diagnosis, treatment, and sometimes correction, of individuals' personalities, behavioural states and, in certain cases, their problems. They include social work, psychiatry, educational psychology, various forms of counselling, and so on, and are seen as having certain characteristics in common with regard to the ways in which they carry out their professional tasks.

By marking off the professions in this way from other kinds of occupations we are acknowledging the peculiar status and power which they possess and which they confer on their members. Later we shall be examining the origins and nature of professionalism as it affects both the practice of work and the recipients of the services which professions offer. This means that we shall be looking at the politics of the internal activities of these occupations — their division of labour, their production of knowledge and control of expertise. We shall also be looking at the ways in which they have become harnessed to a much wider web of power and control in society, acting as 'reality definers' on important issues affecting society at large.

A major theme which will run through this discussion is the idea that professional authority and right to monopoly are strongly legitimated by a well-rooted 'mythology of professionalism' which proclaims the altruism, ethical scrupulousness, and neutrality of expertise which these occupations are reputed to offer. In other words, the expertise

and techniques of the professional group are not normally seen as
serving the interests of that group. In this chapter we examine some of
the sociological literature which has raised these sorts of issues.

A second major theme concerns the relationship between the growth
of professions and the intensification of monopoly capitalism during
the twentieth century. Particularly important here are the ways in
which professional expertise has become harnessed to the operations
of state and local government departments and to the methods of
business production. Through the bureaucratization which now characterizes so much of their work context, professional workers have
become essentially salaried employees – a phenomenon which has
been seen as the 'proletarianization' of the professional.

The corollary of this viewpoint is that professional workers have
become what Baritz has called 'the servants of power' (see Baritz 1960).
In other words, the consolidation of political and economic power in
modern society has occurred through the incorporation of the technical
and scientific skills which are provided by the professions and through
the centralized control of many of their resources. The professions as
key interest groups can therefore be seen as having been co-opted into
governmental decision-making and in some cases as having been allowed
to develop as agents of control for a powerful state.

The discussion has, therefore, a twofold focus: one area of concern
is the inherently political nature of internal professional activity itself;
the second is the significance of professionalism and professional
employment for the wider issue of the location and exercise of political
and economic power in society as a whole.

One of the important features of the various patterns of work in our
society is the existence of status differences between occupations.
Related to these is the varying capacity and success of occupational
groups in exerting their influence and authority over the rest of society
– but within the limits set by the social structure. Quite clearly, the
nature of any kind of work – which includes the conditions under
which it is carried out, the nature of the training required, the difficulty,
or otherwise, of entering the occupation, the life-style and pay which
can be expected from it – is a reflection of its position in the productive system. Generally speaking, mental work has a higher status than
manual work (a notable exception, of course, being surgery which
requires a high level of manual dexterity. It is interesting to remember,
however, that its current high status came only with its incorporation
into a unified medical profession during the nineteenth century.)

Another factor in the different status of occupations is that work for
some people implies a long-term career and the membership of an

occupational community which among other things asserts and protects the rights of its members to exercise authority and expertise.

For many workers, of course, the performance of a job is limited to the processes of a particular firm or plant. Not only in such cases is there likely to be greater insecurity in the face of market pressures on employment, but there is normally no occupational community, nor is work consciousness built around the notion of a progressing career. As Freidson puts, in this kind of work 'the worker and his labour are mere plastic materials for management, materials organized into jobs by managerial conceptions of the tasks necessary for the production of some good or service for the market' (Freidson 1973 p 56).

It would be a mistake, however, to assume that this statement of Freidson's applies to all working-class occupations. Some of the skilled manual crafts, either through long tradition or through unionization, have built up a sense of corporate identity and organization similar to those of the professions which among other things regulate the standards of practice of their members, their entry to the occupation and the rates of pay which they should receive.

Nevertheless, in all industrial societies the positions of prestige and authority in the occupational hierarchy are held by the professions. This fact, as we shall be seeing later, is largely due to their structural position in the economic system by which they are frequently able to define the terms and rules through which production and its administration are carried out. Although they constitute only a small proportion of the labour force, in numerous ways they exert influence and control over the activities and rights of other workers. One of the most significant features of professional practice is its generalized influence on everyday life. To a varying extent, all of the professions are involved in the production and dissemination of knowledge which ultimately structures the modes of thinking which prevail in a society. As McKinlay puts it, professional workers have become the 'Generalized Wise Men' of contemporary society (McKinlay 1973 p 74). In C. Wright Mills's words, 'as critics of morality, and technicians of power, as spokesmen of God and creators of mass sensibility', the members of professions have acquired considerable control and influence over everyday consciousness (Mills 1956 p 4). This means that routine definitions of ill-health, social adequacy, school achievement, degrees of criminality, for example, can be seen as grounded in the specific forms of expertness which at any one time are dominant in society.

This is not to say that the influence of the professions goes entirely unhindered or that these definitions derive from homogeneous or unanimously supported ideologies within them. One of the notable characteristics of professional organization is the existence of counter-groups within the occupational membership which may directly challenge the mainstream practice. The point I wish to make is that any sociological analysis of the professions has to take seriously the view that many of the dominant categories of thought which permeate our commonsense attitudes — as well as the power to enforce them — are to some extent traceable to the political organization of particular occupations.

Perhaps more important is the fact that professional legitimacy is often so strongly embedded and taken for granted that the cognitive frameworks through which we think through various social issues appear entirely self-evident and rational. As Freidson points out in his book *Profession of Medicine* even where a profession's knowledge is almost universally accepted (as in the medical conceptions of 'cancer', for example) it can nevertheless be regarded as having been *socially constructed* through the conceptual and organizational structures of the profession. Notwithstanding the plausibility and predictive power of the biochemical model of medical understanding, it can be argued that it is relative to a particular historical and intellectual focus on human pathology. Moreover, if we were to examine the various specialisms within the medical profession which are involved in the research into the treatment of cancer we would find a wide range of perspectives and views — sometimes conflicting ones — as to its nature. (This idea is looked at in some detail in Philip Elliott's paper 'Professional ideology and social situation' (Elliott 1973).

We have been suggesting so far that, in addition to the sense of community, membership and corporate identity which characterize the professions, they also have a mandate to produce and generate certain kinds of knowledge for society as a whole. Their power and influence clearly lie first in the degree of control which they are able to assume in the management and exercise of this knowledge — and the skills which are based on it — and, secondly, on the level of public acceptance and support for them which they can obtain. Both of these represent important dimensions of control which become crucial to all occupations seeking the status and rights to monopoly practice implied in the title 'profession'. There are obviously considerable variations between a traditional profession such as medicine and an almost marginal or 'semi' profession like social work, but, nevertheless, these elements of 'professionalism' are common to both. The premise from which we are approaching the professions is therefore one which underlines the political nature of their work. As such, it differs from, and is 'sceptical' of, the claims about their function and social value which might be made by the professional bodies themselves. From this viewpoint it appears that the service ethic specific to the professions is, as Halmos puts it in his description of the 'antiprofessional' position, 'a sheer mystification of status claims and a device to silence the critics of monopoly, privilege, and power, to which the professionals are alleged to cling' (Halmos 1973 p 6).

In summarizing the substance of this critical position — in this case in relation to social work — Brian Heraud has suggested that 'Professionalism is seen not as embodying superior knowledge of what constitutes the needs of clients, and therefore of authority based on such knowledge, but as embodying the ideology of the "few" who hold power' (Heraud 1973 p 89).

Similarly, Bennett and Hokenstad refer to the 'gatekeeper' role of the professions in the distribution of society's material and status resources. Talking of the welfare professions they suggest that:

> Whether working in a public welfare agency or a state mental institution, their diagnosis and decisions have a direct effect on the access of their clientele to these scarce commodities in the present and the labels they apply can also affect future access. (Bennett and Hokenstad 1973 p 38)

This critical perspective represents part of the radical theoretical developments which have from the late sixties taken place both in sociology and in some of the professions themselves. Many of the welfare professions, for example, now contain radical groups which are putting forward critical approaches to their professional practice. The efforts of some of these — the anti-psychiatry group, for instance, which has been much influenced by the ideas of Szasz and Laing — have become widely known. The impetus of the critiques has been directed both at the professional labelling which occurs in some occupational practices and in a more general sense at the ways in which the professions articulate and reinforce the class structure.

There are, however, certain dilemmas and paradoxes in adopting this position — particularly with regard to the kinds of alternative organization which are left implicit in the critiques. These dilemmas and paradoxes do not necessarily invalidate the substance of the 'antiprofessional' viewpoint, but they make it essential that the structural analysis of professionalism (in relation, for example, to capitalism, bureaucracy and power) be clearly worked out. There is little point in invoking a somewhat romantic notion of 'deschooling' or disestablishment of the professions if the economic and ideological exploitation on which they are seen to rest is left unchanged. Rather than raise the paradoxes contained in a radical critique at this stage we shall leave them for a fuller discussion until the end of the following chapter by which time it is hoped that the political and economic contexts of professionalism will have become clearer. Before we move into these broader areas, it would be useful for us to look further at the nature of professionalism itself.

1   The nature of a profession: symbol and reality

As I suggested above, one of the most obvious characteristics of professions in our society is that, in comparison with other occupations, they have a privileged status. In terms of their relations with the public, their power of dispensation and the esoteric nature of their knowledge, they represent an ideal for occupations aspiring to professional status.

Not surprisingly, an important aspect of an occupation's power and prestige is its capacity to acquire and demonstrate the trappings of 'professionalism'. For a small number of occupations, notably medicine and law, this normally does not present many problems (although certain branches of them — psychiatry and community law, for instance — may have more difficulty than others in convincing the public of the legitimacy of their work). But for occupations such as teaching, social work, nursing and librarianship, the acquisition of the symbols of professionalism is a major element of their quest for status, internal control of work practice and higher financial reward. 'Professionalism' is one of the most fundamental forms of legitimacy and political control which can be sought in the contemporary organization of work. For this reason, it is important to question the face-value of the *symbols* of professionalism and to remember that they may be somewhat different from the reality.

A good deal of sociological analysis has been devoted to the task of attempting to distinguish the professions from other occupations and to distil the essential qualities of 'professionalism'. Much of it, in fact, has tended to support the professions' own conceptions of themselves as autonomous bodies which dispense high level skills according to the dictates of a strong service ethic. This tradition in the study of professions has been described by McKinlay as the 'inventory approach' (McKinlay 1973). Its main concern has been with the identification of criteria which existing professions are assumed to satisfy, rather than with the examination of them as products of professional ideologies. Not surprisingly, the 'inventories' which have been produced appear to be based on a somewhat idealized conception of the historically preeminent professions, medicine and law, and this has resulted in a set of rather formal characteristics which, as much as anything, give tacit support to the professions' own views of themselves and which they wish to have presented to the public.

One of the most important features of professional practice which is singled out in these accounts is the service ethic. Members of professions are typically seen as motivated by altruism and a high respect for confidentiality in their dealings with clients. Also important is the right of professions to determine their own code of practice, standards of education and training. In the case of the 'true' professions this is concretized in the existence of professional councils or legislatures through which their members are registered. A third significant feature of professional activity is the fact that it is often based on specialist knowledge and technique – usually acquired over a long period of education. Because of this, professions claim the right to act as *guardians* of this knowledge and the means of access to it. For this reason, as well as the other factors listed above, membership of a profession is usually taken to imply a career until retirement.

These characteristics are all part of the 'symbols' of professionalism. They represent the *ideal* base on which the organization, membership, control of work, and relationships with clients can be seen to rest. Using them as a rule-of-thumb guide, it might be thought that occupations which are aspiring to professional status can adjudge their progress in terms of how close they come to fulfilling these criteria.

To concentrate on the symbols of professionalism at the expense of their relevance to practice would, however, be misleading. Not only are they inaccurate as descriptions of the complex nature of professional organization and practice, but, in stressing the *autonomy* of these occupations they direct our attention away from the ways in which they themselves feature in the larger structures of capitalist power and organization. They lead us, in fact, to overlook the ways in which the professions as concentrations of middle class culture have become generators of ideology which legitimates the operation of social order in society. In other words, this approach renders them in some senses as islands of power relatively unconnected with the major sources of political and economic hegemony in society as a whole. An important area to explore, therefore, is the enlargement and incorporation of professional work during the twentieth century, both in economic production and in the formation and implementation of state-controlled social policy. A trend which is becoming increasingly observed is the incorporation of the professions in the wage-labour system – a process which has led to a number of sociologists to refer to the 'proletarianization' of professional workers (see Oppenheimer 1973; Braverman 1974; Aronowitz 1973; and Gorz 1976). From this viewpoint, professional workers are seen as experiencing a steady decline in the control over their work comparable with the 'deskilling' experienced by various groups of skilled workers during earlier parts of the century. This decline, however, is often seen as related to a *consolidation of power* in the agencies which employ them such as the large corporate companies which have arisen during the twentieth century. It is important, therefore, to bear in mind the changing relationship between the professions and the groups which maintain economic and political control in society.

In spite of its apparent plausibility, the 'inventory' approach to understanding the professions is inadequate and misleading. A more important issue is the use which is made by many occupations of the trappings of professionalism as strategy for increasing their influence and power – the unsuccessful attempt during the sixties by the teachers' unions to set up a General Teachers' Council, similar to the General Medical Council, is an obvious example.

One of the earliest critics of the 'inventory approach' to the sociology of the professions was Howard Becker (Becker 1962). In highlighting some of the problems of trying to view occupations in terms of a set of fixed objective criteria, Becker makes the point that the term 'profession' as well as 'describing and pointing to an abstract classification of kinds of work' also 'portrays a morally desirable kind of work'. As such, it is used by occupations themselves in order to secure greater recognition from the public of their status and thereby, hopefully, increased control over their work organization.

Becker argues that it is more fruitful to view the term 'profession' as an honorific label which secures certain political advantages for its possessors than as a neutral, 'scientific' category:

> We can take a radically sociological view regarding professions simply as those occupations which have been fortunate enough in the politics of today's work world to gain and maintain possession of that honorific title. On this view, there is no 'true' profession and no set of characteristics necessarily associated with the title. There are only those work groups commonly regarded as professions and those which are not . . . (pp 32–33)
> Because the symbol legitimates the autonomy of the worker, occupations that are trying to rise in the world want very much to possess it, to be known as professions rather than businesses or sciences (or any of the other alternative stereotypes available to describe kinds of work) . . .
> So we find many occupations trying hard to become professions and

using the symbol of the profession in an attempt to increase their
autonomy and raise their prestige. Optometrists, nurses, librarians,
social workers — these are only a few of the many occupations
engaged in this kind of activity. (Becker 1962 p 39)

An interesting illustration of the point which Becker is making is the
claim which is sometimes made that business management should
become, and should be seen as, professionalized. In the report from *The
Guardian* of a speech made by Sir Frederick Catherwood (see Appendix
on p 372), it can be seen that the appeal of professional status and image
is sometimes felt at top general management and board-room levels. Sir
Frederick Catherwood is speaking here for those who feel that their
moral authority would be strengthened if they could present themselves, not as agents for processing shareholders' profits, but as neutral
professionals co-ordinating a pluralist coalition of 'stateholders'
(employees, shareholders, consumers, suppliers, local authorities,
'public interest') and holding a 'just balance' between the conflicting
claims.

At a later point in his paper, Becker compares the 'reality' of
professional work with the symbol and ideology. In doing so, he draws
attention to a number of ways in which the idealized image of professional authority and autonomy can be seen as inappropriate. In various
ways clients, the organizations which employ professional workers, and,
in some cases, state agencies and legislation all exert varying pressures
on work practice and internal control. Furthermore, because professions are not homogeneous bodies but alliances of smaller occupational
specialisms there are inevitably issues over which different segments
are in competition with one another. This inevitably produces schisms
which can be exploited by other determined groups. (Perhaps the most
notable example of this is Aneurin Bevan's successful policy of dividing
the medical profession while attempting to set up the National Health
Service in 1946. By offering substantial concessions to the powerful
body of consultants he was able to offset the strong opposition of the
BMA to the proposed legislation. (See Forsyth 1966.))

The one area of their activity where professions retain a good deal
of power is in their treatment of clients, and it is here that recent
sociological studies have been more strongly critical than Becker of
the disjunction between the symbol of professional 'worthiness' and the
reality.

One of the most pungent critiques of the 'mythology of professionalism', particularly in relation to the treatment of clients, is that put
forward by McKinlay (1973). In discussing the mechanisms by which
professions maintain their power he suggests that:

Principal among them are the emergence of a mythology concerning
professionalism: the removal of certain activities from external
observability and evaluation; a process by which professionals have
become generalized wise men with an unwarranted mandate to
challenge others; through the accordance of an unprecedented
degree of trust based on ill-founded claims to altruism; and through
the manufacture of artificial needs which render their services
absolutely indispensable. Through such mechanisms it is suggested
that professionals have been accorded almost dictatorial powers
which appear to be cyclically re-employed to protect and even
further enhance the power already vested in them. (1973 p 77)

According to this viewpoint, professionalism is a source of legitimation
for the exercise of occupational influence and monopoly. This is
especially relevant to the professional—client relationship which in
almost all professions rests on an avowed basis of trust. In the course
of his paper, McKinlay puts forward a series of arguments to demonstrate the dubiousness of the professional claim, *credat emptor* ('let
the taker believe in us'). After criticizing the underlying notions of
'vocation' and 'calling' which are sometimes used to describe professional work, McKinlay attacks the fundamental justification for
professional practice and mandate, the service ethic:

[Professions] are commonly depicted as unlike other occupations
in the extent of their selfless devotion to their clients in the pursuit
of some higher ideal. Evidence for the existence of such self-sacrifi-
cial behaviour is to be found in public spirited advertisements which
professional associations sponsor in the news media. A gullible
public tends to forget that these activities promote business of
various kinds and may be generally unaware of the ways in which
they are carefully engineered to perpetuate the myth of altruism. It
is indeed difficult to reconcile this supposed altruism to the ever
increasing exposés of the backstage activities of the professions
regarding fees and fee splitting, unnecessary referral and intervention, ritualistic procedures, or billing for work that was never undertaken, etc. (1973 pp 67—8)

A further criticism which is made of the operation of professionalism
— as distinct from the ideologies which are presented to the public —
is that the client or layman finds difficulty in judging the quality of
the service he is getting. Indeed, according to a number of social
theorists, in some areas of professional practice (for instance, social
work, psychiatry and teaching) the client has few means of redress if
the diagnosis and labelling of his 'problem' goes against his material
and status interests. As McKinlay puts it:

We have a social welfare system which in some cases appears overly keen to intervene and to initiate some morally degrading labelling process . . . The police and certain health agencies appear devoted to the location, apprehension and control of people who engage in supposedly 'deviant behaviour' or who display so-called idiosyncratic signs. In many instances, such activities are actively supported by so-called professionals or are at least condoned by those who, if embodying the knowledge generally imputed to them, ought to respond quite differently. (1973 p 71)

If the service ethic and altruism are suspect as descriptions of professional practice, so also is the other much-cited attribute — the autonomy of the profession in matters of fees, training, curricula, validation, and so on. As we shall be arguing later in the chapter, the conditions of modern industrialization have led to the massive growth of what Aronowitz has called 'the professional servant class' (Aronowitz 1973 p 265). Compared with the independent practitioner of the late nineteenth century, most professional workers are now salaried employees within large organizations. Even in the areas of training, curriculum and validation some professions find that their regulations of entry and practice are determined by state departments rather than by their professional associations (although the associations are likely to be consulted). Thus, one of the paradoxes of the professions is that, although as a whole they constitute an ideologically powerful group, their members act frequently in the role of bureaucratic functionaries.

In the following section we consider some of the reasons for this and the general social influences on the formation of professions.

2 Industrialization and professionalism

It is important for understanding the nature of professional work that it should be seen in terms of the wider 'logics' and relations of production in society. Not only is the existence of professional work itself dependent on large-scale economic forces, but also as creators and purveyors of knowledge about the operation of industrial management, accountancy, company law, urban and industrial building, etc., the members of professions have a major capacity for defining the lives of other workers.

Although the forerunners of contemporary professions were in existence by the sixteenth century (the Inns of Court were established by 1400 and the Royal College of Physicians of London was founded in 1518), large-scale professionalization did not really begin until the mid-nineteenth century. Even in medicine and law, compulsory qualifications were not required for practice until well after 1850. The rapid growth of professional occupations is clearly a phenomenon of industrialization and the concomitant expansion of technological rationalization. Many of the new professional workers, who, unlike their forerunners in medicine and law, are salaried employees working for large organizations, have emerged as providers of services for industrial managerialism. As C. Wright Mills put it in *White Collar*:

> The proliferation of new professional skills has been a result of the technological revolution and the involvement of science in wider areas of economic life; it has been a result of the demand for specialists to handle the complicated institutional machinery developed to cope with the complication of the technical environment. (Mills 1951 p 13)

An illustration of this process is provided in Johnson's discussion of the accountancy profession (whose Institute of Chartered Accountants was founded in 1880) in his book *Professions and Power*:

> The general characteristics of accountancy, as it has developed since the late nineteenth century in Britain, have been such that the occupation has always been subject to a large measure of corporate control. The modern accountancy profession was largely brought into being by the demands of corporate business, first as a form of internal company control and then as a form of accounting to the risk-bearer by means of a public audit. The functions of the accountant in providing the means of cost or management control were regarded as so crucial for the development of capitalist enterprise that Weber defined the capitalist business firm as an 'establishment which determines its income-yielding power by calculation according to the methods of modern book-keeping and the striking of a balance'. Accounting as a form of protecting the risk-bearer arose in association with the public joint-stock company whereby 'independent' auditors or accountancy firms reported on the financial position of a company to stockholders and to the public rather than to management. Despite the fact that all the early accountancy associations regarded themselves as primarily associations for 'independent' public auditors or accountants, their membership always contained a large proportion of employed accountants while many independent firms carrying out auditing services have become increasingly dependent upon a few large-scale consumers of their services. (Johnson 1972 p 66)

In a more recent paper, Johnson has claimed that:

> By the end of the eighteenth century an accountant of some kind, whether he was a lawyer specializing in financial affairs or the

qualified apprentice of a 'writing master' was to be found on the staff of many large mercantile firms. It is estimated that, even by 1775, five hundred young men were studying accounting techniques in the City of Glasgow alone; and accountants were only one occupational group among many which were emerging. Industrialization opened the floodgates of professional growth. Developments in science and technology crystallized into techniques which provided the basis of new professional occupations such as civil engineering and, later, mechanical and electrical engineering. (Johnson 1973 p 125)

Two of the major influences on the growth of professions in the advanced industrial societies have been, first, the rise of corporate capitalism in place of the entrepreneurial capitalism of the nineteenth century and, secondly, the emergence of the ideologies and institutions of liberal welfare policies which have been carried out by various twentieth-century governments. Both of these processes have had the effect of creating and enlarging the scope of two broad types of professional occupation: the industrial managerialist professions such as accountancy, banking, engineering, advertising, surveying, architecture, and industrial psychology, and the various welfare professions such as social work, psychotherapy and, in some respects, teaching. Moreover, as far as the older professions are concerned, it could be argued that law has tended to develop as a supportive occupation for the first type (through the growth of corporation and tax laws, for example) and that medicine has provided some of the ideological content of the second.

3 Corporate capitalism and the growth of 'professional management'

The concentration of capital in large organizations has become a well-attested feature of modern capitalism and has brought with it major changes in the occupational structure. (See on this subject Baran and Sweezy 1966; Sweezy 1971; Mason (ed.) 1961. The most recent studies are those by Braverman 1974, Bowles and Gintis 1976 and Hannah 1976.) This concentration has been slower to take effect in Britain than in the United States — partly due to the greater persistence of the ideology of the family firm — but nevertheless the process has been similar. The greatest industrial concentration in Britain lies in the nationalized industries, but the trend in other areas of industry has been much the same.

The system of entrepreneurial capitalism which has prevailed through the major period of industrial expansion gradually gave way during the late nineteenth century to what has become known as corporate or monopoly capitalism. This process, which has continued throughout the twentieth century, is one in which units of production became larger and more concentrated and in which small producers are taken over by or merged with larger corporations.

One important side-effect of this process is that production and business organization become more bureaucratic. Large organizations invariably operate on the basis of the rational fragmentation and specialization of labour and this in turn produces the necessity for growth in white-collar and professional occupations.

The growth of 'corporatism' in Britain is the subject of a paper by Winkler. He makes the point that, from the end of the nineteenth century in Britain, the state has gradually enlarged its involvement in economic and fiscal planning from a generally *facilitative* role in production and trade to the *directive* role which it now has. This has been accompanied by the consolidation of large firms in the major areas of production. He points out that, according to recent figures, 'the top 100 manufacturing enterprises now account for just about half of all output compared with the 16% they controlled in 1909' (Winkler 1975 pp 24–5). He goes on to suggest that the growth of industrial concentration has stemmed primarily from the political and economic necessity of competing in world markets dominated by the multi-national firms and large corporations.

For our purposes, a major aspect of the growth of corporate capitalism has been the expansion of the range of managerial professions. As management has become more 'scientific' and rational, various specialized work tasks have become institutionalized as occupations. Simple manufacturing has given way to complex systems of production; craft and domestic labour has been replaced by corporate control. As a result of this process, the new occupations — both professional and supervisory — have become part of the expanding system of wage labour — their members are salaried employees. One of the chief characteristics of the social relations of corporate capitalism is that the labour power purchased by the corporation now includes that of white-collar and professional workers. As Braverman puts it:

> The particular management function is exercised not just by a manager, nor even by a staff of managers, but by an *organization of workers under the control of managers, assistant managers, supervisors, etc. Thus, the relations of purchase and sale of labor power, and hence of alienated labor, have become part of the management apparatus itself.* Taken all together, this becomes the admin-

istrative apparatus of the corporation. Management has become *administration, which is a labor process conducted for the purpose of control within the corporation*, and conducted moreover as a labor process exactly analogous to the process of production, although it produces no product other than the operation and co-ordination of the corporation. (Braverman 1974 p 267)

In considering this phenomenon, some sociologists have referred to the new professional workers as representatives of the 'new middle class'. C. Wright Mills, for instance, has claimed that:

In no sphere of twentieth-century society has the shift from the old to the new middle-class condition been so apparent, and its ramification so wide and deep, as in the professions. Most professionals are now salaried employees; much professional work has become divided and standardized and fitted into the new hierarchical organizations of educated skill and service; intensive and narrow specialization has replaced self-cultivation and wide knowledge; assistants and sub-professionals perform routine . . . tasks while successful professional men become more and more the managerial type. (Mills 1951 p 112)

The bureaucratization of professional labour has been the subject of a good deal of discussion in the sociological literature. The two issues which this process raises are first, the problems of identity-management which arise for the professional who may have to divide his loyalties between the organization which employs him and his profession. The second issue is the more structural one which is concerned with the 'increasing' proletarianization of professional labour. One of the best summaries of these issues and the factors involved in the increasing employment of professionals is provided in the following extract from Terry Johnson's paper 'Professions':

Accountants, lawyers, architects, engineers and scientists are today employed in large numbers by business firms. Under this contemporary system of patronage, the independent status of the professional is, in large part, a fiction, but it is a significant fiction. As a result of his socialization into the profession, the organization lawyer or accountant may identify more with the profession than with the firm. This ambivalence in the role of employed professional involves tensions and conflicts. Such tensions, for example, are inherent in the position of the industrial scientist, who may be subject both to professional demands for publication and to commercial demands for secrecy. Similarly the government-employed architect may be subject both to professional aesthetic requirements and to utilitarian demands from his employer.
In all highly industrialized societies the proportion of professionals

in independent practice is declining; in the underdeveloped world the professions have, to a much larger extent, been brought into being by state action, and their members are today employed by government agencies. In neither case is the typical professional an independent practitioner. In Britain in 1960, for example, only one-third of accountants were in private practice. In the case of surveyors the figure was 27 per cent; architects 25 per cent; actuaries 4 per cent; and engineers 2 per cent. Solicitors were unusual in that a majority (62 per cent for England and Wales) was engaged in private practice. In the United States independent professionals make up about 1 per cent of the employed population. The proportion of salaried professionals, however, has risen to at least six times that number. This illustrates how the recent expansion of professional workers in industrial societies has taken place within bureaucratic employment. In other words, not only has bureaucracy invaded the professions – in the form of the law firms, the medical clinic, the management consultancy, and the mass university – but the professionals have infiltrated the bureaucracies. In Britain, the flow of accountants into business bureaucracies, and later into controlling positions on the boards of the corporations, was initiated by the Companies Act of 1867 . . . This Act was a major step towards making audit by a qualified accountant compulsory for public companies. By the first world war accountants were joining the ranks of management in significant numbers. Later in the great economic depression of the 1930's which resulted in the breakdown of *laissez-faire* economic policies, the services of accountants were at a premium. Their special talents as 'fixers', in working out the financial details of mergers, takeovers and price fixing, were in great demand as they have been ever since. Since the 1940's cost accountants have also become an important part of management as the techniques of budgetary control have been developed. Similarly, research and development needs of the large mass-production firm have increased the importance of the scientist and engineer who have in their turn, begun to advance up the ladder of bureaucratic control to join the accountants on the boards. Latest in the line, but increasingly to be found in the higher ranks of management, are the men versed in the mystique of sales and market research – for the expensive, modern automated plant is built only when market research is complete and potential sales are known. This places the market expert at the heart of the decision-making process.

The professionalization of the business bureaucracies may occur not only as a result of the infiltration of the professional, but also through the growing claims to expertise and professional status of general managers. The authority of the general manager does not derive from technical competence but from the position he occupies in the managerial hierarchy. There is, however, an increasing tendency for such managers to call themselves professionals and to behave like professionals, instituting lengthy training schemes and creating professional bodies such as the British Institute of Managers, which was incorporated in 1947 . . .

Another aspect of management's claim to professional status is that it now shares with established professions a dependence upon a complex body of knowledge. Aspects of psychology, economics, sociology and other disciplines are now incorporated into the syllabuses of business studies courses – a rapidly expanding sector of higher education. (Johnson 1973 pp 131–2)

4 The 'proletarianization' of professional workers

One of the paradoxes of the social position of the new professional workers is that they have become both agents of capitalist control and also the professionally trained servants of capitalism. It was this latter feature of their social position which led Baritz to refer to the industrial psychology profession as 'the servants of power' (see Baritz 1960 pp 325–37). In Braverman's words 'Not only does it [the new middle class] receive its petty share in the prerogatives and rewards of capital, but it also bears the mark of the proletarian condition' (Braverman 1974 p 407). He elaborates on this in the following extract:

> For these employees the social form taken by their work, their true place in the relations of production, their fundamental condition of subordination as so much hired labor increasingly makes itself felt, especially in the mass occupations that are part of this stratum. We may cite here particularly the mass employments of draftsmen and technicians, engineers and accountants, nurses and teachers, and the multiplying ranks of supervisors, foremen and petty managers. (1974 p 407)

The point which Braverman is making is true to some extent of the medical and legal professions. One of the characteristics of twentieth-century medical practice in Britain is that it has come increasingly under the aegis of the state – in particular, the Treasury and Department of Health. Following the National Health Service Act of 1946, medicine has become very considerably a field of public employment in which there is a powerful element of lay and governmental control. This has meant that the terms and conditions of work, levels of pay, the training of new doctors and the funding of medical research, have been set by the overall limits on medical resources. The recent growth of unionism among British junior doctors is another indication of an increasing awareness of the 'proletarian' aspects of medical work.

With regard to law, one of the most significant growth areas in this profession – particularly in the United States – has been corporation law. Van Loon, for instance, has suggested that during the twentieth century the legal profession has become a major servant of business, and that, in the eyes of law students at least, the overwhelming emphasis in the law curriculum is on various aspects of business law:

> Curricula offerings illustrate the orientation. In the first year, criminal and personal injury law, affecting great numbers of citizens, receive less thorough treatment than contracts or commercial property transactions; the course on legal procedure draws chiefly on business examples. The second-year law student is advised he is not a real lawyer without the three business-oriented courses known popularly as Making Money, Counting Money, and Keeping It from the Government (Corporations, Accounting, and Taxation). While these three are nominally optional at Harvard, for example, 94 per cent of the student body follows faculty urgings to elect them. Courses on estate planning abound, but few schools teach environmental planning; consumer law is only beginning to receive attention. (Van Loon 1970 p 336)

A similar view is taken by Smigel in his study of *The Wall Street Lawyer* (Smigel 1964). He suggests here that the corporations and the law firms are strongly dependent on each other. The corporations are the most prestigious and lucrative clients of the Wall Street law firm and they themselves rely on the creativity of their lawyers in formulating business policy. It is also quite usual for lawyers to sit on boards of directors and actually participate in business decisions. As Smigel points out, through their various devices for minimizing tax liability and expanding forms of credit, for example, as well as through the creation of industrial case law, the corporation lawyers have had a major responsibility for the nature of contemporary capitalism. Some of the lawyers interviewed by Smigel are quoted as experiencing conflict between their interest in law and their involvement in business. According to one of these informants some lawyers have effectively become businessmen:

> One of the largest areas of conflict arises because some partners feel that they no longer are practising law but are becoming businessmen. This problem seems to have become aggravated with the increase in the size of big business and number of corporations. It is the task of the large firms to tend to the legal problems of these clients. Many partners are asking, 'Are we really practising law?' This question arises on the partnership level because some say much of their work

involves business decisions. As one partner put it, 'We make as many business decisions as decisions about the law.' Or, stated a little more vehemently by another partner:
'We are losing the capacity and status of the old profession now that we deal with corporations. I'm sometimes troubled that maybe we are converting a profession into an area of techniques.' (Smigel 1964 pp 302–3)

These examples provide fairly clear support for the notion that through the logic of capitalism some professions are becoming 'proletarianized' and are simply service agents for the owners of capital, the higher administrators in government departments, and so on. As Martin Oppenheimer puts it in his paper 'The proletarianization of the professional':

The . . . professional is thus caught between the requirements of performing bureaucratic tasks and maintaining the system (and his job) and a professional commitment to do something about social problems, which is presumably what the workplace was set up for. In short, many of the professional and semi-professional jobs in the public sector are related to the oppressive functions of government – keeping welfare clients quiet, policing, regulating – while both the professional's training and the demands of clients emphasize problem-solving and delivering services in a human way. Thus, just as the professional begins to grapple with the real function of the job (as opposed to the rhetoric he has been educated on), that job becomes even more onerous due to deteriorating conditions stemming from budget cuts and other symptoms of the fiscal crises of the public sector. (Oppenheimer 1973 pp 216–16)

It is important to remember, however, that professional workers nevertheless constitute a powerful group – particularly those who are recruited or promoted to higher managerial positions. Certainly, the complaint in the quotation from Smigel's study of Wall Street lawyers draws attention to the loss of control over the profession's knowledge which some lawyers have experienced and that their intellectual skills are being put to use in the service of profit; nevertheless, within the capitalist structure, the corporation lawyer occupies a position of high prestige and considerable power. Like the accountant, in that he provides knowledge and expertise which is relevant to business growth, he becomes a participant in collective capitalist control. It was this interpretation of the corporation lawyer which prevailed for C. Wright Mills; for him, the lawyer should be seen as a member of the 'power elite':

The inner core of the power elite also includes men of the higher legal and financial type from the great law factories and investment firms, who are almost professional go-betweens of economic, political and military affairs, and who thus act to unify the power elite. The corporation lawyer and the investment banker perform the functions of the 'go-between' effectively and powerfully. By the nature of their work, they transcend the narrower milieu of any one industry, and accordingly are in a position to speak and act for the corporate world or at least sizeable sectors of it. The corporation lawyer is a key link between the economic and military and political areas . . . When you get a lawyer who handles the legal work of investment bankers you get a key number of the power elite. (Mills 1956 p 289)

It could be argued that the weight of emphasis on business law and the relative neglect of social-problem oriented law is hardly surprising. It is certainly consistent with the Marxist view of law which sees it – in harness to the power of the state – as the major ideology through which the interests and property of the dominant classes are protected. Indeed, as Taylor, Walton and Young have pointed out, during recent years in Britain increasing use has been made of the law in order to contain industrial 'disruption' – the notable example being the Industrial Relations Act (see Taylor, Walton and Young 1975 p 55). This is a fairly direct and recognizable form of power. It is arguable, however, that professional power is most effectively employed through the monopoly of technical or scientific expertise and in the exercise of the professional mandate. In this sense, social domination becomes self-evidently rational and largely invisible, and the professions are, in effect, surrogate enforcers of the power of the state. In the following section, we examine the significance of the growth of scientific rationality as a major legitimating force in professional work, and at the internal political processes which uphold the professional identity.

4.1 Technocratic rationalization and bureaucracy

The emergence of the professions is a very clear example of the process of bureaucratic rationalization which has become so dominant a feature of advanced industrial societies. Not only have the professional occupations themselves undergone substantial rationalization in organization, curricula and the validation of expertise and qualification, but they have been instrumental in the progressive rationalization of the economic organization of society itself.

If we take first the internal bureaucratization of the professions themselves, it is clear that their organization is built around formal, rational principles. Membership is controlled through examination and qualification; their curricula are validated through the universities or their own qualifying associations; they are hierarchically organized with defined levels of promotion through the various stages of a career; and there are formal councils which decide policy, grant licences to practise, and negotiate with state departments and other official bodies. One other important characteristic is the evolution in most of these occupations of specialist and in most cases 'scientific' knowledge. This is particularly important both for substantiating the occupation's claim to privileged status and for the legitimacy which is conferred on the practice which follows from it. It has also led to the consolidation of what Marcuse calls 'operationalism' (1968 pp 24–6) as the primary basis on which professional solutions to problems are found, that is, the application of ostensibly neutral *technique* to social and organizational policy. The most clear example of this is to be found in the burgeoning of those occupations whose task is to promote 'scientific management' – cost accountancy, data processing, management consultancy, operational research, and so on. In the rational drive for profit maximization, cost reduction and worker motivation lies the objectification of labour – that is the development of a system of control in which labour becomes a unit of cost. Operationalism is also a feature of the welfare professions as we shall see in more detail in the following chapter. Occupations which rely on psychological knowledge, for instance, have been particularly criticized for their tendency to represent human action in terms of diagnostic schemes and systems of variables which take little account of the political and cultural contexts within which they and the individuals concerned exist. (See Ingleby 1974b and Baritz 1960.) In this sense, through its reliance on highly legitimated knowledge, protected by the rituals of expertness and licence to practise, professionalism becomes both an adjunct to bureaucratic administration and a form of political domination. This was well recognized by Weber when he said that:

> Bureaucratic administration means fundamentally the exercise of control on the basis of knowledge. This is the feature of it which makes it specifically rational. This consists on the one hand in technical knowledge which, by itself, is sufficient to ensure it a position of extraordinary power. But in addition to this, bureaucratic organizations or the holders of power who make use of them, have the tendency to increase their power still further by the knowledge growing out of experience in the service. (Weber 1947 p 340)

An elaboration of Weber's ideas on the relationship between bureaucracy and technocratic knowledge and their significance for capitalism is provided in a recent paper by Larson. In the following extract she is concerned to emphasize the political power which is inherent in the legitimation conferred by technocratic expertise:

> For Weber, the process of rationalization has three principal and interconnected historical expressions: industrial capitalism, bureaucratic domination and modern science . . .
> The legitimacy of the bureaucratic form of domination is entirely based on functional efficiency. Bureaucracy shows its superiority over other forms of social organization in its handling of large scale problems, and appears, therefore, as an institutional response to the historical concentration of various kinds of managerial functions. In the West, bureaucracy receives its most decisive impulse from the concentration of the means of administration in the hands of the modern nation-state and from the concentration of the means of production in industrial capitalist economies . . . In the economic sphere, bureaucratization substitutes the professional manager for the capitalist entrepreneur. Therefore, the advance of rationalization also means the emergence of new controlling elites . . .
> The growth of scientific knowledge and the advance of bureaucratization widen the distance between the public and both the scientific and the governing elites. To a large extent the two processes are distinct. They converge, however, when scientifically-grounded expertise enters the political decision-making process . . . What is relevant now is that the concentration of power transforms specialised knowledge into a factor of further power. (Larson 1972)

Larson then goes on to discuss the importance of the university as lending authority to technocratic knowledge:

> The modern university plays a crucial role in this aspect of technocratic development . . . [through its] monopoly on scientific and technical training . . . Because universities monopolize, in our societies, technical and scientific knowledge, the conception of rationality which they transmit can appear 'naturally' as universal rationality. University training and certification not only sanction the 'superior knowledge' of the recipients, but also make them into 'bearers of reason'. (Larson 1972 pp 2–8)

The association between the growth of professionalism and the technocratic rationalization of capitalist society is a complex one. At a general level the relationship hinges on the changes in the nature of the productive process which has come about through the progressive accumulation of capital by large corporations and the consequent demand for (and production of) various kinds of managerial knowledge. On this issue, not unexpectedly, sociologists are divided between those who broadly follow Weber's belief that capitalism and bureaucracy are manifestations of *rationalization* and that modern capitalism (and socialism even more) has to rely on the bureaucratic maximization of efficiency in both production and costing, and those who follow the primacy which Marx gave to the control of capital where bureaucracy is merely the administrative means through which the ruling elites exercise their power. However, the differences are not necessarily as great as they might appear. Some of the recent analyses of contemporary capitalism, such as those of Habermas and Braverman, have attempted to reconceptualize both the nature of production and the control of capital. In both cases, considerable prominence is given to the institutionalized growth of technocratic knowledge as having substantially changed the forces of production and the management of capital. Moreover, the purchase and control of labour power has itself been rationalized and become subject to the dictates of professional methods. As Baran and Sweezy point out, 'the replacement of the individual capitalist by the corporate capitalist constitutes an institutionalization of the capitalist function' (Baran and Sweezy 1966 p 44). A similar view is taken by Braverman:

> The complexity of the class structure of modern monopoly capitalism arises from the . . . [following] consideration: namely, that *almost all of the population has been transformed into employees of capital.* Almost every working association with the modern corporation or with its imitative offshoots in governmental or so-called non-profit organizations, is given the form of the purchase and sale of labor power. (Braverman 1974 p 404)

The immanence of capitalist (and, therefore, rational bureaucratic) domination through the medium of technocratic knowledge is the theme of Habermas's essay 'Technology and science as ideology' (Habermas 1971a. Reprinted in Esland *et al* 1975 pp 33–48). The argument which Habermas is making here is that the process of rationalization has led not simply to the present material structures of capitalism but to a form of technocratic consciousness which pervades the entire symbolic structures of society. As such in Habermas's terms technocratic rationality becomes 'a specific form of unacknowledged political domination' (Esland *et al* 1975 p 33).

4.2 'Conception' and 'execution' in work

No profession can be practised without an underpinning of auxiliary activities. Writs must be served and witnesses notified and sometimes hauled into court. The sick are often incontinent; they must be kept clean, fed, comforted, and even controlled in straitjackets. The deceased must be removed quickly from among the living, and their remains disposed of. Some of these tasks make pariahs of the people who do them. There are no proud professional courses and proud university degrees for those who serve a summons, post bail bonds, or embalm the human body. The people who do these things, in effect, put themselves beyond the pale. These are the people who use the service entrance. (Hughes *et al* 1973 p 6)

Among the manifestations of rationality in the productive process are the principles by which professional occupations are separated from manual labour. One of the most significant of these is what Braverman calls 'the separation of conception from execution' — the principle by which the *conception and organization* of work tasks is assigned to one group of workers (professionalized management) and their *execution* to another. During the early nineteenth century and before, it was fairly usual for the craftsman-worker to be responsible for several stages in the manufacture of his products — from design to completion and selling. With the expansion of corporate capitalism and the extension of the wage-labour system, one of the problems facing capitalists has been the apparent need for controlling a recalcitrant labour force — not only within their own enterprises but in the social system as a whole. The results of this become crystallized in the 'scientific management' movement and developed into a rational fragmentation of work responsibility and the incorporation of various inducements and controls by which the worker might become 'motivated'. As Bowles and Gintis have put it:

> The response by corporate employers to this new reality was to develop a complicated vertical segmentation of the labor force. In the new corporate division of labor power was bureaucratically — not personally — sanctioned. It was wielded in the context of a hierarchically ordered structure of jobs. (Bowles and Gintis 1976 p 184)

The division between work as conception and work as the execution of blueprints laid out by others reproduces a demeaning view of the manual worker, his intelligence and his willingness to sell his labour power. This was perhaps most pungently expressed by the originator of the 'scientific management' movement, Frederick Winslow Taylor:

> I can say without the slightest hesitation, that the science of hand-ling pig-iron is so great that the man who is fit to handle pig-iron as his daily work cannot possibly understand that science; the man

who is physically able to handle pig-iron and is sufficiently phlegmatic and stupid to choose this for his occupation is rarely able to comprehend the science of handling pig-iron . . . The man who is fit to work at any particular trade is unable to understand the science of that trade without the kindly help and cooperation of men of a totally different kind of education . . . (Frederick Winslow Taylor quoted in Bowles and Gintis 1976 p 182)

This mode of thinking has been one of the main legitimations for the emergence of 'intelligence' as a relevant category in schooling and the massive expansion of intelligence testing during the twentieth century. As such, it has brought with it a distinction in the school curriculum — parallel to the industrial division of work — between abstract, theoretical subjects and the manual, practical parts of a school timetable. Along with performance in various kinds of tests these are used as the mechanisms through which children are stratified for the labour market. 'Scientific managerialism' has similarly been influential in promoting the growth of the ancillary professions in education. Increasingly in the twentieth century more of the teacher's responsibilities have been eroded to form the basis of another occupation's activities. So we have a counselling profession, an educational psychology profession, various forms of social work, bodies which deal with curriculum theory, and so on.

The structuring of labour which follows from the rational differentiation of work tasks has had enormous consequences for twentieth-century industrial life. In the Marxist sense, it has increased the alienation of workers of all kinds; it has ratified the higher status of 'mental' work in relation to manual work; and it has legitimized 'scientific' management as a form of capitalist domination. Braverman in the following extract describes some of the characteristics of this process and assesses its impact on the structure of work:

A necessary consequence of the separation of conception and execution is that the labor process is now divided between separate sites and separate bodies of workers. In one location, the physical processes of production are executed. In another are concentrated the design, planning, calculation and record-keeping. The preconception of the process before it is set in motion, the visualization of each worker's activities before they have actually begun, the definition of each function along with the manner of its performance and the time it will consume, the control and the checking of the ongoing process once it is under way, and the assessment of results upon completion of each stage of the process — all of these aspects of production have been removed from the shop floor to the manage-

ment office. The physical processes of production are now carried
out more or less blindly, not only by the workers who perform them,
but often by lower ranks of supervisory employees as well . . . This
paper replica of production, the shadow of which corresponds to the
physical, calls into existence a variety of new occupations, the hall-
marks of which are that they are found not in the flow of things but
in the flow of paper. Production has been split in two and depends
upon the activities of both groups. Inasmuch as the mode of production has been driven by capitalism to the divided condition it has
separated the two aspects of labor *but both remain necessary to
production, and in this the labor process retains its unity.* The separation of hand and brain is the most decisive single step in the division
of labor taken by the capitalist mode of production. It is inherent in
that mode of production from its beginnings, and it develops under
capitalist management, throughout the history of capitalism, but it
is only during the past century that the scale of production, the
resources made available to the modern corporation by the rapid
accumulation of capital, and the conceptual apparatus and trained
personnel have become available to institutionalize this separation
in a systematic and formal fashion. Modern management came into
being on the basis of these principles. It arose as theoretical construct and as systematic practice, moreover, in the very period during
which the transformation of labor from processes based on skill to
processes based upon science was attaining its most rapid tempo. Its
role was to render conscious and systematic the formerly uncon-
scious tendency of capitalist production. It was to ensure that as
craft declined, the worker would sink to the level of general and
undifferentiated labor power, adaptable to a large range of simple
tasks, while as science grew, it would be concentrated in the hands
of management. (Braverman 1973 pp 124—5 and 120—1)

Although we have been talking in general about management, the
essential point is that professionalism has become an adjunct to
managerial ideologies. The status of the new occupations, although
they are in some senses ambivalently poised between clerical white-
collar work and capitalist ownership, to a considerable extent originated
in the separation between work as conception of work and work as
manual execution. The scientific management movement was a
response to corporate capitalism and as such spawned a large number
of service occupations. Having become identified with the causes of
management and science the scene was set for these occupations to
become professionalized and to engender an internal organization
commensurate with their status.

5 The internal organization of professions

So far we have been concerned with the formal characteristics of a profession and the problems which are created if these are seen in relation to actual practice; and we have also examined the economic conditions which have provided the impetus for new occupational groups to seek professional status. It was pointed out in the first section that to acquire this status an occupation usually has to display itself to the public in ways which demonstrate its social responsibility. This and its intellectual seriousness, the necessity for long training, and a fund of socially relevant expertise which cannot (or should not) be acquired by means which are outside the occupation's control are necessary to the public image of most professions. In return for the public's trust, the occupational members allow their work practices to be shaped by a code of ethics – which is itself a means of enlisting support for the occupation's right to control its own affairs. These are obviously profoundly political activities. Not only is there a continuing task of public persuasion, but in all probability competitive relations with other occupations as well.

In order to substantiate and achieve a claim to professional status, most occupations which have tried to do this have had to create some form of internal organization – usually a professional association which legislates for and on behalf of its members. In this section, we shall be looking at three facets of this phenomenon: the professional mandate, professional ideologies and the client relationship. In each of them is revealed the essentially political character of professionalism.

The sociological literature in this area of professional activity is fairly plentiful, much of it in the tradition established by Everett Hughes; but there are in addition the more recent developments in the sociology of knowledge in which a particular concern has been the social organization of professional knowledge. These approaches have to some extent been combined in Freidson's study *The Profession of Medicine.* The following sections will attempt to summarize some of the main contributions in these fields.

5.1 The professional mandate

Professions, perhaps more than other kinds of occupation . . . claim a broad legal, moral and intellectual mandate. Not only do the practitioners, by virtue of gaining admission to the charmed circle of the profession, individually exercise a license to do things others do not do, but collectively they presume to tell society what is good and right for it in a broad and crucial aspect of life. Indeed, they set the very terms of thinking about it. When such a presumption is granted as legitimate, a profession in the full sense has come into being. (Hughes 1971 p 288.)

In this extract from his essay 'Licence and mandate' Hughes is describing one of the mainsprings of a profession's authority — its professional mandate. This and the licence to practise which goes with it are fundamental to the nature of professional work and the work identities of the people who carry it out. The strength of the mandate clearly varies from one profession to another. In some, such as medicine, it is supported by state legislation which forbids any unqualified individual to practise as a doctor (though not, of course, in any of the fringe areas of medicine such as osteopathy or faith healing). Similarly, in Britain only a barrister has the right to represent a defendant in the High Court. In most occupations, however, a licence to practice is not necessarily limited to those with professional qualifications. It is quite possible, for instance, to be described as an accountant without being a member of an accountancy institute, and, in spite of several years of pressure from teacher organizations, it is still possible to be employed as a teacher without being professionally qualified.

All occupations at some point in their growth are faced with the problem of convincing a lay public, and usually a government department, that the nature of their work is such that it can only be entrusted to people who have 'appropriate' qualifications. If it is achieved this claim brings with it a considerable level of internal control over the profession's organization: the profession itself is likely to be able to define its qualifications, to devise the relevant curricula and to register new members. Not surprisingly, in order to legitimate its monopolistic practice it is also likely to create ideologies which combine an emphasis on the potentialities of its knowledge and skills for enhancing human life with an insistence on the dangers which can arise from their misuse. This has to some extent been the pattern for the teaching and social work professions. While, in comparison with medicine, it is difficult for these occupations to suggest 'danger' in the misuse of their knowledge, they have both produced public statements drawing attention to the problems which arise from its *underuse*. For instance, both have propagated ideologies for various kinds of social and individual pathology (handicapped and maladjusted children, educational priority areas, the inadequate mother, the recidivist criminal, the culturally deprived child, and so on) to justify increased intervention in the lives of their 'clients'. Similarly, they have devised more active approaches to schemes of diagnosis and appraisal. In the case of both occupations, however, the struggle for monopoly and internal control has been vitiated by the existence of different interest groups within them and by the fact that a good deal of control and responsibility for initiation of policy lies with state departments.

A major threat in these situations to a claim for monopoly is the existence of other occupational groups claiming similar benefits for society and offering different but apparently equivalent skills. This is particularly true of the various groups which comprise the 'academic' professions, but it has also been a major characteristic of the emergence of the contemporary medical profession. When conflicts of this kind arise they are often waged through campaigns of mutual denigration or, if the plausibility and power of the opposing group are too strong, through co-optation. The current ambivalence of the medical profession towards faith healing, and acupuncture, for instance, is an interesting illustration of an occupation's attempt to extend its licence by means of assimilating alternative conceptions into its mainstream practice.

As Jewson's recent study shows, before its consolidation during the nineteenth century, the British medical profession had been divided by serious differences among its three main constituent groups (Jewson 1974). For at least three centuries, the high-status medical practitioners – the physicians – had attempted to protect the distinctiveness of their training, standards and access to prestigious clients from the more lowly groups of surgeons and apothecaries. Nevertheless, in spite of their cultivation of the aristocracy and gentry, the physicians were unable to prevent their rivals from forming their own professional associations and from continuing to offer medical treatment:

> Medical practitioners [in the eighteenth century] did not comprise an homogeneous occupational group but were divided into several, often warring factions . . . Physicians, surgeons and apothecaries each had distinctive patterns of recruitment, training, occupational associates, skills, patients and statuses. Physicians were the most powerful, prestigious and wealthy of the three, and constituted a tiny elite among practitioners. They attended the upper classes, and had themselves received the education of a gentleman. Physicians eschewed the manual labour of surgery and pharmacy, which they regarded as beneath their professional dignity . . . The surgeon and apothecary had a lower status and income than the physician. The surgeon was irredeemably associated with manual work, and until 1745 was joined in one company with the barbers. His professional domain consisted of all those parts of the body which could be reached with a scalpel. The apothecaries were originally compounders and dispensers of drugs and bore the stigma of trade. In the seventeenth century, however, they rapidly increased in numbers and prestige and began to change their professional function. This

brought them into conflict with the extended powers of the Royal College of Physicians. After the Rose Case of 1703 apothecaries had the legal right to attend and prescribe, but only to charge for the drugs they supplied. Henceforth apothecaries regularly attended the sick, calling in a physician in serious cases or consulting him to receive advice in one of the eighteenth century coffee shops. They were by far the most numerous section of the profession, and varied greatly in the character and quality of their practice. (Jewson 1974 p 374)

Later in the article Jewson makes the point that the physicians of the eighteenth century owed their licence to practise to the patronage system which made them dependent on the support of their upper class patients:

Aristocratic patients were in a position to choose for themselves the most satisfactory or amusing practitioners from among the host of medical men who clamoured for their favours. It was the patient who judged the competence of the physician and the suitability of the therapy. (Jewson 1974 p 375)

In this way, the pre-eminence of the physicians was maintained, but the patronage system also ensured that the conceptions of illness and treatment, as well as of the consultative relationship were those which could be tolerated by the ruling class. As Jewson points out, one of the consequences of this was the neglect of the study of anatomy. At a time when scientific medicine had not yet become established, medical access to the body was regarded as a form of violation, and physicians labouring under the handicap of public distrust of the medical profession were often unable to examine their patients. As Jewson puts it 'the occupational role of medical practitioner did not include a general mandate to undertake free and open clinical inspection of the bodies of patients' (p 381).

Jewson's study provides a very clear example of the social structural elements which are involved in the establishment of a professional mandate. It particularly demonstrates the social class basis of the production of professional knowledge and the importance of occupational strategies which rely on the cultivation of the socially powerful. Although the system of private patronage became less widespread during the nineteenth century, certain of its characteristics persisted. Perhaps the most obvious example is the continuing existence of private practice in medicine. But, as Johnson has argued, patronage in its contemporary form operates chiefly through the institutions of the state and corporate business (Johnson 1972).

A good deal of medical research, for instance, is now financed through bodies like the Medical Research Council, the large foundations such as Nuffield, and by direct grants from industry. Any emerging — or even established — profession has to tailor its claims and stated potentialities to the controls which its patrons are able to exert.

A case study which illustrates this point is that of the British Medical Association which was carried out by Eckstein (Eckstein 1960). Of all the professional associations the BMA has probably been the most publicly prominent and the most active in its dealing with state departments. Its membership in relation to the total number of doctors is also very high. It would appear to be one of the most powerful of the professional associations, and yet on two major pieces of legislation, the National Health Insurance Act of 1911 and the National Health Service Act of 1946, its opposition was overridden by the government.

Few professional associations, if any, have the influence and range of activity which the British Medical Association has had. Indeed for many professions, the status, consolidation of membership and political power of the BMA provide an archetypal ideal. Yet it is important to remember that the professional mandate which it tries to safeguard is under continual pressure from a variety of sources — not least from groups within the profession itself.

The vast majority of professions have evolved some form of professional association with some of the functions of the BMA. The two basic kinds of association are those which offer qualifications such as the Royal College of Physicians, the Inns of Court and the Institute of Chartered Accountants, and the non-qualifying associations such as the BMA and the British Sociological Association. It is impossible to summarize the many differences between professional associations; there are wide variations in the representativeness of membership, the status of the qualifications which are offered, and indeed the force which can be deployed in dealings with other public bodies. Generally, however, the qualifying associations have the more complex structure in view of the fact that they are more directly involved in the licensing of professional members, and therefore in the devising of curricula and examinations.

A further important aspect of professional associations is that to the public they tend to present an image of their occupation which emphasizes its unity. This is particularly true of the question of professional competence. As Everett Hughes puts it, through the system of licensing 'competence becomes an attribute of the profession as a whole rather than of individuals as such'. The profession is thereby protected 'by the fiction that all licensed professionals are competent and ethical

until found otherwise by their peers' (Hughes 1958 pp 141–2). Hughes
has expanded on this point in his article 'Professions' (Esland *et al* 1975
pp 240–57) where he suggests that a central feature of the professional
mandate is that it is based on an ideology of 'trust':

> The client is to trust the professional; he must tell him all secrets
> which bear upon the affairs in hand. He must trust his judgement
> and skill. In return the professional asks protection from any
> unfortunate consequences of his professional actions; he and his
> fellows make it very difficult for anyone outside — even civil courts
> — to pass judgement on one of their number. Only the professional
> can say when his colleague makes a mistake. (p 249)

Corinne Gilb in her book *Hidden Hierarchies* has suggested that the
energies of the professional associations in maintaining the notion of
equal competence of their members effectively reduce the possibility
of redress for the lay public:

> Efforts to reinforce the notion of trustworthiness involve simultan-
> eously individual professionals and the profession as a whole. In the
> elitist era of the nineteenth century professional-association leaders
> did not attempt to justify the whole profession but chose to disting-
> uish themselves from amateurs and quacks. More recently profe-
> ssional associations have tried to preserve a solid front *vis-à-vis* the
> public in general and those who buy or receive services in particular.
> Consequently, most professions have had rules against criticizing
> members of the profession in front of a lay person. The medical
> profession has been the most concerned about maintaining a united
> front, even to the point of discouraging doctors from testifying
> against one another in malpractice suits. Violating the code amounts
> to an appeal to lay rather than peer-group judgements — in opposition
> to the foremost *raison d'être* of the professional association and of
> professionalism. (1966 p 74)

For the members of the established professions (less so in the case of
the newer professions) the fear of exposure to formal public scrutiny is
very much overshadowed by the various forms of internal control. In
his analysis of the medical profession, for example, Freidson has
suggested that, contrary to its public image, there is within the profession a fairly clear awareness of and differentiation between the levels
of achievement and competence of different practitioners. He makes
the point, too, that considerable tolerance is often shown towards
lapses in the technique and medical judgement of other colleagues, and
that doctors are usually reluctant to take steps which would harm a
colleague's livelihood. The most effective device for informal control is,
according to Freidson, the 'personal boycott'. This need not necessarily

be a profession-wide boycott but more usually a boycott by the colleague group.

We have been concerned so far in this section with various features of professional membership and organization and with the professional mandate itself. We have suggested that the production of professional ideology is an important aspect of the attempts by a profession to maintain and in some cases increase its influence over its particular area of social life, and also to substantiate the theoretical basis on which its activities rest. Within this ideological framework the ideology of the client, his 'needs', 'problems' and 'treatment', is a particularly important element in the ongoing production of professional knowledge. It is this area which we shall look at in the following section.

5.2 Professionalism and the client

A major characteristic of the professional mandate is that it is dependent for its justification on a somewhat negative view of the lay public. The clearer the boundary between professional and non-professional areas of operation, the more likely it is that there will be a set of assumptions concerning the means of controlling the lay public. The concept of the 'lay public' is an important one in that it legitimates a profession's *raison d'être* – that is, that it has a right to do things for and to people. A central aspect of any profession's work is the means it adopts for controlling and characterizing its clientele; and here the power of imputation is very significant. The professional practitioner can *presume* to define and prescribe types of treatment for the personal characteristics or conditions of other individuals which the occupational group has itself defined. As Freidson puts it:

> In the modern post-industrial society, the practising professions compose part of the official order and, as Parsons pointed out, are agents for social control. Supported by the power of the state, they have official mandate to apply their knowledge and values to the world about them. Their mandate is to define whether or not a problem exists and what the 'real' character of the problem is and how it should be managed. Given the fact that they have *special* knowledge and values, it cannot fail to be that their conceptions will be different from that of the man on the street: where there are experts, there are laymen by definition. And when experts constitute a profession, their knowledge and values become part of the official order which, however enlightened, liberal and benevolent, is nonetheless imposed on the everyday world of the layman. (1970 p 303)

Another crucial aspect of the mandate is that professions have the power to speak for society on these matters in which they claim to be expert. This is well conveyed in the following quotation from Hughes's article 'Professions':

> Professionals *profess*. They profess to know better than others the nature of certain matters, and to know better than their clients what ails them or their affairs. This is the essence of the professional idea and the professional claim. From it flow many consequences. The professionals claim the exclusive right to practise as a vocation, the arts which they profess to know, and to give the kind of advice derived from their special lines of knowledge . . .
> The mandate also flows from the claim to esoteric knowledge and high skill. Lawyers not only give advice to clients and plead their cases for them; they also develop a philosophy of law — of its nature and its functions, and of the proper way in which to administer justice.
> Physicians consider it their prerogative to define the nature of disease and of health, and to determine how medical services ought to be distributed and paid for. Social workers are not content to develop a technique of case work; they concern themselves with social legislation. Every profession considers itself the proper body to set the terms in which some aspect of society, life or nature is to be thought of, and to define the general lines, or even the details of, public policy concerning it. (Hughes in Esland *et al* 1975 p 249)

These aspects of the professional mandate carry with them a number of consequences for the recipients of professional services. As Becker has pointed out, most professions have developed strategies and techniques (the 'bedside manner', for example) for keeping clients 'in their place' and for minimizing their intrusion into professional definitions and routines of work. Ostensibly, these serve to increase the efficiency of the advice and treatment which are provided and to reduce the emotional involvement between professional and client which is seen as vitiating the effectiveness of the professional service. Indeed, it is often claimed by professional workers that clients prefer and are reassured by an impersonal, clinical relationship where their personal problems can be dealt with in the much wider context of professional awareness and expertise. An interesting example of this is provided in Joan Emerson's analysis of the problems of managing the social relations which arise in the gynaecological examination (Emerson 1970). She makes the point that an important element in sustaining the reality of this encounter — for the doctor as well as the patient — is the necessity for eliminating any undertones of sexuality:

Immersed in the medical world where the scene constitutes a routine, the staff assume the responsibility for a credible performance. The staff take part in gynaecological examinations many times a day, while the patient is a fleeting visitor. More deeply convinced of the reality themselves, the staff are willing to convince skeptical patients. The physician guides the patient through the precarious scene in a contained manner: taking the initiative, controlling the encounter, keeping the patient in line, defining the situation by his reaction, and giving cues that 'this is done' and 'other people go through this all the time'. Not only must people continue to believe that 'this is a gynaecological examination', but also that 'this is a gynaecological examination going right'. The major definition to be sustained for this purpose is 'this is a medical situation' (not a party, sexual assault, psychological experiment, or anything else). If it is a medical situation, then it follows that 'no one is embarrassed' and 'no one is thinking in sexual terms'. Anyone who indicates the contrary must be swayed by some nonmedical definition. (Emerson, in Dreitzel (ed.) 1970 pp 77–8)

The view which Emerson seems to be maintaining in this article is that the medical definition of reality is actually functional to the successful treatment of illness and personal disorders. Although she acknowledges that the treating of a patient as object is insulting she nevertheless tends to leave the problem with the doctor having to combine in his manner both professional detachment and some degree of warmth and reassurance.

Other sociologists have, however, been more critical of the power of professional culture and procedures which they see as tending to *dispossess* the client of his view of himself and his problems. Freidson, for instance, represents medicine as structurally and culturally alienating in that for the most part it is regarded as primarily a scientific field of practice. For the medical practitioners, the reality of illness is one which is underwritten by the objectives, experimentation and commitments of science. For the patient, illness is an existential phenomenon bound up with his personal identity, his work, his family relationships, and so on. As a number of sociologists have pointed out (see particularly Glaser and Strauss 1965 and 1968), on many levels of hospital practice, patients are totally excluded from the medical conception of their illness. They are unable to discover the range of alternatives which are open to the doctor; they may be unaware of the extent to which they are being used for research purposes, and on a more basic level still, they may have little or no idea whether or when they will be allowed to leave the hospital. As Glaser and Strauss have documented at length, the treatment of terminal patients is particularly rife with various cross-currents of collusion in the withholding of information which go on between the doctors, nurses, the patient and his relatives. If he is intent on discovering the true position, the patient may have to do so through learning to recognize an elaborate network of implicit meanings which are played out in the scenario around him. In this, as in several other respects, medical practitioners set the terms on which people are allowed to experience themselves as ill or capable of recovery, and in what period of time and with what degree of dependence. The duration and trajectory of illnesses are defined by medical culture, and some forms of illness may even be regarded as a form of deviance, e.g. alcoholism, misuse of drugs, lung cancer.

The theme of dispossession, or alienation from oneself, is taken up by Taylor Buckner in his article 'Transformations of reality in the legal process' (Taylor Buckner 1970). One of the main premises on which he bases his argument is that any act, which is subsequently seen as criminal and for which an individual is tried, is subject to scrutiny from a number of different contexts — notably those of the police and the lawyers. In examining the translation of a defendant's view of his actions into legal reality, Taylor Buckner suggests that there are a number of social processes at work which dispossess the defendants from control over their public examination and interpretation. The dynamics of court-room procedure, the rituals of legal advocacy and the deals between prosecution and defence lawyers to accept lesser charges are seen as part of a totally alien relevance system for an individual standing trial.

A similar but more critical view of the legal process can be found in Blumberg's article 'The practise of law as confidence game' (Blumberg 1969). Here Blumberg sets out to expose the ways in which the rituals of legal practice obscure the protection of professional interest which underlies them. He points out, for instance, that although in public the prosecution and defence lawyers are seen as antagonists with specific obligations to their respective 'clients', in private there are priorities of colleagueship and the securing of 'economies of time, labor, and expense' which prevail: 'The principals, lawyer and assistant district attorney, rely upon one another's cooperation for their continued professional existence, and so the bargaining between them tends usually to be "reasonable" rather than fierce' (Blumberg 1969 p 326).

One aspect of the professional–client relationship which we have not yet touched on is the extent to which the professional practitioner's choice and characterization of his clients tends to be related to their social class position. Howard Becker, in his article 'Social-class variations and the teacher–pupil relationship', has argued that all professionals uphold some notions of the 'ideal client' and that these seem to follow social-class related typifications (Becker 1952).

Thorne, in his analysis of legal education in the United States, maintains the view that built into its structures of practice, opportunity and reward are a number of means by which class inequalities are reproduced; his general points are plainly applicable to the distribution of legal services in Britain:

> Lawyers, being professional, claim an ideal of service, a concern with the public welfare. But the values and organization of the legal profession favor some clients over others . . .
> Not all clients are equal in the eyes of the legal profession. The fee-for-service system favors those who can pay, and the poor often go without the help of lawyers . . .
> When they do seek private legal services, the poor usually end up with lawyers who are at the lower end of the profession in quality of training . . . In law, as in medicine, the success of a professional is gauged by his income and the status of his clientele. The poor are seen as undesirable clients, and their problems as the dirty work of the profession. The legal problems of the poor are often described as 'repetitive', 'uninteresting', and 'unchallenging'. 'Interesting' problems seem to be a class privilege. According to the traditional values of the profession, a lower-class clientele is a mark of a failure.
> Implicit in the foregoing is a philosophy of distribution − an assumption within the legal profession that the rich have a more legitimate claim to services than do clients from lower socio-economic strata. This assumption runs deep, shaping the very definition of legal services. The law is not a neutral instrument; it is oriented in favor of the propertied, 'those groups or classes in society having the power to bend the legal order to their advantage' (Carlin *et al* 1967 p 4). The law, for example, favors landlords over tenants and those who lend over those who borrow money . . .
> The implicit goal of law school is to create successful lawyers, not to provide an equitable distribution of legal services. The biases of the practising profession are reflected in the law school curricula, in the methods of teaching, and in the career models implicit in the course of training itself . . .
> Law students are rarely introduced to the economic and legal institutions which shape the experiences of the poor − for example, welfare agencies, local police departments, and credit unions. The training of lawyers may make them reluctant to even define the problems of the poor in legal terms; there is a tendency in the legal profession to ignore the legal dimensions of the problems of the poor, to regard these problems as 'basically social or psychological, calling for therapy rather than justice' (Carlin *et al* 1967 p 58). (Thorne 1973 pp 120−3)

The points which Thorne is making are clearly applicable to many of the other professions and bring us back to what has been a major question throughout this chapter — the extent to which the professions have become harnessed to the wider structures of economic and political power in society as a whole. Although they profess help, care and in some cases personal fulfilment, they act as powerful agencies in the legitimation and reproduction of social class and the inequalities which are built on it. Through its reliance on rational, 'value neutral' knowledge, a hierarchized view of expertise, and the right of accredited professional members to define the problems and needs of others, this legitimation exercises a powerful hold over public consciousness. In some professions there are already signs that the contradictions raised by professionalism and professional practice under capitalist conditions are causing the growth of alternative and sometimes radical conceptions of practice. Whether these can be any more than the fringe groups which they now are is unlikely without more fundamental changes in other parts of the wage-labour system. In other words, unless there is a more fundamental reappraisal of the relationship between occupations which manage work processes and those which execute them, there is unlikely to be much possibility of any wider social participation than at present in the activities and monopolies of the professions. This is a question which we shall return to at the end of the following chapter.

CHAPTER 8

Geoff Esland

Diagnosis and therapy

Introduction

Following the discussion in the previous chapter of professional ideologies and the operation of professional power, the intention here is to consider those occupations whose prime task is the diagnosis and reshaping, or 'correction', of other people's behaviour or psychological states. The occupations concerned are mainly in the fields of medicine, education and welfare, and include psychiatry, child psychology, social work and the various forms of counselling. They also extend to certain branches of industrial management – for example, occupational psychology and personnel management. Almost without exception these occupations have come to be regarded as 'professions'. Although they lack the internal cohesion and corporate identity of the established professions, their members have sought the organization, entry qualifications and working conditions which are commensurate with professional status. In most of them there is a structure of degree courses up to postgraduate level and they have been able to exert some influence on the making of official policy in their respective fields.

This group of professions – which Halmos has described as the 'personal service' professions – constitutes an important phenomenon in contemporary society (Halmos 1970). Although their origins are recent (in most cases following the Second World War), their activities have expanded greatly. Health visitors and educational welfare officers are two of the latest of a number of occupational groups which have begun the process of professionalization and gradual enlargement of their domain of practice and concern. Collectively these occupations are now involved in the assessment and treatment of behaviour over a wide area of social life, and, like the other professions, produce knowledge which can be used for a variety of 'official' purposes. A good deal of authority hangs on their judgements. Administrative, judicial, social, educational and employment-selection decisions which relate to the competence, personal adequacy, and even to the sanity, of individuals are now grounded in and filtered through the criteria and diagnostic frameworks which form the ideological substance of these occupations. Not only do their techniques impinge on and define areas of everyday experience, but their assumptions and categories are disseminated through the numerous agencies of the mass media. In this respect, they help to structure the self-experience of an entire population and because they frequently operate on the margins of human crises and problems, the members of the welfare professions have a major institutional significance for policing the line between normality and deviance. As Pearson puts it in his book *The Deviant Imagination*:

> At their back is a shadowy reserve army of misfits: mental patients, sexual deviants, petty thieves, 'delinquents' of all kinds, problem families, deprived children, unemployables ('shirkers', 'skivers' and the 'work-shy'), school truants, baby-bashers, alcoholics, etc. These are the bread and butter of the welfare professions. (1975 p 4)

For the members of these occupations, moral and political questions are converted into technical problems. In this sense, the 'people-working' professions are engaged in a highly political process. Moreover, as Halmos has pointed out, their ideologies and curricula are now permeating other professions such as law and town planning. It is not uncommon for students in these subjects to be provided with courses in psychology or social administration, and to have to consider the implications of these ideas for their own professional practice.

It is not possible here to do more than sketch in the various factors which have led to the massive growth of the welfare occupations, but within their emergence (and here we should include teaching as well) it is possible to discern at least three main strands of influence. The first is the economic changes which occurred during the last of the nineteenth century. As we argued in the previous chapter, the system of monopoly capitalism which began to supersede the entrepreneurial methods of production of the earlier part of the nineteenth century brought with it substantial changes both in the structure of the labour market and in the economic role of the state. The expansion of white-collar labour — both professional and clerical — became increasingly a feature of the more bureaucratic forms of production and distribution. In addition, the state began to develop a more interventionist role in numerous aspects of social and economic policy. The underlying economic conditions were marked by the intensification of economic competition during the late nineteenth century which resulted from the internal expansion and overseas development of various national economies such as Germany and the United States. The resulting struggle for markets and political influence led to the necessity for finding new ways of maximizing productivity and profit, and of minimizing 'wastage', especially through 'inefficient' or 'unmotivated' labour. The bureaucratization of production coupled with the increased consolidation and protection of workers' interests led to the necessity for management to pursue methods of more manipulative and persuasive control rather than coercion and to develop intensive rather than extensive forms of work exploitation. This, as we saw in the previous chapter, was a central element in the ideas of 'scientific management' which were promoted by Frederick Taylor (see Braverman 1974). The armoury of scientifically-derived techniques of behavioural control was gradually extended to the organization of the work process – for example, psychological tests for management appraisal, the development of time-and-motion principles in the interests of job efficiency, and the application of psychology to the problem of worker motivation. Moreover, the economic pressures of the time (particularly after the First World War) underlined the increasing vulnerability of the labour force to competitive capitalism. After the war, Britain could no longer rely on its traditional markets and its economy was increasingly threatened by fluctuations in the trade cycle, culminating in the depression of the thirties. For political as well as social reasons it became necessary for governments, with an eye to wider electorates, to take remedial action against the grosser effects of poverty, unemployment, bad housing, ill-health and so on.

A second major influence on the growth of the welfare professions was the development from the mid-nineteenth century of the biological sciences and psychology which gave rise to 'scientific' modes of assessing and understanding human behaviour. Various types of organization ranging from schools to mental hospitals, from prisons to business companies, have come to find in the methods and potentialities of psychology a practical source of technical assistance in the solving or containing of their problems. Numerous individual and social problems, such as crime and madness, have come to be regarded as amenable to the techniques and experiments of psychology and the biological sciences. Not surprisingly, in conjunction with the economic pressures for expansion and cost reduction, this process has led to the growth of psychology as an applied science in many areas of administration, management and personnel work.

The third strand of influence – which was parallel with the increasing centralization of economic policy — is the growth of state welfare liberalism. During the last third of the nineteenth century, in Britain, Europe and America, there was a massive expansion of state interest in social, educational and health policies.

The outcome of these general influences has been the growth of numerous psychologically-oriented occupations. During the twentieth century a growing number of psychologists, psychiatrists and counsellors have been employed by various kinds of organizations in order to find solutions to the social, political and organizational problems with which they are faced. Although their practical concerns may vary, they are united in their search for a rational means of assessing, shaping and ultimately, in some cases, controlling behaviour. Thus, three generations of educational psychologists have had the task of devising intelligence and attainment tests in order to make the selection and teaching of children more 'rational' and efficient. The energies of occupational psychologists have been similarly directed towards creating programmes of worker motivation, and techniques for assessing management potential and appraising performance. Psychiatrists are called upon by judges to make assessments of a convicted individual's character before passing sentence. A striking example of the trend towards the scientific medicalization of social problems is the practice referred to by Steven and Hilary Rose in which up to a quarter of a million American schoolchildren are given the amphetamine drug Ritalin because they have been diagnosed as being 'hyperactive' (Rose and Rose 1976).

These general and illustrative comments set out the basic context for the discussion in the remainder of the chapter. The themes with which we shall be concerned could perhaps be summarized in the following way:

(i) the growth and spread of technological rationality in relation to the understanding and control of human behaviour, and, following from that, the bureaucratization of this process in specialist occupations;

(ii) the nature of the dominance which arises from the professionalization of social control ideologies and particularly the importance in these of psychology;

(iii) the paradox which exists in the amelioration through welfare of the effects of capitalism and the alienation or oppression which are still perpetrated through its methods;

(iv) the politics inherent in the professional ideologies themselves, including the assumptions which are activated in professional dealings with clients.

We shall explore these issues by looking at certain of the personal-service professions – in particular, psychiatry, child psychology, and occupational psychology. In doing this, we shall be primarily concerned with the *general social and cultural significance* of the growth of these occupations, and particularly with their influence in society at large. We shall not, therefore, be offering a detailed sociological study of their internal operations and separate strands of intellectual interest. For our purposes here, it is relatively unimportant that in child psychology, for instance, there may be striking differences of perspective between the Freudian practitioners, the psychometrists and the behaviourists. Within each of these occupations there will clearly be a wide range of ideological positions including some which would count as radical enough to contemplate the virtual dissolution of the occupation itself. It follows from this that we are not concerned either with considering the relative merits of one set of techniques and prescriptions in relation to another.

What justification is there for treating these occupations as a single phenomenon? First of all, they each had their origins in the same ideological paradox which stems from the claim to be people-helping and to be providing 'therapy' yet being employed by organizations in the interests of creating additional rationality and control. Secondly, they are action-based: they each offer certain kinds of advice and treatment and therefore have built into them notions of pathology, sickness or deviance which require eliminatory action. As Halmos puts it:

> The counsellors' invariable objective is to change the personality of the client or the patient of their ministrations. They wish to change the recipient of their services from condition 'a' to condition 'b', and openly profess that 'b' is preferable, better, or of greater value than 'a'. (Halmos 1970 p 18)

For this reason these occupations are *normative* in that the thrust of their work is towards helping individuals readjust to the requirements of their society. The focus of the various programmes of readjustment and therapy is invariably on the individual and not on the social structure. Collectively, the members of these occupations have become what Baritz describes as the 'servants of power' (Baritz 1960). That is, they act as the rational agents of state policy and the policies of large organizations. They therefore have an implicit political role which is obscured by the ideology of people-helping and welfare.

Perhaps one final point should be stressed. I am not attempting to deny that people suffer from 'problems' for which they are able to obtain relief and assistance from the members of these occupations. It is self-evident that people do experience distress and helplessness over such things as marital and sexual problems, difficulties with children, various kinds of mental stress, persistent truancy, educational 'maladjustment', and so on. What I am concerned with is the social contexts in which people experience certain events as problems, are made to feel that they are problems, and in which it is expected that they will either seek advice or accept it if it is prescribed.

The point I am making is that truancy and school phobia, for instance, arise as problems in a society where schooling is compulsory. People have sexual problems where sexuality is surrounded by culturally established expectations, fears and taboos. One of the chief characteristics of the activities of the personal-service occupations is that they socialize their publics into what have been called 'ideologies of need' (Smith and Harris 1972), that is, they create states of awareness from which people generate both the symptoms and the frames of reference within which they can accept a diagnosis as plausible.

This is exemplified by Pearson in his discussion of Szasz's ideas on the oppressive nature of psychiatry:

> At the microscopic level of human intercourse, for example, he [Szasz] points to the way in which human difficulties of satisfying relationships between men and women are boiled down to a technological 'psychiatric-sexual myth' of simultaneous orgasm. This, he writes, is useful for fostering feelings of sexual inadequacy and personal inferiority. It is also a rich source of 'psychiatric patients'. (Pearson 1975 p 27)

It is the power of professional ideologies in defining the 'needs' and 'problems' of the consumer (that is, the lay public) which has led Illich to describe them as 'addictive':

> Welfare bureaucracies claim a professional, political, and financial monopoly over the social imagination, setting standards of what is valuable and what is feasible. (Illich 1971 p 3)

One major reason for their legitimacy and success as both a bureaucratic and a personal source of containment is their great reliance on the vocabularies and assumptions of medicine. As Pearson puts it,

> Sometimes as an attempt to feed off the authority of the well-established professions, the 'semi-professions' — and in particular social work — adopt a quasi-medical terminology and thereby make a claim to a full-bodied professionalism with technical competence. (Pearson 1975 p 16)

These occupations in fact have a major role in setting the cognitive limits on what it is possible to experience in personal and social life, and as many of the critics of 'welfarism' make clear, it is the apparent benevolence of the claims of these occupations which mystifies their latent role as custodians of the *status quo*. We shall return to this view in a later section, but before doing so we need to look in more detail at the ideological contradictions contained in the liberal basis of welfare.

1 Liberalism and welfare capitalism

One of the central characteristics of the welfare professions is that they exemplify a fundamental contradiction in advanced capitalist (and, in some cases, industrial socialist) society. As I have already pointed out, the critics of the welfare occupations highlight the oppressive, manipulative elements in their practices, yet many people would claim that it is the avowed purpose of these professions to minimize the extremes and excesses of capitalist employment and to offer some protection and tangible advice to the victims of industrial advance. From this perspective, the view is usually taken that the undesirable aspects of economic expansion such as unemployment, job insecurity, increased loss of control over the materials and conditions of work, as well as the psychological and family repercussions of these, are largely dictated by competition from other economies. International capitalist trade is regarded as setting the conditions through which a country's economic and social arrangements have to be made. Under these circumstances, the welfare and educational professions are seen as offering whatever means they have to 'heal' the distress and social dislocation which results from industrial rationalization. Thus adult workers as well as school-leavers are counselled in job opportunities and retraining schemes; the members of 'broken' families are counselled and assisted by social workers and, sometimes, probation officers; extreme psychological stress — in the form of 'mental illness' — is treated through psychotherapy, and so on. As Pearson puts it, 'the welfare professional lays claim to his authority from two sources: he claims to possess a measure of *technical competence*, and he lays claim to *moral veracity*; that is, to being a "good person"' (Pearson 1975 p 69).

This view of welfare and the social conditions which appear to justify its expansion is usually referred to as a form of 'progressive liberalism'. Ideologically, and as the generator of work for occupational groups, it has been a major force in the development of monopoly capitalism and has endlessly facilitated the social acceptance of its profit and efficiency-oriented principles. Its characteristics have been well described by Bowles and Gintis:

> The basic strategy of progressive liberalism is to treat troublesome social problems originating in the economy as aberrations which may be alleviated by means of enlightened social programs. Among these correctives, two stand out: education and governmental intervention in economic life. Figuring prominently in the writings of liberals, both have become essential instruments of economic growth. Both, it is thought, can serve as powerful compensatory and ameliorative forces, rectifying social problems and limiting the human cost of capitalist expansion. (Bowles and Gintis 1976 p 19)

The contradiction to which we referred earlier lies in the fact that the welfare occupations find themselves in the position of attacking the deprivation, alienation and inequalities which accompany monopoly capitalism and of dedicating themselves to the general enhancement of human potential yet remain accepting of the principles and hierarchical social relations which render these aims impossible. In other words, the contradiction lies in their adoption of integrative, egalitarian and liberative objectives in societies whose economic life is organized through the institutions and principles of corporate capitalism. What is often overlooked in the progressive liberal view is that the welfare occupations are not simply engaged in 'healing' but in various ways are also involved in defining and upholding the principles of social order. Some, for instance, are called upon to assist in the administration of the penal system, including the treatment and control of juvenile delinquency; and in certain societies (notably the USSR) people who hold extreme political beliefs are brought within the professional ambit of the therapeutic agencies. Others are used to select, train, appraise and 'develop' the human resources of capitalist organizations.

Two of the chief ideological axes of progressive liberalism are 'reformism' and 'utilitarianism'. Reformism refers to the adoption of social reforms which can be accommodated within the existing economic and political structures, and which do not basically question them. Utilitarianism is manifested in the promotion of policies which maximize 'social usefulness'. It can be seen in the familiar concerns with the need to maximize the potential of everyone, with the need to avoid manpower wastage, with the emphasis on a 'pool of untapped ability' which arose in the Crowther Report (1959) on the fifteen to eighteen-year-olds in schools. It can be seen, too, in the necessity for resocializing and 'curing' individuals who for various reasons are unable to take a productive part in their society. The concept of social usefulness is easily extended into 'economic usefulness'. Much of the liberal reformism in education during the 1960s (such as the promotion of school counselling, careers advice and the creation of 'economically relevant' curricula like Nuffield Science projects, etc.) tended to combine an ideology of personal growth with one of economic rationality.

The importance of the utilitarian ethic in the welfare occupations is discussed by Gouldner in the extract below. In it he makes the point that one of their major aims is the conversion of the socially 'useless' into productive individuals:

A central problem confronting a society organized around utilitarian values is the disposal and control of 'useless' men and useless traits. There are various strategies for the disposal and control of useless men. They may, for example, be ecologically separated and isolated in spatially distinct locales where they are not painfully visible to the 'useful'! They may be placed, as American Indians were, on reservations; they may come to live in ethnic ghettos, as American Blacks do; if they have the means to do so, they may elect to live in benign environments such as the communities for the aged in Florida; they may be placed in special training or retraining camps, as are certain unskilled and unemployed American youth, frequently Black; or again, they may be placed in prisons or in insane asylums, following routine certification by juridical or medical authorities. Transition to a Welfare State does not simply mean transition from a standard of individual to collective utility; it also implies a greater involvement of the State in developing and arranging the disposal of the 'useless'. In some part, the very growth of the Welfare State means that the problem is becoming so great and complex that it can no longer be left to the informal control of market or other traditional institutions. Increasingly, the Welfare State's strategy is to transform the sick, the deviant and the unskilled into 'useless' citizens, and to return them to 'society' only after periods of hospitalization treatment, counselling, training, or re-training. It is this emphasis upon the re-shaping of persons that differentiates the Welfare State's disposal strategies from those that tended to cope with the useless primarily by custody, exclusion, and insulation from society. The newer strategies differ from the old in that they seek to be self-financing; the aim is to increase the supply of the useful and to diminish that of the useless. (Gouldner 1971 pp 76—7)

A point similar to the one which Gouldner is making occurs in Ingleby's article 'The psychology of child psychology' (Ingleby 1974b reprinted in Esland *et al* 1975):

A certain degree of authority is proper to anyone in an advisory role, but the 'people professions' operate with a variety of paternalism that is quite incompatible with their claim to be 'helping people to lead better lives', and betrays the fact that their real duties lie altogether elsewhere. If such were really their aim, then we should expect their voice to be the most insistent in articulating and attacking the ways in which the political system itself systematically limits the quality of their clients' lives: moreover, it would be the latter to whom they would divulge their analyses of the situation, not to the others in authority over them. In practice, they apply their energies to ways of dealing with problems that offer the minimum disruption to the existing order – on peril of their jobs. For if the human wreckage produced by the way society is organized is discreetly removed, processed, and returned in re-usable form by these social garbage-workers, then not only will the service avoid producing disruption itself: it will prevent the disturbance which might result if the evidence of the political system's failure to meet human needs were left in our midst. (Esland *et al* 1975 pp 292–3)

The general influence of utilitarianism in Britain and the interrelationship between welfare and social control has been most strongly represented in the Fabian tradition of the Labour Party. The irony is that in attempting to further its meritocratic aim and its quest for social equality, it embraced the liberal ideologies and machineries of welfare. In so doing, it provided impetus for a new range of middle class occupations and a new form of social control.

One of the prime means by which the contradiction between the overt and the latent operations of the welfare professions is maintained is through what Bowles and Gintis have called the technocratic—meritocratic ideology. They argue that the wide acceptance of meritocratic principles in education has been a major legitimation of inequality and the existing social structure:

> The educational system legitimates economic inequality by providing an open, objective, and ostensibly meritocratic mechanism for assigning individuals to unequal economic positions. Indeed, the more meritocratic the educational process appears, the better it serves to legitimate inequality. For the educational system fosters and reinforces the belief that economic success depends essentially on the possession of technical and cognitive skills – skills which it is organized to provide in an efficient, equitable, and unbiased manner on the basis of meritocratic principle. (Bowles and Gintis 1976 p 103)

The chief vehicle of the technocratic legitimation of inequality during the twentieth century has been psychology. Through its methodology and its apparent value as an ideological resource for so many areas of social policy, psychology has become a favoured handmaiden of the various bureaucracies which process and treat human beings. In almost every one of the people-working occupations psychology has provided the main ideological content. As I argued in the previous chapter, it has become a prime exemplar of what Marcuse calls the 'operationalism' of contemporary society. In its most essential respects it is, in fact, highly congruent with the ethic of rational efficiency which characterizes bureaucratic practice. It is in recognition of this that a number of its critics have come to regard psychology as a mechanized dehumanizing system which renders the individuals it purports to diagnose and treat as reified objects. (This is true of Ingleby's work, for instance; see Ingleby 1970, 1974a and 1974b.)

One of the major principles of psychological practice is that various human attributes can be 'scientifically measured' and placed on a continuum of the psychologist's devising (after he has already decided which attributes are salient and how they and their properties are to be recognized). IQ is the prime example but in recent years other attributes, such as sociability, mental adjustment, extroversion and introversion, social initiative, submissiveness and dominance, group dependency and self-sufficiency, neuroticism and stability, have all been added, along with many others, to the psychologist's battery of 'personality dimensions' which can be assessed through the application of a 'scientific' methodology.

One problem with this methodology is that it takes as given the cultural and political standpoint of the psychologist who makes the measurements and diagnoses. This process represents either an implicit denial of the existence of cultural and structural divisions in society or at least celebrates one set of cultural assumptions and interests against others. As Ingleby has argued in relation to educational psychology:

> Child psychology has wished out of existence the all-important political context of childhood which is usually seen as a source of extraneous variance which must be partialled out of the data to make them truly 'psychological'. (Ingleby 1974b in Esland *et al* 1975 p 288)

In its reduction of politically and structurally located characteristics to the level of individual motivation and personality, it effectively renders the task of psychology as one of technical diagnosis. We should now look at how its latent political purposes become effective.

2 Psychology as professional ideology

Psychology is more than just a professional field of work. It is also a codified ideology and practice that arises from the nature of our capitalist society and functions to bolster that society. Although some of the work of professional psychology and psychiatry is quite overtly oppressive (witness the rise of psychosurgery, electroshock, and behaviour modification for rebellious prisoners), the bulk of psychological manipulation is covert. Hidden below the surface platitudes of social science, industrial psychologists join with the state hospitals in disciplining the working class, creating various devices to stifle popular recognition of oppression and subsequent revolutionary action. (Brown 1974 p 1)

We have so far been suggesting that the ideologies and practices of the 'personal service' professions should be seen in relation to their political and economic contexts. Particularly important is the fact that through the emergence of modern capitalism with its highly bureaucratized system of production, its fragmented division of work and the proliferation of service occupations, many of the 'people-working' professions have come to be regarded as a necessary service in the pursuit of economic rationality – and, therefore, of economic expansion. Coupled with this is the increasing central direction by most western states of various forms of liberal-welfare policy which has led to these occupations becoming key reality-definers for an increasing area of individual and social morality. In other words, they have become the custodians (as well as creators) of rationality and criteria of 'fitness' which are deployed in a variety of official contexts. In the cause of economic and social utility, this group of occupations has acquired the right to be consulted on, and to intervene in, a wide range of issues connected with social order, social productivity and organizational efficiency.

Despite the well-recognized claims that these occupations are explicitly built around a people-helping/improving/caring conception of their function, there is a firm underlying economic rationale to their continuing existence and practice. The effect of this rationale, it was suggested, is to encourage these occupations to support, implicitly at least, the economic and social structures – and notably the class structure – within the wider society. The technocratic–meritocratic ideology which has informed a good deal of the practice of the educational, welfare and personnel professions serves to legitimate the rational allocation and treatment of individuals according to their place in the social structure. This political orientation is also fostered by the necessity for these occupations to compete for public patronage and support and to couch their public pronouncements in terms of the social and economic benefits which their services provide.

This now brings us to the nature of the ideologies themselves, and, in particular, to the social and political consequences which follow from the conceptions of human motivation, behaviour and pathology contained within them. A fundamental feature is that the knowledge which constitutes the ideological substance of the personal-service professions is heavily influenced by various forms of psychological theory. This is not to deny that there may be other theoretical influences operating within them. In addition to theories of individual pathology (e.g. 'maladjustment' or mental illness) there are also theories of *social* pathology which are invoked as explanation for certain social problems. In these cases, the individual's *environment* is cited as the agency responsible for his/her problem condition. Thus, certain difficult schoolchildren are described as coming from 'broken homes' or from 'culturally deprived' families, or from 'overspill' council estates as explanations of their inadequacy. Although these theories do not *individualize* culpability to the extent of more orthodox psychological theories, they are closely related to them in that they similarly fail to connect these descriptions either to the class structure of society or to the cultural viewpoint of the person making them. The power of the psychological paradigm is, however, sufficiently well established for it to have dominated more environmentally based theories, and, in most of the occupations with which we are dealing, psychology has provided the most significant source of ideational content.

A fairly typical progression in the formation of such an ideology is that described by Ginzberg in his review of the history of the vocational guidance service in the United States. He makes the point that psychology has been the 'mother discipline' within the careers counselling profession. Its influence became particularly significant after the widespread use of psychometric testing during the First World War which was designed to classify and assign men to various jobs and ranks in the Army:

> Psychology thus won its spurs. It demonstrated that it had a major contribution to make to the efficiency of large organizations. Small wonder that, during the 1920s, both education and industry attempted to capitalize on it. In addition to tests of intelligence and achievement, the psychometricians developed a wide range of aptitude tests. Once it was postulated that an individual's performance potential could be assessed, and once jobs could be analyzed with regard to the skills required to perform them, the stage was set for turning vocational guidance into a 'science'. (Ginzberg 1971 p 30)

In a later comment in this chapter, Ginzberg underlines the inherent conservatism which is characteristic of a good deal of the practice of the personal service occupations, and which is, in fact, a product of the individualism of psychological theory itself:

> the major varieties of guidance . . . trait-and-factor analysis, and counselling psychology – were all committed to helping individuals make a more satisfactory adjustment to the world in which they must live and work. Time has seen shifts in the emphases that engage guidance specialists – from helping underprivileged children obtain suitable jobs to assisting young people from affluent families improve their decision-making about their life problems. But career guidance has always been concerned with the individual. (Ginzberg 1971 pp 36–7)

The significance of the growth of psychological theory and the techniques which stem from it as a central element of social control in contemporary society has become well recognized in the work of a number of social theorists. It has, for instance, been one of the elements of the 'critical theory' of the Frankfurt school of sociologists. Habermas, for example, in his paper 'Technology and science as ideology' refers to the repression which is implied in the availability and apparent social necessity for psychological controls in society. (See Esland *et al* pp 47–8.) One of the most forceful critics of the effects of the widespread application of psychological techniques to new areas of social life was C. Wright Mills. The following extract from his discussion of twentieth-century 'managerialism' in *White Collar* makes this very clear.

> In modern society, coercion, monopolized by the democratic state, is rarely needed in any continuous way. But those who hold power have often come to exercise it in hidden ways: they have moved and they are moving from authority to manipulation. Not only the great bureaucratic structures of modern society, themselves means of manipulation as well as authority, but also the means of mass communication are involved in the shift . . . Under the system of explicit authority in the . . . nineteenth century, the victim knew he was being victimized, the misery and discontent of the powerless were explicit. In the amorphous twentieth-century world, where manipulation replaces authority, the victim does not recognize his status. The formal aim, implemented by the latest psychological equipment, is to have men internalize what the managerial cadres would have them do, without their knowing their own motives, but nevertheless having them. Many whips are inside men, who do not know how they got there, or indeed that they are there. In the movement from authority to manipulation, power shifts from the visible to the invisible, from the known to the anonymous. And with rising material standards, exploitation becomes less material and more psychological. (Mills 1951 p 110)

The intention behind the sociological critique of the various forms of psychological ideology and practice is to 'restore to consciousness' the political and cultural contexts which are left out of account in the psychological perspectives themselves. This is all the more important given the dependence of various official practices on their assumptions and techniques. The power of the diagnostic and therapeutic professions lies in their mandate for defining the criteria for such qualities as competence, adequacy and responsibility in society. The converse of this is that they have a professional right to label and, in some cases, stigmatize. This mandate is embodied in the professional licence and curriculum and is exercised in harness to a number of powerful institutions backed up in some cases by government legislation. Thus, people can be committed against their will to remain in mental hospitals; convicted offenders can be referred for psychiatric reports; 'inadequate' mothers may be forced to hand over their children to local authority care; children are compelled to undergo various forms of evaluation in schools in order to be ranked for achievement; applicants for certain jobs in industry may have to take a range of psychological tests before their 'suitability' can be decided; the members of some organizations may be told to co-operate in schemes of 'personal appraisal'. Each of these processes is an aspect of institutionalized applied psychology. In this respect it could be argued that social typing or labelling have become legitimated as professionalized processes. Decisions relating to normality, sickness, competence and adequacy have become systematized as various forms of expert knowledge: several kinds of administration have recognized in applied psychology a provider of 'rational' (that is, experimentally validated) knowledge suitable for the selection and management of people. The task of a sociological critique is to bring to the foreground the inherent political nature of these practices.

3 'Scientific psychology'

The status of psychology as a 'science' is one of the principal factors in the general tendency to disregard its inherently political content. As we argued in the previous chapter, a major ingredient in an occupation's claim to professional status lies in its ability to point to a substructure of theory, and preferably scientific theory, on which its practice can rest. As Taylor, Walton and Young put it in their paper 'The appeal of positivism':

> The evocation of natural science presents the positivist with a powerful mode of argument. For the system of thought which produces

miracles of technology and medicine is a prestigious banner under which to fight. It grants the positivist the gift of 'objectivity'; it bestows on his pronouncements the mantle of 'truth'; it endows his suggestions of therapy, however threatening to individual rights and dignity, with the air of the inevitable. (Taylor, Walton and Young 1973 p 32)

Pearson, in his book *The Deviant Imagination*, has attributed much of the influence which welfare ideologies have acquired to their reliance on medical vocabularies and assumptions. He illustrates this in the following passage:

Medicine is a highly legitimate business and its professional empire has colonized many strictly non-medical fields of interest. One of the most important, if not *the* most important, development in the field of deviance has been the 'medicalization' and 'psychiatricization' of social problems: crime, it is said, is an illness; youthful unrest is a maturational phase; political dissent is the result of personality quirks of 'mindless militants'; a poor employment record flows from a disorder of character; poor families, or 'problem families', are low on something called 'interpersonal maturity'. Some critics will say that the worst thing to happen to deviance theory was medicine.
The power of medicine has carried great weight in the control of deviance, and vital to its authority is the fact that medicine – and all its associated vocabulary of 'treatment', 'diagnosis', 'therapy', 'sickness', 'illness' and 'cure' – is judged to be morally neutral. (Pearson 1975 p 15)

As Pearson points out, what are in effect moral and political problems are rendered as technical problems for the members of the welfare professions. As David Ingleby argues in his paper 'The psychology of child psychology', it is the dominance of the scientific world view in psychology which has effectively depoliticized its apparent purpose; this is particularly true of conceptions of the child, his development, his social situations, his relationship with his parents and so on which are contained in it:

. . . child psychology has not looked at its subject-matter in the light of the political system in which it is found: the political order is usually seen as a source of extraneous variance which must be partialled out of the data to make them truly 'psychological' . . . the 'scientific' label is a device for throwing us, ideologically speaking, off the scent: for that which is 'scientific', by definition, does not depend for its authority on the political loyalties implicit in it. My contention was that the social function which determines the spirit of inquiry in psychology – whatever convictions psychologists may

have about it — is the maintenance of the *status quo* . . .
Now the most effective means which psychologists have devised for keeping the political context of childhood out of the picture was the creation of that venerable distinction between 'socialization' and the rest of development, and the regulation of ideology to the waste-paper basket of 'cultural variables'. Having thus disposed of political factors, psychologists have moved increasingly towards areas where these influences are regarded as minimal, and towards a methodology which does not cater for them . . .
Precisely how the prevailing relations of production and consumption will impinge on him [the child] will vary greatly with his class position, but it is those relations which are the most important factors in determining the world in which 'socialization' casts him. (Ingleby 1974b, in Esland *et al* 1975 pp 288–90)

A view similar to the one which Ingleby is putting forward is that of Steven and Hilary Rose. In a chapter entitled 'The politics of neuro-biology: biologism in the service of the state', they point to the numerous ways in which biological assumptions and experimental techniques have been applied to the treatment of social and moral problems. They describe this phenomen of 'biologism' in the follow-ing way: 'Biologism is the attempt to locate the cause of the existing structure of human society, and of the relationships of individuals within it, in the biological character of the human animal' (Rose and Rose 1976).

During the course of their paper, they argue that the *reduction* of social and political issues to the principles of biology (and ultimately physics) has led to their becoming 'locked into the processes of social control'. In other words, explanations of, and treatments for, 'anti-social' or dissenting actions are grounded in biological assumptions of human motivation. Thus, they suggest that:

the importance of biologism is again 'proving' that capitalism and imperialism derive from 'man's innate aggressiveness', that all human experience can be subsumed into categories of stimulus and response, reward and punishment, and that individuals' success or failure in a competitive society, their capacity to revolt against the state, is a result of a flaw in their chemistry or brain structure. This 'proof' both justifies the oppression and, by opposing their struggles with scientific rationality, devalues, divides and demoralizes the oppressed.

These writers provide a number of examples to substantiate their argument, including the widespread prescription of the drug Ritalin to American schoolchildren displaying behaviour problems in school, such as being poor learners, inattentive in class, and disrespectful to autho-

rity. The following extract contains their critique of biological reductionism as applied to schizophrenia and depression:

> The ideological components within the reductionist paradigm are
> apparent: the inborn view of schizophrenia at once refuses to admit
> criticism of social structures, such as the family and alienated work
> forms, whilst at the same time encouraging a manipulative view of
> treatment. This is even more apparent when we look at the respec-
> tive analyses, biochemical or social, as applied to the affective
> disorders such as depression. Those who argue a biochemical cause
> of depression, such as the psychiatrist Sargent, look for treatment
> by way of anti-depressant drugs: treatment is effective if it adjusts
> the depressed individual (typically a woman post-natally or around
> menopause) back into an acceptable social role, such as that of the
> good housewife and mother. The stability and appropriateness of
> the social order is taken as a natural given in this situation, and the
> job of the psychopharmacologist and clinician is to chemically fit
> people into it. (Rose and Rose 1976)

In discussing the centrality of positivism in the ideologies of the
welfare occupations, Taylor, Walton and Young make the point that its
main effect has been to reinforce both a consensual and deterministic
view of normal and deviant development. Through its emphasis on
internal variables (for example, psychomotor skill or cognitive style)
and antecedent influences on behaviour (such as the infant-mother
relationship), psychological theory leaves out of account the cultural
diversity of society and the cultural enforcement which is involved
when the middle class criteria and judgements of the professional are
imposed on the members of another class and culture. In other words,
psychological reasoning and definitions – by individualizing social
problems – legitimate the ethnocentrism of the expert. The following
passage from *The New Criminology* makes this point clearly:

> All three of these strands: consensus, determinism and scientism,
> give weight to positivist rhetoric. What is necessary, at this juncture,
> is to explain why this mode of thought is taken up by the positivist
> and how the interests of the practitioner and the politician mesh
> together. It is important, at the outset, to realize that at the simplest
> level the positivist, by placing himself in the middle of the posited
> consensus, defends the reality of his own world. For example, Dr. R.
> Cockett (Regional Psychologist to the Home Office Prison Depart-
> ment) writes of working-class drug-takers in the Ashford Remand
> Centre [1971 p 142]: '[they]' were shown to be rather more suspi-
> cious and withdrawn than non-drugtakers, more emotionally tense
> and excitable, and more radical or less conservative in temperament,
> but to have relatively poor self-sentiment formation – persistence,

will-power, social effectiveness and leadership.' This was coupled with: 'less emotional maturity and tolerance of frustration', 'intra-punitiveness' and 'a tendency towards paranoid feeling'.

Such 'discoveries' are commonplace in the literature of all forms of deviant behaviour. But behind the neutral language lies, in Cockett's own words, 'what is popularly understood by "inadequacy" and "weakness of character" (p 144). It is a simple translation to inter-pret hedonistic and expressive subcultures as not cultures at all but merely as aggregates of inadequate individuals who are excitable, have a low tolerance of frustration, maturity, etc. Moreover, it is sleight of hand which can conjure what some would term repression into a 'tendency towards paranoid feeling'. All of this reinforces the middle-class professional world of the expert; his stable employment and marriage, deferred gratification and planning are all indices of his own 'strong' personality and social 'adequacy'. By making statements about the deviant he is, inevitably, making valuations about his own world. (Taylor, Walton and Young 1973 pp 32–3)

A similar critical position of scientifically adduced social typing has been adopted by Joan and Stephen Baratz in their paper 'Early child-hood intervention: the social science base of institutional racism'. Here they offer a critique of the assumptions of intervention programmes in the United States which tacitly label Negro behaviour as 'pathological'. They argue that the social typing of black Americans as experiencing various forms of deprivation, which is carried out by professional experts, devalues the culture to which these children belong. The basis of the social typing lies in what the Baratzes call a 'social pathology' model of the black American family and community:

Liberals have eagerly seized upon the social pathology model as a replacement for the genetic inferiority model. But both the genetic model and the social pathology model postulate that something is wrong with the black American. For the traditional racists, that something is transmitted by the genetic code; for the ethnocentric social pathologists, that something is transmitted by the family. The major difference between the genetic model and the social pathology model lies in the attribution of causality, *not* in the analysis of the behaviours observed as sick, pathological, deviant or underdeveloped. (1970 p 32)

One of the chief means by which the pathological model is sustained is through what these writers describe as 'the inadequate mother hypothesis' — a notion which they claim as 'proliferated in the litera-ture of educational psychology':

It is important to understand that the inadequate mother hypothesis rests essentially on the grounds that the mother's behaviour produces deficit children. It was created to account for a deficit that in actuality does not exist — that is, that ghetto mothers produce linguistically and cognitively impaired children who cannot learn. (1970 p 36)

Negative labelling as a function of occupational ideologies has long been an issue of debate in psychiatry. The work of Szasz, Laing and Scheff, among others, has consistently criticized the political basis of psychiatric diagnosis and treatment, and the ethnocentrism which is upheld in the individualist explanations of patients' problems. One study which explicitly recognizes the wider political elements in psychiatric practice is Halleck's book, *The Politics of Therapy* (1971). Halleck, who was himself a psychiatrist, is concerned to provide a critique of the 'official' view of psychiatry. He maintains that this view represents psychiatry as a 'neutral', scientific activity, 'designed to reduce pain and discomfort and to increase the capacity of the individual to adjust satisfactorily'. Against this he wants to claim that 'Therapy has become a commodity, a means of social control' (Halleck 1971 pp xiii—xiv).

One of the examples he provides of the way in which control occurs is through what he describes as the 'repressive use of drugs': 'When a physician prescribes a drug for a patient, he is making a significant social statement to the effect that the patient's problems are internal rather than external. A person who needs pills is judged to be "sick", and his capacity to change the social order is compromised (1971 p 76).

Halleck also refers to the 'double agent' problem, in which the psychiatrist has to act on behalf of an organization and for a patient who may be a member of that organization. This is obviously not true of all institutions; in many, the professional 'personal service' workers insist on their right to preserve the secrecy of their files. According to Halleck, this is not true of prisons. He describes his experience as a psychiatrist in a prison and makes the point that in providing therapy for depressed prisoners he did nothing to change the conditions and oppression of prison life. The converse was, if anything, true:

> By participating in the punishment process, even as a healer, I loaned a certain credibility to the existing correctional system. Prison administrators frequently boast about progress in correctional programs by pointing to the number of therapeutic personnel available. Yet, if such personnel are merely available but do nothing to change the dehumanizing aspects of the system, their very presence makes it easier to rationalize oppression within that system. (1971 p 19)

The net effect of psychiatric practice based on the illusion of political neutrality is, Halleck maintains, to conceal the existence of social conflict and to preserve the *status quo*. He cites a number of instances where students at university or people in particular jobs are more or less compelled by their deans or employers to visit the psychiatrist employed by their organization. At the same time, the psychiatrist may be asked by the employer to provide medical legitimation for getting rid of troublemakers (1971 pp 139–51).

4 Educational psychology

One area of institutional life where psychology has had a major impact is that of education. This is true not only of the diagnosis and treatment of problem and 'maladjusted' children but of the structure of schooling itself. Almost every aspect of school organization is an expression of a psychologistic world view. The grading of children by ability, the structuring of curriculum subjects into age-related blocks, assumptions about learning, motivation and teaching style, even the physical design of classrooms – all embody a number of significant psychological principles.

Educational psychology became particularly important – in both Britain and the United States – during the years immediately after the First World War. Its chief function at that time was to provide material for testing the intelligence of children – an activity which it still continues to serve although in a now much broader context of personality assessment.

Paul Henderson has argued (Henderson 1976) that the grading of children by intelligence testing can be seen in terms of the protection of middle class culture during the rise of mass education. The notion of IQ effectively legitimated the middle class curriculum and downgraded working class culture. Karier's article 'Testing for order and control in the corporate liberal state' (Karier 1972) provides some well-documented analyses of the ways in which psychological testing of schoolchildren in America became firmly sponsored by a number of influential educational and industrial groups (notably the Foundations). Karier argues that the rise of the intellectual testing of children and the institutionalization of vocabularies relating to IQ and achievement should be regarded as an expression of capitalist economic logic. Intelligence tests were seen explicitly by early educational psychologists as a means of legitimating and preserving middle class control of the higher status occupations. He makes the point that the educational

foundations — such as the Carnegie Foundation — sponsored by corporate industry, spent large sums supporting and promoting the work on
testing of people such as Thorndike and Terman:

> It was men like Thorndike, Terman and Goddard, supported by
> corporate wealth, who successfully persuaded teachers, admin-
> istrators and lay school boards to classify and standardize the
> school's curriculum with a differential track system based on ability
> and values of the corporate liberal society. The many varied tests, all
> the way from I.Q. to personality and scholastic achievement, period-
> ically brought up-to-date, would serve a vital part in rationalizing the
> social class system.
> The tests also created the illusion of objectivity which on the one
> side served the needs of the 'professional' educators to be 'scientific'
> and on the other side served the need of the system for a myth
> which could convince the lower classes that their situation in life was
> part of the natural order of things. (Karier 1972)

As Bowles and Gintis have also pointed out:

> I.Q. tests captured the imagination of high-level policy-makers and
> were seized upon by school administrators. In the years 1921–1936,
> over 4,000 articles on testing appeared in print; by 1939, no less
> than 4,279 mental tests were in circulation; a survey of 150 school
> systems, in 1932, revealed that three-quarters were using intelligence
> tests to assign students to curriculum tracks. (1976)

During the 1950s and 1960s the educational psychology profession
has greatly enlarged its activities. The dominance of IQ testing has diminished but the role of the educational psychologist has become much
wider. It now encompasses the diagnosis and assessment, as well as some
of the treatment, of a wide area of children's educational 'problems'.
These range from 'maladjustment' and 'sub-normality' to school phobia
and delinquency. The educational psychologist is also, under the terms
of the Children and Young Persons Act of 1969, part of a much wider
social work organization.

The professionalization of this particular occupational group embodies many of the points which Baritz makes about the massive
expansion of occupational psychologists in industry. In 'The servants
of power', Baritz makes the key point that corporate capitalism has
been significantly dependent in practice on the skills of behavioural
scientists — in particular as a means for increasing worker motivation
and amenability. He suggests that:

> By the middle of the twentieth century, industrial social science has
> become one of the most pregnant of the many devices available to

America's managers in their struggle with costs and labour, government and the consuming public . . . Demanding that the social scientists in their employ concentrate exclusively on the narrow problem of productivity and industrial loyalty, managers made of industrial social science a tool of industrial dominance. (Baritz 1960, in Esland *et al* 1975 p 325)

During the twentieth century an increasing area of human behaviour has come within the ambit of professional inquiry and control. Although this has almost certainly reduced the gross levels of material hardship of the nineteenth century, its dominance as a means of bureaucratic administration and control raises serious questions as to the ways in which the personal service occupations have legitimated and made rational the inequities of the social structure. The concentration on the solving of problems which forms the basis of much of their work safely leaves aside the political implications of their task. As Jack Douglas has put it:

Insofar as social scientists do not initiate and become personally involved in the practical action aimed at solving problems but, rather, await the summons to involvement from men of practical affairs, they not only allow but force the men of practical affairs to define the problems, define the relevance of the social scientists, *define which social scientists* are to be consulted, define the structure of the advising situation, and then, most importantly, force them to pick and choose from that advice those parts which they can interpret in some way which 'helps' them, as they see it, to construct their intended course of practical action. Because of this, it is actually the metaphysics of everyday life or practical affairs which determine most of the impact of the social sciences on everyday life. What has normally happened so far, and what threatens to become even more prevalent, is that the men of practical affairs make use through this consulting process of the prestige of expert scientific knowledge in our society to achieve the goals which they set by the means which they determine: they use the social sciences as a front which helps them to control public opinions and, hence, public responses to what they intend to do. (Douglas 1970 p 267)

5 Radicalism and practice within the welfare professions

For much of this chapter I have been examining the people-working professions from a perspective which seriously puts into question their basic policies and assumptions. By focusing on the contradiction between their ideologies of caring, healing and helping and the structural limitations which substantially constrain what is possible for them to achieve, by highlighting the individualistic basis of their labelling and treatment, we are in effect undermining the 'official' claims through which they present themselves to the public. It is important to be aware of what this entails for the practitioner and the choices which are available to him or her.

Perhaps the first point to make is that in setting out a critical perspective on the practices of these occupations we are not going very far beyond what has been suggested by the radical groups which have grown up within these occupations themselves. In each of them, there are journals, organizations, conferences and even, in some cases, centres of alternative practice, which try to come to terms with the dilemmas of offering remedial services within the structural limitations imposed by advanced capitalism. They are, in fact, well aware of the difficulties of having to balance the need to give short-term assistance to helpless clients with the intellectual quest for the means to change the system itself.

As any student of the recent developments in sociology will know, this is by now a very familiar dilemma to which its radical theories lead. Education, criminology, medicine and science, as well as the professions, have all been exposed to the questioning of assumptions and practice from critical social theory. Brian Heraud's article 'Professionalism, radicalism, and social change' is one of the recent attempts to examine the implications of 'radicalization' for the professions. Starting with the aim of trying to assess the consequences of a radical movement on professional identity, he gives an account of the organizing beliefs of Case Con, the radical movement relating to social work. Founded in 1970, Case Con's main aims are listed as ' "opposition to capitalism . . . the solution of many of the problems facing social workers' clients . . . lies in the replacement through working class struggle of capitalism by socialism" ' (Heraud 1973 pp 88—9).

After reviewing the criticisms and some of the 'revolutionary' practices of radical social workers (such as joining in with squatters against local councils), Heraud remains fairly pessimistic about the impact of such groups within the profession. Perhaps rather blandly he concludes that:

> most professions seem flexible enough to tolerate and even accept a radical wing or segment as part of the price to be paid for change, and hopefully are increasingly sensitive to social movements outside their boundaries. If professions are the 'conscience' of society, they too must have their own 'conscience'. (1973 p 99)

Pearson's article 'Making social workers: bad promises and good omens' provides a rather different view of social workers' attempts to resolve the dilemma which they are forced into as a result of adapting the humanitarian dictates of their occupational task to the pressures of social structures. From interviews with sixty-five social workers Pearson found considerable evidence of what he calls professional 'deviance' and 'sabotage' — that is, complicity on the part of the social worker in law-breaking:

> An area that emerged as being of primary importance, and where rules, training, values and action intersect, was 'industrial deviance' in social work — that is, the bending and breaking of rules and regulations by social workers in order to advance their work with clients, and the turning of 'blind eyes' towards clients who only seem able to 'get by' by 'getting round' the welfare system.
> The most commonly mentioned forms of rule-breaking were in relation to social security benefit regulations. These include:
> 1. People who have undisclosed earnings in excess of the allowed amount while in receipt of welfare benefits. Usually these earnings were thought to be small amounts obtained from jobs such as washing glasses in pubs, part-time work helping out in a shop, house-cleaning or baby-minding.
> 2. Women claimants who receive benefits as single women, or divorced women, but who are nevertheless cohabiting or in a close relationship with a man.
> 3. Clients who attempt to fiddle the social security system through false disclosures, skilful pestering, emotional bullying and other forms of deception. These were commonly described to me as well-meaning rogues who knew their way around the system, although my impression was that much of what I heard was highly dramatized, and possibly even mythical.
> Another main category of official rule-breaking concerned social workers who do not strictly enforce the conditions of probation orders, parole orders and care orders — neglecting, for example, the commission of offences or ignoring residence requirements. (Pearson, in Bailey and Brake (eds) 1975 pp 25—6)

Possible though it is to see 'industrial sabotage' as a collective undermining by an occupation's members of the welfare state and social structure in general, it would be a mistake to see it in those terms. These kinds of incidents, although possibly widespread, are the *ad hoc* attempts by a professional group to assimilate and reinterpret the rules of its own pragmatic codes of everyday practice. They are, in effect, attempts to come to terms with the onerous requirements of heavy caseloads, financial stringency and a range of bureaucratic principles which if adhered to could make the work much more difficult.

Pearson refers also to the 'torment of conscience' which can afflict the social worker leading him to protect the individual against the 'system':

> to the extent that social-work thinking is governed, and flawed, by the false division of the 'individual' and 'society', social work's sabotage can be seen as a continuation of, rather than a departure from, professional consciousness. In its current crises of identity social work rushes to one side or the other of this false split, either to defend 'the system' or, in acts of primitive, bandit-like industrial deviance, to protect 'the individual'. (Pearson, in Bailey and Brake (eds) 1975 p 32)

'Industrial deviance' embodies many of the qualities of a 'hapless reformism' and captures perhaps the sense of futility which may be felt by members of the people-working occupations in the face of the almost unassailable structures of economic and political power and the institutions which legitimate them.

An interesting attempt to go beyond this dilemma, and a critical look at Case Con's proposals for action, is provided in Stan Cohen's paper 'It's all right for you to talk' (1975). After spelling out the possible irrelevance to the clients of social workers (at least in the short term) of radical action based on changing the capitalist system, Cohen proposes a programme which he calls 'The Unfinished'. Drawing on the ideas of the Norwegian sociologist, Thomas Mathiesen, it is based essentially on maintaining the short-term obligations of helping clients without abandoning the commitment to large-scale change. Some extracts from this proposal are set out below:

> The strategy I want to suggest is one which does not (like authoritarian Marxism) make people expendable and which does not write off all short-scale intervention. The long versus short-term issue is critical, because to support . . . the radical view of exploitation, power and inequality should not carry the prescription of abandoning all else . . .
>
> 'The Unfinished' is a programme based on what does not yet exist. From the beginning Mathiesen is quite clear about the dangers of going for short-term goals only: taking up reformist positions in the system — as a humane prison governor, an advocate of inmate councils — cannot but lead to absorption and an abandonment of the long-range goals of changing the system totally. As every social worker well knows, absorption eventually takes place through all sorts of subtle ways of incorporation, initiation into the agency's secrets, compromising for too long. On the other hand there are some very effective short-term possibilities, not just through human-

itarian work but in conscious policies of raiding the establishment for resources, contributing to its crises, unmasking and embarrassing its ideologies and pretensions. Any such effectiveness can be lost by finishing. One must be able to live with ambiguity and refuse to accept what the *others*, the authorities, demand — a choice between revolution and reform . . .

I've suggested this as a paradigm for social-work action. This is not to say it will fit every case, but it seems to me that the notion of 'the unfinished' is the most appropriate one for radical social workers to adopt in welfare-state or social-democratic systems. It has the critical advantage of not exploiting or selling out one's clients. (Cohen 1975 pp 92–4)

For many social theorists, of course, this would not be enough. Cohen's position could, in critical terms, be seen as a form of 'soft radicalism'. In so far as he begins from where the social worker actually carries out his work, it is arguable that he is doing nothing to affect the wage-labour system and the cycles of remuneration, life-style and opportunity which stem from it. In other words, the same wage-labour system, which has given rise to the professions' position as agents of power, is·the means by which *structured inequality* is legitimated and perpetuated. If the aim is to change the basis of opportunity and equality in society then it is arguable that it can be accomplished only through concerted concentration on the structures of work — for example, on changing the distinction in terms of work responsibility between management and worker. This in turn is likely to require the uniting of the practical and theoretical endeavours of diverse groups of workers directed at increasing their control over the means of production and its proceeds. Many of the 'clients' of the personal service occupations are the casualties of a hierarchical wage-labour system which has progressively led to a deskilling of many of its workers and which also makes them acutely vulnerable to fluctuations in the economic cycle.

Although it is not our direct task here to speculate on the various lines of action which might follow from a serious critique of professionalism and power, it is nevertheless important that they can be considered. One of the major points of this and the previous chapter has been that control of large areas of social life and, therefore, of the everyday experiences and potentialities of countless people rests in the hands of a few selective and fairly powerful occupations. Moreover, the dynamic of professional organization and practice is towards the increasing centralization of bureaucratized expertise and the continuing diminution of wider public participation.

Any alternative which insists on counteracting this process must, therefore, focus on means of producing increasing participation in the tasks, policies, knowledge and areas of official pronouncement at present under the guardianship of the professions.

However, it is necessary to remember that the professions themselves are collectively part of a wider power structure (and are themselves in many respects subject to it) which has become embodied in the various organs and agencies of state capitalism. Increasingly, limitations have been placed on the operations of professional groups by central and local state departments, a process which leads us to very necessary questions about the interests — class and cultural — which are dominant in the social groups from which their membership is drawn. However, it is arguable that the professions themselves need to have built into their curricula a view of their practice and social position which does not take the mythology and rhetoric of professionalism for granted but which underlines the very distinct structures which they are helping to maintain. Their increasing political awareness may be an indication that this is slowly happening.

CHAPTER 9

Theo Nichols

Management, ideology and practice

This chapter attempts to situate the ideology of management in a capitalist society in the context of the social relations and forces at work in that society. It notes briefly the diverse means by which management ideology is articulated and the discrepancies which are likely to exist between management ideology and the practice of management. But its particular purpose is to comment on ideas about the 'humanization' of work which have been partly developed by social scientists, and which have been fashionable with some 'progressive' managements.

The seminal work of Harry Braverman, *Labor and Monopoly Capital* (1974) has done much to upset the hitherto conventional interpretation of 'human relations' in industrial sociology (according to which it represented one school of thought among others, including scientific management). In Braverman's words:

> The popular notion that Taylorism has been 'superseded' by later schools of industrial psychology or 'human relations', that it 'failed' — because of Taylor's amateurish and naive views of human motivation or because it brought about a storm of labor opposition or because Taylor and various successors antagonized workers and sometimes management as well — or that it is 'outmoded' because certain Taylorian specifics like functional foremanship or his incentive-pay schemes have been discarded for more sophisticated methods: all these represent a woeful misreading of the actual dynamics of the development of management.
> Taylor dealt with the fundamentals of the organization of the labor process and of control over it. The later schools of Hugo Munsterberg, Elton Mayo, and others of this type dealt primarily with the adjustment of the worker to the ongoing production process as that process was designed by the industrial engineer. The successors to

Taylor are to be found in engineering and work design, and in top management; the successors to Munsterberg and Mayo are to be found in personnel departments and schools of industrial psychology and sociology. Work itself is organized according to Taylorian principles, while personnel departments and academics have busied themselves with the selection, training, manipulation, pacification, and adjustment of 'manpower' to suit the work processes so organized. Taylorism dominates the world of production; the practitioners of 'human relations' and 'industrial psychology' are the maintenance crew for the human machinery. If Taylorism does not exist as a separate school today, that is because, apart from the bad odor of the name, it is no longer the property of a faction, since its fundamental teachings have become the bedrock of all work design. (pp 86—7)

This, however, does not exhaust what there is to be said about 'work humanization' from a Marxist point of view. The French Marxist Bosquet (1972) has, for example, taken it a good deal more seriously, and argued that job enrichment, etc., may in the end boomerang against capital — a view that we will examine later in this chapter.[1]

1　Management and ideology

1.1　The sociology of management and management ideology

It is a notable fact that what may be loosely defined as the sociology of work and industrial relations has been primarily concerned with workers. Prior to the development of industrial sociology proper an overtly managerial perspective held sway, as evidenced, for example, in the Scientific Management of F. W. Taylor. Later on, following the Hawthorne Experiments, the great bulk of the literature of the Human Relations school continued to address itself to the problems of how to make workers work harder and/or more efficiently, though these prime concerns were often pursued in a more covert manner.[2] Latterly, given the pressing need that all capitalist societies have experienced to hold down wage levels and to more firmly institutionalize industrial relations, Durkheimian analyses have appeared (e.g. Fox and Flanders 1969). But these, albeit couched at a higher theoretical level than those dubious derivatives of Durkheimian theory which stress the need for workers to 'belong' and to form primary groups at work, still take as their basic point of departure the problem of how workers are to be *managed.*

It has to be conceded that in recent years this emphasis has been offset by the studies of those sociologists who have been influenced by various currents of symbolic interactionist and phenomenological thought, and above all perhaps by the writings of Everett Hughes. Consequently, there now exists a wide range of occupational studies about workers other than industrial ones. Something of what this has amounted to can be glimpsed from the contents of a new journal devoted to the sociology of work and occupations: the first two issues, for instance, carry articles on priests and medical workers, on 'careers' in symphony orchestras and professional hockey, on footballers (American) and strippers (of clothes, not assets). (*Sociology of Work and Occupations* 1974).

The point to be established right away is, however, that the sociology of management has generally got short shrift. Nor is this all. For aside from inquiries into 'how managers spend their day' (how much time they spend with subordinates/superordinates, on the telephone, etc.; see e.g. Burns 1957, Horne and Lupton 1965, Copeman 1965) the fuller study of what managers do has been left to Management Scientists — that is, has been left to those who are often paid to help show them how to do it better. By contrast, with few exceptions (see Dalton 1959; Winkler 1974), sociologists seem to have been much more strongly attracted to the study of management *ideology.* There is no great mystery about why this is. Quite simply, whatever their validity, statements issued by the powerful are a good deal more accessible than information about how they arrive at decisions.

1.2 Words and deeds

To appreciate that there are reasons why sociologists may tend to study ideology cut free from practice is not to deny that such analyses can be beset by problems: in particular, by the problem of the relationship between words and deeds. This applies whatever the field of research. For though work on ethnic relations has perhaps provided the clearest examples of all[3] there is no shortage of examples of the divergence between words and deeds in the study of management ideology itself. Indeed, according to at least one author (Kolko 1961), Max Weber's *Protestant Ethic* (1930), which, for him, was quintessentially expressed in the person of Benjamin Franklin, was flawed in just this way.

That there can be such discrepancies is worth bearing in mind, not least when the question of business 'social responsibility' is under discussion.

For example, Daniel Bell's discussion of this in *The Coming of Post-*

Industrial Society (1974, Chapter 4) is quite tenable in so far as it rests
on the assumption that an important matter on the agenda of the big
corporation is the question of how the conflict between private appropriation and 'social responsibility' is to be resolved. But Bell's analysis
is of dubious validity in so far as it assumes, on the basis of statements
by businessmen, that they want to act in a socially responsible manner,
without investigating precisely what they mean by this or how their
good intentions are translated into practice.

To take a recent case in Britain: some credence might be given to the
assumption that businessmen want to be 'socially responsible' by the
following declaration of CBI policy which relates to Government plans
for wider disclosure of information (CBI 1973). The Government might
consider, the CBI proposed – thus seemingly tying its own hands –
that there should be a general legislative encouragement for companies:

> to recognise duties and obligations (within the context of the objects
> for which the company was established) arising from the company's
> relationships with creditors, suppliers, customers, employees and
> society at large; and in so doing to exercise their best judgement to
> strike a balance between the interests of the aforementioned groups
> and the interests of the proprietors of the company.

But a little further on in the same document it is made clear that 'This
obviously should not, on the other hand, impose on the company a
duty of general benevolence at the shareholders' expense' (Final Report
of the Company Affairs Committee 1973, paras 15, 23, 24). Throughout the document little relish is evidenced for the piling on of duties
and obligations which interfere with 'the mainspring of private enterprise' (otherwise referred to as 'striving for profit').

To debate the idea of social responsibility, or ideology more generally,
without taking account of this 'mainspring' and such 'strivings' may
therefore be to fail to unmask reality – or even to misunderstand what
businessmen who talk of 'social responsibility' mean.[4] To the extent
Bell does this he stands in a long line of theorists and apologists for
capitalism. But the point to be established here is simply this: that
words can be a poor guide to deeds. And by the end of this chapter it
is to be hoped that it will be apparent why this is likely to be the case
with the talk in company circles about 'industrial democracy', 'participation', and the like.

1.3 Management, ideology and the division of management labour

So far it has been noted that the sociology of management remains a generally neglected subject and that the study of management ideology (especially in so far as it is a substitute for the former) can raise difficult problems about the relationship between words and deeds. But the study of ideology also raises the question 'who?' and 'for whom?' i.e. who articulates the ideology and for which class or stratum.

In the case of business ideologies these are important questions because businessmen-philosophers (like Benjamin Franklin) are in short supply and much of what is conventionally considered as business ideology is not articulated by practising men of business themselves. It is for this reason that a work like Sutton *et al, The American Business Creed* (1958), is not based exclusively on what businessmen said but on thousands of statements from other business commentators as well as businessmen. Yet just because the Sutton study does rest on statements made by persons other than practising men of business it raises the problem of how, and to what extent, the many statements out of which these authors sought to construct the business ideology of the 1940s bore on the conduct of business itself.

The same question surfaces again if we look at the major British study of management thought. For the author of this, John Child, felt bound to state that it was possible that what he termed 'British manage-ment thought' was 'never in fact whole-heartedly accepted by most practising managers' (Child 1969).

Prima facie, of course, Child's admission might seem to considerably undermine the value of his work. This, however, is not the case. Child's approach is a valid one precisely because the formal activity of analy-sing and presenting management values and of developing techniques (especially social science ones) is, in practice, relatively autonomous of the conduct of management itself. For, today, not only has the division of labour in capitalism proceeded to the point where management manages for capital, rather than 'the capitalist' managing for himself, but, over and beyond this, the management function has itself become highly differentiated.

The following are some of the manifestations of this differentiation for the production of ideology:

(i) Public Relations departments

There now exist, within corporations, specialist Public Relations depart-ments: in short, managers exist who are specifically charged to project corporate images and to make their companies appear in the best possible light. When factory chimneys besmirch local townships, when the 'image' of the corporation has itself been sullied or when nationaliza-tion looks possible, the PR departments (and/or specially commissioned

PR agencies) mount offensives (consider, for example, in the last two respects, the 1974—5 media campaigns of ITT and ICI in Britain).

Generally speaking, such advertising seeks to suggest that the companies are efficient and 'progressive': 'progressive' in that they are research-oriented and alive to new technologies, and in that they 'care'. It is not at all unusual for them to hold up for public acclaim the 'contributions' they make via (compulsory) taxes to the Exchequer.

(ii) Occupational specialisms

Within the corporation, the differentiation of management tends to call forth the development of more specialist, *occupational*, management ideologies. It is well attested by many organizational studies that a mixture of 'craft' identification and self-interest is likely to call forth 'sub-unit ideologies' (March and Simon 1963), the emergence of conflicts between staff and line managers (Dalton 1969), the development of sales-centred thinking among salesmen (Sykes and Bates 1962), and so on.

It is even possible that the mode of reasoning and self-presentation that a specialism calls forth in a manager may impress itself deeply on his very self. As a study of salesmen put it (Howton and Rosenberg 1965), the job itself can become 'a very emotional thing', not least because if you believe in your company and the product it is likely to be all the better performed. It is in line with this that examples are to be found of technically qualified managers, paid to manage systems (technical, economic and social), whose thought is impregnated with 'system' categories (see Nichols and Beynon 1977). However, the whole question of just how far the structure of their job activity does imprint itself on the very soul of managers has received scant attention. How many directors consider that 'Ninety per cent of my time at home is wasted on non-productive activity' — as one told Young and Wilmott — and how far managers are, in reality, 'just doing a job' (no matter what apparent psychic involvement they display to their bosses) remain, therefore, open questions (Young and Wilmott, 1973 p 251).[5] In any case, the link between personal character and the social structure of work does not operate in one direction only. (F. W. Taylor, for example, was a man who was devoted to finding the 'one best way', and who subjected workers to the stopwatch. But in his personal life, even as a child, he was given to impose strict rules and exact formulas on his playmates, and he died, so it is said, whilst winding his watch (Merkle 1968 p 60).)

(iii) National propaganda agencies

Bodies like the Economic League and Aims of Industry represent a further aspect of the differentiation of management functions as this bears on the production of ideology. Certainly, the sometimes near-hysterical tone of the League — 'Are we to lose freedom in Britain? The militants who have led the assault on our economy hope so' (Economic League advertisement 1973) — and Aims of Industry's still quite recent declarations to the effect that 'the harsh fact is that the Reds are now in the beds'[6] leave no room for doubt that these organizations perform an ideological function: and, quite obviously, denials notwithstanding, these are political organizations. Most companies, though, seem to give political funds to the Conservative Party direct, or funnel them there indirectly via British United Industrialists and the so-called Industrialists Councils. Arguably, big corporations, like Shell and Courtaulds, even if they do give a few thousands to the League (Courtaulds £1500 in 1973; Shell £6500 in 1974), do not support it with much heart.[7]

Very briefly, then, it may be all too easy to exaggerate the importance of such bodies. As pressure groups they may make so much noise (compared with the generally quieter mode of operation of the CBI, various Trade Associations and of big corporations themselves) because they are empty vessels. British capitalism is shored up ideologically in many diffuse and subtle ways — so much so, that these propaganda agencies (like 'Mr Cube's' comic cartoons) seem to represent awkward intrusions into our particular version of a dominantly bourgeois culture. To identify the outpourings of the Economic League with the thinking that goes on in many British boardrooms could be to make a big mistake. To assume that a book like *The Case for Capitalism* (Ivens and Dunstan n.d.) represents the quintessence of modern management thinking could be to make a mistake of a not dissimilar order.

(iv) Education and the social sciences

The differentiation of management functions has been further evidenced in the splitting of management education from management-as-practice. Aside from professional management bodies — and there has been a growth of such institutions for Sales, Production, Personnel and other managers — a significant part of further education is now geared, directly or indirectly, to management needs. And, of course, this is a development in which the social sciences (including economics)[8] themselves play a part.

Over and above such developments, however, there has developed what can only be termed a minor 'human relations industry'. The 'people-specialists' who staff this industry span industry and the universities, academic work and consultancy, and the most successful of them all market their ideas world-wide.

Such people-specialists do, of course, provide managements with practical techniques, or hope to do so. But they would claim to be 'ideas men' also — and this they are: both as men who claim to understand workers' ideas ('the psychology of the worker') and as men who share management's (ideological) assumption about the need to effectively harness and exploit the labour of others.

Writing of the early years of industrialization, Pollard (1968) noted that the large-scale entrepreneur of the day began with very limited managerial, clerical or administrative staff: he wrote his own letters, visited his own customers, and belaboured his men with his own walking stick (p 232). Today, as we have seen, there has developed a very considerable differentiation of management functions both within and outside the company and extending even to management's ideological function itself. But, nowadays, any sensible employer or manager would think twice before belabouring 'his men' with his walking stick. And, whereas it is true that managements have no lack of negative sanctions, and that many workers know to their cost about unemployment, it is coming to be questioned more and more how far either the stick of unemployment or the carrot of higher wages can secure management sufficient return on its 'investment in people'. Moreover, some of the most sophisticated managements and business commentators suspect that this represents a long-term problem; one that could remain even if the current economic crisis ended tomorrow, and even if days lost by strikes were reduced to a fraction of recent levels. Quite simply, how to make workers work harder and more efficiently is likely to be an abiding problem, and one, therefore, if we wish to glimpse something of management ideology (and practice) that we should look at here. In looking at this problem we will inevitably come across the 'people-specialists' again.

First, though, it is useful to sketch out some assumptions about how managers see industry and also about some of the tendencies at work within capitalism, other of course than the 'striving' we have come across already.

2 Capitalism: the problem of its social means and private purpose

2.1 A management view

Looked at in management terms, industry is typically seen to be a

voluntary, and co-operative, activity; one that is engaged in by individuals, some of whom are workers, some managers, some shareholders,
and so on. That is — though this cannot be adequately demonstrated
here — I believe that it is common for managers to easily fall prey to
the following assumptions:

(i) that just as workers make their 'contribution' (or perform their
'function'), so the shareholders make theirs, management itself
existing to co-ordinate beneficently the effects of others for the
common good;
(ii) that workers, as individuals, 'choose' to work at particular factories and enter into an equal, freely negotiated, contract (are,
in fact, freely associated labour);
(iii) that management's power takes the form of authority, is based on
voluntarily given consent which is given because management's
function is accepted to be a legitimate one.[9]

Formulations of this sort contain more than a grain of truth. Capitalism is not slavery, workers do have a measure of choice about where they
work, can leave, and are not owned by their employers. Again, looked
at from within the given system, management's rules, regulations and
orders do have to be complied with in order that firms may run efficiently. And yes, workers in capitalist firms are dependent upon the
provision of private capital; they do, in this sense, 'need' shareholders.

Against this, though, workers have little real choice about whether to
sell their labour power, or, in practice, even where. And typically, when
they pass through the factory gate for the first time, they are confronted by rules and regulations already devised by management.
Through struggle, these rules and regulations may be modified but in
the absence of effective organization by workers they confront them
as a *fait accompli*. Moreover, since workers exist in relation to capital as
so much labour power, as commodities, there are practical constraints
on the degree to which management can afford to allow them to enter
into decision-making. True, as 'personal' connections and relationships
give way under the impersonal force of capital, it becomes increasingly
apparent that managers *themselves* are — as they sometimes say — also
'employees'; that they are in fact so much (relatively expensive) labour.
But the tighter accountancy and appraisals and monitoring of performance to which they can be subject — to say nothing of management
redundancy — hardly predisposes them to loosen the reins. It is no
accident that managers do not commonly invite workers to make
investment decisions; do not incite them to determine wage levels and

the rate at which they work; do not implore them to determine what happens to the product of their labour.

Yet viewed historically, capitalism, despite its private purpose, is an ever more *social* mode of production. We can see this here in two ways: in relation to investment and in relation to production itself.

2.2 The socialization of capitalism

As capitalism develops, investment becomes less and less strictly private, and takes on a more public, collective nature. So, the early entrepreneur (or owner-manager capitalist) gives way to partnerships. Small partnerships, lacking the wherewithal to finance yet bigger enterprises, and also sometimes lacking necessary technical and managerial expertise, in turn give way to the joint stock company form. This brings together tens of thousands of shareholders, the largest of which, the institutional investors, themselves represent a further depersonalization of capital; it also brings about the further development of the much misunderstood process whereby 'ownership is separated from control'.[10] Then, as we see today, either because the resources of private investors and institutions are insufficient, or because, foreseeing only poor profits, a 'strike' by investors occurs, the state takes on an ever more important planning and investment function and, through investment in private companies, or via outright nationalization, the system of private appropriation becomes socialized even further. Certainly, this process has its setbacks, the nationalization-denationalization-nationalization of steel being a case in point. But though it proceeds in fits and starts, being heightened by depression and lessened by boom, the trend of development remains clear enough.

Socialization proceeds apace in another respect too. As the scale of enterprise extends, the entire capitalist system becomes more highly interdependent. A heightened division of labour in the individual firm, within industries, within national economies, and internationally, makes it increasingly apparent that production is social production. Strikes in small car-component firms halt production in mammoth corporations. Miners find themselves strategically placed in the national economy to 'blackmail' their way (as the Press puts it) to higher wages; and the big corporations themselves switch their labour costs across national frontiers and entire continents.

But this is not the end of the story. For if easy profits are not to be made, it becomes necessary to tighten up on wastage, and, via productivity deals, Measured Day Work and the like, to attempt to *intensify* labour, to make workers work more productively and predictably.

Naked coercion being ruled out, given unionized workforces and other considerations — and bureaucratic control in the end being insufficient anyway, for rules can cut two ways, not only specifying what workers must do but what they need not — it becomes yet more important to call forth a new 'flexibility' in workforces. In short the more far-sighted employers come to more fully appreciate the need to 'involve' workers in their work and to elicit from them, individually and collectively, their productiveness as social labour.

2.3 Partial socialization and 'the problem of motivation'

The argument from socialization — *minus* important qualifications — is of course sometimes used to support the view that capitalism has disappeared, has already transformed itself painlessly into socialism, or has dissolved itself into a generic category of 'industrial society'. But in reality capitalism socializes itself only in an incomplete way. The full development of the forces of production (social and technical) is fettered by the social relations of production (see Chapters 2 and 3). Limits to what is possible are imposed by the need of the individual capitalist to stay in the business of private appropriation or go under, and by the requirement that managements who serve capital must not forfeit control, lest the process of extracting profit for private appropriation be impeded.

All the same, since managements appreciate that an explosive increase in productivity would be possible if only labour acted in an actively interdependent and co-operative way — as truly social labour — a way forward has to be found.

This is why 'the problem of motivation', as some managers call it, is one that now engages the attention of Governments, managements, and their advisers. Certainly, at the present time the problem of motivation is not such a pressing problem as that of holding down wage levels or of getting inflation under control. It is, however, a long-term problem, and one, as suggested earlier, that would remain in a 'post-inflationary' or 'post-militant' situation. To seek to resolve this problem some managements have looked to social scientists: especially, of course, to those of them who basically see capitalism as a 'natural', unalterable system, and who believe that changes in 'people', or forms of organization, or just jobs — rather than in class relations — can afford an answer. Such 'people-specialists' are being sought out world-wide.

In 1972 in America, the problem of 'alienation' amongst workers led Edward Kennedy to propose a Bill to the US Senate — the (to British ears) extraordinarily entitled 'Worker Alienation Research and Technical

Assistance Bill' (US Senate, 14 August 1972). The Bill's purpose was to seek authorization for $20,000,000 to research into the physical and mental ill-health of American workers — workers whose 'alienation' was showing up in poor quality work, high labour turnover, absenteeism, sabotage, and, as the Bill put it, in 'monetary loss to the economy'. All of a piece with this, in 1973, a Special Task Force Report to the Secretary of Health, Education and Welfare was issued (*Work in America* 1973), again concerned with 'the alienation and development of blue-collar workers'. For some time now, indeed, American business commentators and advisers have been addressing themselves to this problem (e.g. Gooding 1970), the disastrous progress of GM's Lordstown plant being a common point of reference for them and for radicals alike.[11]

In France, too, the CNPF (the French employers' federation) has addressed itself to this self-same problem (see Bosquet 1972). In Sweden there has been the much publicized restructuring of assembly line work at Volvo. In Britain, in 1973, the Department of Employment, under a Conservative Minister, published a report on the quality of working life (*On the Quality of Working Life* 1973) which reviewed the current state of social scientific theory, this leading in 1974, under a Labour Minister, to the setting up of a special advisory unit to deal with matters of relevance to worker dissatisfaction, disaffection and alienation. In many countries, in short, the 'problem of motivation' is beginning to loom large and, to a significant degree, Governments and managements are turning to social scientists — and especially to their ideas on 'job enrichment' and 'participation'.

It is extremely easy to exaggerate the extent of these developments. It is probable that most British managements are not interested in worker directors, have only limited participatory machinery in operation and are not familiar with the works of social scientists, let alone being hell bent on introducing job rotation, job enrichment, and the like.[12] But if, for example, Minis and Cortinas are not made in quite the same way as Volvos, Volvo has a good publicity machine and, in Swedish, English and other languages, is simultaneously broadcasting the good news about what is now called the 'humanization of work' (which, incidentally, directs our attention back to the significance of PR departments). Managers are being sent off on courses. More and more academics are flying round the world discussing the 'quality of working life'. And often on the say-so of someone in Head Office — who 'thought there might be something in it' (which points to the stratification as well as the differentiation of modern management noted above) — more managers in big corporations are being paid visits by consultants anxious to sell them the remedies currently on offer in 'behavioural science'.

Generally, the sales appeal of the new remedies rests on the assumption that either workers have not hitherto been properly understood or they have changed. Compared with their fathers, the argument runs, their material needs are now much nearer to having been met and they are now more interested in intrinsic satisfactions, in personal fulfilment and development. Ironically, such an assumption flies in the face of the most influential recent monographs in academic industrial sociology (Goldthorpe *et al* 1968 and 1969). None the less, in management-oriented social science the view seems to be gaining ground that we are in process of seeing a revolution of rising expectations. (It is also gaining ground in some Marxist circles. The work of Bosquet illustrates this and will be referred to below.)

Of all the social scientific theories which have recently gained sway with (at least some) managers, the most appealing has almost certainly been that of the American social psychologist and consultant, Frederick Herzberg. It is of some interest, then, that Herzberg's 'Motivation—Hygiene Theory' (1968) is above all distinctive for the stress it places on the importance of work itself — on the content of the *job*. It has been noted already that 'participation' and greater worker 'involvement' are potentially dangerous remedies. Managements want involved co-operative workforces, but only within limits, for they do not want to forfeit control. Herzberg, however, is fully aware of this. Not only has he gone on record as saying that 'the authoritarian character of American industry will continue despite the propaganda for a more democratic way of life', he has also warned against 'participation' on the grounds that there is no telling where, once set in motion, it might lead (cited in Jenkins 1974 pp 169, 258).

Three assertions then. One: a capitalist mode of production is inherently authoritarian. Two: substantial democratization (as opposed to 'propaganda') threatens its survival. Three: managements and their social science advisers will be lacking in judgement if they ignore this. (And maybe fourthly, by and large they do not ignore this: not in practice.)

3 The new human relations

Managers, being practical men, do not take social scientific theories and implement them root and branch. They select and take out what seems to them prudent and appropriate to their particular needs. It is in keeping with this that 'participation' (in some version or other) and 'job enrichment' (in some version or other) are often introduced together.

Moreover, because there are limits as to how far managers can safely go — either in introducing 'participation' or, because of cost considerations (where, for example, men are cheaper than machines), in 'enriching' jobs — it often appears, not to mince words, that the whole exercise is just a 'sham' or 'con'. The tendency in the not too distant past for such schemes to be introduced hand in hand with productivity deals has only served to make such judgements appear the more apt.

Moral condemnation is not, however, a substitute for sociological analysis. There are good sociological reasons why, on the one hand, managements should want work to become a more truly social (and intrinsically rewarding) activity and why, on the other hand, the socialization process in capitalism should take on a bastardized and incomplete form. Something of this is illustrated by the case of Chemco.

3.1 An illustrative case

The Chemco complex,[13] as it is called here, is part of a large multinational corporation. Its management is a 'progressive' one, which is to say that Chemco managers are generally scientifically qualified and make use of operational research, management by objectives, loss accounting, and so on. They are also familiar with a battery of 'man-management' techniques: at times faddishly contemporary, the company Personnel Department has sponsored various participatory schemes, staff status, grading systems, psychological testing, 'open-door policies', 'Blake's managerial grid', the 'Coverdale system' and T-groups. Chemco managers have read Herzberg, attended courses on 'Motivation—Hygiene Theory', seen him expound his ideas on film and have had his ideas expounded to them by behavioural science consultants. The Personnel Manager is Herzberg's most enthusiastic supporter (a fact which is not out of keeping with the comments made above about occupational specialisms).

During the sixties Chemco experienced problems of labour turnover. This was particularly pronounced amongst workers in the Zap plant — men who did the often heavy and unremitting physical work of bagging, packing, storing and loading the site's end-product. Such men, as opposed to control room operators and maintenance workers, were the bulk of the labour force. They were unskilled, came to Chemco to chase high piecerate earnings and overtime, and tended to move on to other jobs when word got round of better earnings to be had elsewhere.

At the end of the sixties Chemco introduced a productivity deal, as did many other capital-intensive companies. This, it was insisted, was not to be 'just another Fawley'.[14] Rather it was to be seen as the working out of a 'new philosophy of management', as something which would make work a more satisfying experience. The method was two fold: the introduction of new consultative machinery (i.e. more participation) and work restructuring. (It is the latter feature which will be examined in the following pages.) In brief, the deal, as well as abolishing piecerate, introduced a new grading system and higher basic wages; it also brought a package of other 'advanced' policies – generally, 'job enrichment', decreased supervision, an attempt to give more information to workers and the development of plant and site-level joint consultation. In some plants managers claim it paved the way for the introduction of job rotation, the related development of small work teams, and the policy of recruiting more highly qualified and 'flexible' workers. As we will see, some of these claims are of dubious validity, but in any case the context in which such policies to humanize and socialize work were introduced should not be lost sight of.

If capital-intensive technologies are to operate continuously and with a minimum of waste, management has to have an actively involved and flexible workforce. At Chemco, for example, if certain plants come off-line, a chain reaction is set up. This not only means that other plants on site have to stop production (or waste their product) but that plants owned by different firms, which Chemco is contracted to supply, also have to stop production. Very obvious economic considerations like these make management eager to avoid plants coming off-line at all, to get them back on-line as soon as possible, and, when running, given the capital investment at stake, to run them as efficiently as possible.

For all this, even a non-militant workforce that merely 'plods along' and 'gets by' is not enough.[15] Hence what Chemco managers call 'the problem of motivation'. As they see things, this is their number one problem. They are keen to talk about it, to let you know how big a problem it is. So 'if you want an experiment' says one:

> You wait until the 2.00–10.00 shift and say to the supervisor 'You stay there (in the office) and don't go out on the plant'. About 10.00 those blokes will be starting yawning. 'Oh,' they'll say, 'it's about time we were going home', they'll say. Now that's not quite true because at about half past four some curious bugger would say 'What are the bastards up to?' – not because he wants to work mind, no, he won't want to work. He'll just be curious. What he'll want to know is why it is he hasn't been *forced* to work.

Of course things aren't really this bad (for management, that is) but they know that to solve 'the problem of motivation' is to reap rich rewards.

It is worth remembering here that even that demon king of manage-

ment ideology, F. W. Taylor, thought a 'mental revolution' among workers a precondition for maximum efficiency in factory working. (Taylor
1911, see in particular his Testimony to the House of Representatives,
Special Committee, pp 27–31.) But, today, some managements are
beginning to put together again the jobs they earlier disassembled in
following the dictates of Taylorism, and they are doing so precisely
in order to bring about this self-same 'mental revolution' or 'new
psychological contract', as the new generation of business consultants
call it (Paul and Robertson 1970 p 91). If we look at capitalism as a
system in process of partial socialization, this reassembling of work into
larger units, and often allied attempts to involve workers in the management of it, can be seen to constitute in some respects the development
of a kind of mock socialism. It reflects an awareness on the part of
management that the long awaited mental revolution cannot be secured
simply at the level of ideas: that it is not enough for foremen to be
trained in leadership; that it is not enough for managers to ask how the
wife is; not enough to talk of unity of purpose. Things have to be
changed. In particular, managers reason, jobs must be 'enriched' to
make them more meaningful and workers must be given a measure of
participation. At Chemco this reasoning is underpinned by a version
of an argument introduced already – the so-called revolution of rising
expectations argument. Managers say quite explicitly 'you can't treat
labour nowadays like they used to'.

It is arguable, however, that their problem is not so much that
Chemco workers have high expectations of work but rather that they
expect so little. Accepting they are workers, they do not expect their
work to be satisfying, and have entered into a grudging bargain with
their employers. Part of just one more generation of working class men
and women, well used to being denied meaning and control over their
lives, like industrial whores they do enough to get enough. 'It's a job',
they say.

3.2 The meaning of meaning in a job

Chemco management now has a very clear basis upon which to control
the size of the labour force, since there are jointly agreed specified
manning and output levels for each plant. Whatever its psychic benefits,
therefore, job enrichment could, in the long term, amount to job
extension – fewer workers doing more work. But it cannot be taken
for granted that management's policies really have 'enriched' the jobs
that Chemco workers do. Herzberg himself has gone out of his way to
make it clear that job enrichment does not consist of adding more

meaningless bits to already meaningless jobs (1968 p 167). Indeed, it is questionable how many of the changes brought about in his name would, in his view, merit being called 'job enrichment' at all. What happened at Chemco is a case in point.

In the Zap plant, for example, where management is most proud of its attempts to counter boring work, the most that has happened is that men who before might have been expected to spend a whole shift filling hundredweight bags from a spout, or sealing them, or loading them on to lorries, or into rail vans, or weighing them, or operating a palletiser, or driving trucks, or sweeping up, now have to be prepared to carry out nearly all of these activities to qualify for the new, higher grade of pay. The increased variety (in so far as it does represent an increase, for some shifts worked informal arrangements of this kind before the deal) is of course to be welcomed. But it hardly amounts to the creation of an intrinsically interesting or enriched job. As one man summed it up:

> You move from one boring, dirty, monotonous job to another boring, dirty, monotonous job. And then to another boring, dirty, monotonous job. And somehow you're supposed to come out of it all 'enriched'. But I never feel 'enriched' — I just feel knackered.

Not dissimilar feelings seem to have been expressed by ICI workers at Gloucester — the one example Bosquet cites of job enrichment being implemented in Britain, and one which, in America, has been cited in such a way as to make it appear the biggest 'experiment' in 'the humanization of work' yet.[16] A study which monitored this 'experiment' reported, *inter alia*, that the jobs remained essentially monotonous, that the skill level was not essentially changed, and as a worker put it: 'you still do the same job with little bits added on' (Cotgrove, Dunham and Vamplew 1971).

Despite this apparent confirmation of the Chemco case, the question arises whether schemes introduced in other factories have had markedly different results. This is an empirical question which cannot be gone into here (but it is only proper to add that faced with such a claim I would want to look at the evidence very carefully. As can be seen from the boxed quotation, when it comes to 'job enrichment' managers, and those who celebrate their works, can be very imaginative indeed.)

It also needs to be taken into account that even though basic constraints are structured into and fetter capitalist enterprise, the problems which workers pose for particular enterprises can express themselves in many diverse forms. Different workforces and sections of workforces can find themselves confronted by different particular conditions, market

Imaginative Job Enrichment
According to Clark (the man in charge of job evaluation at ICI) the willingness of managers to encourage the radical re-design of jobs was far more important than the grade structure. 'Some of the most enriched jobs I have seen were amongst the lower grades' he said, and cited the case of the lavatory attendant at one works. To his basic job of cleaning were added elements that gave him complete autonomy in his area of work: he was given the responsibility for ordering his cleaning materials and the paper and soap needed in the lavatories; he was given the job of making minor running repairs — replacing tap washers and repairing the 'furniture' — and trained to carry them out. I mention this, in some ways absurd, example because it illustrates well the detailed ways that jobs can be enriched — ways that owe nothing to the complexity of the technology but have much more to do with the completeness of the resulting job and the freedom given to the worker in carrying it out. According to Clark, the result was a far more satisfying job for the lavatory attendant, who is now a man with complete autonomy in his own work area.
'The main limiting factor to job enrichment is the imagination of the manager', Clark says.

From: Joe Roeber (1975) *Social Change at Work: The ICI weekly staff agreement,* p 263.

situations and management tactics. They are composed of workers with particular historical traditions, skills and biographical experiences. As Fox observes in Chapter 6, people differ widely in respect of the personal meanings and aspirations they invest in their labour. It is as a consequence of this that 'the problem of motivation' can be seen to have at least two sides: the one expresses itself in frustrated workforces which include men who resent the lack of scope to exercise their abilities ('men with blocked aspirations and unenriched jobs' as I once heard a manager put it); the other expresses itself in the existence of unco-operative workforces like Chemco's — in workers who are not greatly concerned to affirm or deny management's 'legitimacy' but only to 'get by' and 'plod along' (in management's vocabulary these men are the 'apathetic').

Neither aspect of the problem can readily be solved at the level of the firm. But it is at the level of the firm or factory that they confront the practising production manager and it is here that he must try to deal with them – along with any more or less sustained or sporadic, organized or anarchistic opposition and rebellion ('bloody-mindedness' and 'mindless militancy' are two common management phrases which figure here). Ideally, managements must seek to deal with these problems – of 'motivation' (too much or too little) and of opposition/ rebellion – both *ideologically* and *practically*: ideologically, via a 'mental revolution', by calls for a 'new spirit', by appeals to 'the team' (or to the big team – Lord Robens's 'Great Britain Ltd') and by attempting in various ways to instil 'a sense of responsibility'; practically, by making every attempt to effectively safeguard the managers' 'right to manage'.

The problems – of too little or too much 'motivation', of more or less explicit political opposition – need not of course manifest themselves in a mutually exclusive way. And we should not jump hastily to the conclusion that the new human relations policies are only introduced in workforces engaged in sustained or sporadic open opposition to management, or, as managers see it, which would be likely to become like this in the absence of such schemes being introduced.

Chemco's management acted to 'humanize' and 'socialize' work because, given full employment and heightened competition, it wanted an extra percentage on profit and because it had a prudent regard for the long term. This may be the case quite generally. ICI Nylon Spinners at Gloucester, for instance, probably had a workforce that was less militant than Chemco's. Whereas, to look at the car industry (which serves as Bosquet's key example) is to find, in Britain, that not one employer has been to the fore in implementing changes of the kind he has in mind. Generally speaking, Herzberg's theories have not been put into practice where there are militant workforces. At least, this is what is suggested by his own evidence (Herzberg 1968 p 124) and that of his former associates in Britain (see the studies reported in Paul and Robertson 1970).

To sum up: despite Chemco management's philosophy, the changes in jobs that occurred hardly merit being called 'enrichment'. To the extent jobs were *enlarged*, and workers given a little more say in the organization of work, this hardly evidenced a tendency for them to *take* control. And, despite the broad-ranging examples so frequently cited nowadays about what is happening at Texas Instruments or at A.T. and T. in the USA, at ICI in Britain, at Phillips in Holland, at Volvo in Sweden, and so on, it bears consideration that even some of these now almost mandatory examples of the 'humanization of work' may not, like Chemco's, go very far. There *is* a case for looking at what some managements are doing as a kind of 'mock socialism'. But it must not be forgotten that job enrichment and allied policies, even in their own terms, can be a mockery.

One further point is in order, however. It is this: that even if experiments in the humanization of work are more likely to be geared to increased efficiency and profit in the short run — and a reshaping of workers' consciousness in the longer term — rather than being intended to stave off and circumvent imminent rebellion, the possibility cannot be ruled out that the new human relations remedies may worsen the disease they are supposed to cure. That is, as per Bosquet's argument, as a consequence of management's initiatives, men may come to question not only the meaning but the purpose of work; may look beyond the level of the job to that of class relations; and these policies may boomerang against capital. It is suggested below that a consideration of the relationship of ideology and practice makes this unlikely, at least in the short run.

Conclusion: ideology and practice

As stated at the outset, there is a real danger in attempting to understand the practice of management on the basis of a study of management ideology. For whereas it would be foolish to deny that ideology is part of the fabric of society, ideas do not 'drop from the skies'. Why they are taken up at particular times requires explanation. When bad faith and self-deception appear to be in evidence in the acting out of these ideas in partial or distorted forms this also requires explanation. So, too, does the manipulative and subjectivist nature of the social scientific theories from which these ideas sometimes derive. It is not sufficient to assert merely that much 'participation' in industry is a sham, or that managers are manipulative.

The argument to inform this brief consideration of the new human relations ideology has, therefore, been this: that whereas managements like Chemco's have a definite interest in recognizing more fully that production is social production — i.e. in recognizing that men are not simply commodities but thinking, social beings, with potentially valuable contributions to make, and with the potential to work together more productively — they *also* have an interest in limiting the development of these human potentials. And this is because, though it would suit managements for workers to act *as if* there really were socialism inside work, managers themselves have to operate in a world in which market forces reign and impede the development of the very unstinted co-operation they wish to bring about.

What this can mean in practice may be illustrated here by reference to *other* developments which were taking place at Chemco at the same time workers were having their jobs 'enriched' and being encouraged to think in terms of 'participation'. One such development — which *prima facie* seems to fit well with the idea that in instituting neo-human relations policies management may set in motion forces in opposition to itself — was the strengthening of an only weakly developed rank and file organization. For to implement the deal management had to have someone at plant-level to negotiate with. In some plants, therefore, they pushed for the creation of new shop stewardships. And, at site-level, they allowed a specially founded Shop Stewards' Committee to hold regular and often lengthy meetings in works' time. Both these developments might suggest that thus far we have been too hasty to minimize the unintended consequences of management's new policies.

On closer inspection, though, we find that managers did their best to manoeuvre particular workers into the newly created shop stewardships. What is more, once the deal had been implemented, management put a stop to stewards' meetings in works' time. After the deal management argued such meetings were 'an unproductive use of time' — this being a claim the stewards were still not strong enough to resist.

It is, of course, no accident that Chemco management was quick to nip in the bud the emergent organization of labour they had earlier found it useful to strengthen. But it is most important to appreciate that from the very beginning the deal was introduced in such a way as to deflect attention from deeper issues. The many meetings that were held *could* have amounted to a political education. But it was, above all, *management* who saw the significance of this, and attempted to use them accordingly. By contrast no organized group existed among the men to put an opposing view. The talking points were working procedures, alterations in jobs and the higher satisfaction[17] — and wages — to be had from them. Purpose and profit only appeared on the agenda at plant-level within the terms posed by management itself.

Obviously, the lack of reaction among Chemco workers to their management's attempt to introduce some sort of bastardized social control over production cannot prove the impossibility of workers anywhere ever being led to question private enterprise through the introduction of such policies. What, by contrast, can be said to be illustrated by the case of Chemco is that, whether jobs are enriched and whether workers are offered a limited involvement and participation or not, the possibility of an alternative to private enterprise has to be demonstrated to them. And also, that even though there are men in the union, at both formal and informal levels, who are equally concerned as Chemco management to change these men's thinking, albeit to different ends, they have in Chemco management a competent adversary. These managers are not infallible and they are not all-seeing. But nor do they need to read sociology books to learn about 'unintended consequences'.

Managers' thinking may be ideological, in that they assume capitalism is a 'natural' system, is necessarily here to stay, and in that the truths it expresses are partial truths only. But what others call their 'ideology' managers call 'common sense'. And 'common sense' tells them that they must not forfeit control; that the business of business is profit; and that, whatever ideas they might have in their heads, and whatever enriching or participatory ventures they may institute, there are limits — not of their making — to what they can 'sensibly' do. This is why it is not sufficient to dismiss their espousal of the new human relations as a 'con', and why, also, their words are likely to be only a poor guide to their practice.

Notes

1 For a further Marxist treatment see A. Zimbalist (1975).

2 A sociological and historical analysis of both Scientific Management and of the early Human Relations movement in America is to be found in R. Bendix (1956) Chapter 5. For a history of the uses of social sciences in American industry see Baritz (1960).

3 For a report of LaPierre's classic work on racial prejudice and other evidence, see Irwin Deutscher (1966).

4 I have attempted to argue this elsewhere. See T. Nichols (1969) Chapters 15 and 17.

5 For an examination of the notion that there is an 'executive personality', see Cyril Sofer (1970) Chapter 7.

6 From their attack on the miners, in particular on Michael McGahey and 'his dedicated band', in *Reds under the Bed?*, Aims of Industry pamphlet, 1974.

7 On the best current estimate, 80 per cent of political donations are disposed of in this way. *Big Business and Politics: the functions, propaganda and secret activities of employers' organizations*, pamphlet published by Labour Research Department, 1974 p 7. For details of

business political donations in 1974 — a bumper year with two general elections — see 'Who backs the Tories?'', *Labour Research*, August 1975.

8 On economics as bourgeois science see Bob Rowthorn (1974), especially pp 64—71 on 'Vulgar Economy'.

9 This idea is one well rehearsed in administrative science, as Perrow neatly demonstrates in his consideration of the work of one of its founding fathers, Chester H. Barnard. (Barnard, a senior executive in the Bell telephone system, even quoted a 'notable business executive' and one time World War I officer to the effect that the army is 'the greatest of all democracies' because when the order to move forward was given, it is the enlisted man who has to decide to accept that order.) It is over a century since Marx observed how capitalists assumed they were captains of industry because they were leaders of men, not *vice versa*. Today's 'business leaders' (an interesting phrase this) still seem reluctant to relinquish the habit. See Charles Perrow (1972) Chapter 2 'Managerial ideologies'.

10 For a cogent analysis of the process see M. De Vroey (1975) 'The separation of ownership and control — The Marxist view'.

11 In Britain, for example, Lordstown has been taken up by the Solidarity group: K. Weller (n.d.) *The Lordstown Struggle*.

12 For a review of the British situation, see R.O. Clarke, D.J. Fatchet and S.B.C. Roberts (1972).

13 For a fuller account of what follows, see Theo Nichols (1975).

14 A reference to the productivity deal introduced at Esso's Fawley refinery. This was widely applauded at the time by managers and government spokesmen. See A. Flanders (1964).

15 For a description of how the workers discussed 'get by', and for a systematic consideration of the control situation at Chemco, see Nichols and Armstrong (1976). For more on the management strategy, see Nichols and Beynon (1977) Chapter 7.

16 See *Work in America* (1973), Appendix on 'Case studies in the humanization of work', pp 192—3.

17 It appears the link between the nature of jobs and 'satisfaction' was also a preliminary talking point at ICI Gloucester. Cotgrove *et al* (1971) discuss this as a possible contaminating factor (of a 'Hawthorne effect' kind) in their attempt to monitor the results of this particular productiv-

ity deal-cum-human relations package. It is worth noting, though, that after the deal was put in – a deal on which Cotgrove *et al's* overall verdict was that the gains were limited but none the less real – not one operator 'could remember anybody talking about what makes a worker happy or satisfied at work'! (1971 p 113)

CHAPTER 10

Richard Hyman

Trade unions, control and resistance

1 Job control and capitalism

The central theme of this book is the need to relate an analysis of work to its structural location within the capitalist mode of production; and this is of particular importance in any examination of job control. For the great majority of the 'occupied population'[1] (in Britain, over 90 per cent), work equals wage-labour. Labour relations are thus, at the outset, market relations. The prospective worker must find an employer willing to pay a wage or salary in return for the disposal of his/her skill, knowledge or physical capacities; and can expect such employment to last only so long as this willingness continues. Labour thus has the status of a commodity; and as with all market relationships, the interests of buyers and sellers are antagonistic. The wages and conditions sought by the employee as the means to a decent life, both within and outside work, are a *cost* cutting into the employer's profits. In the absence of specific and untypical countertendencies (the need to recruit and retain scarce categories of labour, or a belief that improved conditions will generate greater worker commitment and productivity), the employer is naturally motivated to resist worker aspirations which are liable to increase labour costs. Moreover, because labour represents a cost to be minimized, it is in the employer's interest to continue a worker's employment only so long as it remains profitable to do so. A decline in demand for the goods and services produced, or the development of new techniques permitting these to be produced more cheaply and profitably, may at any moment lead to managerial decisions which throw men and women out of employment.

If labour within capitalism is in one sense a commodity like any other, in another sense it is quite unlike all other types of commodity. For while the employment contract may well specify precisely what the worker receives from the employer, what he/she provides in return is rarely defined specifically. The worker does not agree to sell an exact quantity of labour; for neither physical nor intellectual work can normally be quantified precisely, and few employers could in any case predict with certainty their day-to-day labour requirements. The employer wishes rather to be able to make flexible use of the labour force as circumstances dictate; and the employment contract reflects the employer's interest by imposing on workers an open-ended commitment. Rather than agreeing to expend a given amount of effort, the employee surrenders his/her *capacity to work*; and it is the function of management, through its hierarchy of control, to transform this capacity into actual productive activity. Hence Marx's vital distinction between labour and labour power: the wage or salary is not the price of labour as such but of labour power, the ability to work; but the realization of this potential is by no means a simple economic exchange, it is a process which occurs 'outside the limits of the market' (Marx 1959 p 175). The cobbler who sells a pair of boots is separated from the commodity after the moment of sale, and is engaged in no necessary and continuing relationship with the customer; but the worker's labour power cannot be detached from his/her physical presence, and this necessitates an ongoing social relationship with the employer (or the employer's agents) throughout the labour process itself. Issues of control inevitably pervade this relationship: the conflictual character of job control and the commodity status of labour are reciprocally dependent aspects of social relations of production within capitalism.

The interdependence of the two elements of the employment relationship — the sale of labour power and the control of the labour process — is apparent in the detail of industrial relations. The worker's standards of acceptable payment are influenced by the nature of the work tasks and the pressure under which they are to be performed: witness the popular slogan 'a fair day's work for a fair day's pay'.[2] An increased workload or speed-up which might otherwise be resisted may be accepted if higher payment is received as compensation (either through a scheme linking earnings directly to output — 'payment by results' — through promotion, regrading, a special bonus or a simple wage increase). Conversely, relatively low pay may be tolerated by some workers if the pressure of work or the exercise of managerial authority is comparatively relaxed. For the employer, this interrelationship is also of crucial importance: the three parameters of level of pay, length of working time and labour productivity together determine the possibility and rate of profit. The drive for profitability will in different contexts focus primarily on one factor rather than another; and historically, improvements won by workers in increasing pay and reducing working hours have been compensated by the employer through more *intensive* exploitation of labour.[3]

This interdependence does not, however, vitiate the analytical utility of the distinction between sale of labour power and control over the labour process. And indeed, there is a further aspect of the work relationship which requires to be distinguished: workers' subordination within capitalist production to an alien *structure* of priorities and decision-making. 'Accumulation for accumulation's sake, production for production's sake: by this formula classical economy expressed the historical mission of the bourgeoisie' (Marx 1959 p 595). The capitalist mode of production involves a built-in compulsion, remote from deliberate human control, to extract profit from workers' labour and to devote this to the accumulation of capital (or in more modern terminology, 'economic growth') — a compulsion sustained by the competitive struggle between productive units, national and international.[4] Workers *have* to be treated as 'factors of production' rather than as men and women with distinctive needs and aspirations. Their upbringing and 'education' often derive from the need to make them in some narrow respect useful to an employer; it is this utility which determines whether they will obtain and retain employment, and which dominates their actual work experience. Utilitarian criteria may prescribe that they perform tasks which are excessively strenuous or degrading — or so monotonously repetitive as to eliminate any scope for creativity. The same principle which justifies the fragmentation of so much work into routine and meaningless tasks also requires that management organize and co-ordinate these fragmented activities into one collective effort on the basis of hierarchy and authority. Sociable relations among workers are normally tolerated only in so far as they do not obstruct the requirements of profitable production; the same is in large measure true of safeguards against accidents and industrial diseases. Or at least, the application of humane priorities in work normally requires the mobilization of power against the *resistance* of employers who (whatever their personal sympathies) must give primary consideration to the requirements of profitability.

The normal priorities of work in capitalism reflect the internal 'logic' of the capitalist mode of production and are thus experienced at the level of the individual enterprise or establishment as inescapable external constraints. These pressures and constraints are, however, mediated by the policies and decisions of top managerial and directorial strata of both private and 'public' organizations. In much of the following discussion it is necessary to refer simply to 'management' without consideration of the divergent orientations and interests associated with different levels and functions of management. But a brief examination of the role of management is essential for any serious analysis of the problematics of control in industry.

The key feature of capitalist management is that it constitutes an *authoritarian hierarchy*. With the subdivision and specialization of tasks, work is productive only through its *collective* character; but each worker surrenders his or her labour power to the employer, who has to realize the potential of the collectivity.[5] It follows that management has a dual function. On the one hand it contributes to the collective process of production through providing overall co-ordination of the diverse activities of other employees, and also other technically valuable services and facilities.[6] On the other it carries out functions of control and surveillance, acting as mediator of the coercive and exploitative dynamic of capitalism. This distinction is developed by Carchedi (1975a). Any sociological analysis of management is complicated by the fact that specific managerial roles often contain a contradictory mix of elements from both functions. Moreover, the size and complexity of many employing organizations necessitate an elaborate managerial structure with many levels between top director and modest chargehands, gangers or section leaders who derive only the most limited power from their toehold in the managerial hierarchy.

It is obvious, then, that 'management' is not a homogeneous group with identical interests or a uniform class position; and indeed, there are many managers whose role includes such contradictory functions that meaningful specification of their class position is in principle impossible. Thus 'personnel management' serves the ends of coercing and manipulating wage-labour, but is not unambiguously repressive. Its 'welfare' functions, designed within capitalism to achieve a tractable labour force, might in a different social context lose their manipulative character. One of the tasks of any effective workplace trade union organization is to identify and exploit the internal divisions within management — the conflicts between staff and line, the disenchantment of junior managers with their superiors, the pressure on particular supervisors to achieve production targets regardless of cost. Yet despite these crucial differentiating processes, all members of management act within the constraints of the overall policy decisions taken by the top strata within the hierarchy; divergence beyond narrow limits invites retaliation. The class position of these top strata is scarcely disputable: they receive rewards far in excess of any identifiable productive contribution; they embrace their role as coercive agents of capital; and they represent, to the ordinary employee, the manifestation of an alien power.* The struggle for job control by ordinary workers — analysed in *general* terms rather than through a detailed examination of the strategies pursued in the individual workplace — involves a confrontation with a managerial hierarchy which, itself controlled from above, constitutes a hostile totality.

2 The sale of labour power

The terms on which labour power is sold are usually set in a highly discontinuous process. In unionized sectors of employment, intermittent negotiations (in Britain, in recent years, typically annually) set the basic rates of wages or salaries for the various grades of labour covered by the resulting collective agreement; and these rates stand until renegotiated. (Historically in Britain, and more notably still in such countries as the United States, such agreements have often run for several years.) Employers of non-union labour often follow wage movements negotiated elsewhere (sometimes as part of a deliberate policy of discouraging unionization); otherwise the pay of unorganized workers is set unilaterally by the employer and altered infrequently, usually in response to labour market pressures or (exceptionally) the individual bargaining of a particularly valuable employee.

By virtue of the character of the collective bargaining process, the opportunities to exert collective control over the price of labour power thus arise only sporadically. Admittedly, this is not without qualification the case. Particular groups with strategic skills or disruptive potential may press 'irregularly' and achieve pay improvements. Others can boost their pay packets through overtime working or piecework earnings. In both instances, higher wages are in theory a compensation for extra labour, on a formula directly related to basic pay. But it is possible for workers (particularly when faced by unsophisticated management information and control procedures) to exert pressure on both the level and the rate of payment for overtime, and to seize the opportunity of changes in piecework tasks to negotiate job times or prices which permit regularly enhanced earnings. (Some managers have referred to piecework bargaining, particularly in certain sectors

* Marx and Engels wrote, in *The Holy Family*, that while the capitalist was alienated — because subject to the determination of externally coercive economic laws — he was 'comfortable and confirmed' in this alienated state. The same is true of top managers and directors today. For an analysis of their beliefs and attitudes — indicating their sense of personal powerlessness and also their commitment to their role — see Nichols (1969).

of engineering, as a 'Persian market'. Brown (1973) analyses the operation of piecework bargaining in such a context.) Hence a substantial gap can exist between formally negotiated wage-rates and actual earnings, particularly in the case of male manual workers; in some cases workers may receive double the basic rate. And movements in pay can involve an inconspicuous process of 'drift' supplementing official bargaining.

Despite the importance of this phenomenon, it remains the case that most collectively organized workers (the large majority of public sector employees and of white-collar staff in private companies, for example) depend on formal and infrequently negotiated agreements for the bulk of their earnings increases. 'Wage drift' in Britain was at its most extensive in the early 1960s; since then, employers have made strenuous efforts to reduce or eliminate the scope for fragmented bargaining over pay on the shop floor,[7] while the size of nationally negotiated increases has risen sharply. Even in those sectors of employment where workplace-generated pay increases are still of substantial importance, the process is nevertheless one of intermittent pressure rather than continuous movement: the concept of 'drift' is misleading both in neglecting the active role of workers in pushing up their earnings, and in failing to indicate that this pressure has its outcome in a series of discrete understandings and agreements between workers and managerial representatives.

The setting of wages and salaries necessarily involves relations of control. The superficial equality of buyer and seller in *any* market transaction conceals inequalities of economic power which often permit certain parties in large measure to dominate the terms of exchange; markets are media of control just as much as they are media of exchange. This is particularly true of the labour market, where the concentrated economic power of capital confronts the far more vulnerable sellers of labour power, and where the most orthodox economic theorists are obliged to recognize a multiplicity of 'imperfections' which represent the impact of institutional and ideological pressures on the interaction of supply and demand. In organizing collectively, workers do not disturb an otherwise evenly balanced labour market; normally they do no more than partially counterbalance the dominance which the employer can exercise over employees as individuals, and the impact of ideologies of occupational worth which reflect the interests of privileged social groups. (The significance of such ideologies is examined in detail in Hyman and Brough 1975.) Control relations also pervade the detail of workplace bargaining on rates of pay, especially under payment by results systems. Historically, many employers introduced such systems in order to divide the labour force, believing correctly that the individual operator faced by the rate-fixer would be in a weak bargaining position. But the growth of shop steward organization allowed in many workplaces a considerable degree of collective control over the rate-setting process. In some cases, rules and practices became established which considerably altered the balance of power in piece rate bargaining: for example, a worker who found the price or time offered for a new job insufficient could reject the company offer and receive payment related to previous average earnings until agreement was reached. Not surprisingly, where workers could establish such controls the rate of wage drift was often particularly high (see Brown 1973); and it was just in such circumstances that employers were often particularly keen to introduce different payment systems.

The discussion of payment questions accounts for the bulk of formal collective bargaining between unions and employer representatives. This same preponderance is reflected in the demands pressed during strikes: in virtually every western country, statistics of strike issues show that well over half concern wages and salaries. (Some of the problems involved in interpreting these statistics are discussed in Hyman 1972 chapter 5.) Not surprisingly, then, trade unions are commonly viewed as institutions exclusively concerned with a struggle for pay increases. This is scarcely remarkable. We live in a society in which the importance of money is pervasively emphasized; in which vast resources are devoted to encouraging new and more sophisticated material aspirations among consumers; but in which workers receive far lower income to satisfy these aspirations than the more privileged social strata. Moreover, the *legitimacy* of wage bargaining as a focus of trade union action is widely accepted, whereas the propriety of demands which challenge managerial authority is more commonly disputed. Hence bargaining over pay is often the line of least resistance for union representatives (a point which is considered further in a later section).

The notion that trade unionism is *exclusively* concerned with wages and salaries would, however, be highly misleading; and the main focus of this chapter is on the less obvious but sociologically particularly interesting aspects of job control not directly related to payment. But one particular feature of the sale of labour power does deserve further consideration, because of its profound implications for the character of the whole trade union movement: the problem of relativities and differentials.

It is clear from chapters in this book that workers do not enter the labour market as an undifferentiated mass. Through education and training (access to which is strongly influenced by class-based advantages), a minority acquire skills, qualifications and knowledge which permit entry to the most privileged occupations. Others acquire through particular on-the-job experience the aptitudes which represent less substantial but, nevertheless, significant advantages in the pursuit of relatively favoured employment. Conversely, those who lack such attributes are virtually disqualified from all but the most undesirable areas of work.

The segmentation of the labour market is reflected in the structure of the labour movement. Trade unions are not cohesive class organizations, uniting all who work for a living behind one common purpose. While class opposition forms the basis of work relations in capitalist society, this is overlaid and often concealed by the immense variety of specific work contexts and distinctive group interests. Hence men and women normally identify themselves first and foremost as members of a specific occupational group, employees of a given firm, or workers in a particular industry. It is within such limited milieux that spontaneous collective organization typically develops. And just as individuals are often most conscious of the narrow area of interests and loyalties lying closest to hand (and hence commonly of what *divides* them from other workers rather than of what unites them), so the policies and priorities of unions often reflect narrow sectional concerns rather than broader class solidarity. (This tendency, it must be noted, is not merely spontaneous in origin; a whole battery of ideological pressures discourages workers from defining their interests in class terms; see Chapter 1.)

Sectional tendencies are particularly apparent in the operation of wage bargaining. One of the most common notions employed in this context is the concept of 'fair comparisons': the pay aspirations of a particular union or group of workers are characteristically framed and justified by reference to the level or movement of earnings among other employee groups. There is considerable sociological evidence that workers commonly assess their economic situation through restricted 'reference groups': limited inequities close to hand appear to generate greater spontaneous discontent than far more substantial but more distant inequalities of class; and collective bargaining often institutionalizes and reinforces this narrow focus. The main basis of contention is typically whether the relative position traditionally occupied by one group – and justified or criticized in the light of its particular skills, expertise, conditions of work or social and economic contribution – shall be sustained or improved in the context of the gains achieved by other groups. Hence wage bargaining typically involves the contestation of the relative economic advantages of different sections of the working class, rather than the *general* process of exploitation affecting all trade unionists. This necessarily obstructs the possibility of workers' self-conception as a class, or of concerted action challenging their subordination to capital.[8]

It can, therefore, be argued that the conventional processes of wage negotiation have a conservative tendency, in that the emphasis on parochial relativities serves to legitimize — if only by default — the broader inegalitarian structure of the overall incomes hierarchy. Yet this is not to suggest that the pursuit of pay improvements by trade unions cannot have disruptive consequences. In Britain since the end of the 1960s (and there have been similar tendencies in other countries), there has been a tendency for trade unionists to frame more ambitious aspirations, and to utilize broader orbits of comparison; and this has been reflected in an unprecedented level of pay demands and pay settlements.[9] Yet this has occurred when the margin for concession — in terms both of the distribution of the total national income, and the rate of profit in individual firms — has been constrained by an economic crisis international in effect but particularly severe in the context of British capitalism. It is this which has made the control of wages and salaries a particularly contentious issue in Britain (and most other countries) in recent years; and it is against this background that the growing interventions of governments in industrial relations and the growing interpenetration of economic and political elements in trade union policy (both discussed in later sections) must be assessed.

3 The control of the labour process

The previous section has considered one aspect of the employment relationship: the economic exchange through which the worker receives wages as payment for his/her labour power. 'What the capitalist obtains from this simple exchange is a use value: disposition over alien labour' (Marx 1973 p 282). The realization of the productive potential inherent in employees' labour power necessitates an elaborate network of roles and institutions ensuring the control of the employer over the labour process. Marx insisted that this control was not merely a *technical* requirement of complex modern industry, but was rather a *social* consequence of capitalist relations of production:

> the labourer works under the control of the capitalist to whom his labour belongs; the capitalist taking good care that the work is done

in the proper manner . . . The directing motive, the end aim of capitalist production, is to extract the greatest possible amount of surplus-value and consequently to exploit labour-power to the greatest possible extent . . . The control exercised by the capitalist is not only a special function, due to the nature of a social labour-process, but it is . . . rooted in the unavoidable antagonism between the exploiter and the living and labouring raw material that he exploits . . . An industrial army of workmen, under the command of a capitalist, requires, like a real army, officers (managers), and sergeants (foremen, overlookers), who, while the work is being done, command in the name of the capitalist.[10]

Why do workers obey such commands? In a real army, a soldier who disobeys an order may be court-martialled and, in extreme situations, shot. Such sanctions are not normally available to employers in modern industry; but what takes their place? Fox indicates a range of both positive and negative sanctions:

> Financial rewards, promotion prospects, praise and approval, transfer to more desired work, and any other form of gratification are positive but also have a negative aspect in that they embody a conditional clause threatening their withdrawal or withholding if the required behaviour is not forthcoming. Conversely, negative sanctions such as reprimands, fines, suspension, dismissal, demotion, or any other form of deprivation all have a positive aspect embodied in a conditional guarantee that they will be lifted or not be imposed if the desired behaviour is followed. (Fox 1971 pp 30–1)

The ability to manipulate such sanctions is, of course, a reflection of the economic (and legal) power on which managements can draw as representatives of capital. Controlling access to the means of production, the employer can ultimately determine whether a worker shall obtain and retain a job and a pay packet or salary cheque.* This dependence on the part of the workers – the need to obtain a buyer for their labour power in order to earn a living – provides the employer with a potent sanction: behind the detail of the control relationship at the point of production stands the threat of the sack.

But the force of this sanction may be attenuated. Where unemployment is low, the threat of dismissal is a lesser deterrent than where jobs are scarce. Its impact is also weakened where workers counterpose the principle of 'one out, all out'. An employer, faced by collective solidarity,

---

* This domination has the curious ideological consequence that the employer can appear to perform the worker a favour by exploiting his/her labour power. In some countries this topsy-turvy viewpoint is built into the language of employment: employers are known as 'work-givers', employees as 'work-takers'.

is unable to coerce employees simply as individuals: any open conflict must needs involve the labour force as a whole. There is a further reason why managements may be reluctant to rely too overtly on the simple threat of the sack. Employers require not merely the passive compliance of their workers with specific managerial orders but their active co-operation, ingenuity and initiative. Within any complex labour process, it is quite impossible to exercise detailed supervision of the performance of every worker every minute of the working day; nor is it possible to provide instruction on how to deal with every conceivable contingency. Bendix cites 'the case of inmates of Nazi concentration camps, who were employed in factories during the war and who sabotaged the production effort by consistently asking for detailed instructions on what to do next' (Bendix 1956 p 204). Without some measure of 'workers' control', industrial and commercial life could scarcely function; hence the chaos when employees withdraw their initiative and 'work to rule'. This becomes increasingly important when workers possess special expertise or skills, or are responsible for sophisticated and costly productive equipment. Yet managerial control based on the blatant exercise of the economic power of capital is necessarily corrosive of employee co-operation, and invites active or passive sabotage when opportunities arise. Significantly, Bendix opens his study with a well-known quotation from Rousseau: 'the strongest is never strong enough to be always master, unless he transforms his strength into right, and obedience into duty'.[11]

Thus the 'problem of order', which has so exercised sociologists in their general analyses of society, is replicated at the level of the workplace; and in both cases, the existence of some form of normative agreement is commonly identified as a necessary basis for stable social relationships. Capitalism is dependent on at least a measure of *self*-discipline, the consciousness of a work obligation which requires the performance of a 'fair day's work' — defined in terms acceptable to the employer. It is clear that powerful social mechanisms exist within our society to encourage such normative commitment on the part of employees. Socialization within the family and the educational system tend to inculcate an assumption that obedience to those in positions of authority is natural and morally proper; and the legitimacy of industrial management is routinely insisted on by religious dignitaries, politicians, judges, editors of newspapers and others with the ability to exert ideological influence. Hence, as Baldamus indicates, workers typically experience feelings of work obligation which provide important social support for the exercise of managerial control (Baldamus 1961, chapter 8).

Yet the acceptance of a generalized obligation to follow managerial instruction does not entail that a worker will accept without question every specific order which any manager may issue. There is a logical gap between generalized social values and specific rules in concrete situations. 'We find it difficult to relate the generalities of a value statement to the complex and specific details of everyday situations' (Becker 1963 p 130). Skilled toolmakers are normally conservative and stolid members of an engineering labour force, unlikely to contest in general terms the right of management to manage; but a supervisor who instructed a toolmaker to sweep the floor would be likely to be told to fuck off. The possibility of resistance to orders which are viewed as unreasonable is increased by the fact that 'legitimacy' is too strong a concept to apply to most workers' conceptions of management. 'Insofar as authority relations do prevail in the industrial organizations of the West,' Fox suggests, 'they are probably most widely characterized, so far as subordinates are concerned, by a low-key acquiescence' (Fox 1971 p 45). The execution of managerial instructions is rarely a matter of conscious choice; the hierarchy of authoritarian control — simply because it exists as a virtually universal feature of employment relation-ships — is typically regarded as natural and inevitable. Hence only when a worker is asked to perform a task which is out of the ordinary does the possibility of disobedience and resistance normally arise. The rare dissident who explicitly denies the authority of the employer to command is confronted not only by the coercive power of the latter but also by the routinized obedience of the mass of his/her fellows; in the normal situation the only choice for such a worker is between isolated and ineffectual protest or prudent acquiescence. Yet precisely because most workers' customary obedience reflects no more than 'low-key acquiescence', the limits of obedience are easily tested. As Fox puts it, there tends to exist a 'zone of acceptance': workers will, for example, normally perform without question tasks which are clearly technically necessary and which come within the customary range of their functions; but as soon as these limits are exceeded their conform-ity becomes problematic.

Capitalism is inherently dynamic: it exhibits phases of gradual and rapid technological change; markets expand or contract; the whole system of economic relations is subject to recurrent crises. In consequence, the patterns of managerial control are necessarily un-stable; and the legitimacy of this control is to this extent exposed to question. In practice, in the typical work situation, managerial control depends on a complex interplay of power, ideology, and the routine of customary forms of interaction. Legitimacy, in other words, should not be regarded simply as the opposite of coercive power: it is socially created from the dialectical interplay of material resources and ideology. This entails that the *processes* through which managers seek to avoid or contain the possibility and reality of worker resistance – while at the same time realizing the goals of profitability which they themselves are required to achieve – demand extremely sensitive sociological analysis. (For an analysis of managerial control in 'processual' terms, see Elger 1975.)

One concept which is useful for this purpose is that of 'negotiation of order'. Originally developed in a study of social relations in a hospital (Strauss *et al* 1971), the term is intended to indicate that where activities within an organization require the co-operation of individuals and groups with divergent attitudes and interests, there is a natural tendency for understandings, agreements and rules to emerge from processes of formal and informal negotiation. In effect, subordinate employees can make their obedience – or more crucially, the intelligent observance of the spirit rather than the mere letter of managerial instructions – a basis for tacit or even overt bargaining. The 'custom and practice' which is of such importance in British industrial relations indicates the significance of precisely this type of relationship. Its origins characteristically lie in recurrent trade-offs between first-line supervisors, themselves under pressure to achieve production targets, and workers conscious of their own ability to frustrate managerial objectives in the day-to-day work process on the shop floor. Thus foremen will purchase their subordinates' goodwill by conceding such demands as special bonus payments, or by showing restraint in enforcing company disciplinary rules. (For a general discussion of custom and practice see Brown 1973 chapter 4.)

Through the process of negotiation of order the 'frontier of control' in each workplace is set. It is a fluid and shifting frontier: the limits of management authority and employee obedience are imprecise and always open to renegotiation. In some situations this instability may take the form of recurrent overt conflict, as either party takes advantage of temporary shifts in the balance of workplace power to alter the basis of the control relationship. Beynon's study is a case in point: the situation he presents as typical is one of 'naked aggression being met by violent defiance' (Beynon 1973 p 139). Such overt and recurrent conflictuality is not, however, the universal pattern: in many work situations, managements interact with subordinates through a relatively accommodative process of give-and-take. In such contexts, temporary changes in the balance of power are less likely to be exploited, precisely because it is recognized that such changes *are* temporary. A relatively stable pattern of reciprocity may thus develop: workers obey orders because managers only *issue* orders which workers find reasonable; and such a relationship may persist at least until an exogenous disturbance (changing demands on management, new aspirations by workers) puts it at risk.

What shapes the detailed power balance through which relations at the point of production are negotiated? Occupational groups clearly vary considerably in respect of the sanctions and resources at their disposal, and also in terms of their readiness to mobilize these in opposition to the power of management.* Variations in the sources and exercise of control by manual work groups are discussed systematically in a valuable article by Hill (1974).

Skilled workers possess labour power of a specialized character, thus rendering the employer more than ordinarily dependent on their cooperation; often in addition they have a pride in their trade, a sense of community and commitment to common craft principles, which support powerful resistance to forms of managerial control which challenge their autonomy in the detailed performance of their work. (Goodrich 1975 discusses in detail the forms of workers' control commonly associated with traditional craft principles. For a recent analysis of craft cohesion in the printing industry, see Sykes 1967.) Other manual workers who, though not craftsmen, fulfil a strategic function in the production process and can easily cause disruption — the Halewood wet-deck team, for instance — also possess sanctions which assist them to negotiate the frontier of control in their favour. The generality of lower-skilled workers are less well placed; though groups like Sykes's navvies, through their manifest refusal to develop a dependent relationship in respect of any single employer, may well fare better than most in asserting an area of control over the labour process (Sykes 1973).**

White-collar employees constitute a heterogeneous stratum (ranging from routine clerical and technical to top managerial and professional occupations) and it is difficult to present meaningful generalizations. It is, however, normally the case that lower-level non-manual workers have

* For workers whose position is in principle strong may fail to recognize their potential strength, or because of an unusual commitment to managerial norms and objectives may fail to apply it in their own interests.
** It might be added that the navvies' readiness to 'jack in' their work could have been encouraged by the buoyant labour market for construction workers at the time of Sykes's research: workers were not dependent on any single employer because they could easily find another. In a situation of recession relationships might well alter significantly.

little ability to cause immediate disruption to production and at the same time — given that literacy alone no longer holds great scarcity value — are comparatively easily replaceable by the employer. Traditionally, such employees have tended to identify more closely than manual workers with managerial values and hence have displayed less will to resist. Yet conversely, employers have often controlled such staff in a less overtly authoritarian manner than in the case of manual workers; much white-collar work cannot be readily characterized as obeying orders. Their subordination, though still real, is often more diffuse. This relationship carries overtones of what Fox terms 'trust': a reliance by the employer less on close supervision than on the employee's own discretion (Fox 1974).* Such a relationship is itself in a sense 'negotiated': discretion is conditional on performance at some point judged satisfactory by the employer and will otherwise be eventually circumscribed. Autonomy is particularly high in the case of the most elevated occupational groups. Professional competence may make 'correct' performance extremely difficult for the employer to assess; more crucially, perhaps, the occupational solidarity of the most privileged white-collar groups, reinforced by their dominant class position, typically protects even incompetent individuals from the type of controls to which ordinary employees would be subject.

In other respects, the negotiation of order in the workplace is subject to broader social influences. It is often suggested, for example, that women workers are more submissive to managerial authority than most men. If this is so — and the evidence of many active and militant female trade unionists shows that it can be no more than a crude generalization — it reflects the subordination imposed on women outside as well as inside work. The material dominance of men, in family and other social relationships, and the ideological pervasiveness of sexist stereotypes necessarily influence the relationship between women as workers and their (usually male) supervisors. (For an elaboration of this point see Acker and Van Houten 1974.) Black workers, too, are commonly affected in their work relations by the fact that they are black as well as workers. Racist stereotypes often shape managerial strategies in dealing with black subordinates. The latter may on occasion tolerate unusually authoritarian treatment precisely because the same is customary outside work; others by contrast, having learned

---

* This distinction, it must be added, does not simply divide manual from white-collar occupations: some of the former enjoy considerable discretion in work performance, some of the latter very little. But the rough generalization remains heuristically useful.

to resist the racism of authority figures in the wider society, may
similarly react against managerial control – even when, exceptionally,
this is not influenced by racism. Racism creates divisions within the
working class which can be viewed as conducive to the stability of
capitalism in that concerted working class action is inhibited. (For a
useful discussion of European experience see Castles and Kosack
1973.) Sexism can have similar consequences. Some writers would
argue that both racism and sexism are at times deliberately cultivated
for this very reason.

With varying degrees of success, then – reflecting both the material
and ideological resources at the disposal of managements and workers
respectively – employees can establish an area of control over the
work process. This autonomy is, however, always conditional. One
condition is that they will continue to contribute to, and certainly
not seriously obstruct, managerial goals of productivity and profitability. Hence groups enjoying significant discretion in the performance
of work tasks must exercise self-discipline in its application; work
groups with the power to obstruct specific managerial decisions cannot
go 'too far' without inviting serious retaliation. To this extent, 'workers'
control' within capitalism is necessarily partial and reactive: a means
of moderating the effects of subordination to the abstract dictates of
capital and the specific domination of hierarchical management, not a
means of enforcing different priorities. Hence Beynon's conclusion that
'essentially the controls obtained over the job by shop floor union
activities involved little more than a different form of accommodation
to the more general controls imposed by management' (Beynon 1973
p 149).

Employee autonomy is doubly conditional in that it operates within an economic, technical and organizational context which can be
expected to persist only so long as the employer is able to derive an
acceptable level of profits. The availability of new technology, a shift
in market conditions, or even a top-level company decision which has
no obvious rationale, can totally disrupt the detailed process of negotiation of order within the workplace. A particular set of work tasks may
be displaced or a whole establishment closed down – sometimes
through a deliberate policy decision that this is the most effective
means of bypassing the controls established by a powerful employee
group. Or economic stringency may lead to the intensification of work
pressure on production workers or the elimination of the elements of
latitude traditionally permitted to white-collar staff.

This helps to underline the fact that control over higher-level policies
and decisions – which set rigorous limits to the workplace negotiation

of order – is remote from the spontaneous processes of workgroup action and resistance. For this reason, the very notion of 'negotiation of order' can be misleading: for exclusive attention to the disposition of power at the point of employment involves the neglect of *broader* structures of power in the economy and society. Workers who establish the most impressive range of controls in their dealings with junior management are nevertheless unlikely to play any positive part in determining what they will produce and in what quality and quantity; which consumers will be catered for, and through which mechanisms (market or otherwise); what establishments will be opened or closed, expanded or contracted; how the collective labour of the totality of employees will be co-ordinated; how profits will be distributed between reinvestment and dividends. (The absence of positive workers' control over such issues is stressed by Goodrich 1975.) Influence at this level would be in principle possible only through a different level of collective employee action: a broader, co-ordinated, consciously formulated strategy to counterpose the interests of workers against the priorities of capitalism, positively and aggressively rather than negatively and defensively. Arguably, it is precisely this function which trade unionism is intended to fulfil. To consider further the possibility of transcending the limitations of the workplace negotiation of order it is therefore necessary to examine explicitly the complex role of trade unionism in the process of job control.

4 Trade unionism and control

Against the background of the previous discussion, the key significance of trade unionism is that it formalizes and generalizes the processes of worker resistance to, and negotiation with, the structure of capitalist domination in the employment relationship.

At the end of 1974 there were in the United Kingdom an estimated 491 trade unions with a combined membership of 11.75 million. Of this large number of unions, the great majority are insignificant in size and influence: half have less than a thousand members, three-quarters less than five thousand. At the other extreme, a mere 25 organizations, each with over 100,000 members, account for over three-quarters of total union membership. The three largest, the Transport and General Workers' Union, the Amalgamated Union of Engineering Workers and the General and Municipal Workers' Union, contain together over four million members. Almost all the major organizations are affiliated to the Trades Union Congress, which in 1975 contained 111 unions with a total membership of 10.4 million.*

Aggregate union membership represents almost exactly half the total labour force; this proportion is the highest ever achieved in Britain. It is high also by comparison with most western nations; though a few countries, such as Sweden or Belgium, can claim unionization of about three-quarters of the labour force, the position in the United States with only a quarter organized is more typical. In part the relative strength of British unionism reflects its deep historical roots. Organization among skilled artisans existed as early as the eighteenth century, surviving and expanding despite severe legal repression. From the 1850s can be traced the consolidation of craft societies into impressive national associations, and the emergence of stable unionization among workers in the large-scale industries of the industrial revolution such as coal-mining, cotton and iron and steel. The turn of the century saw a further wave of unionization, covering in particular the bulk of transport and manufacturing. The extension of organization to white-collar workers — initially primarily in the public sector, but in recent years to a significant extent also in private industry and services — is largely the achievement of the present century.

To a large extent, the current pattern of organization was established in Britain by 1920, when 45 per cent of the labour force was unionized. Mass unemployment between the wars caused severe losses, roughly halving total membership. Since the last war these losses have been more than recovered, though recent progress has been relatively slow. One reason has been the changing structure of the labour force: a decline in employment in industries and occupations (such as coal-mining, cotton textiles, docks and railways) which have been union strongholds; and growth in service industries and white-collar occupations which have traditionally been more weakly organized. Unionization has occurred historically in the face of severe obstacles: forcible opposition by employers, the victimization and blacklisting of activists, the attack of judges, legislators and other agencies of the state. While unions today have won greater acceptance, such forms of resistance remain widespread. Hence it is often extremely difficult to organize in workplaces which are small or isolated, and in industries and occupations with a casual or fluctuating labour force. Conversely, virtual 100 per cent unionization may be maintained in some establishments and occupations through controls which oblige the employer to recruit only

---

* Each November issue of the *Department of Employment Gazette* contains an analysis of the previous year's trade union membership. The affiliated membership of TUC unions is given in the annual Congress Reports.

union members, or at least require that new employees must join the relevant union. In this way, collective control may be self-sustaining.

Trade unions represent a focal point in a complex network of power relations. Their basic rationale is as a source and medium of power: providing a means whereby employees, individually without significant defence against the employer, can achieve more effective collective support. Unions reduce competition among workers in the labour market, confronting the concentrated power of employers with an analogous (though usually far less tightly integrated) combination of labour power. Within the labour process, trade unionism sustains a solidarity which reduces the vulnerability of the individual employee in the ongoing negotiation of the frontier of control. In higher-level decision-making – involving top management, collective organizations of employers and also the various institutions of the state – unions seek to represent the collective interests of their members in influencing the policies and priorities adopted.

Yet the rule of trade unionism in relation to managerial control and the dynamics of capitalist relations of production is essentially ambivalent: a reflection of the multi-directional interaction of power relationships, both internal and external, in which unions are implicated. Trade unions are the institutional meeting point of the contradictory demands and interests of different sectional groups of workers, of employers and state functionaries. Their key task is to mediate and accommodate these conflicting pressures – a task which is at times virtually impossible. This focal role also explains why trade unions are commonly the target of very powerful *ideological* pressures. The pursuit of humane working conditions, a less inegalitarian distribution of economic rewards, increased security of working class life-changes, or greater scope for individual and collective self-determination by working people, conflicts systematically and radically with the priorities of the capitalist mode of production and the interests of those in positions of social and economic dominance within existing society. Hence, not only are very powerful material pressures exerted on the articulation of trade union goals and the selection of specific demands, strategies and tactics,[12] but material power is closely interlinked with the ability to influence the beliefs and perceptions of trade unionists and the 'vocabularies of motive' through which they appraise the actions of employers and their own potential responses. (For an elaboration of this point see Hyman and Fryer 1975 pp 76–8.)

One example of the ideological offensive to which trade unionists are subject is the force of contemporary stereotypes of 'overpowerful' unions persistently engaged in 'militant' and 'irresponsible' actions.

Notions of union militancy lose their plausibility when the objectives actually pursued are measured against the scale of the deprivations and inequalities generated by capitalist wage-labour, and hence the scope of what might potentially be demanded. In assessing union action it is significant that shop stewards — arch-figures in conventional demonology — are viewed by most managers as no more (and often less) militant than the members they represent; and were evaluated by the Royal Commission on Trade Unions and Employers' Associations as 'an accepted, reasonable and even moderating influence; more of a lubricant than an irritant'. (See Donovan 1968 and McCarthy and Parker 1968.) As for the image of 'overmighty' unionism, the comments of Fox are particularly apposite:

> Power and social conditioning cause the employee interests to accept management's shaping of the main structure long before they reach the negotiating table. Thus the discussion may be about marginal adjustments in hierarchical rewards, but not the principle of hierarchical rewards; about certain practical issues connected with the prevailing extreme sub-division of labour, but not the principle of extreme sub-division of labour; about financial (extrinsic) rewards for greater efficiency, but not about the possibility of other types of (intrinsic) reward with some sacrifice of efficiency; about measures which may achieve company expansion and growth, but not about the benefits and costs of company expansion and growth; about how the participant interests can protect and advance themselves within the structure operated by management to pursue its basic objectives, but not about the nature of those basic objectives. (Fox 1973 p 219)

While the precise specification of the relative power of trade unions involves immense methodological difficulties, there is no serious basis for the assertion that this power even approaches, in any general and systematic sense, that of the agencies with which unions are engaged in continuous relationships. To come to terms with the colourful characterizations of union action which are currently prevalent, it is necessary to regard them less as intellectual formulations to be appraised by rational criticism than as ideological weapons in a social struggle aimed at containing the *potentially* disruptive impact of collective worker action within capitalist society.

Central to any serious sociological analysis of trade unionism is the area of institutional autonomy available to union representatives in mediating the conflicting pressures and expectations of members on the one hand and external agencies on the other. Workers as individuals can exert little meaningful control over their work environment; only by submitting to collective principles and decisions can they share in more significant influence over the conditions of their working lives. But in subordinating part of their individual autonomy to collective decision-making processes, they create an institution which (through the activities and initiatives of official representatives and spokesmen) can pursue objectives which diverge from their own interests (see Beynon 1975). If a union is to be effective in wielding power *for* its members and against the employer, the possibility exists that this organizational power will be exerted *over* them, possibly on behalf of external interests. Precisely because the secure existence of unionism appears to require at least the acquiescence of governments and major employers, these 'significant others' can influence union representatives to eschew policies which may invite repression, and even to transmit their own imperatives back down to the membership.

At the very least there exist strong pressures on union officials to act, in Wright Mills's famous phrase, as 'managers of discontent' (Mills 1948 pp 8–9). They express, and in some circumstances actually stimulate, their members' consciousness of grievances; yet at the same time they seek to limit the expression of industrial conflict to forms over which they can exert control, and which do not jeopardize the arrangements and understandings developed with employers. Established union—employer relations may serve, indeed, to transmute the very character of employee grievances, by defining issues within a narrow focus which shapes the parameters for potential resolution; for if fundamental questions of principle are suppressed, the task of achieving compromise may be greatly eased. In such circumstances, far-sighted managements have little to fear in coming to terms with unionism, and may indeed find great advantages in terms of the achievement of a more predictable labour force. This then is the central paradox of trade unionism. Through co-ordinating workers' collective strength, and at times directing this in militant action, unions win significant improvements in their members' conditions (both in the sale of their labour power and within the labour process itself). Against the arbitrary dominance of the employer, they counterpose an 'industrial legality' which represents 'a great victory for the working class' (Gramsci 1969 p 15). Yet in certain forms this 'industrial legality' is acceptable and even advantageous to employers; and trade union representatives are subject to powerful influences to pursue objectives and actions of such character. (For a more detailed discussion of the pressures which limit the effectiveness of collective bargaining in satisfying workers' interests, see Fox 1974, in particular chapter 6.)

It follows that the role of trade unions in relation to job control is inherently ambiguous. As Herding argues, 'job-control rights, and demands for them, may serve the union as an organization, particularly a bureaucratic leadership, or they may be geared to benefit specific strata of workers, or the working class in general. In each case we have to single out how and for whom a job-control measure works' (Herding 1972 p 16). In America, he suggests, the growing involvement of trade unions in negotiations on such issues has centred mainly around demands — the rationalization of personnel administration and the reduction of competition within the labour force — which are not antagonistic to employer interests and may even facilitate managerial objectives. By contrast, unions have achieved few significant concessions on the control of the labour process itself, where the interests of employers and workers are diametrically opposed. Indeed the commitment of unions to the 'peace obligation' inherent in their negotiating procedures has reinforced managerial control of job allocation, production speeds and working conditions by disarming rank-and-file workers; for the only effective response to managerial initiatives which adversely affect the workplace frontier of control is immediate direct action.

In Britain, it is possible to discern some parallels. Many unions have shown a willingness to negotiate over and agree to systems of job evaluation and work measurement; payment by results systems based on work study alone (rather than on 'mutuality' between operator and rate-fixer); and 'productivity' schemes which allocate a range of decisions over the labour process to managerial initiative or formalized collective bargaining. The tendency of all such developments, as Flanders has emphasized, is 'to strengthen managerial control over pay and work through joint regulation' (Flanders 1970 p 204).

Such developments are in general less advanced in Britain than in most other countries. A crucial factor has been the importance of shop steward organization: particularly strong among manual workers in private manufacturing industry, but of growing significance (under a variety of titles) in the public sector and among non-manual employees. The 'challenge from below' discussed by Flanders has created a constant obstacle to the institutionalization and incorporation of trade union action: workplace organization has proved highly responsive to the spontaneous demands of the rank and file, articulating members' aspirations and grievances, where necessary, independently and even in defiance of official trade union channels. Union officials in turn have had to take account of challenges deriving from an independent workplace power base. Hence there has been a considerable tendency for the exercise of job control through trade unionism to retain its autonomous and oppositional character. (For further discussion of this point see Hyman 1971.)

Yet some qualification is necessary. Shop steward organization has normally been less strong in the public sector than the private, in services than in manufacturing, among white-collar employees than manual workers; and the constraints imposed by unionism on managerial initiative have been correspondingly weaker. And even where independent workplace unionism is most firmly established, it is by no means immune from the incorporating pressures diagnosed at the level of official unionism. Workplace representatives are implicated in a two-way relationship of dependence with the offical union hierarchy. The balance of power can vary considerably: reflecting, for example, the strategic position of different occupational and industrial groups, the structure of formal union-employer negotiating arrangements, managerial strategies and preferences, and the constitutional arrangements of union rulebooks; but to a greater or lesser extent all such representatives are necessarily tied into the broader system of union-employer accommodation. This integration is facilitated by the emergent tendencies in most workplace organizations towards an institutional separation of the domestic leadership from the mass of the rank and file, with the development of distinctive perspectives, interests, sanctions and resources; the relationship between members and full-time officials is thus replicated in microcosm. The stability of the domestic collective organization, like that of the larger union, depends substantially on the preservation of established bargaining relationships with the employer (including the tacit or explicit provision of a range of facilities necessary for effective workplace representation). Even an assertive and combative shop steward body, as at Halewood, is constrained by the awareness that carrying resistance to management 'too far' would invite a concerted counter-attack and jeopardize existing achievements. Hence shop stewards too are 'managers of discontent': sustaining job control within the boundaries of negotiation with managerial authority and capitalist priorities, rather than (apart from the most exceptional circumstances) pursuing frontal opposition.

The thesis of this section may appear profoundly pessimistic: the inevitable institutionalization and emasculation of collective resistance by workers to exploitative work relations. Does the study of the politics of work suggest no possibility of a more fundamental and concerted challenge to capitalist work organization? How far trade unionism contains such a potential, and how far the institutionalization of conflict is itself inherently contradictory and unstable, can be assessed only on the basis of a more explicit consideration of the interrelationship of trade unionism, job control, state power and the dynamics of contemporary capitalism.

5 The politics of job control

For Marx, observing the early collective struggles of the proletariat of the industrial revolution, the formation of trade unions was a crucial stage in the growth of class consciousness among workers and presaged an explicit revolutionary challenge to the political economy of capitalism. 'The real fruit of their battles lies, not in the immediate results, but in the ever-expanding union of the workers . . . Out of the separate economic movements of the workers there grows up everywhere a *political* movement, that is to say, a movement of the *class*, with the object of enforcing its interests in a general form, in a form possessing general, socially coercive force.' (In *Manifesto of the Communist Party* and letter to Bolte, 23 November 1871.) (For a discussion of Marx's writings on trade union development see Hyman 1971.)

The actual development of trade unionism has clearly diverged from this model. Sectionalism has not been increasingly transcended by broader unification, an expectation of Marx deriving from his prediction of the rapid erosion of skill distinctions; while some old divisions within the working class have disappeared, others have arisen. As suggested earlier, sectional consciousness is clearly apparent in the typical motivation to collective action; and while sectionalism is not at all times incompatible with broader solidarity, it commonly inhibits class consciousness. Sectionalism is, moreover, often reinforced by the organizational distinctiveness of a multiplicity of competing unions.

Nor has trade unionism developed spontaneously into a political movement. In Britain, indeed (and the same has been even more evident in the United States), trade union representatives have normally insisted on a rigid separation of 'industrial' and 'political' activities. Marx noted the vigorous political campaigns mounted by the early textile unions for statutory limitation of hours of work. Miners were concerned with achieving safety legislation and controls on other conditions of their work. The formation of the TUC in 1868 stemmed primarily from a concern to safeguard the legal position of trade unionism in general. But the premise became rapidly accepted that the industrial strength of workers must on no account be mobilized to force the political authorities to concede their demands. Strikes and related forms of action were legitimate only in the context of the 'industrial' issues which were the unions' central focus of interest; 'political' demands could properly be pursued only through due observance of constitutional proprieties.

This commitment is without rational foundation. The distinction between 'industrial' and 'political' issues is at root merely conventional; there is, as Fox insists, nothing intrinsic in a specific demand which requires it to be classified in one category rather than another. Rather, to call a demand 'political' is simply to assert that unions *ought* not to use all their resources to achieve it. Hence the conventional distinction 'bears an ideological connotation in that it underpins a particular interpretation of the proper role of trade unions in our society' (Fox 1974 p 150). It is, moreover, only the *overt* use of economic pressure on political decision-making that offends conventional notions of 'the sovereignty of a democratically elected government' (Allen 1966 p 35); the power of capital is a permanent constraint on the economic and social objectives which can 'realistically' be pursued. Precisely because a central concern of governments — whatever their political complexion — is to maintain the 'confidence' of those who control industry and to sustain an environment conducive to profitability, the coercive force of those who own and control major economic resources is normally latent rather than overt. (Though on occasion, governments may fail sufficiently to respect capitalist interests and invite the blatant use of economic power: Chile is a case in point. For a general discussion of the relationship between capitalist control and state power, see Miliband 1969.) The traditional self-restraint of British unions has thus seriously inhibited any concerted attempt to counterpose different priorities to those deriving from the pervasive influence of capital.

This ideological segregation of the 'industrial' from the 'political' is reflected in the relationship between the unions and the political organization established largely on their initiative, the Labour Party. While insisting on favourable consideration of 'industrial relations' questions, union leaders have normally been happy to abstain from any initiating role in the formulation of general Party policy. The Party has been correspondingly anxious to establish its autonomy from the unions, and to disavow any interest in 'unconstitutional' forms of political pressure. 'Of political parties claiming socialism to be their aim,' Miliband has argued, 'the Labour Party has always been one of the most dogmatic — not about socialism, but about the parliamentary system. Empirical and flexible about all else, its leaders have always made devotion to that system their fixed point of reference and the conditioning factor of their political behaviour' (Miliband 1964 p 13). Hence the Party leadership has always been concerned to prove its 'fitness to govern' by managing capitalism more efficiently (which often has to mean, in practice, more ruthlessly) than the traditional capitalist parties; while its anxiety to appear as a 'national' rather than class party has limited any special attention to the interests of workers and their families. Certainly Labour leaders have traditionally sought (often quite sincerely) to identify the Party with an idealistic commitment to the development of the welfare state; but their fate has been to achieve office in periods of economic stringency when this goal has proved largely incompatible with the priority of maintaining the viability of capitalism. (For an elaboration of this interpretation see Miliband 1964 and, more recently, Coates 1975. Minkin 1974 analyses the changing relationship between Party and unions during the last decade.)

This conventional segregation of industrial and political goals and strategies invites attention to the orientation often termed 'economism'. Writing at the turn of the century, Lenin argued that workers' industrial struggles led in themselves to no more than 'trade union consciousness': 'the conviction that it is necessary to combine in unions, fight the employers, and strive to compel the government to pass necessary labour legislation, etc.'[13] Any sustained and comprehensive attack on capitalist relations of production, by contrast, required a fully fledged revolutionary consciousness which could not emerge spontaneously from economic conflicts alone but demanded the intervention of a revolutionary party.

A somewhat different conception of 'economism' has been proposed by Mann, who contrasts wage demands with those which focus on control. The former, he suggests, provide a ready basis for compromise, for 'the economic interests of rival parties can in principle be served by increasing the total reward available for share-out by collective cooperation. By contrast, there tends to be a fixed amount of work control available for distribution, and for one party to increase control the other must necessarily lose some of *its* control.' Mann's argument is that 'as trade unions are organized toward the attainment of economic bargaining gains, they tend in practice to lose sight of control issues, whether these concern the immediate work situation or wider-ranging questions of industrial structure'. In consequence 'they operate to *weaken* workers' class consciousness' and integrate them into the structure of capitalist society (Mann 1973 pp 21–3).

While these two interpretations of economism parallel some of the analysis in this chapter, it should be clear from the discussion in the previous sections that any attempt to posit a clear boundary between 'economistic' and 'non-economistic' trade unionism is misleading. Firstly, the *organizational* interests which are particularly salient for union officials necessarily transcend mere economism: they are concerned to establish *procedures* which underwrite union security and status. Even if union members (perhaps encouraged by their leaders) were to see their organization only as a means of pressing a narrow range of substantive demands, the procedural interests of their representatives would necessarily involve explicit attention to control issues. Operating within an environment of power, the right of unions to exist and to operate effectively is necessarily a political question. Secondly, 'pure' economism is in principle impossible because workers do not *merely* sell their labour power; this economic exchange, as was shown in detail earlier, is merely the preliminary to the control relationship in the workplace which inevitably generates conflict which must be the subject of formal or informal negotiation. Thirdly, it is by no means evident that wage demands always permit ready compromise; this can be achieved only when the size of the demands, the resources and determination used in their support, and the margin for concession available in the economy are in some sort of equilibrium. Otherwise even economistic trade unionism will prove economically – and in consequence also socially and politically – disruptive: a point which scarcely requires emphasis in view of the recent history of Britain as well as other western economies. Fourthly, a preoccupation with simple wage-bargaining on the part of union officials presupposes a reasonable balance of supply and demand within the labour market; for otherwise, the *control of employment opportunities* becomes an issue of overt concern for trade unionists. Again, it is quite obvious that in recent years union representatives have been obliged to focus their attention on 'wider-ranging questions of industrial structure' as a precondition of successful negotiation on more limited issues.

Drawing all these arguments together, it is possible to appreciate that trade union economism has always rested on certain *historically contingent* preconditions. The readiness to avoid the use of workers' potential industrial strength in the political arena has been the reciprocal of a parallel abstention by the state in the field of industrial relations: the tradition of 'voluntarism'. Since the mid-Victorian era, *direct* intervention by the law and the state machinery has occurred in Britain usually only on the margins of employment relations; in general, unions and employers have been left free to negotiate autonomously on the main substantive issues of terms and conditions of employment. This 'collective *laissez-faire*' has never been absolute, as the most cursory knowledge of labour history will indicate. More crucially, this tradition (like *laissez-faire* in general) has represented not the neutrality of the state but rather its abstention *in favour* of the stronger party in economic relations: those who own and control capital. (For a development of this argument, see Hyman 1971 chapter 5.) Voluntarism had its roots in an era when unions were relatively weak (through limited membership and often high unemployment) and willing to exercise considerable self-restraint in the use made of power they did possess. The notions of 'responsibility' embraced by trade union leaders ensured a relatively stable pattern of industrial relations: unions pursued wage objectives sufficiently modest to be accommodated within the general framework of economic development (the significance of the ideology of 'responsibility' is explored by Allen 1966, chapter 1) and hence problems of *control* both within the labour process and in relations between unions, employers and the state were only intermittently the subject of large-scale conflict.[14]

Over recent years many of the foundations of voluntarism in state policy and economism in trade union action have been eroded. *Laissez-faire* as a general orientation has given way to government intervention to manage the overall level of economic activity, support specific industries and enterprises, finance costly research and development, guarantee markets and influence investment. Attempts to control labour costs, supply and utilization fit naturally within the logic of this development, and have been apparent in a wide range of government initiatives in Britain in the past decade. The *long-run* trend to interdependence between state and monopoly capitalism is reinforced by more acute economic pressures: after two decades of relatively full employment and sustained expansion, world capitalism — and British capitalism in particular — is beset by an unprecedented combination of recession and rapid inflation. In this unfavourable environment, the economic aspirations of employees appear to have become more ambitious, and union leaders have been forced to sponsor an increased militancy of aims and tactics. *Managerial* attempts to sustain profitability by pushing back the frontier of control on the shop floor ('productivity' bargaining, work measurement, speed-up, new payment systems and work organization) necessarily turn non-economic issues into a major focus of collective bargaining and industrial conflict. Even if the initial stance of trade unionists in such control conflicts is primarily defensive, the experience can stimulate more aggressive and wide-ranging demands for control as the only effective means of defending the existing limited areas of work autonomy. (Hence it is no accident that the revival of interest among trade unionists in theories of workers' control and the possibility of positive strategies of self-management has coincided with employer and government efforts to alter the previously relatively stable frontier of control within production.)[15] Simultaneously, large-scale unemployment and widespread closures and redundancies have thrown into relief the trade union interest in top-level company decision-making and in overall government economic strategies; the distinction between 'industrial' and 'political' concerns loses all credibility. Government attempts to contain the (usually unintended) disruptive consequences of union action challenge the traditional norms of 'free collective bargaining', making the procedural status of trade unions themselves a focus of explicit contention. The fact that Labour governments have been in office for most of the period of these developments has imposed severe strains on the traditional understandings between party and unions: a central theme of Minkin's analysis.

The changing material context of trade union action — which ultimately reflects the contradictory basis of the capitalist mode of production itself — creates a volatile and unstable interrelationship between unions, employers and the state. At times, governments see the only solution in explicit attacks on the procedural status of trade unionism (such as the Industrial Relations Act of 1971); but such strategies necessarily provoke official union opposition which in turn legitimizes more radical resistance by rank-and-file activists. Collaborative strategies — the cultivation of union acquiescence in government economic priorities, as a trade-off for government abstention from repressive measures (and possibly also certain symbolic concessions to the social objectives of the unions) — almost always receive a favourable response from union leaders; but their own limited control over the rank and file entail that they may be unable to guarantee membership compliance. The response of workers themselves — faced by contradictory material and ideological pressures — becomes a critical but unpredictable factor. (For a more detailed development of the points outlined here, see Hyman 1973.)

This discussion does not lead to any tidy conclusions: the analysis is necessarily open-ended, for control relations themselves are fluid and dynamic. The sociologist can seek to assign meanings and discover causes, and can attempt to identify the key problems in the control relations between workers, union officials, managers and state functionaries. But the solution to these problems emerges only in the struggle for control itself.

Notes

1 This official category, comprising employers, employees and self-employed, encapsulates an interesting ideological bias. Those whose

work is not implicated in commercial exchange relations are simply not classed as productively engaged; hence the great bulk of housework, for example, is excluded.

2 Marx and Engels criticize this popular trade union slogan as a 'conservative motto': for notions of fairness typically reflect the assumptions of capitalist political economy and the interests of employers. For a discussion of the significance of ideas of fairness in modern industrial relations see Hyman and Brough (1975).

3 In Marxian terminology, the interrelationships of these three factors (given a particular exchange value of the commodities produced) sets the ratio of *necessary* to *surplus* labour. Necessary labour represents the proportion of working time in which the market value of what is collectively produced compensates the employer for the workers' wages and other necessary costs of production; surplus labour the proportion of which the employer is able to *appropriate* the value added by the workers. Historically, the profitability of early capitalism depended on the *extensive* exploitation of the labour force: surplus value was obtained through low wages and long working hours. As capitalism developed, the tendency has been towards *intensive* exploitation: the length of necessary labour has been sharply reduced by various strategies to increase labour productivity, allowing the maintenance (or even increase) of the rate of surplus value despite higher wages and shorter hours.

4 The process of concentration and centralization of capital, creating large and potent monopolies, overturns the assumptions of a perfectly competitive economic system. Nevertheless, no monopoly is so powerful as to be wholly immune from competitive pressures — particularly given the increasingly overt international character of capitalist production.

5 'The division of labour within the workshop,' wrote Marx (1959 pp 356—61), 'implies the undisputed authority of the capitalist over men, that are but parts of a mechanism that belongs to him . . . By nature unfitted to make anything independently, the manufacturing labourer develops productive activity as a mere appendage of the capitalist's workshop.' It has been argued that historically the development of factory production owed less to the resulting increase in technical efficiency than to the consequential concentration of control in the hands of the employer (Marglin 1974). It might be added that the degree to which this monopolization of managerial power is eliminated is one acid test of any society purporting to have established socialist relations of production.

6 While some such services — e.g. research and development — would

be of value within any social formation, others derive their function specifically from capitalism. Thus 'marketing' is necessary only where the social distribution of products is abdicated to the blind forces of the market; much financial control is similarly specific to capitalist economic relations. (See the detailed discussion in Chapter 11.)

7 An obvious example is the campaign by Chrysler and British Leyland to replace piecework by measured daywork. This trend reflects a growing determination on the part of employers (strongly encouraged by the government, through such agencies as the National Board for Prices and Incomes in 1965−70) to contain and reduce labour costs by reinforcing managerial control over earnings, movements and labour utilization. This tendency is discussed in Cliff (1970).

8 A remarkable historical stability in the share of the national income going to wages and salaries has often been asserted; Glyn and Sutcliffe (1972), in an important analysis, challenge this familiar argument. Their own interpretation appears, however, to require some qualification. Firstly, they put excessive weight on short-run trends; the significant gains by British labour in the late 1960s appear to have been more recently reversed. Secondly, they give insufficient attention to the extent to which the rapidly increasing share of *salaries* may represent, in effect, a reward for the exercise of traditional capitalist functions rather than a return to productive labour. Thirdly, they treat somewhat simplistically the growing interdependence of the state and capitalist industry: a development which arguably renders any simple analysis in terms of factor shares unilluminating.

9 Some of the reasons for this recent 'wage explosion' are discussed in Jackson *et al* (1972) and also in Hyman and Brough (1975).

10 Marx 1959, pp 184−5, 331−2. Here again, Marglin's article (1974) is a notable recent elaboration of the thesis that managerial control in capitalist industry is more a reflection of exploitative social relations of production than of technical necessity.

11 Bendix, p 1. Nor is it necessarily satisfactory for the employer that the worker should fail to view the employment relationship as a coercive subordination to superior power, if he/she regards it simply as an economic exchange. For a purely instrumental orientation fails to engender a normative acceptance of the employer's standards of work performance. For the sake of wages an employee may accept his/her subordination to managerial authority, and agree to perform boring and routine tasks; but any dissatisfaction with the level of pay will corrode any sense of work obligation. 'The "cash-nexus" may snap just because it is *only* a cash-nexus − because it is single-stranded; and if it does snap, there is

nothing else to bind the worker to acceptance of his situation' (Westergaard 1970 p 120).

12 Such material pressures are a central theme of the first extract from the present writer's *Industrial Relations: A Marxist introduction* (1975), and are not discussed further here.

13 *What Is to Be Done?*; for references and discussion see Hyman (1971). It should be noted that 'economism', for Lenin, did not preclude certain forms of political action: he was aware of the practice of Victorian British trade unionism. But he believed (unlike Marx) that such action would not develop spontaneously into a general political challenge to capitalism.

14 This traditional stability should not be exaggerated. The status of trade unions – and hence their legitimate role in control relations involving both individual employers and broader political action – has involved recurrent conflicts with parliament and the courts. 'Public opinion' – the social production of which commonly follows closely the interests of employers – has on many occasions indicated intense hostility to trade union functions. Recognition from employers has more often been the outcome of struggle than of spontaneous acceptance. Control issues at workplace level have not infrequently provoked fierce contention: in engineering, for example, three national lock-outs have arisen from the conflict between managerial control and craft autonomy.

15 One reflection of the growing questioning of traditional authority relations both within the workplace and at higher levels of company decision-making is the current propagation of notions of 'job enrichment' and 'participation': concepts denoting strategies to increase workers' commitment to managerial objectives by giving the *appearance* of enhanced self-determination in work. For a critical appraisal see Fox (1974).

CHAPTER 11

Terry Johnson

Work and power

Work is a relationship of power. The intention in the discussion which follows will be to explore this theme further and in doing so to raise a number of issues which continually surface as unresolved theoretical concerns in the sociology of work.

Given its most general meaning, the statement 'work is a relationship of power' refers to the view that when people enter into relationships of production they are, at the same time, engaged in a political process out of which emerge structures of domination and subordination, mechanisms of social control and forms of exploitation. More specifically, it refers to a process in which power is integral to the social organization of work as occupations, jobs, skills, specialisms, careers, etc. That is to say, the process whereby a new specialism crystallizes in response to technical innovation or an emergent social need is conditioned by and may even transform power relations at various levels of the productive enterprise or bureaucratic hierarchy.

It follows, as a corollary of the opening statement, that the ways in which people relate to one another in work cannot be defined solely in terms of the technical means at their disposal. Computer technology does not, of itself, require the hierarchical ordering of systems managers, analysts, computer programmers, console operators, key punch operators, tape librarians, etc.; nor does it preordain relative rewards in terms of income and status (see H. Braverman's discussion of the 'Mechanization of the office' (1974 pp 326–48)). It may well be that a pre-existing structure of power will effectively determine the boundaries and content of an occupation's technical competence, much as the power of the medical profession has in the past been mobilized to determine the area of competence of auxiliary occupations such as physiotherapy or occupational therapy (see Johnson 1972 pp 57–61) or to exclude osteopaths from the 'profession' of medicine altogether (Inglis 1964). Technical innovation may then create new opportunities for domina- tion, new conditions of exploitation, but such innovations and, more important, their application to work are themselves a product of an existing set of production relations and, therefore, power structures. Technology and its product in machines or instruments of production are, in the end, merely the means by which people actively create and recreate their conditions of life. They are extensions of man; of his capacity to control nature in the pursuit of a livelihood.

We re-emphasize, in this rather obvious fashion, that technology is a product of people's social relationships because it has become part of the conventional wisdom of our own society and an ubiquitous element in dominant ideologies that in the modern world people's lives are increasingly and necessarily subordinated to technique; that in some sense people have become extensions of the machine:

> The attributes of modern society are seen as issuing directly from smokestacks, machine tools and computers. We are, as a result, presented with the theory of a *societas ex machina*, not only a 'determinism' but a despotism of the machine. (Braverman 1974 p 16)

Technique is seen as determining not only work relations but it also operates to shape ideas, mould the contours of political systems and constrain political choice. Whether we seek an understanding of con- temporary society among the critics or celebrants of 'industrialism' or 'capitalism' a similar argument emerges — either 'technological' society involves the inescapable erosion of human freedom or, through its finest technical achievements (usually the computer), it promises a future in which man is finally freed from the coercive exigencies of work.

1 The 'Weberian tradition'

Weber's sociology is pervaded by his 'interpretation' of Western history as a process of demystification: the increasing rationalization of all social relations and institutions. In tracing the path of this historical movement Weber was at pains to stress that such an outcome was the result of a complex conjuncture of ungeneralizable, unique historical conditions. Among such conditions he identified the changing structure of Western religious beliefs, the application to production of improved methods of calculation, the growth of a free market in all goods includ- ing labour, etc.; the latter being the key to the functioning of 'rational bourgeois capitalism'. However, the Weberian tradition in modern sociology while similarly focusing attention on the global process of rationalization locates its major condition in the inherent rationality of technique itself. In effect, the complexity of Weber's analysis of the transition to capitalism is lost when we follow his characterization of capitalist society as increasingly subjected to the tyranny of bureaucratic organization as the expression of rational-legal authority — the most efficient means of co-ordinating advances in the division of labour.

In locating in bureaucratic co-ordination a determining feature of both capitalist and socialist societies, Weber laid the ground for the elimination of the concept 'capitalism' altogether. Thus, theorists who operate within the 'Weberian tradition' direct our attention to what are taken to be the more general processes of industrialization and, more recently, post-industrialization. The interrelated processes of bureaucratization and industrialization (the second often referring to no more than the increasingly detailed technical division of labour within a system of factory production) are viewed as a simple, unilinear development in which the elaboration of technique, conditioned by the input of scientific knowledge and technology, gives rise to an increase in the division of labour which, in turn, calls into being a process of 'imperative co-ordination': a bureaucratic hierarchy in which positions of authority are merely functional in ensuring the co-ordination of fragmented, specialist work tasks. As a result, the social division of labour is reduced to a technical division of labour and, most important for our concerns, the major authority structures are the direct and necessary product of the specialization of work roles. 'One of the central traits [of industrialism] is the inevitable and eternal separation of industrial men into managers and the managed' (Kerr *et al* 1962 p 15). Technique comes to have a logic of its own. It fragments work through the division of labour, blindly seeks the most rational and efficient means of combating problems of co-ordination and in so doing creates structures of authority in its own image. Thus, we can expect, along with Clark Kerr, that all industrializing societies will historically unfold according to the same logic (in fact, history itself dissolves in the face of such a logic, we have no need of it).

The concept of capitalism which, in the Marxist tradition, depends on the specification of antagonistic social relations of production and in Weber's own writings relies on the specification of power relations on the market (life-chances) thus ceases to have any theoretical significance in the face of technical determinism.

The political implications of technical determinism are clear and are given their classic expression in Talcott Parsons's theory of power (1963) and Daniel Bell's heralding of *The End of Ideology* (1961), namely, that the distribution of power is a purely functional consequence and a condition for the maintenance of the division of labour and that any ideological or political attack on the established order is, at best, outmoded and, at worst, the product of diseased minds. Thus, positions of power and privilege are thrown up willy-nilly by the advancing technical division of labour. Such power is unassailable because it is a necessary condition of complexity in the efficient pursuit of material and cultural well-being. Individuals attain such positions of authority because they are able to offer in the market-place those skills and competences which are highly valued and essential to the continuance of such societal well-being.[1]

Elements of this technological determinism, which pervade sociological literature as a set of assumptions rather than an explicit argument, are often found in analyses concerned with the relationship between work and the class structure. Such analyses commonly identify three post-Marxian problems, if not trends: (1) changes in the structure of ownership and control of the productive enterprise; (2) the expansion of the 'new' middle class; (3) the embourgeoisement or, at least, increasing affluence of large sections of the working class. Perhaps the most influential of such discussions has been that of Ralph Dahrendorf (1959), who treats the three 'problems' outlined in a manner consistent with the 'Weberian tradition'. The central significance of authority deriving from 'imperative co-ordination' is stressed as giving rise to status hierarchies which in advanced industrial societies have superseded the single class division of bourgeoisie/proletariat. In fact, he argues that capitalist relations of production were but a short-lived historical moment in the unfolding of a more generic source of social division, differences in authority. Consequently, the source of all social conflicts is man's innate dislike of subordinating himself to authority; the strain for autonomy is seen as an aspect of human nature. Thus, while all forms of despotism are, presumably, bound to founder in the end, authority relations are inherent in the human condition. We are, then, driven back to a speculative anthropology which identifies the condition from which all history unfolds finally expressing itself in the co-ordination of the division of labour. Moreover, the encapsulation of authority relations within specific bureaucratic contexts ensures that societal cleavages of a class nature are rare in modern society. The fine gradations of authority, which proliferate in such organizations, condition the frequency of movement or social mobility, each position being bought with the required amount of education or training. Thus, occupation and education become (as they are in the practice of sociological research) the measures of status.

While for Dahrendorf (1959) the differentiation of co-ordinative functions within the bureaucracy has brought with it both the 'decomposition of capital' in the separation of ownership and control and the 'decomposition of labour' with specialization of occupational function, it is toward a discussion of this latter aspect, particularly as it applies to the expansion of the 'new middle class', that we now turn, and in particular to those occupations conventionally referred to as 'professions', for it is among this group of occupations that we find a fraction of the 'middle class' that has proved remarkably successful in achieving and maintaining powerful and privileged positions without carrying out a directly co-ordinative role in the division of labour. Because professionals do not share this co-ordinative function with the non-owner managers (another important fraction of the 'middle class') the 'Weberian tradition' experiences an initial problem in accounting for their high status. While it is true that within the 'tradition' we can easily explain how individuals attain such positions – they enjoy favourable 'life-chances' as the result of a market capacity based on the possession of educational qualifications (see Giddens 1973) – there remains the problem of determining why such work should offer the possibility of high economic and social rewards if its authority is not derived from functions associated with the co-ordination of the division of labour. The problem is resolved through the claim that the professions are a unique form of organized work in industrial societies. It is this claim to uniqueness which provides the sole basis on which the sociology of professions exists as a separate specialism within the sociology of work.

Let us look at a number of examples of how the 'Weberian tradition' copes with the professions. First, Everett Hughes (1963) claims that the trend toward 'professionalization' is 'a phenomenon of all the highly industrial and urban societies; a trend that apparently accompanies industrialization and urbanization irrespective of *political ideologies and systems*' [my italics]. He argues further that such occupations provide esoteric services based on a body of knowledge that is privy to professional colleagues so rendering the layman client incapable of making a sound judgement about the value of the services received. Thus, the client's need to 'trust' the professional is reflected in the authority accorded to organized practitioners through the mechanisms of 'licence' and 'mandate'.

The general argument (outlined above) which locates the source of authority in the imperative co-ordination of the technical division of labour is, here, simply reversed. Some forms of work are, it appears, naturally resistant to fragmentation and control through specialization. This is so because the knowledge organized as work is so complex that it cannot readily be subjected to the normal processes of routinization and rationalization. As a result certain occupations are 'naturally' resistant to external forms of authority. According to Hughes, then, it is the esoteric nature of an occupation's knowledge which directly explains its authority in relation to the client and is, in turn, the source of power and status which accrue to the organized occupation.

We should also briefly refer to a modified version of this argument introduced by Hughes elsewhere where he claims that the basic problem for analysis turns on the question:

> What are the circumstances in which people in an occupation attempt to turn it into a profession, and themselves into professionals? (Quoted in Vollmer and Mills 1966 p v)

The implications of this question are drawn out by various analysts, including Parry and Parry (1976), Esland (1976) and Becker (1962). The approach appears to depart from the essentialism of the position adopted by Hughes (i.e. explaining the social characteristics of an occupation by reference to its essence — some inherent and unique quality) by questioning the existence of a necessary link between knowledge and authority; and emphasizing the circumstances under which occupations make 'claims' for professional status. This is the case with Parry and Parry whose work is concerned with professionalism as a 'strategy' for controlling practice (p 23) and Becker who argues that it is more fruitful to view the term professional as an 'honorific label which secures certain political advantages for its possessors . . .' (Becker 1962). 'So we find many occupations trying hard to become professions and using the symbol of the profession in an attempt to increase their autonomy and raise their prestige' (Becker 1962 p 39). This point is echoed by Esland when he claims, 'A more important issue is the use which is made of the trappings of professionalism as a strategy for increasing an occupation's influence and power' (p 21).

While there is an attempt here to focus on work as a political process, its inadequacy resides in its failure to theorize the problem of why such 'claims' or 'strategies' succeed or fail. Esland, for example, gives the impression that a successful strategy brings with it authority and status, but what are the sources of power which are mobilized in the struggle? Do all those occupations to which we accord the title 'profession' draw on a common battery of resources? If these questions remain unanswered then we are either reduced to the tautology that the 'claim' to professionalism is the sole condition for attaining it or, more likely, we are driven back to the view that knowledge is the condition for success and, therefore, the major determinant of occupational authority.

It is not suggested that 'professionalism', as an ideology, is unimportant in the political struggle for status nor that the forms and content of knowledge are without influence in this process. Rather (to anticipate the following argument), it is claimed that the influence of such factors can only be evaluated within the context of capitalist relations of production which themselves determine the conditions in which the ideology of 'professionalism' is an effective occupational strategy and the extent to which occupational construction and organization of knowledge can become a relatively autonomous process.

Finally, we can question the claim by Hughes (1963) that 'professional' occupations emerge and exercise authority in industrial societies 'irrespective of political ideologies and systems'. From this premise by Hughes we can only draw the conclusion that whatever variations exist in the *relations of power* from society to society, the *political process* of making a claim for professional status will have the same outcome — the result, therefore, is a depoliticized politics. In effect, we are forced to look for some other determinant which is somehow inherent in the 'nature' of an occupation. It will be noted that the quoted phrase is also redolent of the 'logic of industrialism'.

Any theory which purports to account for occupational power and privilege must explain why it is that certain kinds of work, particularly that associated with the proliferation of technical service occupations, are not, with the 'professions', equally honoured and rewarded. There is no doubt that television and washing machine maintenance men and garage mechanics provide services generally associated with client ignorance and the application of complex bodies of knowledge, yet they are not accorded professional status. Nor do they exercise the degree of occupational authority which characterizes certain professions (a subsidiary problem here is accounting for the heterogeneity of 'professional' occupations which in the literature is often conceptualized by the opposition of such terms as the 'true', 'classical', 'major' and 'full' professions as against the 'lower', 'marginal', 'semi-', 'quasi-', 'auxiliary' professions). In order to solve this problem the 'Weberian tradition' is helped out by the notion of functional significance, explicit in the work of Parsons (1954) and Barber (1963) but implicit in the essay by Hughes. That is to say, while many occupations may carry out esoteric services based on complex knowledge, some of these services are more important than others. In particular, it is argued there are certain functional prerequisites for the maintenance of any society such as the reproduction of its members, and the involvement of medical practitioners in such areas of great moment — affecting questions of individual as well as societal survival — explains the social value placed on their services. So, just as the authority of bureaucratic office is seen as a functional resource in societies characterized by 'imperative co-ordination', so the professionals owe their authority to the functional significance of their work. Lawyers, for example, not only act for individuals at the most important times of their lives — in house purchase, the drawing up of wills, the dissolution of marriage, etc. — but as officers of the courts and upholders of the law they are the guardians of social order, the custodians of 'legal-rationality' and through the doctrine of separation of powers, the jealous protectors of democratic institutions and process.

In short, then, the 'professions' are occupations which provide highly valued services based upon a complex body of knowledge. All such occupations, the argument goes, naturally develop (professionalize) to an end-state of professionalism and as a result enjoy a high degree of autonomy, wield great authority and receive high social and economic rewards. Their autonomy and power is furthered, in so far as the problem of client ignorance is solved, through the setting up of an association of practitioners which guarantees the trained competence of its members: for such associations characteristically monopolize rights to carry out certain kinds of work and wield control over the application of certain kinds of knowledge.

You will notice that the structure of this theory of the professions is very similar to the more general argument relating to authority and the division of labour — despite the paradoxical reversal alluded to on p 339. First, knowledge/technique is the determinant of power relations and secondly, authority — the authority of competence rather than co-ordination — is a functional resource bearing upon dominant, socially shared values. We are back with a modified version of the technological determinism outlined above, in which relationships of power are seen as a direct outcome of knowledge and technique and the functional imperatives associated with the elaboration of the technical division of labour. Once again, in the sociology of the professions, we find a justification of the *status quo* which coincides with the professions' own view of themselves. We have looked at the theory of professions in some detail, largely because in presenting such occupations as a 'unique' case, i.e. in their capacity to resist the rationalizing impetus of industrialization, there accrue very important consequences for an analysis of the relationship between occupation and class.

For example, the fact that the 'professions' are viewed as exercising a form of authority (competence) which is quite different from that (co-ordination) exercised by other high status groups suggests that they can be conceived of as the vanguard of a 'third force' in industrial societies. Being neither capitalist nor worker, in the Marxian sense; superordinate nor subordinate in a Dahrendorfian hierarchy, they function to moderate and humanize the impersonality of bureaucratic structures even where they find themselves (as increasingly they do) functionaries within large-scale organizations. It has even been argued that the very forms of practice ('personal', 'helping', 'altruistic', etc.) dominant in professions such as medicine, law and social work have given rise to a 'personal service ideology' which is increasingly eroding the goal of technical efficiency which has hitherto been a central impulse in industrial societies (Halmos 1970). To some analysts the 'professions' have also suggested the possibility of a 'third road' between capitalist and communist alternatives; providing the social basis of the social-democratic state: a society organized around the production of knowledge and its application, where the most significant social divisions are based on levels of competence and the overriding ethic is that of 'service' (elements of this thesis can be found in Carr-Saunders and Wilson 1964, Lewis and Maude 1952, and Halmos 1970).

2 Relations of production – the Marxian alternative

It may be argued that what has so far been presented is a rather simplified caricature of what is, in fact, a diverse sociological tradition. The procedure can, however, be justified on two major grounds. First, the intention has been to reveal the underlying logic of positions which are otherwise quite diverse in character and which may not make fully explicit or even recognize the full consequences of incorporating elements of this tradition into their assumptions or basic concepts. Secondly, even those sociologists who consciously attempt to rid themselves of such assumptions are often forced back into the paradigm of the tradition by virtue of retaining a concept of the division of labour which is already inescapably wedded to the primacy of technique.

In order to elaborate on these assertions it is now necessary to turn to a consideration of the Marxian concept, mode of production, which, it will be argued, provides a more adequate basis for conceptualizing the interrelationships of technique and power. First, in distinguishing between the forces and relations of production while at the same time identifying the latter as determinant, Marx effectively rejects any attempt to reduce the relations of production to some technical prime mover. Rather, within any given mode of production, such as capitalism, technology is developed and applied in a form consistent with the dominant production relations.

Secondly, Marx distances himself further from any such simple determinism by the way in which he separates out a number of elements and processes within the relations of production themselves.[2] The primary element in capitalist relations is the polarity, producer/non-producer; that is to say the relationship between the producers of surplus value and those who appropriate surplus value.[3] For Marx, it is the dominance of a specific mode of appropriating value which is the determining feature of a type of society or, more properly, social formation. In the feudal mode of production, for example, exploitation takes the form of direct extraction of surplus labour. The serf was not entirely separated from the means of labour in so far as he held a parcel of land, the 'possession' of which was protected by custom. The lord, on the other hand, was the economic owner of the land[4] and extracted surplus labour from his serfs through systems of corveé (direct unpaid labour on the lord's land) or payments in kind.

In the capitalist mode of production the producers are dispossessed of the means of labour having nothing but labour-power which is sold on the market – labour itself becomes a commodity. The extraction of value is achieved in this case not directly, but from labour as a commodity producing surplus value. In capitalist societies, then, it is the appropriation of surplus value which is the determining feature: the basis of the exploitative relations of production and the condition for the emergence of antagonistic social classes. It is important to note here the distinction between relations of production and class, for the characteristics of a social class, such as the bourgeoisie, are formed in the historical context of a developing social formation which is not reducible to the relations of production, even though these relations determine the possibility of its existence, i.e. as non-producers and owners.[5]

It is also important to stress that our insistence on defining capitalism in terms of a mode of appropriation is not mere pedantry but secures the very thesis which is being advanced here in opposition to varieties of technological determinism.[6] For example, it contradicts statements to the effect that the determining characteristic of capitalist society is '. . . that labour [power] itself becomes a commodity, bought and sold on the market' (Giddens p 84). While the buying and selling of labour on the market is a necessary condition for the appropriation of surplus value it does not determine such appropriation. Wage labour can exist without capitalist relations of production. More important for the present argument is that such a definition of capitalism is perfectly consistent with a Weberian rather than a Marxian analysis of the division of labour and social class. It allows, in the work of Giddens (1973), for example, a seeming integration of Marx and Weber. By focusing on labour as a commodity, Giddens is able to stress the market or distributive characteristics of social class rather than on the antagonistic relations of production, so following the Weberian view that 'life chances' are determined by market situation. As a result, Giddens is able to conclude that the middle class (including professionals) owe their class position to their 'market capacity' (Giddens 1973 p 107) based upon *knowledge* and *technical qualifications*. We can presumably extrapolate that the occupational positions these qualifications buy 'demand' such knowledge and such technique. Imperceptibly, we move closer and closer to a restatement of the basic assumptions of technical determinism which underlie the 'Weberian tradition', distorting the relationship between technique and power and flowing from a misplaced determination of the capitalist system.

That these points are made in criticism of Giddens by no means excludes the market or distribution as a significant aspect of the processes of class formation. Such an exclusion would operate to force the analysis into an alternative reductionism. Rather, the Marxian starting point – the social relations of production – eliminates the possibility of conceiving of the market as an arena of individualized 'capacities' or 'skills'. Skill is not a given individual capacity which endows a subject with power in an exchange relationship as Giddens appears to argue. Skill is a product of social power; it is an aspect of the way in which work is organized which structures the market, creating monopolies and scarcities. To suggest otherwise is to relate skill directly to technique and so return us to the reductionist thesis. The market is, as Weber argues, a relationship of power, but power relationships do not originate in the market. Exchange relationships are, as Giddens argues, a process of class formation, but class does not originate in exchange. In Weberian theory exchange is a relationship of equality which functions to create inequalities only because individuals bring differential capacities to the relationship, while Marxian theory attempts to explain why exchange is unequal.

To get back to the elements of the relations of production, the producer/non-producer relationship is associated with the overlapping but non-equivalent relationship of owner/non-owner. There is no equivalence because a non-producer, say a top manager of a productive enterprise, need not own the means of production whilst carrying out the functions of capital in developing and maintaining mechanisms of appropriation (Poulantzas 1975 p 29).

Finally, there is the polarity, labourer/non-labourer, which again overlaps with the former categories without being equivalent. In particular, there would appear to be an identity between producer and labourer. However, while it is true that all producers are labourers the reverse is not the case as not all those who labour are producers of surplus value. This element in the relations of production focuses attention on the *labour process* or that specific aspect of the organization of work which in sociology is normally conceptualized as the division of labour. Thus, while the first element defines the antagonistic relations of production and strategic source of power differentials associated with the production of surplus value, the third element focuses on the labour process: the social division of labour which may affect both parties to the antagonistic relations of production, fragmenting both the functions of capital and labour. However, such processes of fragmentation can only take place within the context of the dominant form of appropriation and power structure which capitalist relations of production imply. Thus, the 'detailed' fragmentation of labour is not the product of technical exigency but flows from the exploitative process of capital appropriation and expansion. 'The first volume of *Capital* may be considered as a massive essay on (among other things) how . . . the social form of capital, driven to incessant accumulation as the condition for its own existence, completely transforms technology' (Braverman 1974 p 20).

Similarly, the fragmentation of the functions of capital does not derive in a simple fashion from the imperatives of changing technique but is conditioned by the inherent tendency in such a mode toward the concentration of capital.

The analytic power of the Marxian concept of relations of production resides, then, in its capacity to generate a theoretical view which comprehends power as integral to the organization of work rather than the effect of a technical cause. While the production of surplus value is enhanced by the continuous revolution in the technical means which is in turn integrated into an increasingly complex labour process, at the same time the input of technology follows the requirements of capital and reflects its basic social divisions. As we pointed out above, the increasingly elaborate hierarchy of occupational functions applied to the running of computers is less a product of computer technology than the tendency of capital to fragment functions in order to reduce the skill content and thus labour costs, while, at the same time, generating surveillance systems which operate to maximize the production of surplus value. Thus, the specific forms of work specialization and fragmentation are to be understood as a product of the antagonistic relations of production, conditioned by the technical means generated by the expansionary dynamics of capital.

3 Production relations and class structure: concepts and problems

We can now look at the implications of this concept of production relations for an analysis of the relationship between work and social class. We have already touched upon certain aspects of this problem as conceptualized within the 'Weberian tradition' and in the following discussion the emphasis on the problem of the 'new middle class' and 'professional' occupations will be continued.

From what has already been said it should be clear that a Marxian analysis conceives of the working class as emerging out of production relations in which it is the producer, non-owner, labourer and exploited. On the other side of these antagonistic relations are the non-producers, owners, non-labourers whose income is derived from surplus value produced by labour; these are the conditions for the emergence of the bourgeoisie.

The dichotomies do, however, provide us with a starting-point for an analysis of the relationship between work and social class, and in order to do this it is first necessary to outline the changing terms of articulation which these primary relationships undergo in the course of capitalist development (Carchedi 1975a pp 13—48).

The first stage of capitalist development has been referred to as the 'formal subordination of labour to capital': a fundamental change in the social organization of production, rather than its technical conditions, involving the subordination of the labour process (including the division of labour) to the process of surplus value production.

The second stage brings the adaptation of labour to the requirements of capital through a continuous revolution in the division of labour associated with the institutionalized application of science and technology. Increasingly, under such conditions, the product is no longer that of an individual but is the outcome of what Marx refers to as the 'collective labourer'. This complex labour process has a dual nature. First, the fragmentation of work is a measure of the increasing extent to which the labour process is bent toward the requirement of capital, for 'The labour power capable of performing a process may be purchased (and reproduced) more cheaply as dissociated elements than as a capacity integrated in a single worker' (Braverman 1974 p 8). Secondly, the labour process takes on an increasingly co-operative form in which productive work is carried out by a wide range of occupations which are integrated into the surplus value producing process as agents of the collective labourer. Paradoxically, then, the labour process, while conditioned by the antagonistic relations of production, at the same time exhibits co-operative forms of the division of labour, including the function of co-ordination. Thus, we can conceive of co-ordinative work which is itself a product of the coercive requirements of capital.

In the final stage, often referred to as 'monopoly capitalism', the functions of capital are similarly collectivized: that is, subdivided into fractional operations. The concentration of capital into larger units involves a diffusion of the functions of capital associated with the appropriation and realization of surplus value as well as the reproduction of capitalist relations of production themselves. Consequently, just as productive labour encompasses a wider range of work activities within the collective labourer, so the functions of capital are dispersed to agents who are not necessarily themselves the legal owners of the means of production but who share the attributes of the non-producers and are, therefore, exploiters, non-labourers and part, at least, of whose income derives from surplus value.

The concentration of capital and the dispersal of its functions generates complex organizational structures through a process of bureaucratization. Thus, the bureaucratization of work also has a dual nature: the result of the co-operative nature of work including the co-ordinative functions of the collective labourer (this process is given primacy in the 'Weberian tradition') and, more significantly (given the determining element of the relations of production), a product of the dispersal of the functions of capital. Work supervision, in so far as it relates to the direct appropriation of surplus value, can then be divided into that of co-ordination and unity on the one hand and control and surveillance on the other (Carchedi 1975a).

It is the analysis of the complex interrelations of these dual processes, it will be argued, which provides us with the means of overcoming contradictions and confusions which are seemingly insoluble within the existing framework of the sociology of work. Let us first look at a few of these confusions. There is little doubt that even a short acquaintance with the sociology of work will impress the newcomer by its capacity to generate contradictions. Among the more common and basic in the literature relating to contemporary 'industrial/capitalist' societies are the following (examples of such problems are located at three levels: the socio-economic structure, the productive enterprise, and occupational function):[7]

1 'Industrial society' is seen as characterized by two contradictory processes:

    i First, there is the empirical generalization that the increasing complexity of production, including its administration and regulation, has led to the continuous upgrading of skills (the process of 'tertiarization') paralleling the growing complexity of machines and reflected in the great expansion of secondary and higher education. This is often linked to theses relating the expansion of the middle-class(es) and the embourgeoisement of the working class.

   ii In total or partial contradiction is the view that the fundamental and growing problem of work in the modern world is its subjection to processes of rationalization and routinization which eliminate the skill content of work. This process is experienced by an increasing army of workers, in commercial and administrative spheres as well as on factory assembly lines, as 'boring', 'unsatisfying', 'alienating', etc. It is often associated with theories stressing the 'proletarianization' of the 'middle class'.

It will be argued that within the concept of mode of production elaborated above such contradictions may be dissolved by recognizing the dual processes of labour and capital while the dominant tradition in the sociology of work finds such a solution unthinkable within its own framework.

2 An example of a confusion arising in the sociology of work and its sister sub-disciplines, industrial sociology and organization theory, is the application of a Weberian concept of bureaucracy to the productive enterprise. Such a concept conceives of bureaucracy as a hierarchy of offices, each subordinated to the authority of another more highly placed in the pyramid, yet, at the same time, exercising authority over lower offices. This model is continually applied as though it is isomorphic with the enterprise as a whole. At the same time, few sociologists would claim that these bureaucratic relationships are, in fact, characteristic of the relations between the bulk of those working within the enterprise: those on the factory floor.

The pyramid has no foundations because the 'Weberian tradition' lacks a means of conceptualizing relationships between the bureaucratic functionaries and the bulk of the workers in an enterprise except by extending into the labour process as a whole the univocal process of specialization—co-ordination, through which all authority takes the same form and has the same origins (given the inapplicability of authority of professional competence, see point 3 below). This issue, like the first, remains unconfronted yet glaringly problematic.

3 Finally, there is the problem of the bureaucratized professional. If we accept, for a moment, an explanation of professional authority and autonomy as emergent from the application of a complex body of knowledge, we are inexorably faced with a further irresolvable confusion. In the 'modern' world a majority of the people engaged in work labelled 'professional' are employed in bureaucratic organizations. They are, at one and the same time, autonomous 'professionals' and bureaucratic functionaries.

The confusion arises from the fact that within the 'Weberian tradition' there is no means of determining the conditions under which the authority of imperative co-ordination rather than the authority of 'professional' competence will operate. Rather, in the literature there is a tendency to back away from the sociological problem into the relative comfort of a derived social-psychological problem – do individual professionals experience bureaucratic employment as a problem? The answer to this secondary question, based on attitudinal surveys, is often taken as a solution to the first, which it is not. In effect, research follows the path laid down by Braverman: '[if] . . . this organization of the labor process is "necessary" and inevitable . . . [then] This leaves to sociology the function . . . of assaying not the nature of work but the degree of adjustment of the worker' (Braverman 1974 p 29).

4 Production relations and class structure: cases and solutions

Let us look at these 'problems' by following through some of the possibilities suggested by the concept of relations of production presented above. In exploring these possibilities the argument will be restricted to a consideration of only certain aspects of three processes which can be identified in Marx's analysis of capital:

1 First, at the level of relations of production we can identify the dual processes of surplus value production and labour, with the former being determinant as a mode of *appropriation.*

2 Second, there is the level of the production process as such which includes, most significantly for the present discussion, that aspect of the *realization* of capital associated with its accounting, allocation and distribution.

3 Finally, there are the processes of *reproduction,* through which the determining relations of production are themselves reproduced in the social formation.

It is suggested that each of these levels of analysis also identifies a distinct function of capital: that is, processes which must be carried out if capitalist relations are to be maintained. Further, it is argued that with the collectivization of labour and the concentration of capital these functions are carried out by distinct structures each generating its own labour process, and representing a mechanism of control. In what follows, therefore, the position of 'professional' occupations in the relations, process and reproduction of capital will be identified. In carrying out such an identification similar questions will be posed in relation to each of these three functions. First, in what sense are certain 'professional' occupations involved in the process of appropriation, and, where they are, is this involvement one of carrying out the 'global functions of capital' or are they merely agents of the labour process which develops as a consequence of the dispersal of such functions? The answer to this question is crucial in theorizing the professions' place in the antagonistic relations of production and, therefore, their place in the class structure.

However, the place of the 'professions' in the class structure cannot be exhaustively determined by reference to appropriation alone since they may also be involved in carrying out the global functions of capital or function as agents of the collective labourer as a result of the way in which their occupational activities relate to the secondary control functions of realization and reproduction. Each of these processes also has a dual structure, involving a social division between those who are engaged in carrying out the functions of capital in respect of realization or reproduction and those who are part of the labour process generated by such functions.

Each of the following three sections presents an analysis of the ways in which various 'professions' differentially relate to the dual structures generated by the antagonistic relations of capital and labour in respect of the primary (appropriation) and secondary (realization and reproduction) functions which generate parallel mechanisms of social control central to the maintenance of the expansionary dynamics of capital.

Finally, in locating the 'professions' in these various processes the analysis suggests a resolution of the types of confusion which were earlier identified as characterizing the sociology of work.

4.1 Appropriation: bureaucracy's other face

Under production relations we can consider the second source of confusion raised above: the tendency in industrial sociology to identify the productive enterprise as a whole with the hierarchical model of bureaucracy. The fundamental fallacy in this procedure arises from the attempt to define an organization (of production) as a structure which is the necessary product of *any* purposive, collective activity; that is, its structure of authority is seen to be inherent in its goal-directedness. The assumption of a single, shared goal implies that a single structure of legitimated authority pervades the enterprise at all levels. As we have already pointed out, this approach locates the source of authority in the co-operative exigencies of specialization in the technical division of labour (for the moment we can exclude the complicating factor of professional/occupational authority). Thus, goal-directedness in concert with imperative co-ordination doubly reinforce the view of bureaucracy as a one-dimensional model, so excluding from consideration the antagonistic relations of production.

However, what Marx calls 'factory despotism' cannot be incorporated into such a concept of bureaucracy, for the social division of labour based upon the appropriation of surplus value is itself a structure of power within the productive enterprise, involving the coercion and surveillance of labour. This crucial division within the productive enterprise is not reproduced within the ranks of the producers (of surplus value) themselves (which may be competitive or solidaristic) nor is it necessarily repeated within the bureaucracy. Bureaucratization is not solely the consequence of the dispersal of the functions of capital it is also a consequence of the extension of the collective labourer. Thus, while the impulse toward bureaucratization must be understood as the outcome of processes relating to the production of surplus value, a consequence of this impulse is to extend the labour process, including its functions of 'co-ordination and unity', as part of the process of bureaucratization.

As a result, antagonistic relations of production can no longer be identified as simply reflected in the social divisions between owner and non-owner, the factory floor and the office, or between 'manual' and 'mental' labour, for the line of this division may be found at various levels of the bureaucracy as well as manifesting itself on the factory floor where agents of the surveillance system operate. Not all of the exploited are on the factory floor nor are all of the exploiters to be found among the shareholders or in the boardroom. Rather, the basic structure of power is expressed in dual authority processes: that of surveillance which is the direct function of capital in the appropriation of surplus value and co-ordination which is the product of the extension of the labour process in the collective labourer, itself generated by the expansionary dynamics of capital.

Let us, then, briefly apply what we have said about the level of relations of production to the problem of the 'professionals'. It has been argued that the bureaucratization of the capitalist productive enterprise involves both an extension of the functions of capital and that of the collective labourer, the former being specifically located (at the level of relations of production) in the structure of appropriation which itself gives rise to those mechanisms of control we are calling surveillance. The question raised here is are the agents of surveillance, in carrying out the global functions of capital, a fraction of the capitalist class? There is no single answer to this question. First, there are agents of surveillance who are merely involved in the functions of capital in so far as their work activities have been transformed into a labour process. Foremen and lower levels of management are, for example, the 'executors' of a surveillance system which is neither their 'conception' nor design.[8] The same is true of those 'professionals' who are involved in the routine execution of systems of quality control; they are non-producers but are engaged in a labour process. At the same time there are 'professionals' who are agents of capital in so far as they are engaged in the conception and design of the systems of surveillance and coercion which facilitate the process of appropriation. Such 'professionals' are the agents of capital and, arguably, at the highest levels participate in real economic ownership, for in a capitalist system the 'power to assign the means of production to given uses' (Poulantzas 1975 p 18) involves the continuous construction and renewal of mechanisms of surveillance in the appropriation of surplus value. The creation of such mechanisms has been a major object of the developing 'management sciences' which have proliferated in the course of the twentieth century. There has been gradual extension of scientized managerial techniques with the object of rationalizing men's physical potentialities in relation to the machine (e.g. time and motion study), exploring their psychological potentialities as well as revealing the social constraints on productivity (e.g. the Human Relations school). This process, particularly the form it took in 'scientific management', is central to the Braverman thesis (1974).

Braverman views this process as the separation of 'conception' from 'execution': the division of the labour process into two. 'In one location the physical processes of production are executed. In another are concentrated the design, planning and calculation and record-keeping' (Braverman 1974 p 124). This separation into 'hand and brain' is not equivalent to the dichotomy presented above for it does not allow us to distinguish between the functions of capital and labour *within* the ranks of those agents we call 'professional'. Within the process of 'conception' we can distinguish between those who are engaged in a labour process and those who carry out the global functions of capital as a consequence of generating and sustaining those definitions and categories which underlie systems of surveillance. Thus, the crucial feature of professional 'monopoly' is occupational control over the forms of knowledge which frame and support the capitalist function of surveillance in the process of surplus value production. Such systems of surveillance have both their 'conceivers' and 'executors'. Those carrying out the routine, day-to-day procedures associated with time and motion studies are the 'executors', engaged in a labour process, whereas those who lay down the principles and formulate the objectives underlying such routines carry out the functions of capital.

These structures of power and their consequences for the organization of work are complicated further if we now move from a consideration of the relations of production alone and continue the discussion at the level of the production process; at which level we can introduce a whole new set of control mechanisms associated with the functions of capital, where, for example, the extension of the labour process is associated with *realization* as a function of capital.

4.2 Realization: accounting value

So far we have been solely concerned with relations of production in the productive enterprise and already the development of these antagonistic relations can be seen to have taken on complex forms. Even greater complexity results when we look in more detail at the dispersal of the functions of capital at the level of the production process: mechanisms through which surplus value is realized rather than appropriated. In the monopolistic stage of capitalism such functions of realization may be carried out by complex organizations external to the productive enterprise including the institutions of finance capital and those organizations executing the fiscal policies of the state. For example, insurance firms are increasingly heavily involved in the process of investment and in so doing, while not directly entering into productive activity, control the flow of capital in certain directions rather than others and preside over the allocation of surplus. State taxation, at the same time, can function to direct and redirect the flow of capital, as can policies associated with the determination of interest rates. An aspect of this process of realization is the accounting and distribution of value, '. . . the means by which surplus value is transferred, struggled over and allocated' (Braverman 1974 p 304).

These are processes which essentially involve all of the complex ramifications of property and ownership claims. Thus, whereas at the level of production relations the appropriation of surplus value involves the direct surveillance and coercion of productive labour in the effort to increase productivity and lower costs, the process of realization introduces new mechanisms of control which have the function of 'watching over capital, of checking and controlling the progress of its enlargement' (Braverman 1974 p 362): of presiding over its allocation. The concentration of capital makes for greater complexity in this process whereby the functions of capital are themselves transformed into a labour process (albeit unproductive).

Within the productive enterprise itself there arise large administrative divisions entirely concerned with the accounting of value: in checking and controlling the flow of stock and cash at each point in the process. Such internal systems of control, ensuring an upward flow of management information, are supplemented by mechanisms of value allocation which meet the requirements of external agencies concerned with securing credit, raising capital, distributing surplus, etc., which centre on the empires of banking, insurance, state taxation, etc. There has emerged then a labour process – the work of a mass of people – producing nothing but increasingly elaborate mechanisms of control associated with realization of capital and its enlargement – 'A vast paper empire [which] separates out the value-form of commodities from their physical form' (Braverman 1974 p 303). Such forms of control are not merely the products of the need for co-ordination deriving from the technical division of labour but are the result of concentration of capital and the consequent need for a large proportion of the work expended to be devoted to the accounting of value. The fact that this is not merely a process of rationalization associated with the need for co-ordination is reinforced when we observe the duplication of these accounting procedures arising out of the competitive principle that no single accounting of value can be taken at its face value. 'The internal record keeping of each corporate institution is, moreover, constructed in a way which assumes the possible dishonesty, disloyalty or laxity of every human agency it employs; this is, in fact, the first principle of modern accounting' (Braverman 1974 p 303). Control, then, rather than the processing of information, is the dominant function of such accounting mechanisms. At the same time the labour process which develops in the implementation of these secondary systems of control is subjected to the same forms of coercive control as are constructed for the direct appropriation of surplus value.

The development of accountancy as an occupation has been tied to the fortunes of capital and, in particular, to the proliferation of the institutions of secondary control. Modern accountancy is the creature of corporate business. First, as a form of internal company control and then as an agency controlling transfers of value following the rise of the joint-stock company. Even more recently it has become a significant mechanism of control in the armoury of the state in, for example, simulating market conditions as a form of legitimation for the reallocation of capital. For example, accountancy procedures are part of the proliferating battery of techniques which are utilized by the state (as well as private firms) as a means of projecting into the future market and general economic trends. These projections are used as an aid to investment decisions on the part of management, planners and government. In effect such techniques simulate unknown market conditions and function in large part to legitimize current decisions affecting capital allocation.

The source and nature of the demand for accountancy services established early on an institutionalized pattern of occupational control based on corporate patronage, whereby large corporate clients determined their own needs, and the manner in which these were to be serviced.[9] I have previously defined corporate patronage as a system of occupational control generating sponsorship in recruitment, a fragmented and hierarchically organized system of practice, particularistic forms of knowledge, etc. (Johnson 1972 pp 65–74). These occupational characteristics relate to the way in which accountancy knowledge is organized as work within the relations of production, the production process and the reproduction of capitalist relations. Corporate patronage as an institutionalized system of the control of accountancy work relates to the determining influence of large-scale business as the major source of demand for such services. The occupation is characteristically fragmented and hierarchically ordered as a result of its functions in respect of both the surplus value producing process and the labour process. The forms of its knowledge are particularistic in so far as business firms require local solutions to local problems rather than universalistic criteria for action. The organized 'profession' relates to the reproduction of capitalist relations in so far as it reproduces through its own multiportal processes of recruitment and training the hierarchical and fragmented relations of accountancy as they emerge in the surplus value and labour processes. The following discussion will take further a number of these points by looking at the processes involved in more detail.

Much of what is conventionally designated as accountancy is more properly characterized as book-keeping: that is a purely technical function relating to the routine day-to-day recording of stock or cash flows. Similar functions are proliferating at the margins of accountancy work with the establishment of new systems of management information gathering and distribution made possible by computerization. Such tasks are essentially part of the labour process even though they are brought into being by the dispersal of the functions of capital and such functionaries find themselves on the lower rungs of the bureaucratic hierarchy. The work activities of book-keepers and other recorders of information may be subject to both coercive control and co-ordinative control. An example of the latter is the consolidation of the various elements of a total record which has been parcelled out as fragmented functions, e.g. the various books and ledgers making up an accounting system. Again, the co-ordinative requirements are not technically determined but result from a fragmentation of tasks imposed by the requirements of capital. Thus, paradoxically, while such agents are part of the mechanism of capital realization, that is, implicated in the functions of capital, they are, at the same time, engaged in the labour process and subject to the forms of exploitation (not appropriation) characteristic of unproductive labour under capitalism.[10] Their implication in the processes of capital realization may, however, have important ideological consequences when it comes to questions of class consciousness — creating the ideological conditions for their self-identification with the bourgeoisie. However, where their function is not directly that of appropriation or where they are merely part of the labour process which has been created as a mechanism of appropriation or realization, the conditions for 'proletarianization' exist, symbolized by the increasing routinization and fragmentation of occupational functions. Despite 'professional' claims for occupational homogeneity and equality of competence the existence of the dual processes of labour and capital within bureaucratic organizations creates the conditions for the fragmentation of the occupation itself; for as well as those accountants who execute the day-to-day routines of cash and stock control there exist those who frame systems of financial and stock control and supervise their implementation. Such accountants may fulfil special functions in relation to the production of surplus and realization of value which, while not necessarily involving them in the

direct personal surveillance of the producer, can involve them in the
creation of those systems of control which in large-scale enterprises are
central to the production (stock systems may operate as much as a
control on production as an accounting of value) or realization of value.

Thus, whether one is concerned with the 'housed' accountant (working as an employee) or the partners of an 'independent' firm, there are
those who create, install and supervise control systems and regulatory
procedures which operate as mechanisms of secondary control associated with the process of realization within the bureaucratic hierarchy
or in the regulation of relationships between the productive enterprise
and external agencies in the distribution and allocation of value.

In so doing accountants are performing the 'global' functions of
capital (Carchedi 1975a) and are, therefore, socially distinct from their
'colleagues' and potentially members of an antagonistic class grouping.
From this it is clear that the conventional distinction between 'line'
and 'staff' management — which depends on the further differentiation
between 'co-ordination' and 'competence' as sources of authority — is
meaningless and fails to conceptualize adequately the position of
'professional' employees. In this case specialist knowledge and professional practice function as components of capitalist control — as an
instrument of 'line' authority if you like.

These very same accountants stand at the apex of an occupational
hierarchy called the 'profession' within which the divisions are based
not only on specialist knowledges and missions[11] but differences in
production relations. Such men command the 'professional' bureaucracies which constitute accountancy firms and man the executive
councils of the most prestigeful accountancy associations. The growth
of large-scale accountancy partnerships on, first, a national and, then,
an international scale has followed the course of business amalgama-
tions, the rise of the holding company and the internationalization of
capital.[12] 'Thus the concentration of economic power brings with it the
concentration of professional services. The concentration of adults as
a corollary encourages the growth of large public practices at the
expense of the small practitioners' (Stacey 1954 p 219). Already by
1929 expansion of such practices had gone so far that in Britain 44 per
cent of all public audits were in the hands of 39 firms. The international movement of capital has drawn these accountancy firms in its
wake, creating a few Anglo-American giants which operate throughout
the world providing not only audit servicing but an increasingly diver-
sified portfolio of 'management' services.

The hierarchical organization of accountancy in Britain has, since the
last quarter of the nineteenth century, been reflected in its fission into

a number of associations of varying prestige headed by the Institute of Chartered Accountants (Johnson 1972 pp 65–74). In recent years this hierarchy has been further fragmented by the moves toward the creation of technician grades within single associations. That partners of the large firms also dominate this hierarchy enables them to control the recruitment, training and work activities (through codes and etiquette) of the colleague-subordinates, thus facilitating the fragmentation and devaluation of certain grades of accountancy work within the production process. As a result the professional association can be viewed as having important political functions in relation to the organization of work; in particular, functions bearing on the reproduction of relations of production. The pluralistic tendencies inherent in the corporate patronage of accountancy (i.e. the tendency of the hierarchical nature of the business enterprise to impose its form on the organization of the occupation) are complete when the differentiation within the occupation at the level of relations of production is expressed at the level of social class formation. Where one segment of the occupation is engaged in carrying out the functions of capital and another segment is involved in the labour process, the conditions for social class divisions within the occupation exist.

Finally, let us be clear about the ways in which this analysis of accountancy differs from analyses of the professions criticized earlier (pp 339–343).

First, it is suggested that the degree of autonomy an occupation enjoys is not directly determined by the complexity of the knowledge it applies nor its functional significance for 'society'. Rather, the very complexity of knowledge, the extent to which it remains 'esoteric', is determined by the degree to which it functions to promote and maintain capital in the course of its appropriation and expansionary dynamics, including its realization. The 'ideology of professionalism' will be an effective strategy only when its claims coincide with and draw upon the dominant ideological processes of capital.

Similarly, work processes organized as accountancy cannot be conceived of as having some general functional significance for 'society' at large: a 'society' which has no historical specificity. Rather, accountancy is viewed as functioning in relation to a specific and determining historical process: the appropriation of surplus value and the accumulation and concentration of capital. Thus, the social organization of accountancy as an occupation, the institutionalized form of control of its work processes (corporate patronage) are elements in the 'social formation' conditioned by the specific processes of capital.

Esland's argument follows this line of reasoning in so far as he sees accountants as 'managerial' or 'bureaucratic' professionals: 'a major aspect of the growth of corporate capitalism has been the expansion of the range of managerial professions' (p 226). The 'professions', he claims, are largely 'service agents' for the owners of capital except, that is, those who are recruited to managerial positions and so participate in 'collective capitalist control'. There is, then, a paradox in the social position of the 'new professional workers'.

The major problem in Esland's argument is that this paradox is never satisfactorily resolved: '. . . they [professionals] have become both agents of capitalist control and also professionally-trained servants of capitalism' (p 229). Under what conditions are 'professionals' one or the other, or both? To claim that they are the 'agents of capitalist control' once they are managers merely begs the question: in what sense are managers capitalists or their agents? A further element of confusion enters Esland's argument in so far as he also relies on Braverman's argument that, 'For those employees the social form taken by their work, their true place in the relations of production, their *fundamental condition of subordination as so much hired labour* increasingly makes itself felt' (my italics). Here the fundamental processes of capital are seen as leading to the inexorable 'proletarianization' of the 'professions'. In following Braverman, Esland has no theoretical means of explaining why certain 'professions' or fractions of professions maintain their privileged positions in the face of their 'true' positions as hired labourers, expecting that they may be individually recruited to managerial posts: posts which are not defined in terms of production relations. For if Esland wishes to explain the privileged positions of certain professionals by reference to their managerial roles then he must indicate why managers themselves are privileged. Are all managers capitalists? Do they all perform the functions of capital? What is their position in the relations of production? Only when we know the answers to such questions can we evaluate the managerial functions of 'professionals'.

This paradox is resolved in the analysis of accountants presented above as a result of distinguishing between the dual processes of capital and labour while insisting on the determinant part played by the former. The work of accountancy is then related to these dual processes. As an aspect of the labour process it is manifested in occupations which comprise fragmented, routinized work roles whose agents are in receipt of wages. On the other hand it is also implicated in the functions of capital in constructing the mechanisms of control associated with the realization of value, so giving rise to an occupational segment which is exploitative rather than exploited and whose ideology of professionalism is coincident with and reinforced by the requirements and ideological processes of capital, so determining the relative success of 'professionalism' as a political strategy. The position of such 'professionals' in the relations of production is not, then, determined by the holding of managerial posts but in respect of their capitalist function in devising and supervising those mechanisms of control associated with realization, the reward of which is income derived from surplus value. In short, through their role in controlling property rights they partake in the income from property.

From the analysis so far we can draw a number of general conclusions bearing on the 'confusions' which were identified above (pp 349–350) as characterizing the sociology of work, i.e. the contradictory processes of skill upgrading and work alienation and the problems associated with the 'professional employee'.

The case of accountants suggests that the seeming contradictory process should be understood as a product of the dual processes of capital and labour operating within the bureaucratic structures of modern industry and business. This double process not only has a differential impact inter-occupationally but can lead to significant forms of differentiation within work activity organized under the umbrella of a single occupational category. In fact the organization of the occupation itself – its controlling body, structure of recruitment, modes of training, body of knowledge, etc. – increasingly reflects and reinforces this trend toward differentiation. While part of the membership is incorporated into the labour process and its activities subject to routinization and fragmentation, a dominant group partakes in the functions of capital not only at the level of the direct appropriation of capital but more importantly, in this case, in the process of its realization.

Similarly, the authority of 'professionals' within bureaucratic contexts will be determined by the manner in which their work activities articulate with or relate to these dual processes: in carrying out the functions of capital or the collective labourer at the level of appropriation or realization. Thus, any analysis of the relationships between the organization of occupational knowledge as work and social class formation must consider the complex outcome of these dual processes: an outcome which cannot be conceptualized by either the one-dimensional model of bureaucratic co-ordination or the single dichotomy of ownership or non-ownership of production.

4.3 Reproduction: occupations and the state

We now come to the final level of analysis distinguished above (p 351):

the reproduction of the relations of production. To focus on the relations and process of production alone would effectively eliminate
from our concerns the ways in which the determining relations of
production are themselves reproduced in the social formation. In
short, we would ignore, or conceive of as residual, major social institutions and political processes in capitalist societies.

By focusing on the notion of reproduction we introduce into the
discussion a new set of control mechanisms which are not directly
relevant to the appropriation of surplus value or its realization but
operate to reproduce the social conditions for the maintenance of such
relationships. In the processes of reproduction both the 'professions'
and the state play a major role, largely by way of their implication in
the reproduction of labour power, including health and education
services, and the institutionalization of knowledge, including science
and those ideological processes consistent with the underlying relations
of production. The following analysis will focus largely on problems
associated with the reproduction of the *agents* rather than positions
of production. (See Carchedi 1975b for the significance of this distinction.) In simple terms the maintenance of capitalist relations depends
on social processes which reproduce not only those agents or actors
who carry out the functions of capital and labour but also social
processes which reproduce the relations or roles themselves. For
example, the application of technology to the division of labour reproduces positions, by way of fragmenting skills in the labour process:

> Translated into market terms, this means labour power capable of
> performing the process may be purchased more cheaply as dissociat-
> ed elements as a capacity integrated in a single worker. (Braverman
> 1974 p 81)

This means that we will be concerned with the way in which the state
and professions are implicated in processes associated with the reproduction of labour power and, therefore, social class formation. The institutionalization of science, on the other hand, would be more directly
implicated in the reproduction of the positions of production.

The increasingly significant role of the state in reproduction of
agents is related to the concentration of capital in the monopolistic
stage of capitalist development, whereby the ensuing rationalization
of production and mobility of capital sets in train the demand for a
labour force which is itself characterized by its mobility or transfer-
ability. The state, in centralizing and formalizing processes of reproduction, such as education, creates a labour force less tied to local and
particularistic cultures; sharing in a common (yet hierarchically organ-

ized) formal socialization process. The state takes on a function, therefore, which cannot be effectively carried out within the confines of a single productive enterprise.

As the state has become more active in this process, heteronomy[13] as an institutionalized form of the control of occupational activities has become increasingly important. Unlike a system of corporate patronage where a corporate client defines its own needs and the manner in which these are serviced by an occupation, heteronomy refers to the intervention of the state to remove from both the occupation and the client (to a greater or lesser extent) the authority to determine the content and manner of practice. There are variations in the extent of this intervention. At one extreme the state may attempt to ensure a desired distribution of occupational services of a determinate kind through the creation of a state agency which is the effective employer of all practitioners who have a statutory obligation to provide the service. Social work is an example of this type as is education (excluding the private system). State heteronomy may be more limited, however, involving, at the other extreme, a minimal encroachment on an existing, institutionalized system of colleague control (see Johnson 1972 pp 51–61) by way of grants-in-aid to means-tested members of the public (e.g. legal aid) or by making resources available to an occupation which (to a greater or lesser extent) continues to determine priorities and the rates of remuneration going to its various membership grades (e.g. medicine in the National Health Service).

Whatever the balance of this intermeshing of state and 'profession', determining the instutionalized forms by which occupational services are controlled, the very services themselves represent mechanisms of control in the processes of reproduction. State heteronomy refers to a situation where occupational definitions of, for example, success and failure in education, sickness and health, deviant and normal behaviour, are subordinated to or derived from 'official' definitions. In the course of the formalization and centralization of such processes of reproduction elements of the state apparatus may arise to impose such definitions upon an emergent occupation, as is the case with social work, or 'recognize' existing occupational definitions, as with medicine in the context of the National Health Service in Britain.

Variations exist, then, in the extent to which the state or a particular occupation monopolizes such definitions and these variations are, in part at least, to be explained in terms of the specific historical conjunctions at which an occupation emerges or the state becomes involved in new areas of social control. For example, the institutionalization of 'colleague' control in medicine took place in the nineteenth century when social conditions associated with the rise of private capitalism were conducive to 'professionalism' (see Johnson 1972 p 52) and occupational definitions of client need. In this field the existence of occupational power has, in the twentieth century, been a limitation to state heteronomy, and it has been the role of the state in the process of reproduction to underwrite existing occupationally generated definitions except where they conflict with the extension of health services to a clientele defined on the basis of citizenship (Johnson 1972 pp 77–9).

The occupation of social work, on the other hand, was largely a creation of the state as its functions were extended to new areas of social control. As a result, the clients of social workers are the creations of the state through official processes of defining client need on the basis of such categories as poverty, deviancy, criminality, etc., and are not (and never have been) autonomously generated as an occupational process.

The distinction between official and occupationally generated definitions is particularly important in the extent to which such definitions, whether generated and sustained by the occupation or the state, coincide with the requirements of capital in the process of reproduction. The strength of the ideological symbols which underpin occupational power and privilege is directly related to the extent to which the occupation fulfils the 'global' functions of capital in the reproduction process or merely applies such definitions as a more or less routine labour process. Thus, the extent to which officially recognized definitions of sickness and health are monopolized by the medical profession, the extent to which they are the outcome of occupationally controlled processes is also the extent to which medicine autonomously carries out the function of capital in the process of reproduction. As a consequence medicine becomes the beneficiary of the whole ideological process of capital which supports its claims to privilege and power – the conditon of a successful strategy of professionalism. In social work the central criteria of occupational judgement – definitions of deviancy, criminality – are generated by state agencies such as the legislature and the courts and in consequence social workers are largely engaged in the labour process of applying such definitions. They are part of the control mechanism of reproduction but do not carry out the functions of capital.

Superficially the relationship between the state and 'professions' presents itself as a series of paradoxes. First, state mediation of the professional–client relationship is represented as an aspect of welfare. The state as benefactor ensures a wider distribution of 'professional' services so providing for those who would otherwise not be able to meet the costs. At the same time, however, the state presents practitioners with a guaranteed clientele, so alleviating the damaging consequences of client choice. For example, client need is essentially defined under conditions of 'professionalism' (colleague or occupational control) by the operation of an occupationally determined fee structure. The choices made by clients, able to meet the costs of the service, favour some practitioners as against others. As a result there are great disparities in the rewards accruing to colleagues whose corporate ideology stresses the equal competence of all members. A 'submerged' segment of the occupation is, consequently, likely to favour a new system of resource distribution such as that promised by state heteronomy. This was certainly one of the conditions operating at the time the National Health Service was successfully launched.

Secondly, the very conditions which are deemed necessary for the 'autonomy' and 'independence' of an occupation include a state guarantee of their maintenance. State credentialism, in issuing to specific occupational associations a monopoly of practice in their fields, is a major condition for colleague control over entry to the 'profession'. Thus, those associations of 'professional' men, which are seen by many as the 'third force' standing out against the dead hand of state bureaucracy, owe their privileges to that very hand. It is the state that ensures that only solicitors may be paid for officiating at the most frequent form of property transfer (conveyancing); that only certain accountants may audit public companies; that only doctors may issue sickness or death certificates, prescribe certain drugs or supervise abortions; that only the signatures of members of the 'building professions' will be recognized in certain planning processes, etc.

Finally, official recognition of occupational definitions of the content of practice (the guarantee of autonomy) may well be the first step in state determination of such content. The close integration of state power and professional privilege illustrated by these paradoxes stems from their involvement in processes of reproduction. It should be pointed out here that the functions of the state are not confined to the reproduction of the relations of production (both agents and positions) but include the functions of appropriation and realization discussed above and certain 'professions' are absorbed into the state apparatus in carrying out such functions either as a labour process (e.g. Tax Inspectors) or in fulfilling the global functions of capital (e.g. civil service heads of the Treasury). However, it could be argued that the dominant role of the state has, with the development of monopoly capitalism, increasingly shifted toward that of reproduction[14] and that, as a result, major fields of class conflict are located at the level of intra-state relations.

This latter point suggests that the intermeshing of state and 'profession' in the process of reproduction cannot be conceptualized as total integration. The state cannot be treated as a monolithic, undifferentiated 'ideological' and 'repressive' apparatus for there is, in the relationship between state and 'professions', at least, an undeniable tension associated with the tendency of the state to continuously centralize and formalize the institutions of reproduction which, while in certain cases bringing with it official recognition of occupational worth, at the same time threatens the power base on which that worth was originally demonstrated at an earlier phase of capitalist development, e.g. the emergence of an institutionalized form of 'colleague control' during the phase of 'private' capitalism. Thus, where state intervention has the consequence of removing from occupational control the monopoly of those functions central to the reproduction of capital it sets in train a process of 'proletarianization' and undermines the foundations of 'professionalism' as a form of control. In such a case 'professionalism' as an ideology is likely to become more strident in the rearguard action mounted by an occupation. This process is not merely to be conceived of as change in the institutionalized forms of occupational control, nor a shift towards bureaucratized practice settings but is a process of class transformation and a sphere of class conflict, located at the level of the state. The recent militancy of junior hospital doctors, the controversy over private beds in national health hospitals, the struggles associated with the contending social work ideologies which focus on an individualized 'case' therapy and 'community' action are all aspects of this tension and reflect the continuous process of class formation.

In looking at the process of reproduction, then, we are once again faced with the complex problem of how an occupational activity articulates with or relates to underlying, determinant processes of surplus value production while at the same time exhibiting structural discontinuities and autonomies, i.e. the processes generated by state intervention in organization of work activities are not directly reducible to the relations of production, while determined by them. In distinguishing between the functions of appropriation, realization and reproduction it is suggested that the institutionalized processes of reproduction, for example, are *relatively* autonomous from those of the determining process of appropriation. That is to say that while the structure of appropriation lays down the conditions for the social reproduction of its own relations, the political and ideological practices that such reproduction processes give rise to are not directly reducible to or deducible from them. Thus, the ideology of 'professionalism' while serving as a tool in the struggle for occupational autonomy and privilege may be reinforced by the general ideological processes reproducing capitalist relations, as is the case with medicine, yet at the same time serve as an effective weapon in those political processes which characterize the relations between 'profession' and state. That state and 'profession' are both implicated in the functions of capital does not then imply a complete identity of interest between the agents involved or a homogeneity of the institutions represented. Rather, it is the ground on which the processes of class fractionalization and alliance take place.

In short, those occupations we call 'professions' are heterogeneous not only as a result of their distinctive functions in relation to the processes of direct appropriation, realization and reproduction but they also exhibit differences of function, power and privilege as a result of the differentiating consequences of each of these processes. We cannot identify these processes by reference to ownership and non-ownership alone nor can we effectively analyse the production process as simply reflecting the rationalized consequences of bureaucratization or the technical exigencies of the division of labour. Nor can we characterize the role of the state as a monolithic undifferentiated apparatus. An adequate analysis of work and power demands an account of the differentiating consequences of each of the processes discussed under the headings appropriation, realization and reproduction, and an assessment of their consequences for the process of class formation.

Notes

1 The most explicit theoretical elaboration of this position is to be found in K. Davis and W. Moore (1967).

2 The discussion in this section relies heavily on the work of G. Carchedi, particularly his article 'On the economic identification of the new middle class', *Economy and Society*, vol. 4, no. 1, 1975, pp 1–86.

3 In the following discussion a distinction is made between 'surplus value' and 'surplus labour'. Modes of production are, according to Marx, structures through which value — the product of labour — is appropriated by agents who do not themselves produce value. The varying structures of appropriation which are dominant in such modes as slavery, feudalism and capitalism determine the fundamental divisions of interest, relations of power and forms of class struggle characterizing each of these modes. While each mode represents then a set of exploitative relations, the form that exploitation takes, through the appropriation of value, varies.

In the case of feudalism value is appropriated as 'surplus labour'; that is to say labour expended in producing value is directly appropriated through institutionalized systems of payment in kind or work on owner's land for which wages are not paid. This form of direct control over labour is characteristic of relations between lord and serf in the feudal mode. Thus, the mechanism of value appropriation is the landowner's call on labour time.

Capitalist relations exist, on the other hand, where value is appropriated not in the form of labour but in the form of surplus value. In this case labour is a commodity, bought and sold on the market like any other commodity, and surplus value is the difference between the wages paid and the value realized in the production process as a result of the application of labour power.

These two mechanisms of appropriation — feudal and capitalist — are, then, distinct structures which are the determinate conditions for distinct economic processes (i.e. the economic, as such, is not then determinate) and social formations, and whose relations (of production) are reproduced through distinct political and ideological practices.

4 The distinction between 'possession', 'economic ownership' and 'legal ownership' is discussed by Nicos Poulantzas (1975), economic ownership being the real economic control of the means of production, i.e. the power to assign the means of production to given uses and so to dispose of the products obtained (p 18). Possession is 'the capacity to put the means of production into operation' (p 18), while legal ownership, in being sanctioned by law, is an aspect of the superstructure rather than the relationships of production and, therefore, does not define class relationships (p 19).

5 See *ibid*, pp 5–10.

6 This insistence is not merely ours: 'The essential difference between the various economic forms of society, between, for instance, a society based on slave labour, and one based on wage-labour, *lies* only in the mode in which this surplus-labour is in each case extracted from the actual producer, the labourer' (Marx, *Capital* vol. 1 p 217).

7 The following is restricted to a discussion of 'western' capitalist societies. Any application to 'socialist' societies would require a complex argument which cannot be embarked upon here. However, it should be clear from the analysis so far which takes the surplus value producing process as the determining feature of the capitalist mode of production, while allowing for the possibility of the dispersal of the functions of capital, that a change in the form of legally defined ownership is not a sufficient condition for the elimination of capitalist relations. For example, Charles Bettelheim (1975) has argued that the USSR is

characterized by a system of State Capitalism with 'effective' private property in the hands of a state bourgeoisie. The role of the state is crucial — 'public ownership' has involved the nationalization of the principal productive enterprises as a limited form of social property: it is social only by virtue of the mediation of the state. At the same time possession of the enterprise is in the hands of managers and labour continues to enter into the production process as a commodity. As labour is separated from the means of production so each enterprise is separated in its organization creating the conditions for the persistence of commodity relations characteristic of capitalism. As a result state property has become a legal fiction and the real economic relations are those of the collective private property of the state bourgeoisie. In the absence of effective ownership by the State the state bourgeoisie become the effective owners.

However, because Bettelheim fails to show that the persistence of commodity relations is a product of a form of the appropriation of surplus labour as surplus value he has not proved the persistence or re-emergence of a fully developed capitalist system in which the 'process of social production as a whole is dominated by capitalist relations of production: that the process of social production is dominated by the capitalist mode of appropriation of surplus labour, that is, by the extraction of surplus-value and its realization for a capitalist class, and further that it reproduces the conditions of existence of this domination' (Hindess 1973 p 392). Thus, in the case which Bettelheim analyses, the existence of a free contractual labour market is not a *sufficient* condition for arguing that capitalist relations exist (see the argument on pp 343–347 above). In order to show that, the 'possession' of the means of production by a 'state bourgeoisie' would also entail an exploitative relationship in which, as the agents of capital, they appropriated surplus value. Where, therefore, one does not show the existence of a structure of appropriation as surplus value, then other features such as commodity relations may involve merely a limitation on the emergence of socialist relations. Or, vice versa, the existence of ineffective state property may, indeed, create the conditions for capitalist possession of property. The significance of private property in capitalist relations lies in the institutional facilitation of the appropriation of surplus value. The question remains as to whether the developing forms of property in socialist societies operate as facilitation or an inhibition of such a structure of value appropriation.

8 This distinction between 'conception' and 'execution' is a major theme developed by Braverman (1974).

9 This point is borne out by the troubled history of company audit disclosure, where the profession has generally stood out against reforms demanding an extension of information provided on grounds of the

need for secrecy in competitive business. See Nicholas Stacey (1954).

10 Coercive control is not here directly surveillance in the appropriation of surplus value, for we are not referring to productive labour. Rather, the forms of surveillance generated in the process of direct appropriation are extended to unproductive labour which arises as a consequence of the surplus value producing process rather than its condition (productive labour). Thus, 'exploitation' in this case refers to an absolute constraint on wages paid from surplus rather than an appropriation of surplus value.

11 The notion of occupational missions which views the heterogeneity of professional groups as deriving from specialist segments attempting to impose their own image on the occupation as a whole is developed by Bucher and Strauss (1961).

12 The concentration of capital has also had implications for the internationalization of the labour process and the reproduction of labour. A particular aspect which is relevant here has been the creation of what has been called a 'transnational elite' through the standardization and reciprocal recognition of 'professional' qualifications. An important effect of this worldwide process has been the phenomenon of the 'brain drain' in which the costs of training skilled manpower, absorbed by highly industrialized capitalist societies, are borne by the underdeveloped countries.

13 The forms of institutionalized control of an occupation in which a third party (such as the state or church) intervenes in the relationship between practitioner and client in order to determine the client's needs and/or the manner in which these needs are to be serviced were previously referred to (see Johnson 1972) as forms of mediation. The term *heteronomy* is now preferred as the general concept, including as subtypes both church and state mediation. The concept is taken from Max Weber: 'A corporate group may be either autonomous or heteronomous . . . autonomy means that the other governing the group has been established by its own members on their own authority . . . in the case of heteronomy, it has been imposed by an outside agency' (1947 p 148). Heteronomy is distinguishable from patronage in my own usage in the sense that it refers to the *order* imposed on a relationship (occupation—clientele) and not the corporate group as such.

14 Implied in this analysis is the suggestion that in the course of capitalist development, the dominant functions of the state change; that is to say, in relation to appropriation, realization and reproduction. This means that while the emergent state is always to some degree involved in the whole cycle of the dynamic of capital at any particular stage in

its expansionary development the frontiers of state development are variously related to one or another of these processes — most recently in relation to reproduction. This provides the basis for a more complex analysis of state functions in relation to capital than is possible when it is conceived of as an undifferentiated structure of repressive or ideological control.

Appendix

Why the bosses need help from a code of conduct

(Source: *The Guardian*, 7 April 1973)

Only commitment to a code of professional standards can give management the moral authority it needs if companies are not to be torn apart by highly organized sectional interests, Sir Frederick Catherwood said in Sheffield last night.

Speaking at the Cutlers' Feast, Sir Frederick expounded a philosophy of management based on the principle of service to the community. He is managing director of John Laing and Son Ltd and a former director-general of the National Economic Development Office.

"Service is the end. Profit is the means to that end. If society wills the end, it must also will the means. At present we are trying to make it will the means without explaining the end," Sir Federick said. The text of his speech follows.

I think that we need a code of professional management which embodies the actual practices of our leading companies. The Confederation of British industry recently published a report in which one of the main conclusions was that there must be drawn up and published a code of corporate behaviour in business which will be adopted and actively supported by as many companies as possible. The British Institute of Management has set up a committee to examine the professional code for individual managers. Similar moves are afoot in Europe where they feel that if their companies are not to be torn apart by highly organized sectional interests, management must have the moral authority which only a commitment to professional standards of service can bring.

Industrial society desperately needs leadership. I believe that it will only accept leadership from those who are publicly dedicated to serve it and that only this dedication will give management the moral authority to fulfil the immense and unprecedented responsibilities which it now has to bear.

So we must not only turn our professional standards into ideals which will inspire management but into a social commitment through which we can give our vision to the society in which we live so that it regains its cohesion and drive and is strongly resistant to the divisive and destructive forces which are now attacking it.

Business is in a troubled state, uncertain of its acceptance in society and under pressure from labour, Government and the public. We are facing an ideological vacuum in which no one way of life has wide enough acceptance to hold society together – and our interdependent wealth-creating industrial society depends utterly on social cohesion and cannot existing without it.

Business has managed to carry on in the past without much ideology. But we live in an age of ideologies and if we are not careful other people's ideologies are going to cast us in the wrong role. It's about time those of us who run British business defined our role more carefully. I think of myself primarily as a professional manager, not as a capitalist. Managers are and must, in my view, be professionals, working to professional standards and must develop and promote professionalism as the standard by which we work and the standard which our society so desperately needs.

What is professionalism? I think that the essence of professionalism is the idea of service. The professional soldiers and public servants serve their country. The doctor serves his patient, the engineer his client, the pastor and priest serve their congregation. The duty of the professional manager is not so simple. Those he serves have conflicting interests which, as part of his professional role, he must reconcile. This means that they need to trust him. So he cannot function unless he has the highest standards of integrity.

If management did not have these professional standards, it would not be trusted with hundreds of millions of pounds, customers would not trust their lives to its products, new generations of students would not trust their careers to its care and workers would not trust its promises across the negotiating table. Professional management exists, it is effective, it contains the vital ingredient of trust which oils the working of industrial society, but its professionalism is concealed behind the confused conflict of irrelevant ideologies and will not make any public impact unless it can be presented in terms of service to the community.

We desperately need a publicly accepted ideology through which we can communicate to the society we serve. In *War and Peace*, Tolstoy asked why the ordinary French soldier followed Napoleon all the way to Moscow. Frederick the Great wondered why his soldiers obeyed him instead of killing him. The answer is that both societies had an ideology through which the military leader could communicate. Professionalism, unlike militarism, is a constructive ideology. The simple ideal of service is hard to dispute or overthrow.

We want to build on the idea of professional service and build on it fast, for we do not have much time.

We all know that we no longer practise old-fashioned capitalism. But we have not given a name or over-riding principle to the things we do practise. And in the absence of a new principle matching and explaining the new practice, we still explain our motives solely in terms of service and the public is confused. We need profits, just as a Communist bank or collective farm needs profits because if their expenditure exceeds their income they cannot go on serving the community. Service is the end. Profit is the means to that end. If society wills the end, it must also will the means. At present we are trying to make it will the means without explaining the end.

Profits for the shareholders, competition for the customers, even incentives for the worker are about separate conflicting interests so they are essentially divisive concepts. We need a unifying ideal. The ideal of professional service, a service which has the twin aims of reconciling different interests and of expanding the real wealth of the community.

There is at least as much professional skill in the management of great economic resources as there is in engineering or medicine, but the traditional professions do not contain the ingredient of economic performance which is at the heart of management. The most vital part of a code of professional management must be that we make the optimum use of the material and human resources entrusted to us.

We not only need to raise the flag of professionalism so that every citizen can see it, we need to write a new constitution, so that the meaning of the flag can be explained.

References

Government documents

CENTRAL ADVISORY COUNCIL FOR EDUCATION (1959) 15–18 (Crowther Report) London, HMSO.

EDUCATION AND TRAINING ACT (1948) London, HMSO.

EDUCATION AND TRAINING ACT (1973) London, HMSO.

NATIONAL YOUTH EMPLOYMENT COUNCIL (1965) *The Future Development of the Youth Employment Service* (The Albemarle Report) London, HMSO.

SOCIAL TRENDS (1974) No. 5, London, HMSO.

SOCIAL TRENDS (1977) No. 8, London, HMSO.

THOMAS, R. and WETHERELL, D. (1974) *Looking Forward to Work – an enquiry carried out on behalf of the Central Youth Employment Executive,* London, HMSO.

References

ABBOTT, C.D. (1948) *Poets at Work*, New York, Harcourt Brace & World Inc.

ABRAMSON P.R. (1971) 'Educational certification and life chances among British schoolboys,' *Research in Education*, Vol. 5, May, pp 52–9.

ACKER, J and VAN HOUTEN, D.R. (1974) 'Differential recruitment and control: the sex structuring of organizations,' *Administrative Science Quarterly*, Vol. 19, pp 152–63.

AIMS OF INDUSTRY (1974) *Reds under the Bed?* (pamphlet), London, Aims of Industry.

ALLEN, V.L. (1966) *Militant Trade Unionism*, London, Merlin Press.

ANTHONY, P.D. (1977) *The Ideology of Work*, London, Tavistock Publications.

ARGYRIS, C. (1964) *Integrating the Individual and the Organization*, New York, John Wiley & Sons.

ARGYRIS, C. (1968) 'The organization: what makes it healthy?', *Harvard Business Review*, Vol. 36, pp 10–16.

ARONOWITZ, S. (1973) *False Promises: The shaping of American working class consciousness*, New York, McGraw-Hill.

ASHTON, D.N. (1973) 'The transition from school to work: notes on the development of different frames of reference among young male workers' in ESLAND, SALAMAN and SPEAKMAN (eds) (1957) pp 147–57.

ASHTON, D.N. (1974) 'Careers and commitment: the movement from school to work' in FIELD, D. (ed.) *Social Psychology for Sociologists*, London, Nelson, pp 171–86.

ASHTON, D.N. and FIELD, D. (1975) *Young Workers*, London, Hutchinson.

BAILEY, R. and BRAKE, M. (eds) (1975) *Radical Social Work*, London, Edward Arnold Ltd.

BAIN, G.S. (1970) *The Growth of White Collar Unionism*, London, Oxford University Press.

BAIN, G.S., BACON, R. and PIMLOTT, J. (1972) 'The labour force' in HALSEY, A.H. (ed.) (1972) pp 97–128.

BAIN, G.S. and PRICE, R. (1972) 'Union growth and employment trends in the United Kingdom, 1964–70', *British Journal of Industrial Relations*, Vol. 10, pp 366–81.

BALDAMUS, W. (1961a) 'Tedium and traction in industrial work' in WEIR, D. (ed.) (1973), pp 78–84.

BALDAMUS, W. (1961b) *Efficiency and Effort*, London, Tavistock.

BARAN, P. and SWEEZY, P.M. (1966) *Monopoly Capital*, New York, Monthly Review Press.

BARATZ, S. and BARATZ, J. (1970) 'Early childhood intervention: the social science base of institutional racism', *Harvard Educational Review*, Vol. 40, No. 1 (Winter) pp 29–50.

BARBER, B. (1963) 'Some problems in the sociology of the professions', *Daedalus*, Fall, pp 669–88.

BARITZ, L. (1960) 'The servants of power' in ESLAND, SALAMAN and SPEAKMAN (eds) (1975) pp 325–37. Reprinted from L. BARITZ, *The Servants of Power: a history of the use of social science in American industry*, New York, Wesleyan University Press.

BASIC STATISTICS: INTERNATIONAL COMPARISONS (1978), Paris, OECD.

BECKER, H.S. (1952) 'Social class variations in the teacher–pupil relationship', *Journal of Educational Sociology*, Vol. 25, No. 4, pp 451–65. Reprinted in COSIN, B.R., DALE, I.R., ESLAND, G.M. and SWIFT, D.F. (eds) (1971) *School and Society: a sociological reader*, London, Routledge/The Open University Press.

BECKER, H.S. (1962) 'The nature of a profession,' in *Education for the Professions*, The Sixty-First Yearbook of the National Society for the Study of Education, Part II, distributed by the University of Chicago Press, pp 27–46.

BECKER, H. (1963) *Outsiders: studies in the sociology of deviance*, New York, The Free Press.

BECKER, H.S. (ed.) (1964) *The Other Side*, New York, The Free Press.

BELL, C., NEWBY, H. *et al* (1978) *Property, Paternalism and Power*, London, Hutchinson.

BELL, D. (1961) *The End of Ideology*, New York, The Free Press.

BELL, D. (1967) 'Notes on post-industrial society,' *The Public Interest*, No. 6, pp 34—48.
BELL, D. (1974) *The Coming of Post-Industrial Society: a venture in social forecasting*, London, Heinemann.
BENDIX, R. (1956) *Work and Authority in Industry: ideologies of management in the course of industrialization*, New York and London, John Wiley.
BENDIX, R. and LIPSET, S.M. (eds) (1967a) *Class, Status and Power*, London, Routledge and Kegan Paul.
BENDIX, R. and LIPSET, S.M. (eds) (1967b) *Working-Class Images of Society*, London, Routledge and Kegan Paul.
BENNETT, W.S. and HOKENSTAD (1973) 'Full-time people workers and conceptions of the professional', in HALMOS, P. (ed.) *Professionalization and Social Change*, University of Keele monograph, No. 20.
BERGER, P.L. (1965) 'Towards a sociological analysis of psychoanalysis,' *Social Research*, Vol. 32, No. 1 (Spring) pp 26—41. Reprinted in ESLAND, G., SALAMAN, G. and SPEAKMAN, M. (eds), (1975) pp 296—305.
BERGER, P.L. and LUCKMANN, T. (1967) *The Social Construction of Reality*, London, Allen Lane.
BERGER, P., BERGER, B. and KELLNER, H. (1973) *The Homeless Mind*, Harmondsworth, Penguin.
BERGER, P. (1964) 'The human shape of work' in ESLAND, SALAMAN and SPEAKMAN (eds) (1975) pp 164—69.
BETTELHEIM, B. (1961) *The Informed Heart*, London, Thames & Hudson.
BETTELHEIM, C. (1975) 'State property and socialism', *Economy and Society*, Vol. 2, No. 4, pp 395—420.
BEYNON, H. (1975) *Working for Ford*, Wakefield, EP Publishing (first published in 1973 by Penguin Education).
BEYNON, H. and BLACKBURN, R.M. (1972) *Perception of Work*, Cambridge University Press.
BIRNBAUM, N. (1953) 'Conflicting interpretations of the rise of capitalism: Marx and Weber', *British Journal of Sociology*, Vol. IV, June, pp 125—41.
BLACKBURN, R.M. and MANN, M. (1973) 'Constraint and choice: stratification and the market for unskilled labour,' paper presented to BSA Conference, March.
BLAU, P.M., GUSTAD, J.W., JESSOR, R., PARNES, H.S. and WILCOX, R.C. (1956) 'Occupational choice: a conceptual framework', *Industrial Labour Review*, Vol. 9, pp 531—43.
BLAU. P. and DUNCAN, O. (1961) *The American Occupational Structure*, London, Wiley.
BLAU, P.M. and DUNCAN, O.D. (1967) *The American Occupational Structure*, New York, Wiley.
BLUMBERG, A.S. (1969) 'The practise of law as confidence game', in AUBERT, V. (ed.) *Sociology of Law*, Harmondsworth, Penguin Books, pp 321—31. Originally published as 'The practise of law as confidence game: organizational co-optation of a profession.' *Law and Society Review*, Vol. 1 (1967) pp 15—39.

BLAUNER, R. (1967a) 'Work satisfaction and industrial trends in modern society' in BENDIX, R. and LIPSET, L.M. (eds) (1967a).

BLAUNER, R. (1967b) *Alienation and Freedom: the factory worker and his industry*, Chicago, University of Chicago Press, Phoenix Books.

BOSQUET, M. (1972) 'The prison factory,' *New Left Review*, No. 73, May–June, pp 23–24.

BOWLES, S. and GINTIS, H. (1976) *Schooling in Capitalist America*, London, Routledge and Kegan Paul.

BRACHER, K.D. (1973) *The German Dictatorship*, trans. Jean Steinberg, Harmondsworth, Penguin.

BRAHAM, P. (1975) 'Immigrant labour in Europe' in ESLAND, G., SALAMAN, G. and SPEAKMAN, M. (eds) (1975) pp 119–33.

BRAVERMAN, H. (1974) *Labor and Monopoly Capital: the degradation of work in the twentieth century*, New York, Monthly Review Press, pp 85–123.

BRITISH LABOUR STATISTICS HISTORICAL ABSTRACTS, 1886–1968 (1971) London, HMSO.

BRITISH LABOUR STATISTICS YEARBOOK 1972 (1974) London, HMSO.

BROWN, P. (1974) *Towards a Marxist Psychology*, New York, Harper and Row.

BROWN, R. and BRANNEN, P. (1970a and b) 'Social relations and social perspectives among shipbuilding workers – part 1,' *Sociology*, Vol. 4, No. 1, January pp 71–84. Also Part 2 *Sociology*, Vol. 4, No. 2, May pp 197–211.

BROWN, W.A. (1973) *Piecework Bargaining*, London, Heinemann.

BUCHEIM, H. (1968) 'The SS-instrument of domination' in H. KRAUSNICK *et al* (1968) pp 127–302.

BUCHEIM, H. (1968) 'Command and compliance' in H. KRAUSNICK *et al* (1968) pp 303–96.

BUCHER, R. and STRAUSS, A. (1961) 'Professions in process', *American Journal of Sociology*, Vol. LXVI (January), pp 325–34.

BUCKNER, H. TAYLOR (1970) 'Transformation of reality in the legal process,' *Social Research*, Vol. 37, No. 1 (Spring), pp 88–101.

BULMER, M. (ed.) (1975) *Working Class Images of Society*, London, Routledge and Kegan Paul.

BURNETT, J. (1974) *Useful Toil: autobiographies of working people from the 1820s to the 1920s*, London, Allen Lane.

BURNS, T. (1957) 'Management in action', *Operational Research Quarterly*, Vol. 8, No. 2, June, pp 45–60.

CANNAN, C. (1972) 'Social workers: training and professionalism', in PATEMAN, T. (ed.) *Counter Course: a handbook for course criticism*, Harmondsworth, Penguin.

CARCHEDI, G. (1975a) 'On the economic identification of the new middle class', *Economy and Society*, Vol. 4, No. 1, pp 1–86.

CARCHEDI, G. (1975b) 'Reproduction of social classes at the level of production relations', *Economy and Society*, Vol. 3, No. 4, pp 361–417.

THE CAREERS SERVICE (1973) *Education*, An 'Education' Digest, 16 November 1973.

CARLIN, J.E., HOWARD, J. and MESSINGER, S.L. (1967) *Civil Justice and the Poor: issues for sociological research*, New York, Russell Sage Foundation.

CARR-SAUNDERS, A.M. and WILSON, P.A. (1964 Reprint) *The Professions*, London, Frank Cass.

CARTER, M.P. (1962) *Home, School and Work: a study of the education and employment of young people in Britain*, London and Oxford, Pergamon Press Ltd.

CARTER, M.P. (1966) *Into Work*, Harmondsworth, Penguin.

CASTLES, S. and KOSACK, G. (1973) *Immigrant Workers and Class Structure in Western Europe*, London, Oxford University Press.

CBI (1973) *The Responsibilities of the British Public Company*, Final Report of Company Affairs Committee, 19 September.

CHILD, J. (1969) *British Management Thought*, London, Allen and Unwin.

CHILD, J. (1972) 'Organisational Structure, Environment and Performance: the role of strategic choice' *Sociology*, Vol. 6, No. 1 pp 1—22.

CICOUREL' A. and KITSUSE, J. (1968) 'The social organization of the high school and deviant adolescent careers' in COSIN, B.R. *et al* (eds) (1971) *School and Society*, London, Routledge and Kegan Paul/The Open University Press, pp 152—9.

CLARKE, R.O., FATCHET, D.J. and ROBERTS, S.B.C. (1972) *Workers' Participation in Management in Britain*, London, Heinemann.

CLIFF, T. (1970) *The Employers' Offensive*, London, Pluto Press.

COATES, D. (1975) *The Labour Party and the Struggle for Socialism*, Cambridge, Cambridge University Press.

COHEN, S. (ed.) (1971) *Images of Deviance*, Harmondsworth, Penguin.

COHEN, S. (1975) 'It's all right for you to talk: political and sociological manifestos for social work action', in *Radical Social Work*, London, Edward Arnold Ltd. pp 76—95.

CONQUEST, R. (ed.) (1967) *Industrial Workers in the USSR*, London, The Bodley Head.

COPEMAN, G. (1965) *How the Executive Spends his Time*, London, London Business Publications.

COTGROVE, S., DUNHAM, J. and VAMPLEW, C. (1971) *The Nylon Spinners*, London, Allen and Unwin.

COULSON, M.A., KEIL, E.T., RIDDELL, C. and STRUTHERS, J.S. (1967) 'Towards a sociological theory of occupational choice: a critique', *Sociological Review*, Vol. 15, No. 3, November. Reprinted in WILLIAMS, W.M. (ed.) (1974) pp 124—32.

DAHRENDORF, R. (1959) *Class and Class Conflict in Industrial Society*, London, Routledge and Kegan Paul.

DALTON, G. (1974) *Economic Systems and Society*, Harmondsworth, Penguin.

DALTON, M. (1959) *Men Who Manage*, New York and London, John Wiley.

DALTON, M. (1969) 'Conflicts between staff and line managers' in BURNS, T. (ed.) (1969) *Industrial Man*, Harmondsworth, Penguin.

DANIEL, W.W. (1969) 'Industrial behaviour and orientation to work: a critique', *Journal of Management Studies*, Vol. 6, October, pp 366—75.

DANIEL, W.W. (1974) *A National Survey of the Unemployed*, London, Political and Economic Planning.
DAVIS, K. and MOORE, W.E. (1967) 'Some principles of stratification' in BENDIX and LIPSET (eds) (1967a).
DAVIS, L.E. and TAYLOR, J.C. (1972) *Design of Jobs: selected readings*, Harmondsworth, Penguin.
DENNIS, N., HENRIQUES, F.M. and SLAUGHTER, C. (1956) *Coal is our Life*, London, Tavistock Publications.
DENZIN, N.K. (1968) 'The self-fulfilling prophecy and patient-therapist interaction', in SPITZER, S.P. and DENZIN, N.K. (eds) *The Mental Patient: studies in the sociology of deviance*, New York, McGraw-Hill pp 349–58.
DEPARTMENT OF EMPLOYMENT GAZETTE (1973) *The Fall in the Labour Force Between 1966 and 1971*, Vol. LXXXI, No. 11, November, pp 1083–87.
DEPARTMENT OF EMPLOYMENT GAZETTE (1973) *Part-time Women Workers 1950–72*, Vol. LXXXI, No. 11, November, pp 1088–92.
DEPARTMENT OF EMPLOYMENT GAZETTE (1973) *Progress Towards Equal Pay*, Vol. LXXXII, No. 8, pp 691–706.
DEPARTMENT OF EMPLOYMENT GAZETTE (1973) *Earnings and Hours*, Vol. LXXXII, No. 12, p 1186.
DEPARTMENT OF EMPLOYMENT GAZETTE (1978) Vol. LXXXVI, Nos 5 and 9.
DEPARTMENT OF EMPLOYMENT (1973) 'On the quality of working life,' *Manpower Paper*, No. 7, London, HMSO.
DEUTSCHER, I. (1966) 'Words and deeds: social science and social policy,' *Social Problems*, Vol. 13, No. 3, Winter, pp 235–54.
DE VROEY, M. (1975) 'The separation of ownership and control in large corporations – the Marxist view,' Working Paper No. 6419, *Economie et Société*, Institut des Sciences Economiques, Louvain, Belgium. Reprinted in *Review of Radical Political Economics*, Vol. 7, No. 2, Summer, 1975, pp 1–10.
DICKS, H.V. (1972) *Licenced Mass Murder*, New York, Basic Books.
DICKSON, D. (1974) *Alternative Technology and the Politics of Technical Change*, London, Fontana.
DONOVAN, (1968) *Royal Commission on Trade Unions and Employers' Associations Report*, London, HMSO.
DORE, RONALD, (1973) *British Factory – Japanese Factory*, London, Allen and Unwin.
DOUGLAS, J.D. (ed.) (1970) *The Impact of Sociology*, New York, Appleton-Century-Crofts.
DOUGLAS, J.W.B. (1967) *The Home and the School*, London, Panther.
DOUGLAS, J.W.B. (1971) *All Our Future*, London, Panther (first published by Peter Davis Ltd., 1968).
DUBIN R. (1962) 'Industrial workers' worlds: a study of the central life interests of industrial workers,' in ROSE, A.M. (ed.) (1962) pp 247–66.
DURKHEIM, E. (1933) *The Division of Labour in Society*, Glencoe, Illinois, Free Press.
DURKHEIM, E. (1952) *Suicide*, London, Routledge and Kegan Paul.

EASTON, L.D. and GUDDAT, K.H. (1967) *Writings of the Young Marx on Philosophy and Society*, New York, Anchor Books.

ECKSTEIN, H. (1960) *Pressure Goup Politics: the case of the British Medical Association*, London, Allen and Unwin.

ECONOMIC LEAGUE (1973) Advertisement appearing in *The Daily Mirror*, 27 December.

ECONOMIC PROGRESS REPORT, *Women in Employment*, Report No. 56, November 1974, HMSO, pp 1–4.

ELDER, Jr., G.H. (1965) 'Life opportunity and personality: some consequences of stratified secondary-modern education in Great Britain', *Sociology of Education*, Vol. 38, Spring, pp 173–202.

ELDRIDGE, J.E.T. (1971) *Sociology and Industrial Life*, London, Michael Joseph.

ELDRIDGE, J.E.T. (1973) *Sociology and Industrial Life*, London, Nelson.

ELDRIDGE, J.E.T. (1975) 'Industrial relations and industrial capitalism' in ESLAND, G., SALAMAN, G. and SPEAKMAN, M. (eds) *People and Work*, London, Holmes-McDougall and The Open University Press.

ELDRIDGE, J.E.T. and CROMBIE, A.D. (1974) *A Sociology of Organizations*, London, Allen and Unwin.

ELGER, A.J. (1975) 'Industrial organizations: a processual perspective' in McKINLAY, J. (ed.) *Processing People*, London, Holt, Rinehart and Winston.

ELLIOTT, P. (1973) 'Professional ideology and social situation', in ESLAND, SALAMAN and SPEAKMAN (eds) (1975) pp 275–86.

ELLIOTT, R.F. (1977) 'The growth of white-collar employment in Great Britain 1951 to 1971', *British Journal of Industrial Relations*, Vol 15, pp 39–44.

EMERSON, J. (1970) 'Behaviour in private places: sustaining definitions of reality in gynaecological examinations', in DREITZEL, H.P. (ed.) *Recent Sociology*, No. 2, New York, Macmillan, pp 74–97.

EMERY, F.E. and THORSRUD, E. (1969) *Form and Content in Industrial Democracy*, London, Tavistock.

ESLAND, G.M. (1976) 'Professions and Professionalism', Unit 12 of DE351 *People and Work*, The Open University Press.

ESLAND G.M. and SALAMAN, J.G. (1975) 'Towards a Sociology of Work' in ESLAND, SALAMAN and SPEAKMAN (eds) (1975) pp 15–32.

ESLAND, G.M., SALAMAN, J.G. and SPEAKMAN, M. (eds) (1975) *People and Work*, Edinburgh, Holmes-McDougall/The Open University Press.

FEST, J.C. (1972) *The Face of the Third Reich*, trans. Michael Bullock, Harmondsworth, Penguin.

FIELD, G. (1974) *Unequal Britain: a report on the cycle of inequality*, London, Arrow Books.

FLANDERS, A. (1964) *The Fawley Productivity Agreements*, London, Faber and Faber.

FLANDERS, A. (1970) *Management and Unions*, London, Faber.

FOGARTY, M., ALLEN, A.J., ALLEN, I. and WALTERS, P. (1971) *Women in Top Jobs*, London, Allen and Unwin.

FORD, J. (1969) *Social Class and the Comprehensive School*, London, Routlege and Kegan Paul.

FORSYTH, G. (1966) *Doctors and State Medicine: a study of the British Health Service*, London, Pitman Medical.

FOX, A. (1971) *A Sociology of Work in Industry*, London, Collier-Macmillan.

FOX, A. (1973) 'Industrial Relations: a social critique of pluralist ideology', in CHILD, J. (1973) *Man and Organization*, London, Allen and Unwin.

FOX, A. (1974) *Beyond Contract: work, power and trust relations*, London, Faber & Faber.

FOX A. (1976) *Man Mismanagement*, London, Hutchinson.

FOX, A. and FLANDERS, A. (1969) 'The reform of collective bargaining: from Donovan to Durkheim', *British Journal of Industrial Relations*, Vol. 7, No. 2, pp 151–80.

FRASER, R. (1968) *Work*, Harmondsworth, Penguin, and *Work 2* (1969) Harmondsworth, Penguin.

FREIDSON, E. (1962) 'Dilemmas in the doctor–patient relationship' in ROSE, A.M. (ed.) (1962) pp 207–24.

FRIEDSON, E. (1970) *Profession of Medicine*, New York, Dodd Mead/TABS.

FREIDSON, E. (1970) *Professional Dominance*, Chicago, Aldine.

FREIDSON, E. (1973) 'Professionalization and the organization of middle-class labour in post-industrial society', in HALMOS, P. (ed.) (1973) pp 47–59.

FRIEDMANN, E.A. and HAVIGHURST, R. (1954) *The Meaning of Work and Retirement*, Chicago, University of Chicago Press.

FROMM, E. (1947) 'Personality and the market place' in WEIR, D. (ed.) (1973) pp 60–3.

GALBRAITH, J.K. (1972) *The New Industrial State*, (2nd ed.) Harmondsworth, Penguin Books.

GALLIE, D. (1978) *In Search of the New Working Class*, Cambridge University Press, Cambridge.

GARFINKEL, H. (1956) 'Conditions of successful degradation ceremonies', *The American Journal of Sociology*, Vol. LXI, pp 420–4.

GARNSEY, E. (1975) 'Occupational structure in industrialized societies: some notes on the convergence thesis in the light of Soviet experience', *Sociology*, Vol. 9, No. 3.

GIDDENS, A. (1973) *The Class Structure of the Advanced Societies*, London, Hutchinson.

GILB, C. (1966) *Hidden Hierarchies: Professions and Government*, New York, Harper and Row.

GINZBERG, E. (1971) *Career Guidance*, New York, McGraw-Hill.

GINZBERG, E. *et al* (1951) *Occupational Choice: an approach to a general theory*, New York and London, Columbia University Press.

GLASER, B.G. and STRAUSS, A. (1964) 'Awareness contexts and social interaction', *American Sociological Review*, Vol. 29, pp 669–79.

GLASER, B.G. and STRAUSS, A.L. (1965) *Awareness of Dying*, Chicago, Aldine.

GLASER, B.G. and STRAUSS, A.L. (1968) *Time for Dying*, Chicago, Aldine.

GLENNERSTER, A., McFARLAND, L., STEELE, R. and STEWART, F. (1966) *Womanpower, A Study Group*, Young Fabian Pamphlet II.

GLYN, A. and SUTCLIFFE, R. (1972) *British Capitalism, Workers and the Profits Squeeze*, Harmondsworth, Penguin.

GOFFMAN, E. (1963) *Stigma*, Harmondsworth, Penguin.

GOLD, R. (1952) 'Janitors versus tenants: a status-income dilemma', *The American Journal of Sociology*, Vol. 57, (March) pp 486–93.

GOLDHAMER, H. (1968) 'Social mobility' in *International Encyclopaedia of the Social Sciences*, London, Macmillan, pp 429–38.

GOLDTHORPE, J.H. (1971) 'Social stratification in industrial society', in THOMPSON, K. and TUNSTALL, J. (eds) (1971) pp 331–47.

GOLDTHORPE, J.H. (1974) 'Social inequality and social integration in modern Britain' in WEDDERBURN, D. and CRAIG, C. (eds) *Poverty, Inequality and Class Structure*, Cambridge University Press, pp 217–38.

GOLDTHORPE, J., LOCKWOOD, D., BECHHOFER, F. and PLATT, J. (1968a) *The Affluent Worker: Industrial Attitudes and Behaviour*, Cambridge University Press.

GOLDTHORPE, J., LOCKWOOD, D., BECHHOFER, F. and PLATT, J. (1968b) *The Affluent Worker: Political Attitudes and Behaviour*, Cambridge University Press.

GOLDTHORPE, J., LOCKWOOD, D., BECHHOFER, F. and PLATT, J. (1969) *The Affluent Worker in the Class Structure*, Cambridge University Press.

GOLDTHORPE, J.H. and HOPE, K. (1972) 'Occupational trading and occupational prestige', in HOPE, K. (ed.) *The Analysis of Social Mobility, Methods and Approaches*, Oxford Studies in Social Mobility, Working Paper 1, Oxford, Clarendon Press, pp 19–79.

GOLDTHORPE, J.H. and HOPE, K. (1974) *The Social Grading of Occupations: a new approach and scale*, Oxford, Clarendon Press.

GOLDTHORPE, J.H. and LLEWELLYN, C. (1977a) 'Class mobility in modern Britain: Three theses examined', *Sociology*, Vol. 11, pp 257–287.

GOLDTHORPE, J.H. and LLEWELLYN, C. (1977b) 'Class mobility: intergenerational and worklife patterns', *British Journal of Sociology*, Vol. 28, pp 269–302.

GOLDTHORPE, J.H., PAYNE, C. and LLEWELLYN, C. (1978) 'Trends in class mobility', *Sociology*, Vol. 12, pp 441–468.

GOODING, J. (1970) 'Blue collar blues', *Fortune*, July, pp 69–117.

GOODRICH, C.L. (1975) *The Frontier of Control: a study in British workshop politics*, London, Pluto Press.

GORZ, A. (ed.) (1976) *The Division of Labour: the labour process and class struggle in modern capitalism*, Brighton, Harvester Press.

GOULD, D. (1975) 'Sickness in the Health Service', *New Statesman*, 12 September 1975.

GOULD, J. and KOLB, W. (1964) *A Dictionary of the Social Sciences*, London, Tavistock.

GOULDNER, A.W. (1954) *Patterns of Industrial Bureaucracy*, New York, Free Press.

GOULDNER, A. (1969) 'The unemployed self' in FRASER, R. (ed.) *Work: twenty personal accounts*, Harmondsworth, Penguin, pp 346—65.

GOULDNER, A.W. (1971) *The Coming Crisis of Western Sociology*, London, Heinemann Educational.

GRAMSCI, A. (1969) *Soviets in Italy*, Nottingham, Institute for Workers' Control.

GRIFF, M. (1964) 'The recruitment of the artist' in WILSON, R.N. (ed.) *The Arts in Society*, Englewood Cliffs, Prentice-Hall, pp 61—94.

GUTSCH, K.U. and ALCORN, J.D. (1970) *Guidance in Action: ideas and innovations for school counsellors*, New York, Parker Publishing Company Inc.

HABER, S. (1964) *Efficiency and Uplift: scientific management in the progressive era 1890—1920*, Chicago, University of Chicago Press.

HABERMAS, J. (1971a) 'Technology and science as "ideology"' in ESLAND, SALAMAN and SPEAKMAN, (eds) (1975) pp 33—48.

HABERMAS, J. (1971b) *Toward a Rational Society*, London, Heinemann.

HABERMAS, J. (1975) *Legitimation Crisis*, London, Heinemann.

HABERSTEIN, R.W. (1962) 'Sociology of occupations, the case of the American funeral director', in ROSE, A.M. (ed.) (1962) pp 225—46.

HADDON, R. (1973) *'Foreword'* to KERR *et al* (1973) pp 1—27.

HALL, R.H. (1969) *Occupations and the Social Structure*, Englewood Cliffs, Prentice-Hall.

HALLECK, S.L. (1971) *The Politics of Therapy*, New York, Harper and Row.

HALMOS, P. (1970) *The Personal Service Society*, London, Constable.

HALMOS, P. (ed.) (1973) *Professionalization and Social Change*, University of Keele, Monograph No. 20.

HALSEY, A.H. (ed.) (1972) *Trends in British Society since 1900*, London, Macmillan.

HANNAH, L. (1976) *The Rise of the Corporate Economy*, London, Methuen.

HARRIS, A. and CLAUSEN, R. (1966) *Labour Mobility in Great Britain 1953—63*, Government Social Survey, London, HMSO.

HAYES, J. (1971) *Occupational Perceptions and Occupational Information*, Stourbridge, The Institute of Careers Officers.

HAYSTEAD, J. (1971) 'Social structure, awareness contexts and processes of choice', *Sociological Review*, Vol. 19, No. 1, February. Reprinted in WILLIAMS, W.M. (ed.) (1974) pp 171—86.

HAYTER, T. (1971) *Aid as Imperialism*, Harmondsworth, Penguin.

HEGINBOTHAM, H. (1951) *The Youth Employment Service*, London, Methuen & Co.

HENDERSON, P. (1976) 'Class structure and the concept of intelligence', in DALE, I.R., ESLAND, G.M. and MACDONALD, M. (eds) *Schooling and Capitalism*, London, Routledge and Kegan Paul.

HERAUD, B. (1973) 'Professionalism, radicalism and social change', in HALMOS, P. (ed.) *Professionalization and Social Change*, University of Keele Monograph, No. 20, pp 85—101.

HERDING, R.G. (1972) *Job Control and Union Structures*, Rotterdam, Rotterdam University Press.
HERZBERG, F. (1968) *Work and the Nature of Man*, London, Staples Press.
HILL, S. (1974) 'Norms, groups and power: the sociology of workplace industrial relations', *British Journal of Industrial Relations*, Vol. 12, pp 213–35.
HINDESS, B. (1973) 'An introduction to Charles Bettelheim, "State property and socialism" ', *Economy and Society*, Vol. 2, No. 4, pp 387–94.
HIRST, P.Q. (1972) 'Marx, law and crime', *Economy and Society*, Vol. 1, No. 1, pp 28–50.
HOBHOUSE, L.T. (1911) *Liberalism*, London, Oxford University Press.
HOESS, R. (1961) *Commandant of Auschwitz*, trans. Constantine Fitzgibbon, London, Pan Books.
HORNE, J.H. and LUPTON, T. (1965) 'The work activities of "middle" managers', *Journal of Management Studies*, Vol. 1, No. 2, Feb., pp 14–33.
HOUGHTON, W.E. (1957) *The Victorian Frame of Mind, 1830–1870*, New Haven and London, Yale University Press.
HOWTON, F.W. and ROSENBERG, B. (1965) 'The salesman: ideology and self-imagery in a prototypic occupation', *Social Research*, Vol. 32, No. 3, pp 277–98.
HUGHES, E. (1937) 'Institutional office and the person', *American Journal of Sociology*, Vol. 43, pp 409–10.
HUGHES, E.C. (1958) *Men and their work*, Glencoe, Illinois, The Free Press.
HUGHES, E.C. (1963) 'Professions', in ESLAND, SALAMAN and SPEAKMAN, (eds) (1975) pp 248–57.
HUGHES, E.C. (1964) 'Good people and dirty work' in BECKER, H.S. (ed.) (1964) pp 23–36.
HUGHES, E.C. (1971) *The Sociological Eye, Vol. 2, Selected papers on work, self and the study of society*, Chicago, Aldine-Atherton.
HUGHES, E.C., THORNE, B., DEBAGGIS, A.M., GWIN, A. and WILLIAMS, D. (1973) *Education for the Professions of Medicine, Law, Theology and Social Welfare*, The Carnegie Foundation.
HUNNIUS, G., GARSON, G.D. and CASE, J. (1973) *Workers' Control: a Reader on labor and social change*, New York, Random House.
HUXLEY, A. (1968) *Brave New World*, Harmondsworth, Penguin.
HYMAN, H.H. (1967) 'The value systems of different classes' in BENDIX and LIPSET (eds) (1967a).
HYMAN, R. (1971) *Marxism and the Sociology of Trade Unionism*, London, Pluto Press.
HYMAN, R. (1972) *Strikes*, London, Fontana.
HYMAN, R. (1973) 'Industrial conflict and the political economy: Trends of the sixties and prospects for the seventies' in MILIBAND, R. and SAVILLE, J., *Socialist Register*, 1973, London, Merlin Press.
HYMAN, R. (1975) *Industrial Relations: a Marxist Introduction*, London, Macmillan, pp 83–93 and 159–71.
HYMAN, R. and BROUGH, I. (1975) *Social Values and Industrial Relations*, Oxford, Blackwell.

HYMAN, R. and FRYER, R.H. (1975) 'Trade unions: sociology and political economy' in McKINLAY, J. (ed.) *Processing People*, London, Holt, Rinehart and Winston.

ILLICH, I.D. (1971) *Deschooling Society*, London, Calder and Boyars.

INGHAM, G.K. (1967) 'Organizational size, orientation to work and industrial behaviour', *Sociology*, Vol. I, pp 239—59.

INGHAM, G.K. (1970) *Size of Industrial Organization and Worker Behaviour*, Cambridge University Press.

INGLEBY, D. (1970) 'Ideology and the human sciences', *Human Context*, Vol. 2, pp 159—80. Reprinted in PATEMAN, T. (ed.) *Counter Course*, Penguin, London.

INGLEBY, D. (1974a) 'The job psychologists do', in ARMISTEAD, N. (ed.) *Reconstructing Social Psychology*, Harmondsworth, Penguin Education.

INGLEBY, D. (1974b) 'The psychology of child psychology' in ESLAND, SALAMAN and SPEAKMAN (eds) (1975) pp 287—95.

INGLIS, B. (1964) *Fringe Medicine*, London, Faber.

INKELES, A. and BAUER, R.A. (1959) *The Soviet Citizen*, Cambridge, Mass., Harvard University Press.

INKELES, S. and ROSSI, P. (1956) 'National comparisons of occupational prestige', *American Journal of Sociology*, Vol. 61, January, pp 329—39.

IVENS, M. and DUNSTAN, R. (eds) (n.d.) *The Case for Capitalism*, London, Aims of Industry in conjunction with Michael Joseph.

JACKSON, B. and MARSDEN, D. (1962) *Education and the Working Class*, London, Routledge and Kegan Paul.

JACKSON, D., TURNER, H.A. and WILKINSON, F. (1972) *Do Trade Unions Cause Inflation?*, Cambridge, Cambridge University Press.

JAHODA, G. and CHALMERS, A.D. (1963) 'The Youth Employment Service: a consumer perspective', *Occupational Psychology*, Vol. 37, No. 1, pp 20—43.

JAQUES, E. (1967) *Equitable Payment*, Harmondsworth, Penguin.

JAY, M. (1973) *The Dialectical Imagination*, London, Heinemann.

JENKINS, D. (1974) *Job Power: blue and white collar democracy*, London, Heinemann.

JENKINS, R. (1970) *Exploitation*, London, Paladin.

JENKS, W. (1972) *Technology for Freedom*, Geneva, International Labour Office.

JEWSON, N.D. (1974) 'Medical knowledge and the patronage system in eighteenth century England', *Sociology*, Vol. 8, No. 3 (September) pp 369—85.

JOHNSON, T. (1972) *Professions and Power*, London, Macmillan.

JOHNSON, T. (1973) 'Professions', in HURD, G. (ed.) *Human Societies: an introduction to sociology*, London, Routledge and Kegan Paul, pp 120—35.

KARIER, C.J. (1972) 'Testing for order and control in the corporate state', *Educational Theory*, Vol. 22 (Spring) pp 159—80.

KEIL, E.T., RIDDELL, D.S. and GREEN, B.S.R. (1966) 'Youth and work: problems and perspectives', *Sociological Review*, Vol. 14, No. 2, July. Reprinted in WILLIAMS, W.M. (ed.) (1974) pp 76—96.

KERR, C., DUNLOP, J.T., HARBISON, F. and MYERS, C.A. (1962) *Industrialism and Industrial Man*, London, Heinemann (reprinted 1973 Harmondsworth, Penguin).

KLEIN, V. (1965) *Britain's Married Women Workers*, London, Routledge and Kegan Paul.

KOHN, M. (1969) *Class and Conformity*, Homewood, Illinois, Dorsey Press.

KOLKO, G. (1961) 'Max Weber on America: theory and evidence', *History and Theory*, Vol. 1, pp 243—60.

KRAUSE, E.A. (1971) *The Sociology of Occupations*, Boston, Little, Brown.

KRAUSNICK, H., BUCHEIM, H., BROZAT, M. and JACOBSEN, H.A. (1968) *Anatomy of the SS State*, London, Collins.

KUMAR K. (1976) 'Industrialism and Post-Industrialism: reflections on a putative transition', *Sociological Review*, Vol. 24, pp 439—78.

KUMAR, K. (1978) *Prophecy and Progress: the sociology of industrial and post-industrial society*, Harmondsworth, Penguin.

LABOUR FORCE STATISTICS, 1961—72 (1974) Paris, OECD.

LABOUR FORCE STATISTICS (1978) Quarterly Supplement to the Yearbook, May, Paris, OECD.

LABOUR RESEARCH DEPARTMENT (1975) 'Who backs the Tories?', Vol. 64, No. 8 (August) pp 162—4.

LABOUR RESEARCH DEPARTMENT (1974) *Big Business and Politics: the functions, propaganda and secret activities of employers' organizations*, pamphlet published by Labour Research Department.

LANE, D. (1971) *The End of Inequality? Stratification under state socialism*, Harmondsworth, Penguin.

LANE, D. (1976) *The Socialist Industrial State, towards a political sociology of state socialism*, London, Allen and Unwin.

LANE, M. (1972) 'Explaining educational choice', *Sociology*, Vol. 6, No. 2, May, pp 255—66.

LANE, T. (1974) *The Union Makes Us Strong*, London, Arrow.

LARSON, M.S. (1972) 'Notes on technocracy: some problems of theory, ideology and power', *Berkeley Journal of Sociology*, Vol. 17, pp 1—34.

LEVENSTEIN, A. (1964) *Why People Work*, New York, Collier Books.

LEVISON, A. (1974) 'The American working class' in *The working class majority*, New York, Coward, McCann and Geoghegan, pp 17—51.

LEWIS, R. and MAUDE, A. (1952) *Professional People*, London, Phoenix House.

LEWIS, R. (1973) *The New Service Society*, London, Longman.

LIPSET, S.M. and BENDIX, R. (1967) *Social Mobility in Industrial Society*, Berkeley, University of California Press.

LITTLER, CRAIG, R. (1978) 'Understanding Taylor', *British Journal of Sociology*, Vol. XXIX, No. 2, pp 185—202.

LINDSEY, A. (1962) *Socialized Medicine in England and Wales*, Chapel Hill, The University of North Carolina Press.

LIVERSIDGE, W. (1962) 'Life chances', *Sociological Review*, Vol. 10, No. 1, March. Reprinted in WILLIAMS, W.M. (ed.) (1974), pp 58—75.

LOCKWOOD, D. (1958) *The Blackcoated Worker*, London, Allen and Unwin.
LOCKWOOD, D. (1966) 'Sources of variation in working class images of society' in ESLAND, SALAMAN and SPEAKMAN (eds) (1975) pp 197–208.
LOWITH, K. (1970) 'Max Weber and Karl Marx' in WRONG, D. (ed.) *Makers of Social Science*, Englewood Cliffs, Prentice-Hall.
LUKACS, G. (1970) *History and Class Consciousness*, London, Merlin.
LUKES, S. (1973a) *Emile Durkheim: his life and work*, London, Allen Lane.
LUKES, S. (1973b) *Individualism*, Oxford, Blackwell.
LUKES, S. (1974) *Power: a radical view*, London, Macmillan.
MACKENZIE, G. (1974) 'The "Affluent Worker" Study: an evaluation and critique' in PARKIN, F. (ed.) *The Social Analysis of Class Structure*, London, Tavistock.
MACKENZIE, G. (1975) 'World images and the world of work' in ESLAND, SALAMAN and SPEAKMAN (eds) (1975) pp 170–85.
MAIZELS, J. (1970) *Adolescent Needs and the Transition from School to Work*, London, The Athlone Press.
MANDEL, E. (1971) *The Formation of Marx's Economic Thought*, London, New Left Books.
MANN, M. (1973) *Consciousness and Action among the Western Working Class*, London, Macmillan.
MANNHEIM, K. (1951) *Freedom, Power and Democratic Planning*, London, Routledge and Kegan Paul.
MANPOWER PAPER No. 9 (1974) *Women and work: a statistical survey*, London, HMSO.
MARCH, J.G. and SIMON, M.A. (1963) *Organizations*, New York, John Wiley and Sons.
MARCUSE, H. (1955) *Eros and Civilization*, London, Sphere.
MARCUSE, H. (1964) *One-Dimensional Man*, London, Sphere.
MARCUSE, H. (1971) 'Industrialization and capitalism', in STAMMER, O. (ed.) *Max Weber and Sociology Today*, Oxford, Blackwell.
MARGLIN, S. (1974) 'What do bosses do?' *Review of Radical Political Economics*, Vol. 6, pp 60–112.
MARTIN, R. and FRYER, R.H. (1973) *Redundancy and Paternalist Capitalism*, London, Allen and Unwin.
MARX, K. (1932) *Economic and Philosophical Manuscripts of 1844*, excerpted in BOTTOMORE, T.B. and RUBEL, M. (eds) (1973) *Karl Marx: selected writings in sociology and social philosophy*, Harmondsworth, Penguin.
MARX, K. (1844) 'Economic and philosophical manuscripts' in EASTON and GUDDAT (1967) pp 283–337.
MARX, K. (1930) *Capital*, 2 Vols, London, Everyman.
MARX, K. (1954) *Capital: A Critical Analysis of Capitalist Production Vol. 1*, Moscow, Progress Publishers.
MARX, K. (1934) Letter to Bolte, 23 Nov. 1871, in *Selected correspondence of Marx and Engels*, London, Lawrence and Wishart.
MARX, K. (1959) *Capital*, Vol. 1, London, Lawrence and Wishart.
MARX, K. (1962) 'Manifesto of the Communist Party' in *Marx-Engels' Selected Works*, Vol. 1, Moscow, Foreign Languages Publishing House.

MARX, K. (1973) *Grundrisse: foundations of the critique of politcal economy*, Harmondsworth, Penguin.

MARX, K. and ENGELS, F. (1956) *The Holy Family*, Moscow, Foreign Languages Publishing House.

MASON, E.S. (ed.) (1961) *The Corporation in Modern Society*, Harvard University Press.

McAULEY, M. (1969) *Labour Disputes in Soviet Russia 1957–1965*, Oxford, Clarendon Press.

McCARTHY, W.E.J. and PARKER, S.R. (1968) *Shop Stewards and Workshop Relations*, London, HMSO.

McINTOSH, M. (1971) 'Changes in the organization of thieving' in COHEN, S. (ed.) (1971) pp 98–133.

McKINLAY, J.B. (1973) 'On the professional regulation of change' in HALMOS, P. (ed.) *Professionalization and Social Change*, Keele, University of Keele, pp 61–84.

McLUHAN, M. (1964) *Understanding Media*, London, Routledge and Kegan Paul.

MECHANIC, D. (1967) 'Some factors in identifying and defining mental illness', in SCHEFF, T.J. (ed.) *Mental illness and social processes*, New York, Harper and Row, pp 23–32.

MERKLE, J.A. (1968) 'The Taylor strategy: organizational innovation and class structure', *Berkeley Journal of Sociology*, Vol. 13, pp 59–81.

MESZAROS, I. (1970) *Marx's Theory of Alienation*, London, Merlin Press.

MILIBAND, R. (1964) *Parliamentary Socialism*, London, Merlin Press.

MILIBAND, R. (1969) *The State in Capitalist Society*, London, Weidenfeld and Nicolson.

MILLERSON, G. (1964) *The Qualifying Associations*, London, Routledge and Kegan Paul.

MILLS, C.W. (1948) *The new men of power*, New York, Harcourt Brace.

MILLS, C.W. (1951) *White Collar*, New York, Oxford University Press.

MILLS, C.W. (1956) *The Power Elite*, New York, Oxford University Press.

MILLS, C.W. (1959) *The Sociological Imagination*, New York, Oxford University Press.

MILLS, C.W. (1963) *The Marxists*, Harmondsworth, Penguin.

MINISTRY OF EDUCATION (1959) *15 to 18*, A report of the Central Advisory Council for Education (England) (Crowther Report), London, HMSO.

MINKIN, L. (1974) 'The British Labour Party and the trade unions: crisis and compact', *Industrial and Labor Relations Review*, Vol. 28, pp 7–37.

MOMMSEN, W.J. (1974) *The age of bureaucracy*, Oxford, Blackwell.

MOORE, Jr., B. (1973) *Social Origins of Dictatorship and Democracy: lord and peasant in the making of the modern world*, Harmondsworth, Penguin University Books.

MOORE, W.E. (1966) 'Changes in occupational structures', in SMELSER, N.J. and LIPSET, S.M. (eds) (1966).

MOORHOUSE, H.F. and CHAMBERLAIN, C.W. (1974) 'Lower-class attitudes to property', *Sociology*, Vol. 8, No. 3, September, pp 387–405.
MORSE, N.C. and WEISS, R.S. (1955) 'The function and meaning of work and the job', *American Sociological Review*, Vol. 20, No. 2, pp 191–8.
MOUZELIS, N.P. (1967) *Organization and Bureaucracy*, London, Routledge and Kegan Paul.
MUSGRAVE, P.W. (1967) 'Towards a sociological theory of occupational choice', *Sociological Review*, Vol. 15, No. 1, March. Reprinted in WILLIAMS, W.M. (ed.) (1974), pp 97–110.
NAIRN, T. (1972) 'The English working class', in BLACKBURN, R. (ed.) *Ideology in Social Science*, London, Fontana, pp 187–206.
NAUMOVA, N.F. (1966) 'Social factors in the emotional attitude towards work', in OSIPOV (ed.) (1966a).
NESS, E. and FRALEY, O. (1967) *The Untouchables*, London, Hodder and Stoughton.
NEWBY, H. (1977) *The Deferential Worker*, London, Allen Lane.
NEWMAN, B. (1968) 'Occupational choice', unpublished paper.
NEWMAN, F.L. (1944) *Behemoth, the structure and practice of National Socialism: 1933–1944*, London, Oxford University Press.
NICHOLS, T. (1969) *Ownership, Control and Ideology*, London, Allen and Unwin.
NICHOLS, T. (1975) 'The sociology of accidents', in ESLAND, SALAMAN and SPEAKMAN (eds) (1975) pp 217–29.
NICHOLS, T. (1975) 'The "socialism" of management: some comments on the new "human relations" ', *Sociological Review*, Vol. 23, No. 2, May, pp 245–65.
NICHOLS, T. and ARMSTRONG, P. (1976) *Workers Divided*, London, Fontana.
NICHOLS, T. and BEYNON, H. (1977) *Living with Capitalism*, London, Routledge and Kegan Paul.
NISBET, R. (1968) *The Sociological Tradition*, London, Heinemann.
NOSOW, S. and FORM, W.H. (eds) (1962) *Man, Work and Society*, New York, Basic Books (quoting from FRIEDMAN and HAVIGHURST (1954).
OAKLEY, A. (1972) *Sex, Gender and Society*, London, Temple-Smith.
OLLMAN, B. (1971) *Alienation: Marx's conception of man in capitalist society*, Cambridge University Press.
THE OPEN UNIVERSITY (1972) D283 *The Sociological Perspective*, The Open University Press.
THE OPEN UNIVERSITY (1974) DT352 *People and Oganizations*, The Open University Press.
THE OPEN UNIVERSITY (1975) D101 *Making Sense of Society*, The Open University Press.
OPPENHEIMER, M. (1973) 'The proletarianization of the professional', in HALMOS, P. (ed.) (1973) pp 213–27.
ORWELL, G. (1962) *The Road to Wigan Pier*, Harmondsworth, Penguin.
ORWELL, G. (1969) *1984*, Harmondsworth, Penguin.

OSIPOV, A.P. (ed.) (1966a) *Industry and Labour in the USSR*, London, Tavistock.

OSIPOV, A.P. (1966b) 'Redistribution of labour and changes in its occupational composition', in OSIPOV, A.P. (ed.) (1966a) pp 37—47.

PARKER, S. (1971) *The Future of Work and Leisure*, London, MacGibbon and Kee.

PARKER, S. (1975) 'The effects of redundancy', in ESLAND, SALAMAN and SPEAKMAN (eds) (1975) pp 88—99.

PARKER, S.R., BROWN, R.K., CHILD, J. and SMITH, M.S. (1977) *The Sociology of Industry*, London, Allen and Unwin.

PARKER, T. and ALLERTON, R. (1962) *The Courage of his Convictions*, London, Arrow Books.

PARKIN, F. (1971a) 'Class stratification in socialist societies', in THOMPSON, K. and TUNSTALL, J. (eds) (1971) pp 348—62.

PARKIN, F. (1971b) *Class Inequality and Political Order: social stratification in capitalist and communist societies*, London, MacGibbon and Kee.

PARRY, N. (1973) 'Power, class and occupational strategy', Paper presented at the British Sociological Association's Annual Conference.

PARRY, N. and PARRY, J. (1976) *The Rise of the Medical Profession: a study of collective mobility*, London, Croom-Helm.

PARSONS, T. (1948) 'Social classes and class conflict in the light of recent sociological theory', in THOMPSON, K. and TUNSTALL, J. (eds) (1971) *Sociological Perspectives*, Harmondsworth, Penguin, revised edition.

PARSONS, T. (1954) 'The professions in the social structure', in *Essays in sociological theory*, rev. edn, Glencoe, Free Press.

PARSONS, T. (1960) 'Some principal characteristics of industrial society', in *Structure and Process in Modern Societies*, Glencoe, Free Press.

PARSONS, T. (1963) 'On the concept of political power', *Proceedings of the American Philosophical Society*, Vol. 107, pp 232—62.

PAUL, W.J. and ROBERTSON, K.B. (1970) *Job Enrichment and Employee Motivation*, London, Gower Press.

PAYER, C. (1974) *The Debt Trap, the IMF and the Third World*, Harmondsworth, Penguin.

PEARSON, G. (1975) *The Deviant Imagination*, London, Macmillan.

PEARSON, G. (1975) 'Making social workers: bad promises and good omens' in BAILEY, R. and BRAKE, M. (eds) *Radical Social Work*, London, Edward Arnold Ltd.

PEARSON, M. (1972) *The Age of Consent*, Newton Abbot, David & Charles Ltd.

PEDLEY, R. (1969) *The Comprehensive School*, Harmondsworth, Penguin, revised edition.

PERROW, C. (1972) *Complex Organizations: a critical essay*, Illinois, Scott Foresman and Co.

PETTIGREW, A.M. (1973) 'Occupational specialization as an emergent process', in ESLAND, SALAMAN and SPEAKMAN (eds) (1975) pp 258—74.

POLLARD, S. (1968) *The Genesis of Modern Management*, Harmondsworth, Penguin.

POLLNER, M. (1974) 'Sociological and commonsense models of the labelling process', in TURNER, R. (ed.) *Ethnomethodology*, Harmondsworth, Penguin, pp 27—46.

POULANTZAS, N. (1975) *Classes in Contemporary Capitalism*, London, New Left Books.

PRICE, R. and BAIN, G.S. (1976) 'Union growth revisited: 1948—1974 in perspective', *British Journal of Industrial Relations*, Vol. 14, pp 339—355.

REISS, A.J. (1964) 'The social integration of queers and peers', in BECKER, H. (1964) pp 181—210.

RIESMAN, D. (1950) *The Lonely Crowd*, New Haven, Yale University Press.

RIESMAN, D. (1955) 'The themes of work and play in the structure of Freud's thought', in *Individualism Reconsidered*, New York, Anchor Books.

ROBERTS, K. (1968) 'The entry into employment', *Sociological Review*, Vol. 16, No. 2, July. Reprinted in WILLIAMS, W.M. (ed.) (1974), pp 138—57.

ROBERTS, K. (1971) *From School to Work: a study of the Youth Employment Service*, Newton Abbot, David and Charles.

ROBERTS, K. (1975) 'The developmental theory of occupational choice: a critique and an alternative', in ESLAND, SALAMAN and SPEAKMAN (eds) (1975) pp 134—46.

ROEBER, J. (1975) *Social Change at Work: the ICI weekly staff agreement*, London, Duckworth.

ROETHLISBERGER, F.J. and DICKSON, W.J. (1939) *Management and the Worker*, Cambridge, Mass., Harvard University Press.

ROLPH, C.H. (1955) *Women of the Streets*, London, Secker & Warburg.

ROSE, A.M. (1962) *Human Behaviour and Social Processes*, London, Routledge and Kegan Paul.

ROSE, M. (1975) *Industrial Behaviour: theoretical development since Taylor*, London, Allen Lane.

ROSE S.P.R. and ROSE, H. (1976) 'The politics of neurobiology: biologism in the service of the state', in ROSE, H. and ROSE, S.P.R. *The Political Economy of Science*, London, Macmillan.

ROSZAK, T. (1970) *The Making of a Counter-Culture*, London, Faber and Faber.

ROWTHORN, R. (1974) 'Neo-classicism, neo-Ricardianism and Marxism', *New Left Review*, No. 86, July—August, pp 63—87.

ROYAL COMMISSION ON TRADE UNIONS AND EMPLOYERS' ASSOCIATIONS (Donovan) (1968) *Report*, London, HMSO.

SALAMAN, J.G. (1970) *Work organizations: resistance and control*, London, Longman.

SALAMAN, J.G. (1974) *Community and Occupation*, Cambridge University Press.

SALAMAN, J.G. (1975) 'Occupational community, culture and consciousness', in BULMER, M. (ed.) *Images of Society*, London, Routledge and Kegan Paul, pp 219—36.

SALAMAN, J.G. (1978) 'Towards a sociology of organizational structure', *Sociological Review*, Vol. 26, No. 3, pp 519—54.

SCHACHT, R. (1971) *Alienation*, London, Allen and Unwin.

SCHMIDT, A. (1969) *The Concept of Nature in Marx*, London, New Left Books.

THE SCHOOLS COUNCIL (1972) *Careers Education in the 1970s*, Working Paper 40, London, Methuen Educational.

SCHUMACHER, E.F. (1973) *Small is Beautiful*, London, Blond and Briggs.

SEEAR, N. (1968) 'The position of women in industry', in WEIR, D. (ed.) (1973) *Men and Women in Modern Britain*, London, Fontana, pp 231—44.

SEMYONOV, V.S. (1966) 'Soviet intellectuals and white-collar workers' in OSIPOV, A.P. (ed.) (1966a) pp 130—41.

SENNET, R. and COBB, J. (1973) *The Hidden Injuries of Class*, New York, Random House.

SHARPE, S. (1976) *Just like a girl – How girls learn to be women*, Harmondsworth, Penguin.

SHERLOCK, B. and COHEN, A. (1966) 'The strategy of occupational choice: recruitment to dentistry', *Social Forces*, Vol. 44, pp 303—13.

SHROYER, T. (1970) 'Toward a critical theory for advanced industrial society' in DREITZEL, H.P. (ed.) *Recent Sociology, No. 2: Patterns of communicative behaviour*, New York, Macmillan, pp 209—34.

SHUBKIN, V.N. (1966) 'Social mobility and choice of occupations', in OSIPOV, A.P. (ed.) (1966a) pp 86—98.

SMELSER, N.J. and LIPSET, S.M. (1966) 'Social structure, mobility and development', in SMELSER, N.J. and LIPSET, S.M. (eds) *Social Structure and Mobility in Economic Development*, pp 1—50.

SMIGEL, E.O. (1964) *The Wall Street Lawyer: professional organization man?* Glencoe, Illinois, The Free Press.

SMIRNOV, G.L. (1966) 'The rate of growth of the Soviet working class and change in its composition with respect to occupation and skill', in OSIPOV, A.P. (ed.) (1966a) pp 86—98.

SMITH, G. and HARRIS, R. (1972) 'Ideologies of need and the organization of social work departments', *British Journal of Social work*, Vol. 2, No. 1 (Spring) pp 27—45.

SOCIAL TRENDS (1977) No. 8, London, HMSO.

SOFER, C. (1970) *Men in Mid Career: a study of British managers and technical specialists*, Cambridge University Press.

STACEY, N. (1954) *English Accountancy*, London, Gee and Company.

STRAUSS, A., SCHATZMAN, L., EHRLICH, D., BUCHER, R. and SABSHIN, M. (1971) 'The hospital and its negotiated order' in CASTLES, F.G., MURRAY, D.J. and POTTER, D.C. *Decisions, organizations and society*, Harmondsworth, Penguin.

STRAUSS, G. (1963) 'Some notes on power-equalization' in LEAVITT, H.J. (ed.), *The Social Science of Organizations*, Englewood Cliffs, New Jersey, Prentice-Hall.

SUPER, D.E. (1957) *The Psychology of Careers: an introduction to vocational development*, New York, Harper and Row.

SUPER, D.E. (1968) 'A theory of vocational development' in HOPSON, B. and HAYES, J. (eds) *The theory and practice of vocational guidance: a selection of readings*, Oxford, Pergamon Press in consultation with the Vocational Guidance Research Unit, University of Leeds, pp 13–24.

SUTTON, F.X., HARRIS, S.E., KAYSEN, C. and ROBIN, J. (1958) *The American Business Creed*, Cambridge, Mass., Harvard University Press.

SWEEZY, P.M. (1971) *Modern Capitalism*, New York, Monthly Review Press.

SYKES, A.J.M. (1967) 'The cohesion of a trade union workshop organization', *Sociology*, Vol. 1, pp 141–63.

SYKES, A.J.M. (1973) 'Work attitudes of navvies' in WEIR, D., *Men and Work in Modern Britain*, London, Fontana, pp 203–20.

SYKES, A.J.M. and BATES, J. (1962) 'A study of conflict between formal company policy and the interests of informal groups', *Sociological Review*, Vol. 3, No. 10, November, pp 313–27.

TAWNEY, R.H. (1938) *Religion and the Rise of Capitalism*, Harmondsworth, Penguin.

TAYLOR, I., WALTON, P. and YOUNG, J. (1973) *The New Criminology: for a social theory of deviance*, London, Routledge and Kegan Paul.

TAYLOR, I., WALTON, P. and YOUNG, J. (1975) *Critical Criminology*, London, Routledge and Kegan Paul.

TAYLOR, F.W. (1911) *Scientific Management*, New York, Harper and Bros.

TERKEL, S. (1975) *Working*, London, Wildwood House.

THOMPSON, E.P. (1968) *The Making of the English Working Class*, Harmondsworth, Penguin.

THOMPSON, K. and TUNSTALL, J. (eds) (1971) *Sociological Perspectives*, Harmondsworth, Penguin.

THORNE, B. (1973) 'Professional education in law', in HUGHES, E.C. *et al*, pp 101–68.

TUNSTALL, J. (1962) *The Fishermen*, London, MacGibbon & Kee.

TURNER, H.A. (1962) *Trade Union Growth, Structure and Policy*, London, Allen and Unwin.

TURNER, R.H. (1961) 'Modes of ascent through education: sponsored and contest mobility' in HALSAY, A.H., FLOUD, J. and ANDERSON, C.A. (eds) *Education, economy and society*, Glencoe, The Free Press, pp 121–39.

UDY, Jr., S.H. (1970) *Work in Traditional and Modern Society*, Englewood Cliffs, New Jersey, Prentice-Hall.

UNITED STATES SENATE (1972) 'Worker alienation research and technical assistance bill', 14 August.

VAN LOON, E.E. (1970) 'The law school response: how to make students sharp by making them narrow', in WASSERSTEIN, B. and GREEN, M.J. (eds) *With justice for some: an indictment of the law by young advocates*, Boston, Beacon Press.

VENESS, T. (1962) *School leavers: Their Aspirations and Expectations*, London, Methuen & Co.

VOLLMER, H.M. and MILLS, D.L. (1966) *Professionalization*, New Jersey, Prentice-Hall.

WEBB, S. and WEBB, B. (1920) *History of Trade Unionism*, London, Longman.

WEBER, M. (1930) *The Protestant Ethic and the Sprit of Captialism*, Talcott Parsons (trans.), 'Foreword' by R.H. TAWNEY, London, George Allen & Unwin (reissued, 1965, Unwin University Books).

WEBER, M. (1947) *The Theory of Social and Economic Organization* (trans. A.M. HENDERSON and T. PARSONS: ed. T. PARSONS), New York, Oxford University Press.

WEBER, M. (1968) *Economy and Society*, 3 vols., Totowa, New Jersey, Bedminster Press.

WEDDERBURN, D.L. (1974) *Poverty, Inequality and Class Structure*, Cambridge University Press.

WEDDERBURN, D. and CRAIG, G. (1974) 'Relative deprivation in work', in ESLAND, SALAMAN and SPEAKMAN (eds) (1975) pp 59—69.

WEIR, D. (ed.) (1973) *Men and Work in Modern Britain*, London, Fontana.

WEISS, R.S. and RIESMAN, D. (1963) 'Social problems and disorganization in the world of work' in MERTON, R.K. and NISBET, R.A. (eds) *Contemporary Social Problems*, London, Rupert Hart-Davis.

WELLER, K. (n.d.) *The Lordstown Struggle*, London, Solidarity.

WESOLOWSKI, W. (1969) 'The notions of strata and class in socialist societies', in BETEILLE, A. (ed.) *Social Inequality*, Harmondswoth, Penguin, pp 122—45.

WESTERGAARD, J.H. (1970) 'The rediscovery of the cash nexus', in MILIBAND, R. and SAVILLE, J. *Socialist Register 1970*, London, Merlin Press.

WHYTE, W.H. (1960) *The Organization Man*, Harmondsworth, Penguin.

WILLIAMS, L. (1965) *The Changing Pattern of Women's Employment*, Eleanor Rathbone Memorial Lecture, Liverpool. Liverpool University Press.

WILLIAMS, W.M. (ed.) (1974) *Occupational Choice*, London, Allen and Unwin.

WILLIS, P. (1977) *Learning to Labour*, Farnborough, Saxon House.

WILSON, N.A.B. (1973) *On the Quality of Working Life*, Manpower paper No. 7, London, HMSO.

WILSON, R.N. (1964) 'The poet in American Society' in WILSON, R.N. (ed.) Inc. pp 1—34.

WILSON, R.N. (1964) *The Arts in Society*, Englewood Cliffs, Prentice-Hall.

WINKLER, J (1974) 'The ghost at the bargaining table: directors and industrial relations', *British Journal of Industrial Relations*, Vol. 12, No. 2, July, pp 191—212.

WINKLER, J. (1975) 'Corporatism', Unpublished paper presented to the Annual Conference of British Sociological Association, University of Kent.

WORK IN AMERICA (1973) *Report of a Special Task Force to the Secretary of Health, Education and Welfare*, Cambridge, Mass., MIT Press.

YOUNG, J. (1971) *The Drugtakers*, London, Paladin.
YOUNG, M. and WILMOTT, P. (1973) *The Symmetrical Family*, London, Routledge and Kegal Paul.
ZDRAVEMYSLOV, A.D. and YADOV, V.A. (1966) 'Effect of vocational distinctions on the attitude to work', in OSIPOV (ed) (1966a).
ZIMBALIST, A. (1975) 'The limits of work humanization', *Review of Radical Political Economics*, Vol. 7, No. 2, Summer, pp 50–59.

Index